Cambridge studies in medieval life and thought

Edited by WALTER ULLMANN, LITT.D., F.B.A.
Professor of Medieval History
in the University of Cambridge

Third series vol. 7

THE POLITICAL THOUGHT OF
WILLIAM OF OCKHAM

CAMBRIDGE STUDIES IN MEDIEVAL LIFE AND THOUGHT

THIRD SERIES

THE POLITICAL THOUGHT OF
WILLIAM OF OCKHAM

PERSONAL AND
INSTITUTIONAL PRINCIPLES

ARTHUR STEPHEN McGRADE

CAMBRIDGE UNIVERSITY PRESS

Published by the Syndics of the Cambridge University Press
Bentley House, 200 Euston Road, London NW1 2DB
American Branch: 32 East 57th Street, New York, N.Y.10022

© Cambridge University Press 1974

Library of Congress Catalogue Card Number: 73-86044

ISBN: 0 521 20284 1

First published 1974

Printed in Great Britain
at the University Printing House, Cambridge
(Brooke Crutchley, University Printer)

Vestra (potestas) est verbalis,
nostra autem est realis.

Pierre de Flotte to
Boniface VIII

CONTENTS

Contents

PREFACE

This book is an account of Ockham's political principles, the central ideas about individual action and governmental institutions elaborated in the large body of polemical writings he produced at Munich in the two decades from 1328 until his death. I have tried to provide as clear an account of these ideas as possible and to do so from Ockham's own standpoint. This has proved a difficult and lengthy enough task to require omitting other important matters or treating them all too briefly. Thus, comparisons of Ockham's ideas with the classical and earlier medieval traditions as well as with the political thought of his contemporaries have been greatly restricted. My main concern with the political and spiritual movements of the time has been to see them, if I could, as they appeared to Ockham, not as they were *in rei veritate*. Little is said in this study about Ockham's use of canon and civil law sources. I have also omitted any assessment of his influence on later thought and action. Although I have explored the relations between Ockham's political works and his nominalist speculative writings, I am certain that further detailed investigation in this area, too, would be rewarding.

Regarding all of these matters, however, I believe that the subjects treated here have some claim to priority. For example, Ockham's extensive and sometimes original use of legal materials should be more understandable if account has been taken of the place of law and lawyers in his broader scheme of thought. His relations to earlier, contemporary, and later thinkers and events can be interpreted correctly only if we understand the distinctive structures of his own thought. Connections between his academic and polemical writings should be considered in the light of his conceptions of government and the political rights and powers of the individual. In general, since Ockham was in so many ways a pivotal figure, it is naturally tempting to pass over the substance of his political thought rather

ix

quickly, in order to grasp its external relations. These important relations should not be ignored, but perhaps more attention should first be given to isolating Ockham's thought in its own terms. That, at any rate, is what has been attempted in the present study.

It is a pleasure to acknowledge the aid of various kinds which I have received in preparing this study. Major material support has come from the National Endowment for the Humanities, the Society for Religion in Higher Education, and the University of Connecticut Research Foundation. The American Council of Learned Societies and King's College, Cambridge have also made helpful contributions. The bibliography for this volume, which includes several items not available to me earlier as well as sources for aspects of Ockham's political thought beyond the limits of this study, was completed in 1972–3 in Tübingen, where I had the pleasure of holding an Alexander von Humboldt fellowship.

The staffs of the University and King's College libraries, Cambridge, and the Wilbur Cross Library at the University of Connecticut, Storrs, have been of invaluable assistance. I must also thank those who have helped me at Merton College and the Bodleian Library, Oxford, the Universitätsbibliothek and Institut für Spätmittelalter und Reformation (especially the Abteilung Spätaugustinismus), Tübingen, the Bibliothèque Nationale and Mazarine and Arsenal libraries, Paris, the Biblioteca Laurenziana, Florence, the Ambrosian and Municipal Libraries, Milan, the Biblioteca Vaticana, and the libraries at the Universities of London, Yale, and Harvard. For the discriminating labors and always constructive spirit of the editorial and production departments of Cambridge University Press, I am most grateful.

The interpretations offered in this study and its many shortcomings are my own. If I have succeeded at all in putting Ockham's ideas in a clearer light, that is largely due to the exceptional opportunities I have had to learn from others. My former teachers, Alan Gewirth, George Lindbeck, and Richard McKeon, have found time to discuss aspects of Ockham, medieval politics, and philosophy with me in the last few years, as have many of my colleagues at Storrs, especially Garry and Joyce Brodsky, Michael Simon, Len Krimerman, Fred Cazel, and Daniel Kelly. I have also benefited from stimulating conversations with H. S. Offler, Steven Ozment, and M. J. Wilks.

Preface

Dr Wilks has provided detailed and highly perceptive comments on an earlier version of this research which he and T. M. Parker were kind enough to read in its entirety. I am grateful to Brian Tierney for a *précis* of his recent study of papal infallibility and to Stefan Kuttner for a significant detail bearing on Ockham's activity as a canonist.

From beginning to end, Walter Ullmann has been not only a shining example of the intellectual insight required and merited by medieval political ideas, but also a constant source of encouragement, learning, and fresh thought in relation to my own research. It would be difficult to imagine a more able tutor.

Concerning so great a matter as the deliberations of a general council of the church, Ockham contended that when the wisdom, goodness, or power of women was necessary for a discussion of the faith, they should not be excluded. I am happy that the same principle could be applied in the lesser matter of this book. Without the intelligence, affection, and manifold scholarly abilities of my wife, without her longstanding and substantial contributions to its thought and expression, the present study could scarcely have been completed. It is only as the most modest thanks, then, that I dedicate the final version: to Jo.

Storrs, Connecticut
November 24, 1973

ABBREVIATIONS

AFH   *Archivum Franciscanum Historicum*

An Princeps   Ockham, *An Princeps pro suo Succursu, scilicet Guerrae, Possit Recipere Bona Ecclesiarum, etiam Invito Papa*

BF, v–vi   C. Eubel (ed.), *Bullarium Franciscanum sive Romanorum Pontificum Constitutiones, Epistolae, Diplomata Tribus Ordinibus Minorum . . . Concessa*, v–vi (Rome, 1898–1902)

Brev.   Ockham, *Breviloquium de Principatu Tyrannico super Divina et Humana, Specialiter autem super Imperium et Subiectos Imperio, a quibusdam Vocatis Summis Pontificibus Usurpato*, ed. Scholz

DA   *Deutsches Archiv für Erforschung des Mittelalters* (before 1951: *Deutsches Archiv für Geschichte des Mittelalters*)

Imp. Pont. Pot.   Ockham, *De Imperatorum et Pontificum Potestate*, ed. Scholz

i–iii *Dialogus*   Ockham, *Dialogus*, Parts i–iii. The two tracts of iii *Dialogus* are indicated by large roman numerals (iii *Dialogus* i and ii), books and chapters by arabic and small roman numerals. Folio and column references are to Trechsel's edition. Thus, 'iii Dialogus ii, 3, vi, fol. 263vb' refers to the left-hand column on the verso side of folio 263 of the Trechsel volume; the passage indicated is in chapter 6 of Book 3 of iii *Dialogus*, Tract ii

FcS   *Franciscan Studies, New Series*

FzS   *Franziskanische Studien*

La naissance, iv–v   Lagarde, *La naissance de l'esprit laïque . . .*, iv: *Guillaume d'Ockham: défense de l'empire*; v: *Guillaume d'Ockham: critique des structures ecclésiales*

OND   Ockham, *Opus Nonaginta Dierum*

OP i–iii   *Guillelmi de Ockham Opera Politica*, i–iii (Manchester, 1940, 1963, 1956)

OQ   Ockham, *Octo Quaestiones de Potestate Papae*

Sent. i–iv   Ockham, *Scriptum in Quattuor Libros Sententiarum*, Books i–iv, prologue and Book i, distinctions 1–3 ed. G. Gál and S. Brown; balance of Book i and Books ii–iv ed. Trechsel

xiii

Chapter 1

OCKHAM AS A POLITICAL THINKER

'There seems to be no way round Ockham. Sooner or later he confronts every worker in late medieval history.'[1] Unfortunately, Ockham seems not only unavoidable but also enigmatic. He has been seen as the destroyer of the high scholastic synthesis of faith and reason, yet his personal orthodoxy has seldom been questioned in recent times, and the avowed target of his critical attacks was the 'common opinion of the moderns' rather than traditional theological systems. He was involved in a literary war with the popes at Avignon that rivaled in length and bitterness any previous contest between empire and papacy,[2] yet he has also been described as 'a constitutional liberal . . . not an anti-papal zealot'.[3] If we restrict our attention to the content of Ockham's political writings and consider his life,[4] his speculative thought,[5] and the world around

[1] E. F. Jacob, 'Ockham as a political thinker', in *Essays in the Conciliar Epoch*, rev. ed. (Notre Dame, Indiana, 1963), pp. 85–105 and 246–8; p. 85.

[2] As 'the obvious, or it might almost be said the inevitable, representative of the Fraticelli among the supporters of Lewis of Bavaria', according to C. H. McIlwain, *The Growth of Political Thought in the West* (New York, 1932), p. 293.

[3] Jacob, 'Ockham as a political thinker', p. 15.

[4] Ockham was born between 1280 and 1290, studied and taught at Oxford in the years prior to 1324, when he was summoned to the papal court at Avignon for an examination of his doctrines. He fled Avignon in 1328, taking refuge with the Emperor Ludwig of Bavaria. He died at Munich in 1349. The primary sources for Ockham's life were explored by J. Hofer, 'Biographische Studien über Wilhelm von Ockham O.F.M.', *AFH*, VI (1913), 209–33, 439–65, 654–65. For studies of the proceedings against him at Avignon, see note 22 below. On the traditions concerning his death, see below, note 89. Recent comprehensive studies of Ockham's life and the literary history of his writings are Léon Baudry, *Guillaume d'Occam: sa vie, ses œuvres, ses idées sociales et politiques* (Paris, 1949) and, largely replacing Baudry, Jürgen Miethke, *Ockhams Weg zur Sozialphilosophie* (Berlin, 1969). The best short life of Ockham is by Philotheus Boehner in his edition of *The Tractatus de Successivis Attributed to William Ockham* (St Bonaventure, N.Y., 1944), pp. 1–15.

[5] The interpretation of Ockham's speculative thought has been much disputed. For the view that Ockhamism leads to skepticism or destroys the medieval synthesis

him[6] only as they clarify the inner structure and meaning of these works, difficulties still remain in even outlining our subject, let alone providing a finished account. Indeed, it has proved so hard to mark off the politically significant elements in Ockham's gigantic body of writings that some scholars have doubted he was a political thinker at all. We may begin with this problem, which is both important in itself and connected with other issues.

A nominal definition of Ockham's political work is easy to give: it consists of those treatises that have appeared or are to appear in the

of faith and reason, see E. Gilson, *The Unity of Philosophical Experience* (New York, 1937), pp. 61–91; R. Guelluy, *Philosophie et théologie chez Guillaume d'Ockham* (Louvain, 1947), pp. 375–6; G. Leff, *Bradwardine and the Pelagians* (Cambridge, 1957), pp. 188–210; T. K. Scott, 'Nicholas of Autrecourt, Buridan and Ockhamism', *Journal of the History of Philosophy*, IX (1971), 15–41. Ockham's good standing as a scholastic philosopher was ably defended in many articles by P. Boehner, *Collected Articles on Ockham*, ed. E. M. Buytaert (St Bonaventure, N.Y., 1958), while the constructive aspects of nominalist theology have been brilliantly expounded by H. A. Oberman in *The Harvest of Medieval Theology: Gabriel Biel and Late Medieval Nominalism* (Cambridge, Mass., 1963). Also see P. Vignaux, *Nominalisme au XIVe siècle* (Montreal, 1948) and H. Junghans, *Ockham im Lichte der neuren Forschung* (Berlin, 1968), a synthesis based on Boehner's work. Other scholars have found it fruitful to approach Ockham from the standpoint of empiricism and modern philosophical analysis: E. A. Moody, *The Logic of William of Ockham* (London, 1935); M. M. Adams and N. Kretzmann, *William Ockham: Predestination, God's Foreknowledge, and Future Contingents* (New York, 1969). Also see A. C. Crombie, *Robert Grosseteste and the Origins of Experimental Science* (Oxford, 1953). As could be expected of a movement that dominated European academic thought for a century and a half, Ockhamism, or nominalism, had a varied development. On types of nominalists, see D. Trapp, 'Augustinian theology of the fourteenth century', *Augustiniana*, VI (1956), 146–274; W. J. Courtenay, 'Nominalism and late medieval religion', C. Trinkaus and H. A. Oberman (eds.), *The Pursuit of Holiness in the Late Middle Ages and the Renaissance* (Leyden, 1974), pp. 26–59.

6 Studies of Ockham that pay detailed attention to the historical context are G. de Lagarde, *La naissance de l'esprit laïque au déclin du moyen-âge*, especially vol. IV of the first edition, *Ockham et son temps* (Paris, 1942) and vols. I and II of the second edition; I: *Bilan du XIIIe siècle* (Paris, 1956), II: *Secteur social de la scolastique* (Paris, 1958); and Miethke, *Ockhams Weg*. The editors' introductions to the works that have appeared in the modern edition of Ockham's *Opera Politica* (see the following note) detail the circumstances of ecclesiastical and secular politics surrounding the composition of each work. For the context of political thought in which Ockham wrote, briefly summarized below (pp. 82–4), see W. Ullmann, *Principles of Government and Politics in the Middle Ages*, 2nd ed. (London, 1966), especially Part III; A. Gewirth, *Marsilius of Padua, the Defender of Peace*; vol. I: *Marsilius of Padua and Medieval Political Philosophy* (New York, 1951); M. J. Wilks, *The Problem of Sovereignty in the Later Middle Ages* (Cambridge, 1964); G. Leff, *Heresy in the Later Middle Ages* (2 vols., Manchester, 1967).

edition of his *Opera Politica*, which will include nothing that he wrote
at Oxford or Avignon and everything, with the exception of two
logical treatises, that he is known to have written in his twenty years
at Munich.[7] The problem arises when we seek common themes or
principles in this material. It is a strange political work that spends
200 pages on the question, whether a person can licitly eat a piece of
bread without having any legal rights in it,[8] and a still stranger one
that is devoted to proving that a particular individual died believing
the souls of the blessed would enjoy the vision of God only at the end
of the world.[9] On the other hand, certain theses advanced by Ockham earlier, in his speculative or academic, apparently non-political
works,[10] are of interest from a political standpoint; for example, the
thesis that only acts of will (in contrast with overt behavior – *actus
exteriores*) have intrinsic moral value,[11] or that respect for right reason
is required in any virtuous act.[12] But aside from the problems involved in interpreting the speculative works, how are we to determine their bearing on Ockham's politics if we do not know what is
essential in the political treatises themselves? The difficulty of
such questions is reflected in the present unsettled state of Ockham
scholarship, and a review of major issues in current interpretation
will prove helpful in charting our course. First, however, it will be
well to consider Ockham's complicated involvement in politics on a
more concrete plane through a brief survey of his life and works.

7 *Guillelmi de Ockham Opera Politica*, vol. I, ed. J. G. Sikes, H. S. Offler, and R. F.
Bennett, vol. II, ed. J. G. Sikes and H. S. Offler, vol. III, ed. H. S. Offler (University
of Manchester Press, 1940, 1963, 1956). This edition will be referred to as *OP*, with
volume and page numbers. Individual works are discussed below.
8 Ockham, *Opus Nonaginta Dierum*, cc. 2–32; *OP* I, 301–74; *OP* II, 375–509.
9 Ockham, *Contra Ioannem*, *OP* III, 19–156. The so-called *De Dogmatibus*, always
printed as the second part of the *Dialogus* (cited below, note 61) deals with John
XXII's adhesion to this error before his death.
10 For a detailed enumeration and discussion of these works, see Baudry, *Guillaume
d'Occam* and Miethke, *Ockhams Weg*. On the range of scholarly interpretation of
them, see above, note 5.
11 *Scriptum in Quattuor Libros Sententiarum* (to be cited as *Sent.*) III, q. 12, especially
sections E–G. Ockham's commentary on the *Sentences* of Peter Lombard, his most
important theological and philosophical work, occupies vols. III and IV of Trechsel's edition of Ockham's *Opera Plurima* (Lyon, 1494–6; Gregg Press facsimile,
London, 1962). In the *Quodlibeta Septem* (Strasbourg, 1491; facsimile by Éditions
de la Bibliothèque S.J., Louvain, 1962), see, besides IV, 6 (almost identical with
Sent. III, 12), I, 20; II, 16, and III, 13–14.
12 *Sent.* III, 12, CCF–FFF; A–G.

OCKHAM'S INVOLVEMENT IN POLITICS

'I call God as my witness that I have never desired anything after the salvation of my soul as much as I have desired that man's salvation, so that he would return to the bosom of holy mother church.'[13] This remark, attributed to Clement VI, the pontiff reigning at Avignon at the end of Ockham's life, indicates that he was a political figure at least in the sense of being considered important by a 'political' pope.[14] Clement's remark was in fact apposite in half a dozen ways, for Ockham was roughly in succession a premier theologian and logician, a personally alienated intellectual, a Spiritual Franciscan, an implacable enemy of three Avignonese popes (John XXII, Benedict XII, and Clement himself), a propagandist for the imperial rights of the excommunicate Ludwig of Bavaria, and the proponent of a secular world government essentially independent of traditional ecclesiastical sanctions. Significant issues for the study of his work are posed by the presence or absence of political factors in each of these phases of Ockham's life.

It is commonly held that nominalism was the death of scholasticism and that Ockham's political ideas were destructive of the medieval social order. Hence, it is important to recognize that at the beginning of his career Ockham was very much a part of the religious and academic establishment. In his early work at Oxford he explicitly disagreed with such figures as St Thomas and Duns Scotus on fundamental points of metaphysics and epistemology, but he discussed their views, especially those of Scotus, in detail and with respect.[15] Indeed, it has been argued that Ockham's aim was to maintain the intellectual standard of his great predecessors against the 'second-rate' scholasticism current in writers like Egidius Romanus. 'His criticisms are rarely directed against the "ancients" . . . Ockham's unnamed adversary, for whom he has little sympathy and less

---

13 Pope Clement VI, as quoted by Conrad of Megenberg, *Tractatus contra Wilhelmum Occam*, in R. Scholz (ed.), *Unbekannte kirchenpolitische Streitschriften aus der Zeit Ludwigs des Bayern (1327–1354)*, II (Rome, 1914), 364.

14 See, for example, G. Mollat, *The Popes at Avignon*, transl. Janet Love (New York, 1965), pp. 37–43.

15 For example, in treating the problem of universals, Ockham went to considerable trouble to lay out the position of Scotus, 'qui alios in subtilitate iudicii excellebat'. *Sent.* I Di. 2, q. 6B.

respect, is the *communis opinio modernorum.*[16] Especially on the point which most sharply divides *nominales* from *reales*, the issue of realism itself, Ockham claimed to proceed constructively, for he held that it was realism, not nominalism, that destroyed the possibility of genuine knowledge. To posit non-singular things outside the mind was, he said, not only absurd, but it destroyed the whole of Aristotle's philosophy and all science, truth, and reason. This opinion was not only the worst error in philosophy, but those holding it were incapable of grasping scientific knowledge.[17] It is unnecessary to accept these claims in order to appreciate the affirmative spirit in which Ockham made them. In this spirit, too, we are entitled to interpret the widespread acceptance of his ideas in academic circles within his own lifetime, in spite of their having come under examination at Avignon, and in spite of Ockham's excommunication on other grounds in 1328. Such acceptance, which at first met opposition, to be sure,[18] would scarcely have been possible if these ideas had been generally perceived as a skeptical threat to the established intellectual

16 E. A. Moody, 'Ockham and Aegidus of Rome', *FcS*, IX (1949), 414–42; p. 442. For Ockham's reference to the 'detestanda praesumptio' of certain 'moderni', who slander any opinion differing from their own, see *The De Sacramento Altaris of William of Ockham*, ed. T. B. Birch (Burlington, Iowa, 1930), p. 444; see pp. 166 and 126 for similar expressions.

17 Ockham, commentary on Aristotle's *De Interpretatione*, cited by E. A. Moody in his preface to Ockham's *Expositionis in Libros Artis Logicae Prooemium et Expositio in Librum Porphyrii de Praedicabilibus* (St Bonaventure, N.Y., 1965), pp. xviii–xix. Ockham presented his own work in logic as an instrument of scientific knowledge, not as a weapon for skeptics. Logic, he said, was the 'most apt instrument' of all the arts. Without it no science could be perfectly known. *Summa Logicae, Pars Prima*, ed. P. Boehner (St Bonaventure, N.Y., 1957), *Proemialis Epistola*, p. 7. Cf. Baudry, *Guillaume d'Occam*, p. 23n. Comparisons of Ockham with Hume (as by Gilson in *The Unity of Philosophical Experience*) should be balanced by attention to contemporary nominalism, which shares Ockham's logical and scientific interests more than Hume did and which, though rigorously critical, is certainly not skeptical in its philosophical program (as yet, to be sure, it has no theological program). See Nelson Goodman, *Fact, Fiction, and Forecast* (London, 1955) and 'A world of individuals' in *The Problem of Universals* (Notre Dame, Indiana, 1956), pp. 13–33.

18 Conrad of Megenberg, writing against Ockham shortly after his death, compared him with the dragon of the apocalypse and estimated that a third part of the world had apostatized from sound philosophy to follow him. *Tractatus contra Wilhelmum Occam*, in Scholz, *Streitschriften*, II, 347. On official reaction to this trend at the University of Paris, see R. Paqué, *Das pariser Nominalistenstatut (1340)* (Berlin, 1970).

order.[19] There is a similar apparent innocence in the relation between Ockham's early work and the established moral and institutional order. Although he put forward basic theses in psychology and ethics which might affect the way men thought of themselves and their moral obligations, he said nothing to change the outward content of those obligations.[20] There is nothing in his early writings remotely resembling an attack on the dominant secular or ecclesiastical powers of the day – in contrast with the dissident and heretical movements of Italy and southern France, he presents no indictments of the carnal institutional church[21] and no apocalyptic schemes of history. In short, while the importance of Ockham's early work for the history of thought can scarcely be exaggerated, he was not in the

[19] 'Le caractère scandaleux de la doctrine d'Occam est une découverte toute moderne; du XIVe au XVIIe siècle, personne ne s'en est aperçu.' E. Gilson, 'La philosophie franciscaine', in *Saint François d'Assise: son œuvre, son influence* (Paris, 1927), pp. 148–75; p. 171. As E. A. Moody has argued ('Empiricism and metaphysics in medieval philosophy', *Philosophical Review*, LXVII (1958), 145–63), the critical empiricism of such thinkers as Ockham was quite consistent with the deeper motives of scholastic theology. The widely held belief that scholastic theology was primarily interested in philosophy as a source of support for its own positions is appropriate only to a much later historical situation. In the fourteenth century, the purely rational speculative metaphysics of the Greeks and Arabs presented itself more as a rival to theology than as its handmaid. Hence, the 'anti-metaphysical' aspect of Ockhamism should not uncritically be taken as a sign of theological decay. For the spread of nominalism see F. Ehrle, *Der Sentenzkommentar Peters von Candia, des Pisaner Papstes Alexanders V, FzS, Beiheft* IX (Münster, 1925), 112–251; G. Ritter, *Studien zur Spätscholastik*; I: *Marsilius von Inghen und die ockhamistische Schule in Deutschland* (Heidelberg, 1921); II: *Via Antiqua und Via Moderna auf den deutschen Universitäten des XV. Jahrhunderts* (Heidelberg, 1922); G. Leff, *Paris and Oxford Universities in the Thirteenth and Fourteenth Centuries: an Institutional and Intellectual History* (New York, 1968), pp. 248–55.

[20] Ockham's discussions of the moral virtues (see notes 11–12) obviously presuppose that such virtues exist. Cf. his affirmative answer to the question, whether there can be a science of morals (*Quodlibeta Septem*, II, 14).

[21] See especially the expressions of respect for the authority of the Roman church quoted by Lagarde, *La naissance de l'esprit laïque*, new ed., IV (Paris, 1962), 18n. It is difficult to attach much significance, except after the fact, to Guelluy's judgment that 'la rigueur de ses critiques [in Ockham's commentary on the *Sentences*] laisse présager la violence de ses futures attaques contre le pape' (*Philosophie et théologie chez Guillaume d'Ockham*, p. 359). Equally sinister omens might be found in the works of many a theologian who never came into conflict with the papacy. Ockham's most eminent theological follower in the late fifteenth century, Gabriel Biel, was also a notable defender of papal prerogatives. See his *Defensorium Obedientiae Apostolicae et Alia Documenta*, ed. H. A. Oberman, D. E. Zerfoss, and W. J. Courtenay (Cambridge, Mass., 1968), pp. 3–55.

beginning a political person. He began as an academic theologian with strong interests in logic, psychology, and the philosophy of science.

In 1324, after teaching at Oxford for some years but apparently before receiving the doctorate, Ockham was summoned to the papal court at Avignon to answer charges of heresy brought against some of his doctrines by a former chancellor of the university, John Lutterell. The proceedings at Avignon have been extensively discussed elsewhere.[22] We need only note various features of the case which suggest that ecclesiastical politics played a part. Thus, there is some evidence that Ockham's accuser, Lutterell, who had been so unpopular among the regent masters at Oxford that he was expelled as chancellor there, went to Avignon in hope of ecclesiastical preferment, which he eventually received.[23] At any rate, although Lutterell was a doctor of theology, the set of purportedly Ockhamist theses he prepared shows a surprisingly poor grasp of Ockham's views – the papally appointed examining commission had to revise the list substantially before it could begin its own inquiry.[24] The two verdicts reached by this commission in successive years also count against the objectivity of the proceedings. Out of fifty-one

22 Besides the works of Hofer, Baudry, and Miethke already cited, see A. Pelzer, 'Les 51 articles de Guillaume Occam censurés en Avignon en 1326', *Revue d'histoire ecclésiastique*, xviii (1922), 240–70; J. Koch, 'Neue Aktenstücke zu dem gegen Wilhelm Ockham in Avignon geführten Prozeß', *Recherches de théologie ancienne et médiévale*, vii (1935), 353–80, and viii (1936), 79–93, 168–97; Gordon Leff, *Bradwardine and the Pelagians*, pp. 189–92; C. K. Brampton, 'Personalities in the process against Ockham at Avignon, 1324–1326', *FcS*, xxv (1966), 4–25; D. Burr, 'Ockham, Scotus and the censure at Avignon', *Church History*, xxxvii (1968), 144–59; C. J. Chambers, 'William Ockham, theologian: convicted for lack of evidence', *Journal of the History of Philosophy*, vii (1969), 381–9.

23 Lutterell was removed from the chancellorship by the bishop of Lincoln at the express request of the Oxford regent masters. There had been complaints that his actions threatened to excite a schism dangerous to the whole English church. See Miethke, *Ockhams Weg*, pp. 46–74, for the best account of the matter, many details of which are still obscure. On Lutterell's purposes at Avignon, see Brampton, 'Personalities', pp. 13n., 12.

24 Brampton ('Personalities', p. 24n.) quotes G. N. Buescher's conclusion (*The Eucharistic Teaching of William of Ockham* (St Bonaventure, New York, 1950)): 'After placing Lutterell's articles and accusations side by side with Ockham's teachings, it is bewildering to attempt an understanding or an explanation either of the ex-chancellor's accusations or of his attitude towards the Venerable Inceptor's Eucharistic teachings. That Lutterell did not have first hand information concerning Ockham's doctrine is hardly believable.'

articles considered in 1324–5, the examiners found many to be erroneous but not one heretical. The commission was then set to work on a second inquiry, this one resulting in a finding of heresy in connection with ten articles. We can only speculate as to whether John XXII's recent and continuing attacks on the Spiritual Franciscans were important in stimulating a second and harsher examination of the order's most brilliant theologian. To Ockham, suspicions of this sort would have been natural, especially since his examiners appeared so unwilling to understand the theological system whose theses they condemned. The report of the second examination begins with a new, fairly detailed discussion of an article on justification, but its main difference from the first report is the finding of heresy where previously there had been only error. Both reports have been criticized for dealing with Ockham's views on the basis of snippets taken out of context and badly understood at that.[25] The examining commission submitted its second report to the pope in 1326.[26] Thereupon the documents in the case were turned over to Jacques Fournier (later Benedict XII) for his opinion. No further action had been taken, as far as we know, by the time Ockham fled from Avignon nearly two years later. Indeed, there was no subsequent formal action of any kind. In a letter to the king of Bohemia, the pope was willing to brand Ockham a heresiarch for the ideas on which he had been examined at Avignon, but his excommunication was based on his having fled the papal curia with Michael of Cesena, not on the results of Lutterell's process against him.[27] The objective orthodoxy

[25] Brampton, 'Personalities', pp. 13–14. The sixteenth article of the first report is moved up to first place and criticized much more extensively. It is no longer called Pelagian in one sense and erroneous in another, but 'erroneus et sapit heresim Pelagianam vel peius' (Koch, *Neue Aktenstücke*, III, 84ff.). See also Burr, 'Ockham and censure at Avignon', and Miethke, *Ockhams Weg*, p. 64, n. 230. Lagarde (*La naissance de l'esprit laïque*, IV, p. 19) characterizes the examining commission as 'passablement malveillante'.

[26] Pelzer, 'Les 51 articles de Guillaume Occam', p. 242.

[27] *Bullarium Franciscanum sive Romanorum Pontificum Constitutiones, Epistolae, Diplomata tribus ordinibus Minorum . . . concessa*, V–VII (Rome, 1898–1902) [*BF*], V, 480. In a general letter of May 1328 John asserted that by fleeing Ockham had rendered himself guilty of the crime of heresy for which he had been delated to the curia ('occulte absque licentia nostra recesserit, se de dicto crimine reddendo convictum', *ibid.*, p. 346a), and in the bull of 6 June 1328 in which he deposed Michael and excommunicated him, Ockham, and Bonagratia he again referred to Ockham as a heretic (*ibid.*, p. 348b), but when he came to the sentence of excommunication

of Ockham's doctrine of justification is still in dispute,[28] but there is no doubt that the manner in which his teaching was examined would have strained even a patient man's confidence in the established system of justice. All in all, that process appears to have been a needless humiliation of an original but very cautious theologian. Although there are no direct references to it in his later writings,[29] such an ordeal must surely have reinforced the other, more important grounds for dissatisfaction with the papal government which were becoming evident to him at the same time.

John XXII thought at first that Ockham had fled the curia because of a bad conscience about the heresies for which he had been delated there, but he soon learned of Ockham's association with the Franciscans' minister general, Michael of Cesena. Early in May, 1328, Michael, Ockham, and a few other friars secretly left Avignon and took refuge with Ludwig of Bavaria, first in Italy and then, for the rest of Ockham's life, in Munich. The reason for Ockham's flight was his duty, as he saw it, to defend Franciscan devotion to poverty as a Christian ideal against no less a danger than papal heresy.

Francis of Assisi had found in the poverty of Christ and His apostles the pattern for a whole and perfect way of life, for which he himself provided a model to his followers by his own life and in the rule he laid down for the Franciscan order. Nothing in Ockham's early writings suggests a preoccupation with the contentions over this rule which had torn the order and engaged the concern of many other Christians for nearly a century.[30] To judge from his later works,

---

he proceeded against Michael and all his accomplices on the same ground, that they had left Avignon without his permission and had refused to return when summoned to do so (*ibid.*, p. 349*a*).

[28] Thus, H. Oberman concludes, against Seeberg and Vignaux, that Ockham taught a doctrine of predestination *post praevisa merita* (*The Harvest of Medieval Theology*, p. 211).

[29] Miethke (*Ockhams Weg*, p. 74) suggests that this was because Ockham saw that the matters at stake in his polemical works went beyond questions of academic theological correctness.

[30] Discussed most recently and provocatively by Gordon Leff (*Heresy in the Later Middle Ages*, pp. 51–255) and Brian Tierney (*Origins of Papal Infallibility, 1150–1350* (Leiden, 1972), pp. 171–237), both of whom find the conflict between John XXII's pronouncements and even the moderate Franciscan doctrine approved by previous popes irreconcilable. In Tierney's view John exercised the sovereign power of one pope to correct the mistakes of his predecessors, while the Michaelist rebels' insistence on the irreformability of the earlier decrees was an important step in the

he believed that the church was definitively committed to poverty as a spiritual ideal, as set forth in Bonaventure's *Apologia Pauperum* and Nicholas III's bull, *Exiit qui seminat*.[31] At the same time he may well have thought that the dispute between the majority of the order and the chiefly French and Italian *zelantes* who demanded that this ideal be concretely and strenuously implemented in the details of the friars' lives had been terminated by the debates at the Council of Vienne (1311–12) and the bulls issued there by Clement V, *Exivi de paradiso* and *Fidei catholicae fundamento*. Shortly before Ockham's arrival at the curia, however, John XXII, having reopened the whole question and solicited theological opinion outside the Franciscan order as well as within it, had issued the first in a series of bulls which, in the judgment of some historians, 'effectively destroyed Franciscan poverty', 'placed the friars in an impossible position', or 'looked like turning them into heretics'. In *Ad conditorem canonum* (8 December 1322),[32] John began by acknowledging that Nicholas III had been moved by pious consideration in ordaining that the Roman church should hold legal title (*proprietas* and *dominium*) to the things used by the Franciscans. Experience had shown, however, that this arrangement was an impediment both to the friars and to others.[33] John found, indeed, that even as an ideal complete legal poverty was contrary to law and reason, for concerning things which are consumed in being used, such as food and clothing, rightful use cannot be separated from ownership ('quod in talibus rebus usus iuris vel facti separatus a proprietate seu dominio possit constitui,

origin of the (unfortunate) doctrine of papal infallibility. Tierney regards Ockham's case against John XXII in the *Opus Nonaginta Dierum* as a tissue of illogical deductions and subtle points of interpretation. An excellent discussion of the poverty controversy with special regard to Ockham is provided by Miethke, *Ockhams Weg*, pp. 348–427. The controversy had considerable impact outside the Franciscan order. According to E. Jordan (as quoted by L. Oliger, 'Spirituels', *Dictionnaire de théologie catholique*, xiv.2 (Paris, 1941), cols. 2522–49; col. 2545), 'On peut dire, au moins pour le midi de l'Europe, que tout le monde, à ce moment, a dû plus ou moins prendre position dans la controverse, et qu'on ne connaît vraiment un homme de la première moitié du XIVe siècle que lorsqu'on sait dans quel camp il s'est rangé.'

31 Bonaventure, *Apologia pauperum*, in *Doctoris Seraphici S. Bonaventurae Opera Omnia*, ed. PP. Collegii a S. Bonaventura, viii (Ad Claras Aquas, 1898), pp. 233–330. Nicholas III, *Exiit qui seminat*, in A. Friedberg (ed.), *Corpus Iuris Canonici*, 2nd ed. (2 vols., Leipzig, 1879), ii, cols. 1108–21 (*Sext.* v, xii, 3).

32 *BF*, v, 233–46.   33 *Ibid.*, p. 235.

repugnat iuri et obviat rationi'),[34] and some kind of right of use (*ius utendi*) is connected with the licit use of anything whatever: 'simplex usus, idest sine iure utendi ... haberi nequeat'.[35] On the basis of these considerations, John renounced papal ownership of goods used by the Franciscans.[36] A year later, in *Cum inter nonnullos* (12 November 1323), he declared it heretical to deny that Christ and his apostles 'had' anything or to deny that they had any *ius* in the things they used, including the right to sell them or give them away.[37] The extent to which this bull ignored the theological complexities of the question and the authentically religious claims of the Franciscan position was little short of brutal. John proceeded as if the friars had denied any and every kind of 'having' to Christ and the apostles and then used the fact that Scripture often refers to their having things as a pretext for branding the assertion of absolute poverty as an attempt to destroy the catholic faith: 'scripturam sacram ... supponat continere mendacii [*sic*] ac per consequens, quantum in ea est, eius in totum fidem evacuans, fidem catholicam reddat ... dubiam et incertam'.[38] John's discussion of the *iura* of Christ and the apostles was hardly more subtle: the Franciscan denial of *iura* evidently supposed that Christ and the apostles were not just (*non iusta*) in their use of things.[39] '*Ad conditorem* had turned the friars into possessors; *Cum inter nonnullos* now looked like turning them into heretics.'[40] This was a remarkable way to handle an order which, along with an overly complex theory of poverty and undeniable afflictions of spiritual pride, had given so much to the church in its efforts to fulfill a particular dominical precept: 'If you wish

---

[34] P. 237.

[35] P. 241. John's most important argument for this more basic thesis was that *usus* without *ius* would be *iniustus*: 'Si simplex usus absque iure utendi haberi posset ab aliquo, constat, quod non iustus esset actus utendi huiusmodi reputandus, cum ille usus fuerit, cui non competebat ius utendi' (p. 242).

[36] Leff's judgment, that in *Ad conditorem canonum* John 'effectively destroyed Franciscan poverty' (*Heresy in the Later Middle Ages*, I, 165), may seem too strong, since John avowedly wished to stimulate the friars to 'real' rather than 'simulated' poverty (*BF*, V, 244–5), yet this recommendation is not easy to take at face value from one who had violently repressed the Spirituals for their adherence to the *usus pauper*. Bishop Moorman's judgment is close to Leff's: John placed the friars 'in an impossible position' (J. Moorman, *A History of the Franciscan Order from its Origins to the Year 1517* (Oxford, 1968), p. 317).

[37] *BF*, V, 256–9.   [38] *Ibid.*, pp. 256–7.   [39] Pp. 258–9.

[40] Moorman, *A History of the Franciscan Order*, p. 317.

to be perfect, go and sell all that you have, and give to the poor' (Matthew 19: 21). Near the end of 1324, in *Quia quorundam*, John claimed both that his previous pronouncements were consistent with *Exiit qui seminat* and that his own authority was sufficient to deal with such matters.[41] Ockham later asserted that he had only encountered these constitutions ('or rather, heretical destitutions') some years after coming to Avignon, when Michael of Cesena ordered him to study them. He had not read them earlier because he had not wanted to believe too easily that a person placed in so great an office would promulgate heresies.[42] Exactly this belief was forced upon him, however, for when he finally read John's pronouncements, he tells us, he found, 'quamplura haereticalia, erronea, stulta, ridiculosa, fantastica, insana et diffamatoria', which were patently against the orthodox faith, good morals, natural reason, certain experience, and fraternal charity.[43] Convinced that the pope had fallen into heresy, Ockham set his face against John's errors 'like the hardest rock', taking up an intensely personal opposition that was to shape decisively the rest of his life and work.[44]

There is a bitter irony in the resistance activities of the Michaelists, for until their break with the pope Michael of Cesena and Bonagratia of Bergamo, the lawyer in the group of friars fleeing from Avignon, had been leaders of the established order against the *zelantes*, even taking the initiative in measures which led to the burning of four of these Fraticelli or Spiritual Franciscans in 1318. They now felt

41 10 November 1324. *BF*, v, 271–80.
42 'Nolens leviter credere quod persona in tanto officio constituta haereses definiret esse tenendas, constitutiones haereticales ipsius nec legere nec habere curavi.' *Epistola ad Fratres Minores*, *OP* III, 6. No Franciscan wanted to believe that the pope would err in this matter. On Michael of Cesena's extended, desperate effort to reconcile John's pronouncements with previously accepted doctrines, see Tierney, *Origins of Papal Infallibility*, pp. 197–200.
43 *Epistola ad Fratres Minores in Capitulo apud Assisium Congregatos*, *OP* III, 6.
44 Ockham vowed that nothing short of physical coercion would stop him from attacking and refuting John's errors as long as he could write. 'Nam contra errores pseudo-papae praefati *posui faciem meam ut petram durissimam*' [Isa. 50: 7, with the continuation, 'et scio quoniam non confundar.' The preceding verse: 'Dominus Deus auxiliator meus, ideo non sum confusus.']. *Epistola ad Fratres Minores*, *OP* III, 15. If Ockham had not joined Michael of Cesena in the spring of 1328 there would probably be no *opera politica* of his now. When he wrote to the friars at Assisi, however, his overt political interests still extended no further than the defense of Franciscan poverty and the struggle against a heretical pope – this after six years under the protection of Ludwig of Bavaria.

obliged to act as defiantly as the more extreme friars[45] in defense of a position which seems comparatively bloodless – one can almost imagine an Angelo Clareno or Ubertino di Casale agreeing with John XXII that the poverty defended by the Michaelists was purely verbal. The propriety of describing Ockham as a Spiritual Franciscan is therefore debatable. Certainly the Michaelist movement must have had the sympathy of many friars in its early years, since, in contrast with earlier dissident movements, it stood for principles previously accepted by all Franciscans.[46] Indeed, Michael's constant theme was that the question of poverty had been clearly determined by the church in *Exiit qui seminat* and at Vienne and that he himself had 'legitimately' appealed against John XXII. His main writings are *Appellationes* based on the orthodoxy of previous official pronouncements, not expressions of private insight.[47] On the other hand, it is significant that Ockham never attempted to fix a gulf between his group and the extreme figures in the order. On the one occasion when he discusses the orthodoxy of Peter John Olivi's teachings, the moral and intellectual inspiration for so many of the Franciscan Spirituals, he presents several opinions without choosing among them. There are some, he says, who regard Olivi's whole teaching as catholic. Others find no clear heresy in it, but much that is false and fantastic, especially when Olivi predicts the future. Others reckon that his doctrine contains manifest heresies.[48] Although this survey shows at best a tolerance of Olivi's views rather than agreement with them, it should restrain us from drawing a sharp line between Ockham and the original Spirituals. If we are to describe the final struggle over Franciscan poverty in political terms, we can only

---

45 The Michaelists wrote more in these years than all of Munich's inhabitants since the city's founding, according to S. Riezler (*Geschichte Baierns*, II (Gotha, 1880), 561).

46 Cf. the friars' unanimous declaration at Perugia in 1322 and their re-election of Michael as minister general in 1328 in the face of strong papal pressure to depose him (Moorman, *A History of the Franciscan Order*, pp. 316ff.).

47 *Appellatio in Forma Maiori* (Pisa, 18 September 1328), in S. Baluze (ed.), *Miscellanea, novo ordine digesta et . . . aucta opere ac studio J. D. Mansi*, III (Lucca, 1764), 246–303. *Appellatio in Forma Minori* (Pisa, 12 December 1328), *ibid.*, 303–10; also printed in *BF*, v, 408–25.

48 I *Dialogus*, Book 2, c. xxiii, ed. Trechsel (cited below, note 61). At another place (I *Dial.* 4, xx, fol. 29r *ab*) he uses both Olivi and Joachim of Flores to illustrate the distinction between the condemnation of a person and the condemnation of doctrines asserted by him.

13

place John XXII at one extreme (a radical extreme, surely, in view of previous papal pronouncements), the friars burned at Marseilles at the other extreme, and the main body of the Franciscan order in the center.[49] John's policy – both his doctrine and his way of enforcing it – drove men like Ockham in the direction of the *zelantes*.

Turning now to the content of Ockham's writings on poverty, we find ideas of great potential interest for political thought – but the potentialities are not developed. Thus, in his first polemical work,[50] the *Opus Nonaginta Dierum*,[51] an exhaustive criticism from the Michaelist standpoint of John XXII's *Quia vir reprobus* (itself a detailed reply to Michael's criticisms of John's earlier constitutions),[52]

---

[49] Although the Michaelist movement is often presented as a spiritual and practical failure, its resemblance to the comparatively effective reform movement of the *Osservanti* in the early sixteenth century should not be overlooked. Decima Douie, *The Nature and Effect of the Heresy of the Fraticelli* (Manchester, 1932), p. viii; Moorman, *A History of the Franciscan Order*, p. 580.

[50] Leaving out of account the *Allegationes Religiosorum Virorum*, a joint response by several of the Michaelists to the election, in 1329, of Gerald Odonis as minister general of the Franciscans in place of Michael of Cesena (*BF*, v, 388a–396b), and a brief Minorite defense of Ludwig of Bavaria in 1331 (ed. W. Preger, 'Beiträge und Erörterungen zur Geschichte des Deutschen Reichs in den Jahren 1330–1334', *Abhandlungen der historischen Klasse der königlich bayerischen Akademie der Wissenschaften*, xv.2 (1880), 76–82).

[51] *Opus Nonaginta Dierum* [*OND*], *OP* i, 287–374 (cc. 1–6), *OP* ii (cc. 7–124). The *OND* is generally dated between 1322 and 1334 (nearer to 1332, according to Miethke, *Ockhams Weg*, p. 83; in 1333, according to Baudry, *Guillaume d'Occam*, p. 153). For the sources of the *OND* see *OP* ii, xv–xix. For an excellent discussion of the work, see Miethke, *Ockhams Weg*, pp. 428–535.

[52] 16 November 1329. *Quia vir reprobus* is a complex document. One of its more interesting contributions to the poverty controversy is a discussion of the 'keys' of *potestas* and *scientia*. In *Quia quorundam* (*BF*, v, 273) John had rejected the Michaelist contention that some papal determinations are made *per clavem scientiae* (these being irrevocable) and others *per clavem potestatis* (these being revocable by the pope or his successors). Without committing himself, John had presented the opinion that the spiritual key was in no way a *scientia* but a *ligandi atque solvendi potestas* (p. 272), and had pointed out that there is no mention of *scientia* in the primary Petrine text, Matthew 16: 18 (p. 273). Now, in *Quia vir reprobus*, he gave a more positive account of the *clavis scientiae*, but it is a markedly moral or devotional interpretation, not on the surface very scientific. According to the gloss, John says, the key of science is Christ's humility. He who has this has an open door to understanding the scriptures (p. 448). Or again, faith may be called the key of science. It was this that Peter had before the Lord promised him the keys of the kingdom of heaven. Peter had humility, too. Otherwise it would not have been revealed to him that Christ was the son of God, for God customarily reveals such things to little ones, that is, to the humble (p. 449). As to the Michaelist claim that no pope

Ockham notes that John's ascription of universal temporal monarchy to Christ implies that the pope, as Christ's vicar, would also have such power.[53] This is not his main objection to John's thesis, however, and Christ's temporal kingship is not the major topic of the *Opus Nonaginta Dierum*.[54] (It may be noted in passing that only in *Quia vir reprobus* did John himself go on to his more extreme claims concerning Christ's universal *dominium* and *regnum*. As he pointed out, he had asserted in *Cum inter nonnullos* only that Christ and the apostles had had *some* right in the things they used. There was no mention of *proprietas* or *dominium*. The issue having been raised by Michael, however, John was ready to proceed with it.)[55] Likewise, there are interesting discussions of the primitive church as a community deliberately setting up its own legal and economic institutions,[56] and passages on *ius naturale* which may represent Ockham's most original contribution to the controversy.[57] It can even be said that the whole debate is of great potential interest for legal and political theory, since ownership is treated in depth in all its aspects, economic, moral, legal, metaphysical, and religious. It remains the case, however, that neither in the *Opus Nonaginta Dierum* nor in any of his other works does Ockham attempt to construct a political theory on the basis of Franciscan poverty. There is no wholesale criticism of the institutional church and no suggestion that the poor should rule the world, or even govern the church. Perhaps this is entirely natural,

can revoke the definitions of his predecessors on matters of faith and morals, John's position here (as in *Quia quorundam*) is that it has yet to be shown that the question of whether Christ and the apostles had only 'simplex usus facti' is a matter of faith and morals. 'Dicant nobis assertores huiusmodi', he says, quoting *Quia quorundam* (p. 279) 'ubi legunt, quod ad fidem vel ad mores pertineat, Christum et apostolos non habuisse in iis, quae habuerunt, nisi simplicem facti usum' (p. 449).

53 *OND*, c. 93. *OP* II, 686–9.
54 It occupies Ockham for but three chapters (93–5), though they are certainly substantial chapters (pp. 670–729 in *OP* II).
55 *BF*, V, 439. After refuting Michael's claim that property was first introduced *iure humano*, John argued that Christ had universal *regnum* and *dominium* as a gift from God the Father from the moment of his conception. Christ's kingdom was not *from* the world, but it extended universally over the world.
56 *OND*, cc. 4–9 (*OP* I, 332 – *OP* II, 405). Cf. the treatment of the question, '*quo iure sit ius proprietatis seu dominii introductum*' (*OP* II, 655–70, cc. 88–92). The Michaelist answer: *iure humano*.
57 *OND*, c. 65 (*OP* II, 573–80). Leff, *Heresy in the Later Middle Ages*, I, 251. Miethke, *Ockhams Weg*, pp. 477–502.

for the polemical thrust of much of the work was to defend a way of life that had no legal standing. As his definitions of the key terms *ius utendi* and *dominium* make clear, the issue of Franciscan poverty was for Ockham not merely a matter of the friars' subjective renunciation of possessions (perhaps only a frame of mind) but also a matter of objective disengagement from the legal order, not as being outlaws, of course, but has having no legal recourse. *Ius utendi* is a licit power of using an external object, the unwarranted denial of which can be prosecuted in court; *dominium* (in the sense of the term most central to the dispute) is a 'principal power' of laying claim to a temporal thing in court.[58] In a sense the Franciscan ideal, even in its Michaelist form, was by nature 'non-political'. At least in Ockham's discussions of poverty, there is no effort to exploit the topic for broader institutional applications, and no sustained attempt to place it in the context of a broader Christian social theory.[59]

If the content of the poverty controversy was in essential respects non-political, its form raised an issue of tremendous political import. Ockham had not wanted to believe that a person holding the papal office would promulgate heresies as catholic truth. On reading John XXII's constitutions, however, he concluded that just this had

58 *ius utendi*: 'potestas licita utendi re extrinseca qua quis sine culpa sua et absque causa rationabili privari non debet invitus; *et si privatus fuerit, privantem poterit in iudicio convenire*' (*OP* I, 304). *Dominium* (among many senses the one most relevant to the dispute): 'Potestas humana principalis *vendicandi et defendendi in humano iudicio* rem aliquam temporalem' (*OP* I, 308), or, more strictly, 'potestas humana principalis rem temporalem *in iudicio vendicandi* et omni modo, qui non est a iure naturali prohibitus, pertractandi' (*OP* I, 310). Also see the discussion in cc. 108–19 (*OP* II, 782–823) of the question, whether it was licit for the apostles to litigate over temporal things. It has been argued (by M. Villey, 'La genèse du droit subjectif chez Guillaume d'Occam', *Archives de philosophie du droit*, IX (1964), 97–127) that in treating a right (*ius*) as a power of action of the individual rather than part of an (objective) common good, Ockham achieved a Copernican revolution in jurisprudence (p. 126), a revolution which has triumphed in the modern world due to a combination of egoism and a deformed extrapolation of Christian ideas (p. 97). We shall return to this criticism. It should be noted now that for Ockham a *ius* is always a licit power of action (and not merely what an individual is able to get away with) and that, however subjective or objective his idea of *ius* may have been in the OND, he did not use the idea there to criticize existing political institutions.

59 This is not to deny the political significance of many ideas discovered or developed by Ockham in the course of the poverty controversy. Thus, Miethke (*Ockhams Weg*, pp. 502–35) has found in the OND the beginnings of Ockham's later conception of the church.

occurred. The problem thus posed, the problem of papal heresy,[60] is the central concern of Ockham's longest and most complex polemical work, the first part of the *Dialogus* (1 *Dialogus*).[61] Once again, it will be helpful to determine in a preliminary way wherein this work is and is not political.

While John XXII and his doctrines are the formal subjects of such works as the *Opus Nonaginta Dierum* and the *Contra Ioannem*, they are mentioned only incidentally in the body of 1 *Dialogus*. It is made clear at the outset, however, that the current controversy among Christians about the catholic faith centers around John's orthodoxy. This is the moving cause of the entire discussion and was to have been explicitly dealt with in a second major part of the work. One of the two interlocutors, the student, has observed the other, the master, anxiously reading everything written against the pope and wants to question him about the whole matter of papal heresy. At the same time, the student expresses his own confidence in the pope's orthodoxy. Respecting the student's position, the master does not raise the issue of poverty and does not try to show that John is a heretic. As a result, the discussion proceeds generally and impersonally, and yet with fateful awareness of a particular crisis in the real world to which the theses discussed are highly relevant.[62]

---

[60] The term *papa haereticus* is so convenient that it is used even by Ockham, yet it is misleading. As we shall see (pp. 51–2 below), Ockham accepted the view that a person who had been duly elected pope ceased to be pope *ipso facto*, without need of formality, if he became a heretic. On this view, the phrase 'heretical pope' is a contradiction in terms. To be precise, we would need to speak of a pope who may become a heretic, or of a heretic who was once pope, but never of a person who is at one and the same time both pope and heretic.

[61] 1 *Dialogus* is used here in the Gregg Press facsimile edition (London, 1962) of Trechsel's edition of Ockham's *Opera Plurima* (Lyon, 1494), in which it occupies fols. 1–165 of vol. I. The work was also published by Stol (Paris, 1476) and M. Goldast (*Monarchia Sancti Romani Imperii* (3 vols., Hanover and Frankfurt, 1611–14; reprinted Graz, 1960)), II, 394–739.

The work must have been completed by the end of 1334 and presumably follows the *Opus Nonaginta Dierum*. (See Miethke, *Ockhams Weg*, p. 85, with references; and Baudry, *Guillaume d'Occam*, p. 163.) For a useful summary, see Jacob, 'Ockham as a political thinker', pp. 91–7.

[62] Although he is a 'sincerissimus zelator' of the pope and heartily detests his adversaries, the student is evidently torn between this loyalty to the pope and his respect for the teaching of the master, a motive which leads him to request at first that the master refrain from asserting his own views, lest his authority coerce the student's understanding. Then, however, he asks that the master open his mind to

A serious problem of interpretation is thus posed. It is not merely a matter of identifying Ockham's own opinions in the welter of views canvassed in this gigantic work. That is a sometimes complicated but rarely impossible task, one made easier by an indication in the prologue that Ockham's position will always be included among the theses presented on each issue. Using this indication along with our knowledge of Ockham's situation and his other works, we can proceed by eliminating clearly non-Ockhamist views with a high likelihood of finding Ockham's opinion in the remainder.[63] A more significant problem is to determine why Ockham chose to write in this unusual fashion. Although close study will usually reveal it, his position is not always immediately apparent. Yet we know that Ockham considered John XXII's pontificate a menace which urgently required action for the good of the church. Why, then, since he was already personally implicated and was convinced of the need for effective action, did he produce such an elliptical work? The perplexing relation between abstract format and concrete problems is a difficult and distinctive problem in understanding I *Dialogus* as a political work. A further problem is posed by the peculiar subject of the work.

In the context of medieval political thought, any work centering around the papacy is necessarily political, for whatever other vital forces may have been present in medieval history, the development of a hierocratic ideology centered around the papal monarchy was a potent factor in Western politics, in practice, in the science of jurisprudence, in political theology, and so on.[64] From this standpoint, I *Dialogus* is highly political simply in being concerned with the

him before the end of the work and not think that he will incur any fault for doing so. I *Dialogus, prologus*, fol. 11a. This balancing of personal attitudes, respect for professional competence, and awareness of grave issues in the world outside is surprisingly subtle in a writer so little practiced in literary devices. It deserves to be taken seriously.

63 'Quamvis enim velis [velim?] omnino ut cum diversas et adversas assertiones fueris discursurus *tuam conclusionem minime praetermittas*, quae tamen tua sit, nullatenus manifestes' (I *Dialogus, prologus*, fol. 11a). The importance of this passage as a basis for identifying Ockham's views in the *Dialogus* was first noticed by Y. D. Knysh, 'Political authority as property and trusteeship in the works of William of Ockham' (University of London Ph.D. thesis, 1968).

64 W. Ullmann, *The Growth of Papal Government in the Middle Ages*, 4thed.(London, 1970). L. Buisson, *Potestas und Caritas: die päpstliche Gewalt im Spätmittelalter* (Cologne, 1958).

papacy. At the same time, and indeed because of the power of the hierocratic standpoint, 1 *Dialogus* may be described as the most thoroughly anti-political work of the later middle ages. This is because of its peculiar subject, the problem of the heretical pope or, more precisely, the heretical pseudo-pope. If a political work is one which concerns a scheme of government, then the thinker who considers this unique problem with full seriousness in a hierocratic context may seem committed to anarchy rather than politics. Many students of Ockham have found 1 *Dialogus* unassimilable. This is in part because the work is large, apparently ill-organized, apparently inconclusive, and available only in manuscript and in the unsatisfactory editions of Trechsel and Goldast. More important than any of these sources of difficulty, however, is the vertigo produced by a work centered on an absolute monarch who is not even a citizen, a *caput ecclesiae* who is not even a Christian. If Ockham had been ready to propose a regular alternative scheme of government for the church, or if he had been willing to submerge the church in a secular state after the manner of Marsilius of Padua, there would have been a stable *point d'appui* for dealing with papal heresy. Recent studies have suggested, however, that Ockham was not a conciliarist,[65] and in 1 *Dialogus* there is no theory of the secular state.[66] Hence, in

---

[65] B. Tierney, 'Ockham, the conciliar theory and the canonists', *Journal of the History of Ideas*, xv (1954), 40–70 (now reprinted with a useful introduction by H. A. Oberman, Facet Books, Historical Series, xix (Philadelphia, 1971)); *Foundations of the Conciliar Theory* (Cambridge, 1955, reprinted 1969); J. B. Morrall, 'Ockham and ecclesiology', *Medieval Studies Presented to Aubrey Gwynn, S.J.*, ed. J. A. Watt, J. B. Morrall, F. X. Martin (Dublin, 1961), 481–91; G. de Lagarde, *La naissance de l'esprit laïque*, discussed below (pp. 29–34; conciliarism on pp. 30–1). The absence of a conciliar theory of church government in 1 *Dialogus* is all the more significant (as Morrall suggests, 'Ockham and ecclesiology,' p. 485) in view of the schemes afoot at the time for bringing John XXII to trial before a council. For these schemes, which centered around Cardinal Napoleon Orsini, see C. A. Willemsen, *Kardinal Napoleon Orsini* (Berlin, 1927), pp. 115–29; O. Bornhak, *Staatskirchliche Anschauungen und Handlungen am Hofe Kaiser Ludwigs des Bayern* (Weimar, 1933), 37–43; Miethke, *Ockhams Weg*, pp. 85–7.

[66] Emperors, kings, and other secular rulers enter into the work, especially in Book 6, cc. 1–9, 53–4, 57, 62, 83–5, 89, 91–100; and in Book 7, cc. 35, 52–5, 69. Except perhaps in the inconclusive discussion of the emperor's jurisdiction over the pope (Book 6, cc. 2–9), however, no systematic conception of the essential nature of these secular offices is employed. In the sense of 'secular politics', then, 1 *Dialogus* is much more political than the *Opus Nonaginta Dierum*, but still falls far short of such later works as III *Dialogus*, the *Octo Quaestiones*, and the *Breviloquium*.

the major work of his first decade of polemical activity, there is a severe tension between the political importance of the subject treated and the apparently irresponsible or at least unsystematic position taken concerning it.

It is agreed that the year 1337 was a turning point in Ockham's career as a publicist. It was in the *Contra Benedictum*, written at this time, that he first attempted to determine the limits of the power of even an orthodox pope, a problem henceforth never far from his mind and one which was indubitably political in every sense of the term.[67] The central difficulty was to form an adequate conception of the distinctive 'fullness of power' – *plenitudo potestatis* – traditionally attributed to the pope. After raising this problem in the *Contra Benedictum*,[68] Ockham treated it intensively in each of the important works which followed: III *Dialogus*,[69] the *Octo Quaestiones*,[70] and

---

[67] *Contra Benedictum*, ed. H. S. Offler, *OP* III, 157–322. The dating of the work should perhaps be extended to early 1338 (Offler, *OP* III, 162). Book VI is 'Ockham's first known excursion into the contemporary political debate between the papacy and the empire' (*ibid.*, p. 159). 'In books VI and VII of the *Contra Benedictum*, he approaches directly for the first time the political problem posed by that conflict between papacy and empire which was the background of his later life and which did something to guarantee him freedom of expression. Thus the *Contra Benedictum* is the bridge over which Ockham passed from ecclesiology to a developed interest in political matters' (*ibid.*, pp. 162–3).

[68] *Contra Benedictum*, Book 6, cc. 2–4; *OP* III, 273–7. The problem of *plenitudo potestatis* had been very lightly touched on in I *Dialogus* 7, lxvii, fol. 160rb.

[69] The incomplete third part of the *Dialogus* (III *Dialogus*), used here in the edition of Trechsel (*Opera Plurima* I, fols. 181–276), consists of two tracts, one on the power of the pope and clergy, the second on the rights of the Roman empire. *Plenitudo potestatis* is the subject of Book I of the first tract (III *Dialogus* I, I). III *Dialogus* is variously dated from 1338 to 1346. Miethke, who discusses the problem in detail (*Ockhams Weg*, pp. 121ff.), thinks it possible that the first tract was completed before 1342, but finds no basis for setting narrower limits to the dating of the second tract than 1341–6 (p. 125). I am inclined to accept the somewhat earlier dating proposed by Baudry (*Guillaume d'Occam*, pp. 214–16) and accepted by Lagarde: 1339–41 for the two tracts together, for the third of the *Octo Quaestiones* would seem to be a more mature treatment of the problem of governmental unity under discussion at the end of III *Dialogus*. But the *Octo Quaestiones* was completed no later than 1342 (see next note).

[70] *Octo Quaestiones de Potestate Papae* [*OQ*], ed. J. G. Sikes, *OP* I, 1–221. This work can be quite confidently dated between 1340 and 1342. In an essay demonstrating, among other things, that the *quidam vir venerabilis* who posed the eight questions to Ockham was not Ludwig of Bavaria, H. S. Offler gives reason to narrow the dates further to between the fall of 1340 and the summer of 1341 (H. S. Offler, 'The origin of Ockham's *Octo Quaestiones*', *The English Historical Review*, LXXXII (1967), 323–32; p. 332). *Plenitudo potestatis* is the main subject of *Quaestio* I.

the *Breviloquium*;[71] he presented his views finally and more concisely in the *De Imperatorum et Pontificum Potestate*.[72] In each work the problem is posed in terms of substantially the same extreme hierocratic thesis, the thesis that the pope has such plenitude of power in both spiritual and temporal matters that he can do anything not expressly contrary to divine law or natural right, even things contrary to generally accepted human law (*ius gentium*), or to civil or canon law.[73] Although Ockham sometimes considers as many as eighteen arguments in favor of this thesis, the balance of his discussion is always heavily against it and in favor of a more moderate view. A limited conception of papal power implies that there are other powers which do not emanate from the pope. Accordingly, as the usual sequel to his refutation of extreme papalist claims about *plenitudo potestatis* in general, Ockham goes on to show that the

71 *Breviloquium de Principatu Tyrannico super divina et humana, specialiter autem super imperium et subiectos imperio, a quibusdam vocatis summis pontificibus usurpato* [*Brev.*], ed. R. Scholz, with an essay by Scholz on *Wilhelm von Ockham als politischer Denker* (Leipzig, 1944; unaltered reprint, Stuttgart, 1952). Future references will be to this edition. The work has also been edited by L. Baudry (Paris, 1937). It is generally dated 1341–2 (Miethke, *Ockhams Weg*, p. 116; Baudry, *Guillaume d'Occam*, p. 218). Book II of the *Brev.* is concerned with *plenitudo potestatis*.

72 *De Imperatorum et Pontificum Potestate* [*Imp. Pont. Pot.*], ed. Scholz, *Streitschriften*, II, pp. 453–80. Also ed. C. K. Brampton (Oxford, 1927). Both Scholz and Brampton worked from a single manuscript. W. Mulder (*AFH*, XVI (1923), 469 92; XVII (1924), 72–97) gave additional material from the other known manuscript of the work. Unless otherwise noted, references will be to Scholz's edition. The *Imp. Pont. Pot.* is generally dated 1347 (Baudry, *Guillaume d'Occam*, p. 232; Miethke, *Ockhams Weg*, p. 133). Offler (*OP* III, 164) more cautiously suggests 1346 or 1347. It is thus Ockham's last significant political work (leaving aside the brief and somewhat dubious *De Electione Caroli Quarti* and assuming that Ockham did no significant work on III *Dialogus* after that date). The papalist view of *plenitudo potestatis* is dealt with in chapter 1. Ockham tries to determine the proper limits of papal power in succeeding chapters.

73 'Papa in spiritualibus et temporalibus habet talem plenitudinem potestatis, ut omnia possit quae non sunt expresse contra legem divinam nec contra ius naturae, licet sint contra ius gentium, civile vel canonicum'. *OQ* I, 2; *OP* I, 15. Similar formulations are to be found in I *Dialogus* 7, lxvii, fol. 160rb; *Contra Benedictum* VI, 2 (*OP* III, 273) (the only case I have found in which Ockham used the expression *potentia absoluta* in connection with papal power); III *Dialogus* I, I, i, fol. 181va; *Brev.* II, I, p. 53; *Imp. Pont. Pot.*, c. I, p. 455. Ockham's formulation of the extreme papalist idea of *plenitudo potestatis* as a power to do anything not expressly contrary to divine or natural law has been criticized as idiosyncratic. For similar formulations in Egidius Romanus and Augustinus Triumphus, see below, chapter 4, note 16.

empire in particular is not 'from the pope', but, in a carefully specified sense, 'solely from God'.[74]

Besides his treatment of *plenitudo potestatis*, another indication of the specifically political character of Ockham's later polemical works is the fact that some of them defend particular policies in secular affairs. The *Octo Quaestiones* is in effect a defense of the German nation for treating Ludwig of Bavaria as emperor in virtue of his election in 1314 by a majority of the imperial electors but in the absence of papal approval.[75] The brief *Consultatio de Causa Matrimoniali*[76] defends Ludwig's politically significant annulment of the countess of Tyrol's marriage to the second son of the King of Bohemia. The *De Electione Caroli Quarti* attacks the electors' withdrawal of support from Ludwig and their election of the King of Bohemia's eldest son in his place.[77] In all of these works, as well as in his defense of Edward III's right to impose a war tax on the English churches without the pope's consent,[78] Ockham wrote in favor of Ludwig of Bavaria, and in some accounts this personal bond figures as the most important factor in his career as a political writer.[79] There is reason to doubt, however, that Ludwig had much

[74] *OQ* II; *OP* I, 69–97. *Brev.* IV–VI, pp. 141–207. *Imp. Pont. Pot.*, c. 19, pp. 472–3.
[75] Questions IV and VIII. On Questions V–VII, however, see note 148 below.
[76] Ed. H. S. Offler, *OP* I, 273–86. Written before 10 February 1342. *Ibid.*, p. 274.
[77] Contained only in Conrad of Megenberg's *Tractatus contra Wilhelmum Occam* (Scholz, *Streitschriften*, II, 346–63. For the dating (late 1347 or early 1348) and slightly dubious authenticity of this work, see Miethke, *Ockhams Weg*, pp. 135–6.
[78] *An Princeps pro suo succursu, scilicet guerrae, possit recipere bona ecclesiarum, etiam invito papa*. Ed. H. S. Offler and R. H. Snape, *OP* I, 223–71. For the dating, see Professor Offler's introduction. For the political situation see also H. S. Offler, 'England and Germany on the eve of the hundred years war', *The English Historical Review*, LIV (1939), 608–31; F. Bock, *Das deutsch-englische Bündnis von 1335–1342*; I: *Quellen* (Munich, 1956).
[79] On Ludwig's struggle with the curia for recognition of his authority as emperor, see H. O. Schwöbel, *Der diplomatische Kampf zwischen Ludwig d. Bayern und der römischen Kurie im Rahmen des kanonischen Absolutionsprozesses* (Weimar, 1968); F. Bock, 'Die Prokuratorien Kaiser Ludwigs IV. an den Papst Benedict XII', *Quellen und Forschungen aus italienischen Archiven und Bibliotheken*, XXV (1933), 251–91. H. S. Offler, 'Über die Prokuratorien Ludwigs des Bayern für die römische Kurie', *DA*, VIII (1950), 461–87 and 'Empire and papacy – the last struggle', *Transactions of the Royal Historical Society*, Series V, 6 (1956), 21–47. For Ludwig's disclaimers of sympathy with the rebel Franciscans on the poverty question – he protested that he agreed with them only in things pertaining to the imperial jurisdiction and the preservation of his own rights – see O. Berthold, *Kaiser, Volk und Avignon* (Berlin, 1960), pp. 210–14. On his undertaking to surrender Ockham,

interest in the Franciscan campaign against John XXII on the poverty question except as it provided collateral support for his own struggle with John over the empire. His later willingness to offer up the friars at his court as a part of a reconciliation with the papacy adds yet another shadow to the picture of Ludwig and Ockham as devoted mutual defenders. On Ockham's side, too, there are signs of an independent approach to the issues at hand. The *An Princeps . . .*, Ockham's tract for the English king, begins with an encomium of Edward markedly more enthusiastic than any reference to Ludwig in his more important pro-imperial treatises.[80] Ockham's refutations of the hierocratic idea of *imperium a papa* correspond, of course, with Ludwig's persistent efforts to maintain his imperial rights in the face of papal opposition, and Ockham may have had an important role in formulating Ludwig's claims at the historic national assemblies of Rhens and Frankfurt in 1338.[81] Even here, however, the coincidence of views was probably not complete. It is doubtful, for example, how seriously Ludwig wished to be regarded as a successor to the pagan Caesars in the sense Ockham was to give that succession.[82] He has been praised as a German lawgiver,[83] but also treated

Marsilius of Padua, and the other heretics and schismatics at his court if he could not lead them back to the church with him, see *ibid.*, pp. 210–11 and 220.

[80] The point is noted by C. K. Brampton ('Ockham, Bonagratia and the Emperor Lewis IV', *Medium Aevum*, XXXI (1962), 81–7; 81–2) as evidence against the view of Ockham as merely a defender of his protector's interests.

[81] Although it did not last long, the widespread support given the emperor at this time marks an important stage in the development of German national self-consciousness. F. Bock, *Reichsidee und Nationalstaaten* (Munich, 1943); E. E. Stengel, *Avignon und Rhens* (Weimar, 1930). For the sources, including the imperial constitutions *Fidem catholicam* and *Licet iuris*, see Berthold, *Kaiser, Volk und Avignon*. For discussion and references concerning Ockham's influence, see Miethke, *Ockhams Weg*, pp. 101–4 and H.-J. Becker, 'Das Mandat *Fidem Catholicam* Ludwigs des Bayern von 1338', *DA*, XXVI (1970), 454–512.

[82] As Wilks notes (*Sovereignty in the Later Middle Ages*, p. 191), Ludwig did much to nullify the effect of his coronation 'by the Roman people' in 1328 when he subsequently submitted to a second coronation by the anti-pope Nicholas V. There is not a word in *Fidem catholicam* about the universal authority of the empire. In *Licet iuris*, the claim that 'eidem [scil. imperatori] omnes subsunt nationes' and the reference to rendering unto Caesar what is Caesar's are balanced by repeated assertions of the more limited claim that 'eidem *ab omnibus subiectis imperio* debeat obediri' (Berthold, *Kaiser, Volk und Avignon*, p. 284). Ludwig was in no position to assert more.

[83] H. Lieberich, 'Kaiser Ludwig der Baier als Gesetzgeber', *Zeitschrift der Savigny-Stiftung für Rechtsgeschichte*, LXXXIX, *Germanistische Abteilung* LXXVI(1959), 173–245.

simply as a dynast.[84] He sometimes showed a pathetic eagerness to be accepted in the established order but seldom a deep desire to change it.[85] All in all, then, Ockham's writings on particular secular matters show an undeniable involvement with forces at work in the world around him, but the way he saw those forces was not entirely determined by his position as an apologist for Ludwig of Bavaria. To understand how he viewed the problems of his age, we must attend to his own distinctive forms of argument, including many theoretical passages which have no immediate bearing on current issues.

The final evidences of Ockham's specifically political concerns after 1337 are an entire tract of III *Dialogus* on the rights of the Roman empire (III *Dialogus* II) and extensive passages of the *Octo Quaestiones* devoted to topics in general political theory.[86] Although Ockham had planned to recount in III *Dialogus* the deeds of those involved in current controversies about the orthodox faith, the two existing tracts of the work are something else: the most systematic political treatises he ever composed. Even Tract I (III *Dialogus* I), on the power of the pope and clergy, has long passages that would be easily recognized as 'political' by either a classical philosopher or a modern political scientist. There is a whole book on the question, whether it is expedient for the whole community of believers to be subject to one head, ruler, and faithful prelate under Christ,[87] in which the crucial chapters are an exposition of Aristotle's *Politics*.[88]

[84] Denys Hay, *Europe in the Fourteenth and Fifteenth Centuries* (London, 1966), p. 191.

[85] In his efforts at reconciliation with the papacy under Clement VI, Ludwig expressed himself even more abjectly than he had toward Benedict XII. 'Wie ein Säugling nach der Mutterbrust', he wrote in 1343, 'so sehnt sich unsere Seele zur Gnade Euerer Heiligkeit und der römischen Kirche zurückzukehren', and his willingness to accede to papal demands is reported so to have astonished pope and cardinals that they thought he had gone mad from anxiety. Riezler, *Geschichte Baierns*, II, 481. A stronger Ludwig is presented by Professor Offler in the articles cited in note 79.

[86] Besides Questions I and II, see especially Question III, cc. 4–12, on the question, 'quod ad optimum principatum, praelationem, rectoriam seu regimen requiritur, quae sibi repugnant et quae sibi compossibilia debeant reputari'.

[87] 'An expediat toti communitati fidelium uni capiti principi et praelato fideli sub Christo subiici et subesse'. III *Dialogus* I, 2.

[88] *Ibid.*, iii–viii. In an appendix to *The Growth of Political Thought in the West* (pp. 400–3), C. H. McIlwain reprinted all of chapter 6 as 'the fullest and clearest discussion of these important distinctions [concerning types of polity] that I have found in the political writings of the fourteenth century'.

The second tract of III *Dialogus*, on the rights of the empire, begins with the question, whether it pertains to the commodity and utility of all mankind for the whole world to be under one emperor or secular prince in temporal matters, while later books deal with the rights of the empire in temporal and spiritual affairs. The work breaks off during a discussion of the emperor's judicial power over the pope. Even in its incomplete state, this tract, along with the first tract and certain passages in the *Octo Quaestiones*, provides us with a considerable body of systematic political thought, part, at least, of a political philosophy.

In the decade after 1337, then, Ockham 'went political' in various ways: by treating questions of church government in a partly political style, by supporting particular courses of action in secular affairs, and by explicitly considering basic questions of political theory. This is not to say that earlier 'non-political' or only ambiguously political phases of his career are without interest for the present study, but we must acknowledge the changes in Ockham's interests – indeed, an attempt must be made to explain these changes, as well as to identify permanent underlying principles.

There is a tradition that Ockham sought reconciliation with the papal church at the end of his life but died in 1349, possibly from the Black Death, before the process could be completed.[89] The main evidence for this is a form of submission transmitted to the minister general of the Franciscans, William Farinier, by Clement VI. After confessing himself to hold what the holy mother, the Roman church, believes, holds, and teaches, Ockham was to deny as heretical that the emperor has authority to depose the pope and to elect or create another, and he was to swear not to adhere to the heresies, errors, opinions, and rebellions of Ludwig the Bavarian and Michael of Cesena.[90] The theological ideas for which he had been examined at Avignon are not directly mentioned. Aside from the thesis about the emperor's power over the pope there is no specification of *which* opinions and actions of Ludwig and Michael are to be repudiated as erroneous and rebellious, and no peculiarly Ockhamist political ideas are named. Although it was apparently not a response to Ockham's

---

[89] Hofer, 'Wilhelm von Ockham', pp. 654–64; Baudry, *Guillaume d'Occam*, pp. 240–2; Jürgen Miethke, 'Zu Wilhelm Ockhams Tod', *AFH*, LXI (1968), 79–98 – the best treatment of the subject.   [90] *BF*, VI, 231.

own initiative, this fairly mild formula of submission may at least be taken as showing Clement VI's order of priorities. In focusing on the matter of imperial power over the papacy, did Clement show political astuteness, or was he blind to genuinely subversive tendencies in such works as the *Dialogus*? In completely ignoring Ockham's early writings, did he tacitly acknowledge their orthodoxy? If so, was he blind again, this time to ideas more potent to dissolve the medieval world view and the social order based on it than any error of Michael of Cesena or Ludwig of Bavaria? The pope's list of conditions for Ockham's reconciliation is more precise, it has a narrower emphasis than the expression of his concern with Ockham's salvation cited earlier, but both statements suggest questions about the 'political' in Ockham that force us to consider other areas of existence as well.

Instead of finding in our survey of his life and writings a single sharply-defined idea of the political which can be deduced from his philosophy and theology and used to explain his *opera politica*, we have found that Ockham became involved in politics in an unruly variety of ways. As a theologian who had said nothing directly relevant to public affairs, he was subjected to political proceedings against his own ideas – political in the sense that the special interests of powerful individuals and factions played a prominent role. As a Franciscan, he became engaged in a dogmatic controversy which had broad practical repercussions, disturbing and dividing Christians throughout the Western church. As a member of Ludwig of Bavaria's 'Munich academy', he composed political treatises ranging in level of concreteness from apologies for specific actions of the emperor and his allies, to treatises on the spiritual government of all believers and the secular government of the human race. Along with the variety of ways in which he became involved in politics, our survey has also come upon a certain non-political tendency in Ockham's thought. Not to mention the lack of explicitly political content in his speculative writings, such a tendency can be found even in some of the more important polemical works. For example, the defense of Franciscan poverty in the *Opus Nonaginta Dierum* was non-political, in content if not in form, for the ideal upheld there entailed a conceptually absolute renunciation of legal standing. Again, the treatment of papal heresy in I *Dialogus* provides no political solution to that problem – that is, no set of permanent institutions designed to replace the church's existing government. The recurrence of this non-political tendency in so many contexts prompts the question, whether it may also be a factor elsewhere, for example, in the discussion of secular government or papal *plenitudo potestatis*.

The complexity of Ockham's political life suggests as a point of method that special attention be given to the quite different levels of polemic and abstraction at which he wrote in different periods and works. For example, it may be prudent to treat personal and institutional politics separately. Thus, it seems clear that Ockham's opposition to John XXII and his successors was intensely personal – not necessarily in the sense that his own case at Avignon significantly affected his political works (about this we can only speculate, and speculate better after studying his writings than before), but in the sense that he spent an enormous amount of effort and ingenuity attempting to show that these particular men, John, Benedict, and Clement, were heretics and so could no longer occupy the papal office. On the other hand, in such works as III *Dialogus*, the *Octo Quaestiones*, and the *Breviloquium*, emphasis falls on the powers attached to the papal and imperial offices, not on the character of their occupants. To be sure, what Ockham had to say about ridding the church of particular evil rulers is unlikely to prove intelligible except on the basis of certain assumptions about governmental institutions in general, while in writing about institutions he can hardly have disregarded the effects of institutional ideas on the men and policies guided by them. Furthermore, in trying to understand Ockham in his own terms, we must not accept those terms as being necessarily correct. It has seemed to many readers that his personal attacks on the pontiffs at Avignon were in fact thinly disguised assaults on the whole traditional system of ecclesiastical authority, on the papacy as well as on (pseudo-)popes. It has been suggested by others that Ockham's opposition to papalist political theory and his general discussions of spiritual and secular government were only devices for furthering the personal interests of Ludwig of Bavaria – here it is the institutional aspect that becomes illusory. Or it could be said that although men and offices were both important enough for Ockham himself his ideas on both subjects were equally out of touch with reality: to some scholars his polemics against the popes and in defense of the emperor have seemed logically incoherent, while his abstract discussions of institutional questions have often been seen as empty ideology, an irrelevant attempt to revive a political order long outmoded. Such criticisms, as we shall soon see, are important in current views of Ockham. Nevertheless, these very difficulties show the need to approach the personal and institutional sides of his political thought with greater discrimination than has usually been observed in these problems.[91] Only thus can we hope to arrive in the end at a reasonable assessment.

A second point of method suggested by a survey of Ockham's life and writings has to do with the relation between his political and speculative thought. It is natural when dealing with a medieval theologian and philosopher to attempt to explain his political thought by deducing it from his more general speculative world view. There are, however, at least three difficulties with such a plan in Ockham's case: the intrinsic difficulty of correctly interpreting nominalist theology and philosophy, the nearly total absence of explicitly political passages in the speculative works, and a corresponding paucity of specifically nominalist passages in the political works. While we must seek links between the two halves of Ockham's career,[92] we should be cautious in looking for the straightforwardly deductive connection presented by earlier medieval thinkers. But on this problem, too, light is shed by contrasting current interpretations.

THREE CURRENT INTERPRETATIONS OF OCKHAM'S THOUGHT

It is hardly surprising that Ockham's life and writings should have aroused controversy in the fourteenth and fifteenth centuries. More surprising is the sharp scholarly disagreement about his work which

91 Ockham is often granted or emphatically denied the status of a revolutionary. It may be pertinent to recall here Aristotle's distinction between basic types of revolution. Some are directed to a change of persons, others to a change of institutions. *Politics*, v, 1 (1301*b* 5–13).

92 Miethke's work, *Ockhams Weg zur Sozialphilosophie*, is an excellent example of the more traditional approach to Ockham's political thought by way of a detailed preliminary exposition of his speculative ideas. For evidence that Ockham did not abandon his speculative interests in later life, at least in the area of logic and semantics, see Robert Price, 'William of Ockham and *suppositio personalis*', *FcS*, xxx (1970), 131–40; 139–40.

28

persists today. Thus, for Georges de Lagarde, Ockham was the great theoretician of the last debate between papacy and empire, a laicist, the chief intellectual source of an anarchism which destroyed the medieval social order. For Richard Scholz he was not a *Politiker* at all, but a theologian, hardly interested in political problems and inclined, when circumstances forced him to deal with such issues, to apply theological principles in resolving them. To still other scholars Ockham has appeared variously as a constitutional liberal, a reverent upholder of medieval tradition, or the exponent of such classical and modern ideas as equity, public utility, and reason of state. A review restricted to salient points will hardly do these interpretations justice, but it will serve well to indicate topics needing investigation in the present study.

For Lagarde, then, the only purpose of Ockham's political writings was to proclaim the empire's independence of papal authority – 'Elles n'ont été écrites que pour cela.'[93] Lagarde devotes an entire volume to Ockham's defense of the empire, considering even his treatment of the vexed question of papal *plenitudo potestatis* within this narrowly political context. Although willing to concede that he was haunted by the abuses of curialism, Lagarde nevertheless finds that in Ockham's many confrontations with this ideology, his only firm conviction concerned the perfect legitimacy of Ludwig of Bavaria's empire.[94] To Lagarde, however, Ockham's attempt to construe this empire as a successor to that of the ancient Caesars seemed to rest on a total misapprehension of the realities of a developing social milieu, a fault all the more striking in an apologist for empiricism in philosophy and the established order in secular politics.[95]

Although, as Lagarde acknowledges,[96] Ockham never presented a systematic exposition of the nature and structure of the church, Lagarde's own second volume on Ockham is concerned with his presumed *Critique des structures ecclésiales*. The first ecclesiastical

---

[93] *La naissance de l'esprit laïque au déclin du moyen-âge*, new ed.; IV: *Guillaume d'Ockham: défense de l'empire* (Paris, 1962) ; V: *Guillaume d'Ockham: critique des structures ecclésiales* (Paris, 1963). These volumes will be referred to as *La naissance*, IV and V. Also see the volumes cited in note 6 above, as well as the fourth and fifth volumes of the first edition (Paris, 1946), V: *Ockham: bases de départ*; VI: *Ockham: la morale et le droit*. The phrase quoted is at *La naissance*, IV, 132.

[94] *La naissance*, IV, 247, 91.

[95] *Ibid.*, pp. 253, 247ff., 261ff.   [96] *La naissance*, V, 30.

structure considered is the general council. Correcting the mis-
conceptions of earlier generations, Lagarde shows that Ockham was
not a conciliarist in any positive sense, although his criticisms of
pontifical power were to prove useful for the negative side of conciliarism.[97] With respect, next, to the primacy of the Roman see,
Lagarde sometimes attributes to Ockham a genuine, anguished
ambivalence: he was opposed to curialism, but he firmly believed
that papal primacy was a truth of faith sealed by the consent of the
universal church.[98] Elsewhere Lagarde writes in a darker vein of
the 'subtilité insidieuse' or 'respectueuse impertinence' of Ockham's
positions on papal primacy, which go much further than his timid
observations about general councils.[99] Lagarde is especially vehement
about the destructive tendency of Ockham's treatment of the pope's
doctrinal *magisterium*. He comments that it would at least be frank
to say with Luther that there *is* no doctrinal authority except the
Bible illuminated by the Holy Spirit. But Ockham

maintient le principe de l'autorité, mais en ruine si bien la substance que
sa reconnaissance n'est qu'une occasion d'organiser la méfiance, la suspicion et, le cas échéant, la révolte de la chrétienté en face d'elle. Le
docteur enseigne, contrôle et condamne le pontife. Le laïque surveille et,
s'il le faut, punit le docteur, le clerc, l'évêque ou le pape. Au nom de la foi,
on a justifié un activisme anarchique et désordonné de tout le corps ecclésial,
et la logique du système interdit qu'une institution quelconque puisse le
contrôler efficacement . . . Ockham . . ., en prétendant sauvegarder le
principe de toutes les institutions traditionnelles, en sape irrémédiablement
la base.[100]

This indictment is rendered yet more extreme by Lagarde's contention that Ockham's theses on the *magisterium* are rigorously coherent
with the principles of his epistemology, his metaphysics, and his
social thought.[101] In asserting this linkage Lagarde at once magnifies
the menace of Ockham's anarchic activism and, for many readers,
discredits the speculative thought that leads to such disastrous
practical conclusions.[102]

[97] *Ibid.*, p. 86. On this point Lagarde contrasts Ockham with the other Michaelists
(pp. 54–5). On Ockham's conciliarism – or lack of it – also see note 65 above.
[98] *Ibid.*, p. 98.   [99] *Ibid.*, p. 126.
[100] *Ibid.*, p. 164.   [101] *Ibid.*, p. 128.
[102] In contrast with this destructive treatment of the *magisterium* is the relatively
moderate position on papal jurisdiction that Lagarde attributes to Ockham.

Notwithstanding his description of Ockham as a 'grand theorician' of papal–imperial affairs, a central conclusion of Lagarde's first volume is that Ockham's writings contain no coherent philosophical or theological basis for politics. Ockham's reflections on the foundations of political authority are dispersed and disparate, to all intents and purposes 'sans jointure et sans équilibre'.[103] Ockham is said to oscillate between rational philosophy and positive theology,[104] but on the former head Lagarde finds no clear development of any of the lines of justification for political authority, rights, property, etc. considered by Ockham.[105] Even his doctrine of popular consent impresses Lagarde as only another means of supporting the established secular order, not as a sign of rationality or enlightenment.[106] Lagarde's failure to discover a coherent rational basis for political institutions in Ockham led him to place correspondingly greater stress on the other side of the oscillation, to find a strange combination of positivism and theologism.[107] Instead of basing secular authority on philosophical principles or common sense, Ockham is said to have felt the need for an indisputable charter or legal privilege, the result being an appeal to the Bible to attest the legitimacy of the empire. The reference to Scripture becomes so imperious as to transform the theory of free human institutions into a new theology of politics and the political order.[108]

In a series of chapters towards the end of his second volume on Ockham, Lagarde completes his picture of Ockhamist politics as at once philosophically groundless and philosophically well supported: groundless in the sense that Ockham fails to provide any affirmative speculative basis for his political conclusions, even when those conclusions are eminently capable of such support; but well supported in the sense that Ockham's politics are strikingly parallel with (if not necessarily determined by) his formidable epistemology and metaphysics. Thus, for example, Ockham took more care to criticize

Although 'seduced' by radical formulas at the beginning of his careeer, he did not assert them even then, and in later years he retreated to a middle position which, he thought, would allow him to reconcile the traditional position with at least some of the new theses. *Ibid.*, p. 175.

103 *La naissance*, IV, 193. Cf. pp. 234 and 254.
104 *Ibid.*, p. 204.   105 *Ibid.*, pp. 195, 224, 225.
106 *Ibid.*, p. 230.   107 *Ibid.*, p. 260.
108 *Ibid.*, p. 261. Lagarde refers for support here to the essay by Scholz discussed below.

the superficiality of earlier distinctions between the spiritual and the temporal than to find more satisfactory philosophical criteria.[109] Hence, we are to suppose that Ockham envisaged Christian society as a relatively undifferentiated community of believers – not as church and state, certainly, for these would only be two aspects of a single reality.[110] It is true that on one occasion Ockham presented a defense of the independence of the supreme spiritual power from the regular jurisdiction of the supreme lay power. Since, however, Lagarde regards it as rather contradictory to recommend such magnanimity to a ruler after showing that sharing power is repugnant to any government, he hesitates to see in this passage – this 'étrange plaidoyer' – an expression of Ockham's own thought.[111] Lagarde also laments the lack of any affirmative rational basis in Ockham for the autonomy of civil power, attributing this defect to a willful misappreciation of Thomism.[112] Lagarde concludes, then, that political Ockhamism was without a sound philosophical foundation. At the same time, however, he argues that there is a 'parallélisme . . . indiscutable' between Ockham's philosophy and his politics. The latter, therefore, is not philosophically unfounded. Worse yet, it is philosophically ill-founded.

Ockham le philosophe a eu pour tâche essentielle de montrer le peu de solidité des synthèses du savoir édifiées par les théologiens de la fin du XIIIe siècle . . .

Ockham le polémiste exerce la même critique sur les justifications juridiques ou rationnelles qu'on donnait des institutions de la chrétienté médiévale.[113]

Lagarde makes it clear that Ockham did not himself present his political and ecclesiological positions as a straightforward application of philosophical principles. Accordingly, he goes on to trace connections between philosophical and political Ockhamism which may hold good logically even though Ockham did not have them

---

[109] *La naissance*, v, 204. Cf. 213–14.
[110] *Ibid.*, p. 264. Whether consciously or not, Lagarde here makes Ockham sound like Hooker or Hobbes. Cf. Richard Hooker, *Of the Laws of Ecclesiastical Polity*, Book VIII, chapter 1 (Hooker's *Works*, ed. J. Keble (3 vols., Oxford, 1874), vol. III, p. 330); Thomas Hobbes, *Leviathan*, ed. M. Oakeshott (Oxford, 1957), p. 306.
[111] *La naissance*, v, 258f. The passage referred to (OQ III, 12; OP I, 116–24) is discussed below, p. 129.
[112] *La naissance*, v, 271.   [113] *Ibid.*, p. 282.

consciously in mind. On the side of speculative principles, he finds in Ockham a rejection of anything which might lead us to reason about the world or about values as if they were necessary, a still more fundamental doctrine of the omnipotence and absolute liberty of God, and, finally, an extreme metaphysical individualism. All these principles are said by Lagarde to have applications in Ockham's polemical works.[114] On the relation between philosophy and politics in Ockham, Lagarde presents us, in effect, with a dilemma: there is either no connection or, if one exists, it is a relationship between unsound philosophy and subversive, anarchic politics.

Both the coherence and the weakness of Lagarde's interpretation stem from his having used a structure of questions and a set of historical assumptions that Ockham himself would surely have rejected. We may agree that there are close relationships among Ockham's various works and thus also agree that an adequate understanding of his thought demands broad interpretive questions and categories as well as detailed study of successive treatises, but this does not force us to adopt a standpoint essentially external to Ockham himself. We need not, for example, consider Ockham first as a defender of the empire of Ludwig of Bavaria and then as a critic of ecclesiastical structures without asking whether these topics or their sequence correspond either logically or chronologically with Ockham's own commitments. On Lagarde's own showing, the stages of his polemical activity were, first, 'le cycle de la querelle autour de Jean XXII' and only then 'le cycle de la controverse impériale'.[115] In the former phase Ockham presented, not a criticism of ecclesiastical *structures*, but a sustained attack upon a *person* whom he believed to be no longer even a member of the church. And far from it being the case that belief in Ludwig of Bavaria was his only firm conviction in the struggle with curialism, we find that even as late as 1342 in the *Octo Quaestiones* he adopts a deliberately impersonal format – presenting reasons for contrary opinions without formally determining among them. What is more, the one direct reference to Ludwig in this work carries only a very tentative endorsement of his legitimacy. He is the lord Ludwig of Bavaria, 'whom some call

---

[114] *Ibid.*, pp. 282ff.   [115] *La naissance*, IV, 15.

Bavarum, some *imperatorem'*.[116] I do not mean to suggest that Ockham had serious doubts about the legitimacy of Ludwig's empire, or that he was driven into controversy over the empire against his will. What should not be taken for granted, however, is that the defense of the empire or the criticism of ecclesiastical structures were as central in Ockham's thought as in Lagarde's, who wished to trace the birth of laicism and hence of 'l'esprit politique de la Réforme'.[117]

A similar criticism can be made of Lagarde's approach to Ockham's philosophical and theological first principles. Whatever the outcome of current scholarly controversies over his speculative thought, the historian must note that Ockham considered his own positions the constructive ones and regarded the doctrines he opposed as not merely false or indemonstrable but also negative and destructive. If Ockham's speculative intentions were ultimately constructive, may not the same be true of his intentions in politics? If so, there would be a 'parallelism' very different from the one proposed by Lagarde.

Lagarde's work is by far the most incisive and stimulating of current interpretations of Ockham, and it also exhibits admirable courtesy in the face of a doctrine which the author found profoundly disturbing. Nevertheless, it has not gained general acceptance. Since the appearance of the first edition of *La naissance*, its main theses have been criticized by J. B. Morrall and W. Kölmel,[118] while H. A. Oberman expresses a reaction to Lagarde's work that is no doubt widely held when he remarks that 'one wonders, after arriving at the last page of this impressive work, how it is possible that though the text is well documented, the texture of Ockham's thought has not come through'.[119]

While Lagarde was developing his interpretation of Ockham as the main progenitor of Reformation laicism, Richard Scholz pub-

---

[116] *OQ* VIII, 2; *OP* I, 183. The point is made by H. S. Offler in 'The origin of Ockham's *Octo Quaestiones*', p. 324.

[117] Previously described by G. de Lagarde in *Recherches sur l'esprit politique de la réforme* (Paris, 1926).

[118] J. B. Morrall, 'Some notes on a recent interpretation of William of Ockham's political philosophy', *FcS*, IX (1949), 335–69; W. Kölmel, *Wilhelm Ockham und seine kirchenpolitischen Schriften* (Essen, 1962). Lagarde replies to Morrall and Kölmel in the notes to his second edition.

[119] H. A. Oberman, 'From Ockham to Luther – Recent studies', *Concilium*, VII.2 (1966), 63–8; 66.

lished quite a different interpretation in his short but pregnant essay, *Wilhelm von Ockham als politischer Denker*.[120] According to Scholz, there is something of a contradiction in writing about Ockham as a *Politiker* or in expounding his doctrine of the state, for he was a theologian, and nothing can lead to greater errors than considering his political views apart from his theological starting point.[121] In a sense, of course, Lagarde gives ample attention to Ockham's theological and philosophical points of departure, but Scholz ascribes to him a much more positive religious stance. He concedes that Ockham pushed aside previous systems of eternal truths and conceptual essences in developing his own central idea, the concept of divine omnipotence,[122] but the idea of God as pure will (*reine Willkür*) leads to doubt and to a lack of rational pattern only with respect to the external, physical world. In the inner world of the individual, Ockham is said by Scholz to present us with a wholly different view. Here there is certainty.[123] Following Augustine, Ockham holds that man must orient himself in all moral questions from his own inwardness, but in Scholz's account the result of this orientation from the 'subject' is not arbitrariness or relativism, but an awareness of the immutable laws of human nature as God created it, laws revealed in Scripture and providing a basis for moral regulations which only God himself could revoke if it were reasonable to do so.[124] Ockham's theology is positive for Scholz not only in the sense that it is solid and affirmative, but also in the sense of emphasizing the divine revelation of the Bible. The inner world of the individual, where one finds the unique certainty of experience, is also the world of revealed faith.[125]

Scholz's account of Ockham as a political thinker is thoroughly consistent with this view of his philosophy and theology. He stresses the lack of political content in the doctrines for which Ockham was denounced at Avignon.[126] Ockham became familiar with Aristotle's *Politics* and with the canon and civil law because these happened to be the weapons used in controversies in which he found himself

---

[120] Richard Scholz, *Wilhelm von Ockham als politischer Denker und sein Breviloquium de Principatu Tyrannico* (Leipzig, 1944, repr. Stuttgart, 1952).
[121] *Ibid.*, p. 1. [122] *Ibid.*, p. 21.
[123] *Ibid.*, pp. 21–2. [124] *Ibid.*, p. 22.
[125] 'Es ist die Welt des Glaubens, der durch Gott in den heiligen Schriften offenbart ist.' *Ibid.*, p. 22. [126] *Ibid.*, pp. 3–4.

2-2

involved, not because of their intrinsic relevance to a speculatively based politics of his own.[127] In going through Ockham's admittedly voluminous[128] political writings, he emphasizes their concern with the author's personal position, and especially his position as a Franciscan in the poverty controversy. Only in three or four cases did Ockham take up his pen to support the emperor or some other political personage. His other writings, and especially the most important ones, owe their origin in Scholz's opinion to Ockham's own initiatives and show more concern with his personal and theological interests than with the empire. The chief problem was the relation of faith and reason, not the right or wrong of the empire or a search for the best order of the state and its relation to the church.[129] Although Scholz has some sympathy with Stengel's conjecture that Ockham played an active part in advising the emperor during the politically important years around 1338,[130] his essay ends as it began by stressing Ockham's basically non-political nature. The standpoints of Marsilius of Padua and Lupold of Bebenberg were equally foreign to him. He was neither an Aristotelian nor a jurist. He remained 'der Jünger des Franz von Assisi'.[131]

It is in this basically non-political, theological context that we must understand Scholz's account of Ockham's political doctrines. Two points stand out. One is the continued emphasis on the positive will of God. State and church, papacy and empire are not free human creations, but divinely willed orders whose truth and validity must always be based on the Bible and other revelations of God's will.[132] The other crucial point is Scholz's repeated application of the distinction between the 'inner' moral world and the 'outer' natural world. It is because, and in so far as, state and church belong to the moral order that they fall within the region of faith and divine revelation. *Per contra*, to the extent that these institutions belong to the objective, outer world, they are subject to the failings of human will

---

[127] *Ibid.*, p. 5.
[128] 'Folgen sie sich ... in rascher Folge und in einem Umfang, daß man immer wieder nicht so sehr über die Fruchtbarkeit, denn die Probleme und Gedanken wiederholen sich unaufhörlich, als über die Möglichkeit staunen muß, eine solche Schreibarbeit in so kurzer Zeit bewältigen zu können. Ockham muß viel Muße für seine Arbeit gehabt haben.' *Ibid.*
[129] *Ibid.*, p. 6.
[130] *Ibid.*, p. 10.
[131] *Ibid.*, p. 27.
[132] *Ibid.*, p. 22.

and knowledge. This distinction between the moral and natural orders, when combined with an emphasis on the divine will, produces a radically critical spirit *vis à vis* historic institutional forms. To be sure, Scholz's Ockham is a practical conservative, notwithstanding this critical radicalism.[133] Especially in his conception of the church, however, Ockham is said to aim at constant correction of merely human external forms in accordance with the will of God. The sphere of secular politics is treated in close connection with the religious sphere. In particular, emperor and prince have an office in the universal church on earth. They have both a religious basis for their authority and a divinely willed duty in the exercise of it.[134]

Underlying the great differences between their negative and affirmative interpretations of Ockham's speculative thought and their widely differing estimates of the relative importance of theology and politics for Ockham, there is important agreement between Lagarde and Scholz that Ockhamist politics is in some way a function of Ockhamist philosophy and theology. This basic contention is called into question by several other studies which together build up a picture of Ockham as a constitutionalist.

The description of Ockham as a constitutional liberal is due to E. F. Jacob, but before we review Jacob's essay it will be convenient to consider an article on Ockham's political ideas by the leading rehabilitator of his logic, epistemology, and metaphysics, Philotheus Boehner, O.F.M. To Boehner the attempt 'to base Ockham's political ideas on, or to develop them from, his so-called Metaphysics . . . appears . . . more as an adventure and certainly as a construction of the writer'.[135] Boehner does not deny that there are inner connections to be seen, if the philosophical and theological system of Ockham is correctly interpreted, but he does not believe that Ockham's speculative thought provides a basis for deducing a set of political ideas markedly different from those that could be grounded on other scholastic systems. 'Ockham's political ideas in their great outlines could have been developed, so far as we can see, from any of the classical metaphysics of the 13th century; for . . .

---

133 The notion that in Ockham there is a 'Vereinigung von kritischem Radikalismus und praktischem Konservatismus' is Seeberg's (quoted by Scholz, *ibid.*, p. 20).
134 *Ibid.*, p. 25.
135 P. Boehner,' Ockham's political ideas', in P. Boehner, *Collected Articles*, pp. 442–68 (originally published in the *Review of Politics*, v (1943)), pp. 445–6.

they coincide with a sound Catholic political theory.'[136] Instead of beginning with Ockham's 'so-called Metaphysics', Boehner attempts to set out from Ockham's own starting point, his notion of the limits of papal power.[137] After indicating some of Ockham's grounds for opposition to the 'usurped and tyrannical power of the Pope', which was 'in reality an absolutistic and universal supremacy... which, in its fantastic exaggerations, had been developed by the so-called Curialists',[138] Boehner presents an exposition of Ockham's own more moderate opinion of the extent of papal authority, an exposition closely based on the sources and quite consistent with his description of Ockham as presenting 'sound Catholic political theory'. The pope's power is not *plenissima* (it is limited to those things which are necessary to be done or omitted and does not extend to commanding works of supererogation), but it is 'grand, singular and very great'. The pope possesses the same right and privilege as Peter. He has regular supreme power in all spiritual matters, including some regular coercive power. He is not subject to any secular power or jurisdiction, and has the right to the temporal support necessary for his divine work.[139]

To be sure, as Boehner notes, Ockham stresses the idea of a *ministerium* of the pope rather than a *dominium*, but in this he follows St Bernard, as Dante did also. In Boehner's exposition, Ockham's concern with the limits of papal power was the main reason he eventually gave direct support to Ludwig of Bavaria, for both the Franciscan Order and the emperor were, as Ockham saw it, struggling for inviolable, lawful rights against the unjust claims of the papacy.[140] While they may have been parts of a sound and orthodox political

---

[136] *Ibid.*, p. 446.

[137] '... the only logical and psychological starting-point, even of a short outline of Ockham's political ideas'. *Ibid.*, p. 445.   [138] *Ibid.*, p. 448.

[139] *Ibid.*, pp. 450–2. Boehner relies primarily on III *Dialogus* I, I, xvii and the *An Princeps*. Although he uses the *Octo Quaestiones* mainly to corroborate points based on other sources, Boehner states the most accurate brief formula for identifying Ockham's own opinions among those presented in this work: 'That opinion which, in comparison with the others, is disproportionately more developed and proved represents Ockham's own opinion'. 'Ockham's political ideas', p. 447. This corresponds with J. Haller's suggestion (*Papsttum und Kirchenreform*, I (Berlin, 1903), 77, n. 2) that Ockham's view is always to be found 'in dem "Respondetur" am Schlusse der Erörterung' (that is, just after the initial presentation of contrary opinions, not at the end of the *Quaestio*).

[140] Boehner, 'Ockham's political ideas', p. 444.

theory, however, Ockham's views on the rights of property and dominion, the divine right of secular power, and the just constitution of a commonwealth bear little resemblance in Boehner's exposition to the theologized politics attributed to Ockham by Scholz.[141] Thus, Boehner stresses that, although for Ockham the right (*potestas*) to acquire private property and set up temporal rulers was in some sense God-given as a remedy for sin, the actual appropriation of temporal things and establishment of government is ordinarily the act of man and of human law. Similarly, the divine right of secular power consists of the fact that only God is superior to the secular power. Such power is ordinarily the concession, donation or resignation of other men – it is truly conferred by the people. In contrast with both Lagarde and Scholz, Boehner asserts that 'Ockham certainly arrived at a clear distinction between secular and ecclesiastical power.'[142] Boehner immediately goes on to argue for a coordination and collaboration between church and state in Ockham, a position which he admits is not systematically developed by Ockham himself, but which he supports by a brief survey of the mutual relations of the two powers. This survey shows that, although the two powers may in cases of necessity (*casualiter*) interfere with one another, this is not a regular matter. Boehner concludes his exposition by remarking that, although Ockham was driven into political discussions by personal necessity and in defense of his unjustifiable disobedience to a pope, he 'remained moderate in his theory'. It would not be far wrong to describe Boehner's Ockham as a constitutionalist,[143] in contrast with Lagarde's secularist Ockham and the 'theologizing' Ockham of Scholz.

'Constitutionalist' certainly describes the Ockham presented by E. F. Jacob in his essay, 'Ockham as a political thinker'.[144] This essay,

---

[141] *Ibid.*, pp. 454–63. Boehner used mainly the *Breviloquium* here, the work to which Scholz's essay was offered as an introduction, and again his exposition is almost literal.

[142] Boehner, 'Ockham's political ideas', p. 464.

[143] Boehner's Ockham is a medieval constitutionalist in the essay just summarized. Ockham assumes a more modern guise in Boehner's excellent biographical sketch (in P. Boehner (ed.), *The Tractatus de Successivis Attributed to William Ockham* (St Bonaventure, N.Y., 1944), pp. 1–15), which describes him (p. 15) as 'a brilliant man whose political views were in advance of his time'.

[144] In Jacob, *Essays*, pp. 85–105 and 246–8. This essay first appeared in the *Bulletin of the John Rylands Library*, xx (1936), 332–53.

rich in historical detail for its brevity, includes a useful summary of
I *Dialogus*. It reaches the conclusion that, 'in spite of the extreme
bitterness which he feels against Avignon, he [Ockham] is never
extreme. It is the view of a constitutional liberal, not of an anti-
papal zealot, that demands our scrutiny.'[145] In this respect, Jacob
contrasts Ockham, whose arguments 'are not unaffected by the
older, historic claims of a deeply-rooted religious society', with
Marsilius of Padua, 'the brilliant and revolutionary Italian. To Marsilius the Church was a department (*pars*) or organ of the State.'[146]
Although Jacob finds a similarity of method between Ockham's
non-polemical works and his political writings, he is at one with
Boehner in locating the doctrinal roots of Ockham's political ideas
in more traditional sources. He specifically cites the organization
and practice of the early church and the proclamations of the
supremacy of law made by thirteenth-century Franciscans. Like
Boehner, too, Jacob emphasizes Ockham's idea of papal government as a 'principatus ministrativus', and he uses precisely the same
passage from the *Dialogus* that Boehner does to present Ockham's
moderate but by no means nugatory conception of papal
power.[147]

The fact that scholars of such different interests and *milieux* as
Boehner and Jacob should independently characterize Ockham as a
political moderate whose views in practical matters were relatively
independent of his speculative philosophical and theological commitments argues strongly against Scholz's judgment that such a view
is simply grotesque.

C. C. Bayley's useful essay, 'Pivotal concepts in the political

---

[145] Jacob, 'Ockham as a political thinker', p. 103. Scholz, *Wilhelm von Ockham*, p. 15,
dismissed this description as 'grotesk', without, however, discussing the evidence
adduced by Jacob in support of it.
[146] Jacob, 'Ockham as a political thinker', p. 89. On Marsilius, whose vehement
Defensor Pacis was the purest statement of a secularist political theory in the middle
ages, see A. Gewirth, *Marsilius of Padua, the Defender of Peace*; vol. I: *Marsilius
of Padua and Medieval Political Philosophy*; vol. II: *The Defensor Pacis* (New York,
1956). Marsilius was an influential counsellor of Ludwig of Bavaria during his
Italian campaign of 1327–9 and returned with him to Munich, where he remained
until his death (1342–3).
[147] III *Dialogus* I, I, xvii. 'The almost painfully careful wording, and the emphasis
laid upon the gradual historical evolution of the papal prerogatives, are worth
notice.' Jacob, 'Ockham as a political thinker', p. 98.

philosophy of William of Ockham',[148] makes some concessions to Lagarde's picture of Ockham as an unrestrained secularist, but its net effect is to confirm the accuracy of the picture drawn by Boehner and Jacob. Bayley's central thesis is that the ideas of *epieikeia, bonum commune*, and *necessitas* make up a 'formidable trinity of weapons' which Ockham constantly draws on to defend the imperial cause against papal encroachments. It is true that Ockham uses these ideas to justify departures from regularly established legal and political procedures. Bayley even concludes that it would be fascinating to study the contribution of these Ockhamist concepts to the doctrine of *ragione di stato*. And yet, as Bayley makes clear throughout, each of these pivotal conceptions has roots in, or affinities with, such respectable sources as St Thomas and the Roman and canon law. 'His theme was compounded of strictly orthodox concepts.'[149] Further, Bayley finds more to say about Ockham's possible influence on conciliarists such as Conrad of Gelnhausen, Dietrich of Niem, and Cardinal Uguccione, than about his suggestion of the suspicious doctrine of reason of state. Due to the later work of Lagarde and Tierney, it is necessary to be cautious about Ockham's influence on conciliarism in its details, but this does not entirely offset the more general claim that Ockham's ideas were admirably adapted to furnish 'intellectual underpinnings' for conciliar theories of church government.[150] In any case, Bayley's linking of Ockham with conciliarism tends to support the constitutionalist interpretation of Boehner and Jacob, who also associated Ockham with forces of moderation in later time.

Boehner, Jacob, and Bayley all present Ockham's political ideas as both independent of his speculative thought and comparatively lacking in order on their own level. Thus, although Bayley's object is to discuss 'general points of vantage' assumed by Ockham, the pivotal concepts he selects, equity, utility, and necessity, are not

---

[148] *Journal of the History of Ideas*, x (1949), 199–218. Bayley's presentation of the *Octo Quaestiones* (pp. 206–15) is helpful in placing that work among the larger currents of papal, imperial, and nationalistic thought, but H. S. Offler has demonstrated ('The origin of Ockham's *Octo Quaestiones*', pp. 328–30) that the fifth, sixth, and seventh questions were concerned with the coronation of Charles of Moravia as hereditary king of Bohemia rather than with Ludwig's much earlier, elective accession to the office of emperor.

[149] Bayley, 'Pivotal concepts', pp. 215, 200–1.

[150] *Ibid.*, pp. 215–17.

developed very systematically even by the standards usual in political theory, much less by those customary in scholastic metaphysics or theology. It would seem that for Bayley's Ockham politics is largely a matter of acting reasonably (equity) in response to emergencies (necessity), in order to promote a somewhat vaguely conceived social goal (the common welfare). A similar lack of system marks the interpretations of Boehner and Jacob. For all his conviction that Ockham had some conception of an 'order' of 'coordination' and 'collaboration' between secular and spiritual power, Boehner must confess that the proofs for such an order 'are not systematically developed by Ockham'.[151] Jacob does not claim to discern even an informal general conception of the political 'order' (or orders) in Ockham. To be sure, none of these interpretations makes use of the one Ockhamist treatise in which a system of politics is most likely to be found, III *Dialogus* II, on world government and the rights of the Roman Empire. As things now stand, however, the constitutionalist interpretation seems to be caught on one horn of Lagarde's dilemma: although the separation of Ockham's political ideas from his speculative thought avoids Lagarde's imputation that the political ideas are philosophically *ill*-founded, it seems only to reinforce Lagarde's alternative contention, that the political ideas are philosophically *un*founded. Of course, this criticism will not seem damning to anyone who doubts that politics in truth ought to be systematic or ought to be based on metaphysics or theology. Nevertheless, when the subject of our study is himself a metaphysician and theologian, we cannot help wanting to know why his political ideas are *not* systematic, if, indeed, they are not, and why they are *not* based on, or illuminated by, his speculative ideas, again assuming that they are not.

The constitutionalist interpretation of Ockham can also be criticized for not giving due weight to the fact that Ockham was an agitator,[152] that he not only lived in a time of crisis, but was personally involved in the partisan politics of his day. Thus, although Boehner, for example, reports that Ockham regarded John XXII as a heretic, his account of Ockham's attempts to determine the limits of papal power tends to ignore this decisive initial stimulus. In

---

[151] Boehner, 'Ockham's political ideas', p. 465.
[152] The word is Scholz's, in the foreword to *Wilhelm von Ockham*.

treating his disobedience to John XXII as a purely personal matter, something that 'cannot be justified', but needs to be understood in terms of the 'confusion' from which he (along with many others of his day) suffered concerning the power of the pope,[153] Boehner makes Ockham too tranquil. Ockham's own starting point, logically as well as psychologically, was an apparently clear case of papal heresy, not a set of 'notions' concerning the limits of papal power. It was not a matter of setting bounds to the authority of a true pope, but of taking action against a pseudo-pope. Ockham may indeed show the temperate constitutionalism which Boehner, Jacob, and others attribute to him, but this moderation must be understood in terms of the rest of his thought and action. His revolutionary agitation was not merely an unfortunate episode in his personal life, but an integral part of his whole involvement in politics. Or to put the suggestion in different terms, it was Ockham's fate to live in a time of constitutional crisis. Hence, his own constitutionalism was of necessity critical and creative.[154]

THE PLAN OF THIS STUDY

Current scholarly interpretations of Ockham present us with a laicist, a pure theologian, and a constitutionalist. One is tempted to ask whether these are three individuals or one. As we saw earlier, however, Ockham's involvement in political issues was complex, for he acted and wrote at many levels of concreteness and abstraction, passion and reflection, individuality and group loyalty. Perhaps the apparently contradictory descriptions of him – as laicist, son of St Francis, agitator, positive theologian, anti-papal zealot, sound catholic, constitutionalist, proponent of reason of state – can to an extent be reconciled if some are applied on one level, some on others. Indeed, the preceding review already suggests how this might be done for the two aspects of Ockham's political thought distinguished

[153] Boehner, 'Ockham's political ideas', p. 446.
[154] In this as in other respects Ockham may be compared with Locke, whose major essay in temperate, balanced political thought, the *Second Treatise of Government*, proved extraordinarily useful in justifying the revolution of 1688–9 and provided much of the theory for the American Declaration of Independence. For the general comparison of Ockham with Locke, see Gewirth, *Marsilius of Padua and Medieval Political Philosophy*, p. 258.

earlier, the personal and the institutional. Roughly speaking, we may expect to find that Ockham's reflections on governmental institutions have a significant liberal or constitutionalist component, while his campaign against John XXII and his successors, radical as it was in practice, would naturally involve radical theoretical argumentation as well. It is not enough to offer this distinction in general, of course. It must be tested by a detailed examination of texts. Furthermore, dividing Ockham's political thought into different levels of abstraction will not ultimately be helpful unless we also ask how consistent he was between levels. Still, such a division seems worth attempting as long as these requirements are kept in mind.[155] Hence, in the present study succeeding chapters will be devoted to the problem of radical action and to the basis and functions of governmental institutions, an order which corresponds in chronological emphasis as well as logically with the order of Ockham's work.[156]

Certain problems posed by the relationship between Ockham's speculative and political thought have already been mentioned. The preceding survey of scholarly opinion underlines both the importance and the difficulty of satisfactorily defining this relationship. Since careful students of Ockham have concluded, variously, that there is a somewhat sinister relationship, a positive and constructive relationship, or no noteworthy relationship at all between his academic theology and philosophy on one hand and his political ideas on the other, it is necessary to be very cautious about attempting to deduce Ockhamist politics from specifically nominalist first principles. It is surely significant that a writer like Boehner, who was far more familiar than most scholars with Ockham's metaphysics and epistemology, found it proper to consider the political thought apart from such a speculative basis. At the same time, the findings of Lagarde and Scholz compel us to take seriously several matters which Boehner ignored. Thus, although there is little in Ockham's speculative writings which entails particular solutions to political problems,

---

155 On the usefulness of distinguishing various senses of the political for purposes of modern analytical social and political philosophy, see A. Gewirth's essay, 'Political justice', in R. B. Brandt (ed.), *Social Justice* (Englewood Cliffs, N.J.; 1962), pp. 119–69, especially pp. 119–22.

156 On the need to consider the sequence of Ockham's changing interests, see H. S. Offler, *OP* III, vii.

these works provide abundant original material for reflection on the place of politics in the broader context of human life. To cite but one example, there are numerous passages in the theological works concerned with the question, whether only acts of will are intrinsically morally good or bad. This immediately brings us to grips with basic problems about the relations of politics, law, and morals. If politics is concerned only with overt behavior (*actus exteriores*), and if only inner (volitional) acts are morally good or bad, then the whole political domain might seem to be morally neutral or meaningless, and morality would become a radically private affair. Or again, Ockham's intricate discussions of the place of *recta ratio* in virtuous action surely have at least indirect implications for politics,[157] though to judge from some previous studies the very existence of rationalistic or 'objectivist' passages in Ockham is cause for wonder. Finally, as Scholz emphasized, Ockham was primarily a theologian. He was first propelled into a polemical career by his religious commitments, and he submitted to religious criteria at the end of his life, offering to account for his actions since joining the Franciscan order so that all believers might see if anything could be proved against him because of which he ought not to be counted among the sons of light.[158] It is thus clearly appropriate to compare Ockham's faith with his actions. Beyond this, there is the relevance of theology to political thought in the middle ages generally. If there should prove to be no connection between Ockham's theology and his politics, this very lack of connection would deserve explanation.

Perhaps the best course is neither to ignore Ockham's academic writings nor to start from them. By examining the polemical works in their own terms first, we may hope to discover exactly what in Ockham's political thought needs speculative explanation or justification, and this should put us in a better position to assess such support as his earlier thought actually provides. In following this

---

157 I know of no passage later than I *Dialogus* 6 that shows a significant direct dependence on Ockham's speculative doctrines. As Miethke has pointed out (*Ockhams Weg*, p. 301, n. 571), Ockham's discussion of criminal moral psychology there (I *Dialogus* 6, lxxvii–lxxix, fols. 89vb–95rb) corresponds with the treatment of 'the connection of the virtues' in his academic writings (*Sent.*, III, 12), but even on this matter the student in the *Dialogus* leaves the detailed discussion of different opinions to the curious, because it seems to him to have little utility, 'but in this work I think only useful things should be taken up' (fol. 90va).

158 *Imp. Pont. Pot.*, c. 1, pp. 453–4.

45

order we may anticipate ignoring much in Ockham's theology and philosophy that is important from a non-political standpoint and finding much in his political works that does not 'follow' simply from speculative general principles. So untidy a result may, however, be the correct one.

Chapter 2

THE PROBLEM OF RADICAL ACTION

Nam contra errores pseudo-papae praefati
'posui faciem meam ut petram durissimam'.

For against the errors of the forenamed
pseudo-pope 'I have set my face like a
flint'.

Epistola ad Fratres Minores (OP III, 15)

Pauci non deberent de victoria desperare,
immo unus solus de victoria sperare deberet.

A few ought not to despair of victory. Even
one man alone ought to hope for victory.

1 *Dialogus* 7, xlvii, fol. 147ra

The starting point for Ockham's political thought both logically
and psychologically was the problem of papal heresy. More precisely,
he sought to bring about the downfall of John XXII, whom he
regarded as a pseudo-pope because of his teachings on evangelical
poverty and, later, the beatific vision. Before we consider Ockham's
treatment of basic political institutions an attempt must be made to
understand this striking initial 'personal' project. As a theologian and
philosopher among a small group of excommunicate friars, how did
Ockham think to bring down the reigning head of the Roman
church? How could he think himself morally justified in such an
undertaking? What obstacles did he recognize? How did he seek to
overcome them? What significance does this venture in revolutionary
ecclesiastical politics have for politics in general? These are the
questions of the present chapter.

47

AUTHORITY AND UNDERSTANDING IN THE PROCESS
OF DOCTRINAL CORRECTION

By the time he reached the sixth and seventh books of 1 *Dialogus*, Ockham was ready to discuss action against a heretical pope and his followers as if such action could be taken without seriously disturbing the life of the church. In Book 5 he had asked who could be tainted with heretical depravity. His answer was, very nearly everyone. The faith will endure until the end of the world. Christ's promise assures it. But this promise is fulfilled if there is even one catholic Christian. Certainly the pope can become a heretic,[1] and so can the college of cardinals,[2] as for that matter can a general council,[3] or even all the clergy.[4] Indeed, all Christian men can fall into heresy.[5] One could even imagine the Christian faith being preserved only in the soul of a single baptized infant.[6] In Book 6 Ockham went on to discuss the punishment of heretics and especially of the pope, if he should become a heretic,[7] and in the seventh and last book of 1 *Dialogus* he turned to the believers, favorers, defenders, and receivers of heretics.[8] Here he issued a call to arms of virtually all classes of Christian society and an accusation of those who might fail to respond.[9] The simplest layman is in some cases bound to take action against the supporters of a heretic, even one who occupies the papacy.[10] With such recommendations Ockham reached the

[1] 1 *Dialogus* 5, i–iii. Seven *auctoritates*, eight examples, and fifteen *rationes* are given for the thesis that a canonically elected pope can err against catholic truth and adhere pertinaciously to heretical depravity.

[2] *Ibid.*, vii.   [3] *Ibid.*, xxv.

[4] *Ibid.*, xxix.   [5] *Ibid.*, xxxii.

[6] *Ibid.*, xxxv, *ad fin.* For the tradition that the church consisted of one person, Mary, during the three days between Christ's death and resurrection, see Y. M.-J. Congar, 'Incidence ecclésiologique d'un thème de dévotion mariale', *Mélanges des sciences religieuses*, VII (1950), 277–92.

[7] 1 *Dialogus* 6, especially lxxiv–lxxxii.

[8] *Ibid.*, 7, i–lxix.

[9] '*Discipulus*: Volo de Christianis diversorum statuum et graduum quomodo doctrinae pestiferae papae haeretici valeant favere interrogare quamplura. Propono inquaerere singillatim de episcopis et praelatis [chapters 35–41], de doctoribus et magistris [chapters 42–50], de religiosis [chapter 51] et regibus principibus et publicis potestatibus et de dignitatibus [chapters 52–5] et ultimo de laicis et simplicibus nullam potestatem habentibus coactivam [chapter 56].' *Ibid.*, xxxv, fol. 137ra.

[10] *Ibid.*, lvi, fol. 152rb–va. Also see 1 *Dialogus* 6, xci–c. These chapters are the *locus classicus* for Ockham's laicism.

extreme of radical anti-establishment ecclesiastical politics. And yet, as we have remarked, he discussed these matters as if action could be taken against a heretical pope without seriously disturbing the life of the church – or at least without disturbing it as much as the continued dominance of a papal heretic. To understand how Ockham thought himself able to proceed on this footing will be partly a matter of making clear some institutional assumptions that he himself did not articulate until later in his career. So far as the argument of I *Dialogus* is concerned, however, we can make considerable headway if we read the highly dramatic later books in the light of an earlier portion of the work whose significance is often overlooked, the discussion of pertinacity in Book 4.

This discussion has, first, an important moral bearing on the whole matter of heresy. Even apart from its anarchic institutional implications, Ockham's opposition to John XXII and later popes must impress the modern reader as morally dubious. Current uncertainty about truth and falsity in religion in general combines with the special opacity of the poverty controversy and the special bitterness of Ockham's style to make such works as the *Contra Ioannem* and *Contra Benedictum* look like fanatical attacks on men whose theological opinions happened to disagree – and disagree trivially, it often seems – with Ockham's own. Perhaps nothing should entirely erase this impression, yet it must be pointed out in Ockham's defense that the argument of I *Dialogus* is directed against obdurate rejection of the very basis of Christianity, not against innocent blunders or theological ineptitude. According to Ockham, as we shall see, a professing Christian can be mistaken even about major articles of the faith without thereby being a heretic.[11] The question is whether his faith in the general veracity of scripture and the whole church is stronger than his attachment to some particular proposition which is in fact contrary to such catholic truth.[12] To describe a man as an

---

[11] Note 38 below.

[12] 'Ille est censendus catholicus qui integram et inviolatam servat catholicam fidem ... Servare vel tenere catholicam et integram fidem, continet omnia quae ad fidem pertinent orthodoxam explicite vel implicite fideliter et absque ulla dubitatione credere ... Credere implicite est credere alicui universali ex quo multa sequuntur firmiter assentire et nulli contrario pertinaciter adhaerere. *Et ideo qui firmiter tenent omnia tradita in scriptura et universalis ecclesiae doctrina esse vera et sana et non adhaerent pertinaciter alicui assertioni contraria[e] veritati orthodoxae fidem catholicam inviolatam tenent et integram sunt catholici censendi.*' I *Dialogus* 3, i, fols. 17vb–18ra. A heretic,

errans leaves this question open. To accuse him of being pertinacious or a heretic is to assert, rightly or wrongly, that his adherence to some error contrary to divine revelation is so strong that he would rather reject the general principle of God's veracity than give up his own opinion.[13] In these terms, Ockham's insistence on orthodoxy as a condition for genuine papal authority was an insistence on openness to the basis, or bases, of Christian truth,[14] not a demand that the pope have the one right answer to every detailed question in academic or pastoral theology. His conviction that John XXII was a heretic, however unjustified it may have been, was thus far more serious than a mere denial of John's omniscience.

Similarly, the phrase 'heretical depravity', prominent as it is in 1 *Dialogus* 5, indicates that Ockham subscribed in that book to the possibility of a virtual abandonment of Christianity by one or another ecclesiastical official or group of Christians. He envisaged the defectibility of various parts of the church and not merely their technical theological fallibility.[15] None of this makes 1 *Dialogus*

on the other hand, is someone truly baptized or bearing himself as baptized who pertinaciously doubts or errs against catholic truth (*ibid.*, iii, fol. 18va). Ockham gives most of the particulars in this description little comment, but the need to include 'pertinaciter' in the description of a heretic occupies him for several chapters (*ibid.*, v–x).

13 'Tripliciter potest quis pertinaciter errare in mente, et primo quidem, si quis non obstantibus miraculis quae audiuntur fuisse facta pro fide firmanda putat fidem esse falsam vel incertam. *Secundo si in generali credit totam fidem esse veram, alicui tamen errori in speciali* (quam nescit ad fidem explicite pertinere) *adhaeret tam fortiter quod quantumcunque sibi ostenderetur ad fidem pertinere errorem nullo modo dimitteret huiusmodi, sed ante putaret fidem esse falsam* ... Tertio ... si alicui errori inhaeret et negligit quomodo et quando debet quaerere veritatem, quia talis non est paratus corrigi si persistit in errore quem debet de necessitate salutis dimittere.' 1 *Dialogus* 4, ii, fol. 22vb. Cf. the discussion of virtue and vice, including heresy, as involving good or bad dispositions towards *all* good acts or *all* evil acts (*ibid.*, 6, lxxvii–lxxix, especially lxxvii–lxxviii, fols. 90rb–93ra). According to Ockham's earlier treatment (*Sent.* iii, q. 8 L–N), *fides* (*infusa*) has as its immediate object the one general proposition, 'omne relevatum a Deo est verum, sicut revelatur esse verum'.

14 On the complex subject of Ockham's account of the sources of Christian truth, see Oberman, *The Harvest of Medieval Theology*, pp. 361–422; Miethke, *Ockhams Weg*, pp. 245–99.

15 On the distinction between indefectibility and infallibility, or inerrancy, see Tierney, *Origins of Papal Infallibility*, pp. 31–9, It should be noted that the term 'heretical depravity' was not Ockham's coinage but had been the official papal terminology since the twelfth century, if not earlier.

enjoyable reading, but attention to the central place of pertinacity in Ockham's account suggests that at least by medieval standards his approach to the problem of heresy was neither pedantic nor perverse.

Besides setting the moral context for the whole of 1 *Dialogus*, the treatment in Book 4 of the various modes of convicting someone of pertinacity[16] is of considerable practical import. It is the fulcrum with which the discussion of heretical *doctrines* in Book 2 can be brought to bear effectively on the *holders* of such doctrines in the ways put forth in Books 5–7. The need for practical effectiveness must be emphasized. As the work of Tierney and Wilks has made abundantly clear, the problem of papal heresy was not a new one in theory.[17] It had received increasingly detailed treatment from the twelfth- and thirteenth-century canonists and had a place in the writings of such contemporary hierocrats as Augustinus Triumphus and Alvarus Pelagius. By Ockham's time one common opinion held that a heretical pope was automatically deprived of all ecclesiastical authority – just as a dead man is not a man, so a pope fallen into heresy is not a pope and is *ipso facto* deposed. Such a man was indeed 'less than' any Christian.[18] These striking formulations express what

16 Another person's inner pertinacity, *pertinacia in mente*, cannot be directly known, but Ockham considers no fewer than twenty ways in which someone might reasonably be judged pertinacious on the basis of his words or actions.

17 Tierney, *Foundations of the Conciliar Theory*, pp. 8–9, 60–7, 214–15. 'The Decretalists were apparently quite happy to discuss in the abstract the theoretical limits of the Pope's powers but extremely reluctant to admit that there could be any human authority competent to enforce such limitations in practice', p. 96. Cf. Wilks, *Sovereignty in the Later Middle Ages*, pp. 455–78, 502–3. Although the possibility of papal heresy was widely taken for granted when Ockham wrote, the frame of mind which led one of his contemporaries, Guido Terreni, to a finished doctrine of papal infallibility was also not a new one. On Guido, see Tierney, *Origins of Papal Infallibility*, pp. 238–69. On earlier developments, see Ullmann, *Government and Politics in the Middle Ages*, Part 1.

18 1 *Dialogus* 6, lxvi–lxxiii. *Epistola ad Fratres Minores*; *OP* III, 15. *OND*, cc. 1, 124; *OP* I, 296–7 and II, 853–4. *OQ* I, 17; *OP* I, 60–1. *Imp. Pont. Pot.*, c. 27, ed. W. Mulder, *AFH*, XVII (1924), 72–97; p. 97 (the last words Ockham is known to have written). Augustinus Triumphus, *Summa de Ecclesiastica Potestate* (Rome, 1479, 1584), q. 5, a. 1, p. 50 (quoted by Wilks, *Sovereignty in the Later Middle Ages*, p. 502n.): 'sicut homo mortuus non est homo, ita papa deprehensus in haeresi non est papa, propter quod ipso facto est depositus'. For the earlier development of this idea by the canonists, see Tierney, *Foundations of the Conciliar Theory*, pp. 9, 62–3, 214–16. For Ludwig of Bavaria's use of the theory in 1328 as basis for setting up a rival pope to John XXII, see Wilks, *Sovereignty in the Later Middle Ages*, p. 516. According

might be called the spiritual death theory of papal heresy, a theory which may appear both decisive and inevitable from a theological point of view. For all its theological value, however, this idea provided little help in doing anything about a heretic actually occupying the papal throne. One might know perfectly well in general that a heretic could not 'really' – that is, from the standpoint of abstract theological truth – be pope, but this theoretical conviction could not effectively remove anyone from the exercise of the papal office. In order to take action against a false pope it was first necessary to determine that the individual in question was a heretic, but no guidance had been offered for reaching such a determination. This problem needed to be handled if the general notion of papal heresy (and hence, correlatively, papal orthodoxy) was to have more than nominal significance.

The difficulty was in taking due account of the authority of a pope who *is* pope. The papacy is normally the supreme authority in matters of faith, and this fact can readily be used to justify an authoritarian power structure in which no one can do anything about heresy 'at the top', since *ex hypothesi*, no one has 'authority' to question the supreme authority. From the standpoint of action there is an impasse.[19] Thus, for example, even though John XXII's Michaelist attackers had at length become painfully convinced of his heresy and regarded themselves as obliged to resist

to Alvarus Pelagius, a general council does not depose the pope (for it has no jurisdiction over him), but tells him, 'Ore tuo iudica causam tuam . . . ex ore tuo condemnaberis' (*De Planctu Ecclesiae*, ch. 6 (Wilks, *Sovereignty in the Later Middle Ages*, p. 503n.)). Cf. Gratian's *Decretum*, Dist. 21, cc. 7–9. According to Augustinus Triumphus, 'si notabiliter praeciperentur inconsueta, et dissona a praeceptis Dei, et praeceptis legis naturae; cum papa sic praecipiendo esset infidelis, seipsum iudicaret, quia qui non recte credit, iam iudicatus est', *Summa de Ecclesiastica Potestate* q. 22, a. 1, *ad* 2, p. 130.

19 The impasse is similar to that experienced by churchmen of the conciliar epoch. The obvious means of ending papal schism was a general council, but traditionally only the pope could convene a council (W. Ullmann, *The Origins of the Great Schism* (London, 1948), pp. 178ff.). The same dilemma is put forward by the student in a discussion of 'spiritual warfare' against papal heresy in 1 *Dialogus* 7, xliii–xlv. He objects that a man cannot rightly go to war unless summoned to do so by his commander in chief. Hence, one can never go to war against the pope, since he is the spiritual commander in chief. By this stage in the *Dialogus* Ockham is easily able to dispose of so 'frivolous' an objection. Our central problem is to understand how this genuine practical difficulty was turned into a frivolous objection.

him,[20] there was no generally accepted procedure through which their convictions could be put to a fair trial. There was not even a coherent set of ideas on the subject. The bare request for a neutral, impartial hearing of their charges could be rejected out of hand as a rebellion against divine order. So, while a good catholic could admit the theoretical possibility of papal heresy, the relative ecclesiastical standing of John and his attackers posed an enormous practical obstacle for the Michaelists to overcome.

To sum up a complicated course of argument in the simplest terms, we may say that Ockham attempted to overcome this obstacle by transforming the concept of legitimate doctrinal correction. By treating the process of correction in primarily cognitive terms rather than as an exercise of institutional power, he provided at least in theory a means for examining authoritative pronouncements without already having decided that the authority in question was corrupt. Aside from its direct contribution to the logic of the Michaelist resistance to John XXII, we shall find that this treatment of doctrinal correction also helps explain the perplexing impersonal format of some of Ockham's most important works.

The topic of legitimate correction is introduced in connection with one of the many modes of convicting someone of pertinacity: an *errans* may be considered pertinacious if he does not revoke his heresy after being legitimately corrected for it.[21] The student raises two questions on this matter. To whom does it pertain to correct an *errans*? What sort of correction should be regarded as legitimate and sufficient? Significantly, the master first offers an account of the correction itself and only then goes on to discuss the corrector. A correction should be counted sufficient and legitimate, he says, only if it is clearly shown to the *errans* (*qua aperte erranti ostenditur*) that his assertion is against catholic truth, so that in the judgment of those who understand (*iudicio intelligentium*) he cannot by any tergiversation deny that this has been sufficiently and clearly shown to him.[22] After the briefest illustration of what is meant by clearly showing

---

[20] *OND*, *passim*, especially cc. 123–4; *OP* II, 837–57.
[21] I *Dialogus* 4, xiii.
[22] *Ibid.*, fol. 26va. Cf. *OND*, c. 124; *OP* II, 852: 'Illa correptio est censenda legitima qua evidenter erranti ostenditur quod suus error regulae fidei contradicit.'

someone that his assertion is contrary to catholic truth,[23] the master proceeds to the other main topic, the *corripiens*, and here he makes a distinction: some correct by rebuking and punishing with due penalty, others by charitable admonition and by merely reproving the error; the first way pertains to prelates and those who have jurisdiction, the second to any Christian.[24] Thus the stage is set for a reversal of the relative credibility of John XXII and his attackers. Although the distinction between authoritative and fraternal correction was a traditional one,[25] when it is coupled with the requirement that an *errans* be shown his error before his correction is sufficient and legitimate, the result is revolutionary.

The direction of the argument becomes clear at once in Ockham's treatment of authoritative correction. The student asks whether all the learned know (*an omnes sciant litterati*) that an *errans* corrected by his own prelate or by someone else having jurisdiction over him is bound to revoke his error even if he has not been shown that it is against catholic truth. The question is whether he ought to revoke his error solely at his prelate's admonition or rebuke.[26] In contrast with his usual procedure, Ockham elaborates only one answer to this question, the negative one: an *errans* is *not* bound to give up his error immediately on the bare rebuke of an ecclesiastical superior. The fact that the superior is right and the inferior wrong does not by itself impose an obligation upon the latter to change his views. The student raises many objections to this assertion, but since they are all answered and no independent arguments are given for the contrary opinion, Ockham's own position is clear.[27] As far as I have been able to determine, this well articulated defense of the rights of an erring inferior in the face of rebuke from an orthodox religious superior is without precedent in the publicistic literature.[28]

---

[23] By showing him, for example, a text of the gospel or of the proceedings of the council of Ephesus which is directly contrary to what he has said. I *Dialogus* 4, xiii, fol. 26va.

[24] *Ibid.*

[25] Cf. Thomas Aquinas, *Summa Theologiae* IIa IIae, q. 33, esp. aa. 1, 3, and 4.

[26] I *Dialogus* 4, xiv, fol. 26va.

[27] When Ockham presents only one view on a subject in the *Dialogus*, it is almost certainly his own. See above, chapter 1, n. 63.

[28] Ockham's view differs especially from that of the Inquisition. Cf. Bernard Gui's *Manuel de l'Inquisiteur*, ed. G. Mollat (2 vols., Paris, 1926–7), 1, 4: 'Eo ipso iam [aliquis] haereticus censeretur quo errorem defendere niteretur.' Only authority

Ockham's first and most detailed argument in this defense is an application and amplification of a celebrated canon law text, Distinction 20 of Gratian's *Decretum*. Gratian had said that it is one thing to bring ecclesiastical controversies to an end (*causis terminum imponere*) and something else to expound sacred scripture. Hence, even if those who treat of the scriptures have not attained to the height of pontifical dignity, if they surpass the pontiffs in knowledge (*scientia*) their expositions of scripture should be preferred, though in settling cases they deserve a place after the pontiffs. Ockham uses this text to argue that, if teachers (*doctores*) are to be preferred over pontiffs in the exposition of scripture, they are not bound to give up their opinions at a pontiff's correction unless the errors in these opinions are clearly shown to them.[29] It has been asserted that Ock-

has rights in the 'Summula Inquisitionis . . . (1361)', ed. L. Oliger (*Antonianum*, v (1930), 475–86), especially p. 483: 'quod laicis non licet disputare de fide'.

[29] More precisely, Ockham argues that those who are of greater authority in a given matter ought not to be subjected in that matter to those who are 'less' in it. He cites Gratian to show that many of those who have dealt with scripture have used greater reason, and hence that their words have greater authority (*maioris auctoritatis eius verba esse videntur*). The nerve of the argument is Ockham's treatment of *auctoritas* here as a specialized rather than a comprehensive notion. Whatever Gratian meant by the term, Ockham clearly employs it to designate the theologian's special competence as an expositor of the Bible, not any charismatic or juridical power. The full text will serve as an example of Ockham's ingenious though somewhat mechanical style of argument and of his use of a major canonistic source. 'Illi qui in expositione scripturae divinae, et per consequens in traditione eorum quae ad fidem pertinent orthodoxam praeferuntur praelatis et iurisdictionem habentibus non tenentur nec debent si erraverint ignoranter opiniones suas tanquam haereticas (licet sint in rei veritate erroneae) revocare, quamvis correpti fuerint a praelatis vel aliis, nisi eis patenter fuerit ostensum quod opiniones suae veritati obviant orthodoxae, quia qui maioris auctoritatis est in aliquo nequaquam in hoc minori subiicitur, ergo qui praeferuntur praelatis in expositione scripturae divinae non subiiciuntur eis in hoc; sed doctores et tractatores scripturae divinae praeferuntur praelatis et iurisdictionem habentibus in expositione scripturae divinae, et per consequens in traditione illorum quae ad fidem pertinent orthodoxam, igitur doctores non tenentur opiniones suas licet sint erroneae revocare si fuerint a praelatis correpti nisi probatum fuerit eis evidenter quod eorum opiniones obviant veritati. Maior est certa. Et minor probatur primo auctoritate Gratiani in Decretis, di. xx, c. i, qui ait, *aliud est causis terminum imponere aliud scripturas sacras diligenter exponere* et ita patet *quod divinarum scripturarum tractatores si* [etsi ed. Friedberg] *scientia pontificibus praeemineant licet* [tamen quia ed. Friedberg] *dignitatis eorum apicem non sunt adepti in sacrarum litterarum expositionibus eis praeponuntur, in causis vero diffiniendis secundum post eos locum merentur.* Ex his patenter habetur quod doctores in expositionibus scripturae pontificibus praeferuntur. Quod etiam ratione eiusdem Gratiani ostenditur, quam ponit sub his verbis,

ham's conclusions are a 'véritable contresens' to the intended meaning of Gratian's text.[30] Although it is true that Gratian's aim is to show that 'potestas' is needed to decide disputes – that 'scientia' is not sufficient – that is not contradicted by Ockham's contention that something like *scientia* is *necessary* in certain cases, if justice is to be achieved. So far as Ockham's thesis is concerned, *scientia* may not be sufficient, but *potestas* alone is not sufficient either (an issue Gratian silently avoids). Ockham's purpose is thus very different from Gratian's, but not inconsistent with it, so far as we have seen. At any rate, whatever the level of endorsement Gratian can be made to provide for the principle that doctors are to be preferred to pontiffs, we would miss the point of Ockham's discussion if we interpreted it as solely an elitist defense of academic theologians against inexpert prelates.[31] For Ockham himself raises an objection along this line and replies by boldly extending his argument to cover, first, those simple persons who may have followed the errors of experts, and then all *simplices*, since all would seem to have the same right.[32] The text from Gratian thus turns out to be only an entering wedge. Ockham's final development of the argument also takes in illiterate *errantes* at odds with ecclesiastical authorities who perhaps could explain their errors to them but choose instead to act in an arbitrary manner. In addition to this reasoning, three further arguments are offered against the thesis that an *errans* is automatically bound to give up his views on being rebuked by a superior. In none of these is there any suggestion of a privileged status for *doctores*.[33]

> quia *quicunque maiori ratione utitur eo maioris auctoritatis eius verba esse videntur. Plurimi autem tractatores (quia sunt pleniori gratia Spiritus Sancti et ampliori scientia aliis praecellentes) rationi magis adhaesisse probantur, unde nonnullorum pontificum constitutis Augustini, Hieronimi atque aliorum tractatorum dicta videntur esse praeferenda.* His verbis ostenditur quod in his quae ad fidem pertinent doctores sunt pontificibus praeferendi et ita nisi fuerint ab eis correpti legitime modo praeexposito non tenentur opiniones suas si fuerint erroneae revocare' (1 *Dialogus* 4, xiv, fol. 26vb). The first citation is from Part II of Gratian's Dictum to Distinction 20; the second is a nearly verbatim quotation from the beginning of the same *Dictum Gratiani*. Ed. Friedberg, I, 65.

30 Lagarde, *La naissance*, v, 144.   31 *Ibid.*, pp. 39n., 49, 144, 158–60.

32 'Eadem ratione nec simplices peritorum sequaces tenentur opiniones quas de peritioribus acceperunt aliqualiter revocare ... Ex quo sequitur quod etiam alii simplices non tenentur (nisi correpti legitime) suas opiniones erroneas revocare, quia omnes simplices consimili iure censeri videntur.' 1 *Dialogus* 4, xiv, fol. 27ra.

33 A person is not bound to give up his views merely on being rebuked by (1) someone whose own opinion he is not bound to believe without doubt, (2) someone

This is not to deny that the role of the *doctor* or theological *peritus* is a crucial one in Ockham's anti-papal campaign. Close attention will be given to this function later in our discussion, when it will be necessary to specify exactly who these experts are. At no point, however, does Ockham appear to adopt the academicism sometimes ascribed to him.

Demolition of the authoritarian thesis that erring subjects are bound to give up their views at the mere rebuke of an ecclesiastical superior occupies Ockham for several chapters. By comparison, his treatment of the person corrected by a friend or someone else who holds no jurisdiction over him is quite brief. The thesis developed here is equally radical, however: an *errans* whose errors are clearly pointed out to him is bound to give them up at once, no matter who has corrected him, whether a friend, a subject, or anyone whatever.[34] As the student fairly remarks at this point, there seems to be no difference left between a person corrected by his prelate and one corrected by someone who is not his prelate, possibly even by his own subject. The master points out that a prelate can cite those over whom he has jurisdiction, constrain them to give information, and compel them to public recantation or mete out punishment if he finds them pertinacious or rebellious. He is bound to admit, however, that so far as the *errans'* obligation to give up his error is concerned, there is no difference at all: 'quantum ad hoc quod error dimittatur non est differentia'.[35] In this all-important respect, the traditional distinction between authoritative and fraternal correction has been effectively collapsed. The concept of a cognitively legitimate correction – a process in which the *errans* is clearly shown his error – has superseded it.

We can now begin to see the relevance of this whole discussion to the Michaelists' basic problem in resisting John XXII. Michael of Cesena and his associates did not, of course, present themselves as *errantes*. Quite the contrary, they regarded themselves as defenders of catholic truth against an erring pope and claimed that they had

who should be ready to satisfy those asking for a *ratio de fide* (unless he gives such a *ratio*), or (3) someone from whose sentence it is licit to appeal. *Ibid.*, xv, fol. 27ra–va.

34 *Ibid.*, xxi. On earlier, less decisive attempts to apply the idea of fraternal correction to the problem of papal heresy, see Buisson, *Potestas und Caritas*, pp. 166–215.
35 1 *Dialogus* 4, xxi, fol. 29va.

'legitimately' corrected John.[36] By enforcing his errors on others and by refusing to accept legitimate correction, even though this was offered by his inferiors, John became no longer simply an *errans* but a *pertinax*, hence a *haereticus*, hence no longer pope but pseudo-pope, and inferior to any Christian. Crushing as this series of inferences seemed to the Michaelists, however, something more was needed to make other churchmen even pay attention to their specific doctrinal charges against John, let alone act on them. The great disparity between a reigning pope's inherent trustworthiness and the credibility of a small group of excommunicate friars was not reduced by the fact that this excommunication was mutual. We must therefore look back to the earlier part of Ockham's discussion of correction for a significant contribution to the problem of action.

What we find there is a conceptual basis for examining authoritative pronouncements without presupposing their falsity, and hence without commitment to the personal heterodoxy of the authority issuing them. For the first part of Ockham's discussion assumes that the authoritative *corripiens* may be right and his subject wrong in the doctrinal issue between them. Hence, recipients of an accusation against the ecclesiastical authorities would no longer be called upon to decide at once as to the orthodoxy of those authorities. There was room to suppose them sound in faith but arbitrary and dictatorial in repressing their subjects' opinions without rendering them an adequate explanation. Since the obligation to correct 'legitimately' falls on the pope as well as on other prelates,[37] the case of John XXII and the Franciscans would obviously be covered. The burden of proof has thus been subtly shifted. Since the prelate's orthodoxy is no longer the sole issue, it is not necessary for his attackers to demonstrate his heresy in order to be justified in maintaining their own beliefs. Rather, on the line of argument presented in the last several pages, it is the responsibility of one in authority to correct his inferiors legitimately before they can rightly be stigmatized as *pertinaces* and *rebelles*. Instead of presuming that the inferior is guilty until he has managed to demonstrate the guilt of his superior, we

---

36 *OND*, c. 124; *OP* II, 853: 'Nam constat quod iste impugnatus per plures scripturas istius appellantis et aliorum legitime est correptus, quia in pluribus scripturis, *quas vidit et legit, evidenter ostenditur* quod errores sui regulae fidei contradicunt.'
37 1 *Dialogus* 4, xx.

are now invited to presume that the inferior is innocent (not of error, but of *pravitas haereticalis*) until his error has been clearly shown to him. In such a situation a good catholic could sympathize in some measure with both sides.[38]

Has Ockham here substituted the private judgment of the individual for the judgment of the church? Does his discussion point to the result that each man must be his own church? Are we landed here in a morass of total subjectivity? Such assessments fit well with both the laicist and the purely theological interpretations of Ockham. One might naturally look for the seeds of Ockham's presumed anarchism in a doctrine of the rights of individual error against ecclesiastical correction or, alternatively, one might expect the certainties of the inner world of the individual to manifest themselves in a rejection of supervision from the outer world of fallible officials. For better or worse, however, these interpretations prove unfounded. There is clear evidence that Ockham meant to avoid arbitrary individualism as much as arbitrary authoritarianism. By following this issue we shall gain light on Ockham's view of his own role in the process of doctrinal correction, both as an individual Christian and as a theological expert.

The issue is raised in 1 *Dialogus* after the discussion of correction by superiors has reached the papal level. Perhaps, the student suggests, someone defending his own opinion would say, even after his opinion had been proved heretical, that it had not been shown *to him* that it was against the orthodox faith, and so he could never be convicted.[39] The master's reply clearly treats the legitimacy of the

---

[38] There are other signs of Ockham's dissatisfaction with the arbitrariness of current procedures for doctrinal correction. Thus, he argues at length (*ibid.* 2, xviii–xxiv) that bishops and inquisitors can legitimately proceed only against the holders of heresies already explicitly condemned by the church; persons defending errors that have been condemned only implicitly must be referred to pope or general council. Even when the *errans* holds an explicitly condemned view, he is not bound to give it up unless he is corrected legitimately (*ibid.* 4, xvi–xix, fol. 28v*ab*). Accordingly, Ockham scathingly criticizes the practice of treating such persons as manifest heretics even if they are ready to be corrected. Some inquisitors and prelates proceed unfairly and unjustly, he says. Many of them are simple and uneducated. Blinded by avarice, they try to condemn those accused of heresy to acquire their goods. Hence, the practice of such men is no objection to the requirement that doctrinal errors be adequately explained to those who hold them. (*ibid*, xviii, fol. 28 r*ab*)

[39] *Ibid.*, xx, fol. 29r*a*.

process of correction as an objective, publicly observable fact. It is not up to the *errans* to settle the question, whether he has been legitimately corrected. The judgment of experts must be relied upon (*cogitur stare iudicio peritorum*). If they regard it as sufficiently proved that the opinion is heretical, he is bound to revoke it or be counted among the pertinacious and heretical.[40] What if the experts and all the masters of theology should err, and the pope as well? The master does not deny that such a case could arise. After suggesting that an innocent person who has been condemned may be able to appeal his case, the master concedes that if such an appeal should not be heard, there remains nothing for the man to do but commit himself to the divine grace and not fear to be cut off by an unjust judgment from the society of men.

Although it is not conclusive, as we have seen, the appeal to expert judgment is of considerable importance in Ockham's overall argument. The 'doctor' or expert plays a role not only in assessing the legitimacy of doctrinal correction but in other situations as well. More generally, Ockham's habit of phrasing the questions in this dialogue between master and student in terms of what the 'litterati' think about this or that issue is symptomatic of a general attitude towards truth as a possession of the learned rather than the inspired or the authorized. It is important, therefore, to understand who and what the Ockhamist expert is and what sort of power he is supposed to have. Once again, the appeal to Gratian's Distinction 20 is enlightening. When the master uses this text to show that *doctores* should not be required to give up their views on the simple rebuke of an ecclesiastical superior, the student objects that Gratian spoke only of doctors approved by the church, not about modern doctors.[41] The master readily replies that Gratian was speaking in terms of a general comparison between the 'status' of *doctores* and the 'status' of *pontifices*: 'comparat enim in genere statum doctorum ad statum pontificum'.[42] However venturesome this reply may be as an interpretation of Gratian, it leads Ockham to a highly revealing characterization of the *doctores* who he himself thinks should nowadays be preferred to pontiffs. Just as, in ancient times, *doctores* were to be preferred to pontiffs in passing on (*traditio*) things pertaining to faith, he says, so now *doctores* are still to be preferred to

---

[40] *Ibid.*   [41] 1 *Dialogus* 4, xiv, fol. 26vb.   [42] *Ibid.*, fol. 27ra.

modern pontiffs as long as they are doctors because of their outstanding knowledge (*scientiam excellentem*) and laudable life, but not if they have been elevated to the *rank* of master because of gifts, improper entreaties, or human favor. Gratian was certainly not talking about doctors such as those who bear the *name*, but about those who treat of divine scripture with understanding, whether they are *called* masters or students (*intelligentibus scripturae divinae tractatoribus sive magistri sive discipuli appellentur*).[43] Even in the course of defending the claims of the *status* of doctors, Ockham has, so to speak, de-institutionalized that *status*. Just as the person who bears himself as pope and is generally acknowledged as such may fail really to be a pope (if he is a heretic), so he who is called a *doctor* may fail to be one, in the sense required by Ockham's argument from Gratian, if he is lacking in *scientia excellens* and *vita laudabilis*, if he fails to be an *intelligens tractator* of divine scripture. Ockham has thus substituted primarily cognitive criteria for institutional criteria in defining the *doctor*, and there can be little doubt that he would have us supply the same cognitive criteria for the *periti* who are to judge the legitimacy of papal acts of correction.[44]

It is here, perhaps, more than anywhere else that Ockham's view of the expert differs from that of Marsilius of Padua, the writer with whom he is most frequently compared. While both thinkers distinguished sharply between the judgment of experts or teachers on one hand and the judgments of those in positions of authority on the other,[45] Marsilius is much readier than Ockham to allow judgments of the latter class to determine who is to be considered a good judge in the first sense. To be sure, Marsilius did not advocate the selection of experts on the basis of bribery and other such manoeuvres. Yet he

43 *Ibid.*
44 I *Dialogus* 4, xx. See above, p. 60. Also see *OQ* I, 16; *OP* I, 59; I *Dialogus* 7, xiii, xlii, xliii, xlvii; I *Dialogus* 6, xciv; III *Dialogus* I, 3, xxv (all cited by Lagarde, *La naissance*, v, 158–60).
45 For Ockham's distinction between defining by the authority of an office (*auctoritate officii*) and by way of teaching (*per modum doctrinae*), see I *Dialogus* I, i, fol. 1va: 'Diffinire plures habet significationes, de quibus ad propositum duae videntur pertinere. Contingit enim aliquid diffinire auctoritate officii, et sic diffinire quae est assertio haeretica quae catholica est censenda, ad summum pontificem spectat et concilium generale. Aliquando contingit diffinire per modum doctrinae quomodo magistri in scholis quaestiones diffiniunt et determinant, et sic accepto secundo modo diffiniendi circa propositam quaestionem diversimode sentiunt litterati.' Cf. *Defensor Pacis*, II, ii, 8; I, xv, I; II, xxx, 4.

clearly accepted an institutional or political definition of the official *status* of the expert rather than a purely cognitive one. Thus, for example, he emphasizes that it is up to the people to choose the experts who shall investigate what is useful for the state, and that only the consent of the people gives legal force to expert recommendations.[46] In the matter of heresy in particular, he insists that the competence of priests as experts on matters of orthodoxy and heresy does not by itself provide a basis for coercive action. Only the power of the people gives force to the correction of heretics in this world, not any qualifications the experts can claim for themselves apart from recognition by the state.[47] No doubt, Marsilius was primarily concerned to rule out papal claims to coercive power, rather than claims to expert knowledge which might be put forth by Ockham's *intelligentes tractatores* of scripture.[48] Here as elsewhere, however, Marsilius' position is a mirror image of the papalism he opposed. John XXII's insistence on keeping the *clavis scientiae* firmly under control by the *clavis potentiae*[49] is reflected in the Marsilian subordination of expert knowledge to the power of the people. The locus of power has been changed, but not its relation to expert knowledge. On a practical level, then, Marsilius and Ockham are brought close together by their common opposition to extreme papalism. Theoretically, however – and fundamentally – Ockham's conception of the relations between political power and 'scientific' knowledge is about as distant from Marsilian as from papalist ideas on the subject.

It seems wrong to characterize this independent position as a shift from the authority of institutional superiors to the authority of individual conscience or even the authority of experts. For if the

---

[46] *Ibid.*, I, xii, 1, 3, 4, 7, 8.

[47] *Ibid.*, II, x, 5, 6; II, vi, 12; II, xvii, 14; II, xx, 2, 3, 5.

[48] Marsilius constantly illustrates his distinction between the non-coercive judgment of the expert and coercive political judgment by reference to the non-coercive nature of a physician's diagnosis of leprosy if there is no law requiring the separation of lepers from the community (see, for example, *Defensor Pacis*, II, vi, 12). As a physician himself, he presumably did not believe that medical judgments were 'relative', scientifically speaking, to the dictates of those in power. For the anti-papalist direction of Marsilius' distinction of expert from coercive judgment, see Gewirth, *Marsilius of Padua and Medieval Political Philosophy*, pp. 226–7. Other aspects of Marsilius' doctrine here are discussed by Gewirth on pp. 168–9, 188–9. For Gewirth, Marsilius' distinction 'means not that the ruler lacks knowledge, but that knowledge is not essential to him as such' (p. 227).

[49] See above, chapter 1, note 52.

private judgment of the individual were the criterion of legitimacy, then no amount of explanation would be 'sufficient', so long as the individual refused to change his views. His beliefs would be 'true for him' so long as he maintained them. But Ockham rejected this view, as we have seen. On the other hand, experts are not to be relied upon as authorities in the institutional sense, where the authorities are those who have been duly appointed to their office or are officially recognized as having a certain competence.[50] It is more accurate to describe Ockham's treatment of correction as a shift in emphasis from authority of any kind to understanding.

His solution to the practical impasse caused by papal supremacy was to transform the concept of legitimate correction from a primarily disciplinary or authoritative concept to a primarily cognitive one. This transformation had two aspects. On the one hand, actions by duly constituted ecclesiastical authorities (superiors) lost much of their value if they were attempts to impose doctrinal opinions arbitrarily without clearly showing the truth of those opinions. On the other hand, corrections *of* ecclesiastical superiors gained decisively in value if they *were* cognitively sufficient. In thus transforming the concept of legitimate correction, Ockham greatly narrowed the traditional distinction between 'authoritative' and 'fraternal' correction. The consequences of this step radiate throughout the plans of action developed in the rest of the *Dialogus*.[51]

[50] On the 'authority' accorded the master by the student within the imaginary context of the *Dialogus*, see the prologue of that work (see above, pp. 17-18, n. 62). Ockham also picks out and uses the term *auctoritas* in the argument from Gratian discussed earlier: 'qui maioris auctoritatis est in aliquo nequaquam in hoc minori subiicitur'. The word itself is not decisive. What counts is that the so-called *auctoritas* of the *doctor* is not dependent upon his holding an acknowledged office in some institutional structure such as a church or a university.

[51] Before considering how Ockham's treatment of legitimate correction contributes to the practical import of the surrounding books of 1 *Dialogus*, we should note that this discussion occupies a central place in the argument of Book 4 itself. The ways of convicting someone of pertinacity that are treated before the discussion of legitimate correction bear equally on heretics of any station, high or low. In connection with some of these, Ockham specifies exceptions (c. 5), makes allowances for ignorance (cc. 6 and 8), or expounds a contrary position (c. 11). The modes of conviction treated *after* the discussion of legitimate correction, however, are for the most part only relevant to heretics in positions of power or authority: a person can be convicted of pertinacity if he tries to compel others to defend his error by commands, threats, penalties, rewards, promises, oaths, or in any other way (c. 22); if he forces someone to abjure catholic truth (c. 23); if he pursues, molests, or impedes

OCKHAM'S DOUBLE ROLE IN THE PROCESS OF CORRECTION

This transformation of the concept of legitimate correction helps to explain how Ockham thought of himself and his polemical activities. It also has consequences for the courses of action he recommended to others. As for Ockham's conception of his own activity, the following hypothesis is proposed. Ockham conceived of himself in two distinct but mutually consistent ways: as a faithful Christian and as an expert in theology. The individual Christian must bear witness to the truth as he sees it, while the theologian must make clear the reasons for the truth. This dual conception roughly corresponds with the division between Ockham's personal works, in which he wrote as a Christian, and the impersonal works, especially 1 *Dialogus*, in which he wrote as a theological *peritus*.

We have already noticed that Ockham extended immunity from arbitrary coercion in matters of faith to the *simplex* as well as the *peritus*. Along with this right to reasonable treatment from his ecclesiastical superiors, the individual Christian has an obligation to maintain the truth of faith as he sees it – until and unless he comes to see that his views are wrong. Ockham's clearest exposition of this obligation is his discussion of the question, whether the pope should give sentence in accordance with the judgment of all of the learned

those defending catholic truth or attacking heretical depravity (c. 25); if, in favor of heretical depravity, he forbids the reading of catholic scriptures or the preaching or publishing of catholic truths (c. 28); if, as pope, he solemnly defines an error to be held by all Christians (c. 29); if he consents to such a papal definition by counseling or cooperating in the process (c. 30), or if, as an inferior bishop, he defines or determines that an error should be held (c. 30); or, finally, if, having the power to do so, he does not resist heretical depravity (c. 31). In none of these cases is the *errans* allowed any extenuation. The pattern is not perfect but it is impressive. The theoretical possibilities for pertinacity in high places are great and are treated severely by Ockham; the transformation of the concept of legitimate correction has served as a fulcrum, so that the full rigor of 'convicting' people of pertinacity can now affect the powerful as well as the weak.

The last chapters of Book 4 have a relentlessness that is typical of Ockham's explicit attacks upon John XXII and Benedict XII. He appears to be disproportionately harsh to those in high places. In the context of Book 4, however, the effect is natural. Since an *errans* by the very nature of the case cannot give a 'sufficient' explanation of the errors of those who oppose him (since it is he that is in error, not they) it follows that he will never be justified in using coercion to enforce his own views.

doctors at a general council if he himself does not see the truth of the proposed sentence. Going directly counter to the text, 'doctores sunt pontificibus praeferendi', Ockham argues that the pope should not give judgment in matters of faith unless he is persuaded of the judgment's truth in his own conscience. For it is possible, according to Ockham, that all the experts might be wrong and only the pope right. Remarkably enough, then, the closest thing to a defense of 'private judgment' that can be found in Ockham is offered on behalf of an imagined pope in conflict with the judgments of everyone about him![52] There can be no doubt, however, that Ockham considered it the duty of other Christians as well as the pope to defend the truth as they saw it. In addition to the sense of personal responsibility expressed in various passages in his works, we may refer to the discussion at the end of 1 *Dialogus* of the qualifications (*praerogativae*) needed by attackers of a heretical pope. Among the foremost of these is a commitment to catholic truth so strong that not even the tongues of angels, let alone the multitude of human voices, can turn the attacker from his course.[53]

The individual Christian must be absolute in his commitment to catholic truth. Those things which are from God he must submit to the correction of no man – and yet he must be ready for correction wherever he may have erred.[54] How is this to be managed? Here we

[52] The student marvels at the presumptuous suggestion that one man, no matter what his office, ought to prefer his own imaginings to all the learned and wise men gathered at a general council ('miror quomodo isti dogmatisare praesumunt, quod unus homo mortalis quacunque praeditus dignitate magis debet adhaerere propriae fantasiae, quam omnibus viris litteratis et sanctis ad generale concilium convocatis'), but this, according to the master, is to miss the point. The pope should not follow his own *fantasia*, but conscience. Because of the words of men, he should not condemn any assertion against conscience or beyond his own conscience ('propter verba hominum nullam debet assertionem contra conscientiam vel praeter conscientiam propriam damnare') 1 *Dialogus* 2, xxix, fol. 16rb. In effect, Ockham requires that the theologians or other wise and learned men be able to *explain* their results to the pope if he is to give them official standing.

[53] The truths contrary to the heretical pope's errors should not be submitted for correction by anyone, because they are received, embraced, and reverenced not as from men but as from God, who needs no correction ('illas veritates non tanquam ab homine sed tanquam a Deo qui correctione non eget traditas suscepit, amplectitur et veneratur') 1 *Dialogus* 7, lxxi, fol. 163ra.

[54] In the prologue to the *Breviloquium*, Ockham shows both readiness to be corrected (he will disclose with fear – *cum timore* – what at present – *pro nunc* – seems to him to be consonant with the truth, as he wishes to be reproved by a wiser judgment

must attend to the other aspect of Ockham's dual role, his status as an expert. If we are to take the discussion of legitimate correction as a guide, the chief function of theological experts is not to be authorities from whose lips the simple Christian may unhesitatingly receive the truth. The function of a *peritus* or *doctor* is to lay out reasons for the truth. Thus, when Ockham argues in Book 7 that *doctores* are the principal combatants (*bellatores principales*) in the spiritual warfare that needs to be waged against a heretical pope,[55] his aim is not to set up a new source of inspired truth in the church or a new source of coercive power. It pertains to the office of doctor to *confute* heretical depravity, not to provide an original revelation or to assume an executive role.[56] The point is made yet more directly in the prologue to the *Dialogus*, where the student proposes a format that will set aside the master's *auctoritas* and allow the student to be 'moved' only by the reasons the master sets forth.[57] From this point of view, the theologian's personal convictions are immaterial. If, before a Christian is entitled to take decisive action for a proposition, he must see and understand for himself that it is a catholic truth, then the pronouncements of official teachers will be irrelevant if they are accepted simply from respect for the teachers. Even for the expert himself there must be submission to the test of argument, lest he cling to his opinions because they are his own, rather than because of their evident truth.[58]

if he is wrong) and firmness in what is certain and needs no correction ('quae autem per scripturas sacras vel per rationem evidentem aut quocumque modo sunt certa, nullius correctioni subicio, quia illa approbanda sunt et nullatenus corrigenda') (*Brev., prol.*, p. 40). Cf. *Imp. Pont. Pot.*, c. 1, p. 455.

55 1 *Dialogus* 7, xlvi–xlviii.

56 *Ibid.*, xlvi, fol. 145va. On the distinction between 'definition' *auctoritate officii* and *per modum doctrinae*, see note 45 above. Knowledge gives only the 'power' to refute error. A. Van Leeuwen's conclusion, that from a doctrinal standpoint pronouncements of the church's *magisterium* were not essentially distinct for Ockham from those of theologians, must be understood in this light ('L'église, règle de foi, dans les écrits de Guillaume d'Occam', *Ephemerides Theologicae Lovanienses*, XI (1934), 249–88; 287.

57 See above, chapter 1, note 62. Cf. the prologue to the *Octo Quaestiones*; *OP* I, p. 13.

58 The theme of testing propositions by constructing arguments for and against them occurs more than once in Ockham's writings. Besides the prologues to the *Dialogus* and *Octo Quaestiones*, see, for example, his approval of the gloss on 1 Thess. 5: 21 in the prologue to the *Opus Nonaginta Dierum*; *OP* I, 293: 'omnia esse probanda, id est, *ratione discutienda*'.

Readiness to argue and to be argued against was perhaps the only safeguard

All in all, then, the impersonal format of Ockham's major polemical works should not be thought of as an incidental by-product of his academic background (in his academic work he was quite forthright, after all) or as a result of fear for his personal safety (he was thoroughly compromised already). Still less should his impersonality be dismissed as a way of avoiding involvement in the problems of his time. On the contrary, Ockham's view of the situation of contemporary Christians called for just such an approach. The greatest practical problem, as he saw it, was to induce men to act from regard to Christian truth rather than illusory political practicality.[59] It would be disingenuous to suggest that Ockham experienced any uncertainty in his view of John XXII after the *Opus Nonaginta Dierum* at the latest. In a material sense, then, his objective was always to generate a similar conviction in his readers. At the same time, since he believed that John's heterodoxy was subject to strict demonstration, the means by which Ockham hoped to produce conviction cannot be disregarded.[60] Notably unattractive by literary standards, his work shows an intellectual passion of rare intensity.

available to Ockham in his own case. Since he was doubtful of finding an impartial judge in the institutional church ('nemo est iudicis exercens officium ... nisi adversarius manifestus et publicus hostis'), he could only defend his innocence informally by bringing his views to public knowledge ('ad publicam ... notionem'), so that all the orthodox who might wish to do so could consider whether they were from God. *Imp. Pont. Pot.*, c. 1, p. 454.

59 The importance Ockham attached to the cognitive aspect of orthodoxy and heresy, as opposed to the juridical or authoritative aspect, is also illustrated by the brief but important first book of 1 *Dialogus*, where the student asks whether it principally pertains to theologians or canon lawyers to define what and who should be regarded as heretical or catholic. Especially pertinent is the discussion in chapters 7–10 of the question, to whom it pertains to *understand* the canons themselves. In these chapters understanding is played off against memory. Ockham grudgingly admits that modern canonists may have a good memory for what is written in their lawbooks, but he argues that they do not understand these laws. This is in contrast, he tells us, with the early authors of the canons, who had expert knowledge of theology and moral philosophy. Although, therefore, legal experts should be called on to deal with the procedural details of heresy trials, questions of substance fall within the competence of theologians. Heresy, for Ockham, is not primarily a legal but a moral and religious problem.

60 In the prologue to the *Octo Quaestiones* (*OP* I, 13), Ockham expressed fear that his enemies might try to distort even assertions that seemed true to them if he made them. This motive for adopting an impersonal format would presumably not have operated so strongly at the time of 1 *Dialogus*.

ACTION AGAINST THE HERETICAL POPE

Besides helping to explain the format of some of his own writings, Ockham's transformation of the idea of legitimate doctrinal correction clarifies his approach to the practical problem of anti-papal action. An important peculiarity of the struggle in which the Michaelists were involved was its intra-institutional character. Michael's appeals and Ockham's anti-papal writings were circulated within the church. They were in no sense an abandonment of the institutions of Western Christendom. But *to* whom exactly were these documents addressed? On the surface, of course, 1 *Dialogus* does not take John XXII's heterodoxy for granted. Ockham at times uses considerable skill to avoid denying the supreme spiritual authority of an orthodox pope over all other Christians, whether considered separately or all together. The pope, then, or pope and council, would normally be the supreme tribunal in cases of heresy. Yet it would hardly be reasonable to suggest that the occupant of the papal chair should be the recipient of such an accusation when he was also the person accused. A general council would be suitable if one were in session, but even then the remedy might be ineffective, since a council can err, too. The Michaelists proceeded on the assumption that it 'must' be possible to do something about a heretical pope, but, we must ask, *who* can or should act in such a situation?

According to the common theory of papal heresy discussed earlier, any Christian who has the physical power to do so may rightly take action against a heretical pope, for such a man has *ipso facto* ceased to be pope and is immediately deprived of all ecclesiastical dignity and honor without need of formal judicial procedure. What Ockham saw, perhaps more clearly than any of his contemporaries, is that if this theoretical point of view is consistently accepted, the practical problem of dealing with papal heresy takes a radically new turn. Instead of being a matter of institutional authority, it becomes primarily a matter of discovery and communication – a cognitive problem. In accordance with this insight, the essential conclusion of Ockham's long and complicated discussion in 1 *Dialogus* 7 of the various kinds of supporters and attackers of papal heresy is apparently that any Christian who knows the pope to be a heretic not only may, but must, take action against him.[61] Secular rulers are excused from doing so if it appears that prohibiting publication of the heretical pope's doctrine in their realms will bring no spiritual or temporal utility to the faithful, but only disturb catholics and turn many from the faith.[62] The individual simple Christian is sometimes excused from opposing the pope if his own isolated effort will be ineffective.[63] Not even the fear of death can excuse the theologian or preacher from mortal sin if he fails to voice his opposition on a particular occasion unless saving his life then is likely to make more effective opposition possible in the future.[64] By their very weakness, the exceptions prove the rule. The responsibility to act does not depend on a person's institutional status but on his state of knowledge – those who know must act. Any catholic whatever ought to oppose an erroneous judgment of the pope against the faith – if he knows the judgment to be erroneous. 'Sententiae erroneae papae contra fidem debet quilibet catholicus (qui scit sententiam eius esse erroneam) obviare.'[65]

---

[61] Furthermore, there is little room to avoid the responsibility for action by remaining in a state of ignorance about the pope's errors. Ockham finds it difficult to give a certain rule as to the particular times at which someone is bound to listen to those wishing to divulge a heretical pope's perfidy. It can be said, however, that each man is bound to listen unless he has a reasonable excuse for not doing so – 'Potest tamen dici quod tunc ad hoc tenetur unusquisque quando non habet rationabilem excusationem, quare tunc eos minime audire teneatur' (I *Dialogus* 7, x, fol. 119*vab*).

[62] *Ibid.*, lii, fols. 149*vb*–150*ra*.

[63] In many cases *simplices* having no power over others are not bound to resist the heretical pope's teaching when princes and other public powers are bound to do so. Still, if there is so great a multitude of such individuals as to allow effective resistance ('si est tanta multitudo quod cum fructu spirituali potest doctrinam papae erroneam prohibere'), failure to resist amounts to favoring heretics and heresy. Even one man alone, if he could fruitfully resist and provoke others to resistance, would be a favorer of heretical depravity if he did not resist. *Ibid.*, lvi, fol. 152*ra*–*va*.

[64] *Ibid.*, xlviii, fol. 148*ra*.

[65] *Ibid.*, i. fol. 113*rb*. Naturally enough, then, when he comes to weigh the sins of the heretical pope's various supporters, Ockham begins with the assertion that, among the believers (*credentes*) of heretics and heresies, the educated sin more than the uneducated ('gravius peccant litterati quam illitterati') because, other things being equal, they can more easily know the truth. Again, theologians sin more gravely than others, other things being equal, and among the theologians those sin more gravely who have been more nurtured in the contrary truth. *Ibid.*, lxix, fol. 161*ra*. It is true that kings and princes who by reason of their temporal power could resist the heretical pope without any danger are discussed first among the favorers (*fautores*) of papal heresy, but even here the responsibility of the learned is great. Monks, superiors, and teachers who would be out of danger even if they attacked

Quite in line with this cognitive orientation, the labyrinthine exploration of anti-papal action in i *Dialogus* 6 and 7 is guided by considerations of credentials and credibility. The desirability of formal legal procedures is by no means denied. Indeed, Ockham insists on distinguishing between the credence sufficient for a judicial decision and that which one 'friend' should give another. There can be no doubt, however, that Ockham regarded this less formal *credulitas* as a step towards the institution of effective formal proceedings. The degree of credence sufficient for a judge's decision should not be given to those claiming that the pope is a heretic unless the fact is notorious or is proved in a proper judicial process (*iudiciario ordine observato*).⁶⁶ As to the credence appropriate to a friend, however, the situation is different. Although one is not *bound* to believe a single person asserting that the pope is a heretic, no matter what that person's reputation,⁶⁷ one *may* without sin believe an individual of good reputation.⁶⁸ If many upright and sane men offer to show with complete certainty (*per certam scientiam*) that the pope is a heretic, one is obliged to give them credence.⁶⁹ Indeed, if such men proceed only on the basis of the pope's public reputation they should be believed,⁷⁰ and even criminals defaming the pope should be believed if they provide legitimate documents to support their charges.⁷¹ This last conclusion is an especially striking indication of the extent to which Ockham proposed to substitute considerations of knowledge for considerations of institutional authority in dealing with the problem of papal heresy. Still clearer is an argument he offers in connection with an earlier conclusion, the proposition that we are bound to believe many men of good reputation when they defame the pope. This is based on the appealingly simple ground that the testimony of many men is more likely to be true than the testimony of one. As Ockham construes the situation, then, the pope's word

the heretical pope (reading *impugnarent* for Trechsel's *non impugnarent*) sin more gravely by favoring him than do kings and princes, for they have greater knowledge of the truth and are more strictly obligated to spiritual works. *Ibid.*, fol. 161va.
⁶⁶ i *Dialogus* 7, xiii, fol. 122ra.
⁶⁷ *Ibid.*, xiv, fol. 123ra.   ⁶⁸ *Ibid.*
⁶⁹ i *Dialogus* 7, xv, fol. 123va.   ⁷⁰ *Ibid.*, xvi, fol. 124rb.
⁷¹ *Ibid.*, xvii, fol. 124va. Hence, presumably, someone who suspected the Michaelists of being criminals would still be obliged to pay attention to their proofs of the pope's heresy.

alone should not be believed over that of his many attackers. The pope is only one man. If there are many who assert that he is a heretic, they ought to be believed even if the pope himself denies it.[72] Has Ockham forgotten that it is he and his friends and not John XXII who hold the minority position? That would seem strange, all things considered, and so we read with interest the student's objection: 'That reasoning proves nothing, because sometimes one man should be believed rather than many.' It is in reply to this objection that the non-institutional character of Ockham's attack on papal heresy receives one of its clearest expressions:

> If more credence should be given one man than many this is not especially because of his greater position (*maiorem dignitatem*), because anyone placed in a high position can be convicted by the testimony of many . . . Therefore, if the one is to be believed more than the many this is because he has a better account (*meliorem rationem*) to give for himself, because of his better life, because he is better instructed about the case, or for some similar reason. If, therefore, the pope is not of better life than the many who say he is a heretic, or more learned in divine scriptures, or outstanding in anything else except the papal dignity and things annexed to it, then he should not be believed rather than the many.[73]

When it comes to questions of truth, then, institutional authority is a secondary consideration, one which must in some cases be entirely disregarded.[74]

THE GENERAL POLITICAL SIGNIFICANCE OF OCKHAM'S ANTI-PAPAL STRUGGLE

In the first book of I *Dialogus* Ockham advances arguments which are relevant to the general question of freedom of expression.[75] For the most part, however, he is concerned in this work with the specifically Christian problem of papal heresy. Hence, caution must be observed in drawing conclusions of universal 'political' significance from what he says here. On the other hand, since the papacy was a major force

---

[72] *Ibid.*, xv, fol. 123va.   [73] *Ibid.*, fol. 123vab.

[74] Or more than disregarded. Thus, in I *Dialogus* 7, xxv, fol. 130rb, it is argued at some length that more credence should be given to the adversaries of a rich and powerful pope than to the adversaries of paupers, for there is less to restrain men from attacking paupers than from attacking the pope.

[75] I *Dialogus* 2, xix–xxxii, especially xxii–xxiv.

in European affairs when Ockham wrote, his struggle against what he regarded as corruption at the top of the ecclesiastical power structure can hardly be passed over in even the most narrowly conceived history of political thought. Furthermore, in spite of the distinctively religious content of the issues between Ockham and the papacy, the formal features of his idea of legitimate correction have important consequences for the general notion of political action, consequences more novel than Ockham himself at first recognized.

Before Ockham, the tendency of medieval political thinkers was to suppose that persons in authority held places in a divinely ordained structure whose intrinsic value prohibited protest or change except through channels provided by the structure itself. For Ockham, on the other hand, everyone is potentially active in matters concerning the government of the church, at least in the extreme case of papal heresy. In such a case plans for public action will start from individual awareness of values or facts that ought to be the concern of everyone, not only of officials in the established order. To be sure, previous thinkers, from Leo I in the fifth century on through the medieval period, had insisted on the importance of a distinction between office and person.[76] The distinction was also emphasized by the curialists of Ockham's time. Augustinus Triumphus, for example, distinguished between the papal office, which is perfect, and the holder of that office, who may fail to live up to it.[77] In such applications of the distinction, however, the office is always a position of authority, and the moral generally drawn is that one should accept the defective office-holder out of respect for the office. In other words, the person may fall short of his office, but is partly redeemed by it. In Ockham's early polemical writings it is the other way around. Here the 'office' in question may be the comparatively low status of 'simplex laicus', and the holder of this low position is asked to rise

---

76 On Leo I, see W. Ullmann, 'Leo I and the theme of papal primacy', *Journal of Theological Studies*, n.s., XI (1960), 25–51. For Gerhoh of Reichersberg in the eleventh century, see Ullmann, *Papal Government*, pp. 410–11. On the distinction between mortal rulers and their immortal offices as a theme in medieval political theology, see E. H. Kantorowicz, *The King's Two Bodies: a Study in Medieval Political Theology* (Princeton, 1957).

77 Augustinus Triumphus, *Summa de Ecclesiastica Potestate*, q. 20, a. 6. It is on the basis of such a distinction that papalist writers could hold that a heretical pope condemns himself: the office condemns the man (see above, note 18).

above it, to take an active part in affairs that are normally beyond his competence. In the special or irregular situation in which Ockham made his appeal, he asked individuals to rise above the social categories normally defining them. To be sure, the appeal was made only in an extraordinary situation, and its basis was that other individuals, those in positions of authority, had fallen short of the demands of their offices (the traditional distinction), and yet Ockham did not support an alternative ideology in which some other *office* was superior to the papacy. This was the path of those royal and imperial political theories which used the sacral character of the king's office or the lay ruler's protective function as *tutor ecclesiae* to make him, rather than the pope, the foundation of ecclesiastical order.[78] Such a path was closed to Ockham by the fallibilism defended in 1 *Dialogus* 5. Since no part of the church can be identified with the whole church, no part can lay claim to the inerrancy which has been promised to the whole church.[79] Hence, there can be no 'fail-safe' ecclesiastical constitution, no purely constitutional solution to so radical a crisis as papal heresy. Accordingly, although Ockham made systematic reference to the *officia* of *doctor, rex, princeps, praelatus*, and so on, in the course of insisting upon action against the heretical pope, his ultimate appeal was for the individual to act in spite of his position, not because of it.[80]

[78] Cf., for example, the Norman Anonymous of the twelfth century, who states the key premise in Ockham's position in 1 *Dialogus* 5 when he asserts that no part of the church is the church, but in spite of this responds to the developing papalist ideology by attempting to find some part of the church – other than the pope – which *could* for practical purposes be equated with the whole church. By emphasizing the regal rather than the priestly aspect of the image of Christ as *rex–sacerdos* the Anonymous sought to substitute the supremacy of the king for that of the priesthood (Ullmann, *Papal Government*, pp. 395–9). On medieval sacral kingship in general, see Ullmann, *Government and Politics in the Middle Ages*, pp. 117–211; O. Höfler, 'Der Sakralcharakter des germanischen Königtums', in Th. Mayer (ed.), *Das Königtum: seine geistigen und rechtlichen Grundlagen* (Darmstadt, 1965), pp. 75ff. On the lay ruler's tutorial function, see W. Ullmann, *The Carolingian Renaissance and the Idea of Kingship* (London, 1969), pp. 122–4, 176ff.

[79] This is the major argument in each division of 1 *Dialogus* 5 (see above, p. 48). As we shall see in the next chapter, Ockham's markedly non-sacral conception of secular government provides a powerful additional explanation for his failure to appeal to the office of king or emperor as a reliable basis for ordering the church.

[80] As we shall see in the next chapter, Ockham also utilized the more traditional idea that in some circumstances one office-holder might take extraordinary or 'casual' action in another office-holder's normal sphere of jurisdiction. The remarkable

73

If Ockham did not propose a new order of offices for the *societas Christiana*, was he after all an anarchist? When he addressed his appeal for action even to individual *simplices* having no power over others, did he thereby set the individual over and against society? The answer to such questions depends on what is meant by 'society'. If the term is used to refer to a particular government, a concrete group of persons actually engaged in ruling society, then Ockham did indeed attempt to set the individual against society. This, however, may equally well be construed as a matter of arousing society to take action against a set of corrupt individuals. As we shall soon see, Ockham may have greatly underestimated the difference between his own approach to concrete political problems and the attitudes generally prevailing. Nevertheless, his professed enemy at this stage was not an institution but a particular set of persons, John XXII and his followers. It would seem, then, that a proper assessment of individualism as against corporatism in Ockham's thought must wait until we have seen what he had to say about society in the institutional sense.

One thing is certain, however. On the level of personal action, Ockham was prepared to be as radical as necessary to bring about the downfall of his papal antagonists. Although we have yet to consider his attitude towards the papacy as an institution, it is clear that his opposition to the individual popes of his time was far from conventional. It was a matter not of inner anguish but of practical outrage, and involved not only stubborn adherence to his own dogmatic views but the construction of an original and impressively coherent rationale for active resistance to the apparent head of the whole church.

THE TURN TO INSTITUTIONS

In Ockham's original plan for the *Dialogus*, the third and final part was to be an account of the *gesta* of those presently altercating about the Christian faith. At the beginning of Part Three we learn that he intended to discuss the deeds of six individuals (John XXII, Ludwig of Bavaria, Benedict XII, Michael of Cesena, Guiral Ot, and himself) and then, in a final tract, the actions of other parties involved

thing about the argument of 1 *Dialogus* is the extent to which it goes beyond all considerations of office whatever.

74

in the current disturbances. Such a continuation of the *Dialogus* would have been entirely in keeping with the personal or individual emphasis of Ockham's struggle against John XXII and his successors. Yet the balance of the evidence suggests that this plan was not carried out. None of the proposed 'historical' tracts is to be found.[81] What we have of III *Dialogus* is a pair of quite substantial introductory tracts on spiritual and temporal power *in general*, one on the power of the pope and clergy, another on the rights and power of the Roman Empire. Assuming that the historical tracts were never written, we must ask why. What prompted so relentless and indefatigable an author as Ockham to abandon an important part of the original plan for his major work?

The answer cannot be that he softened in his attitude towards the contemporary papacy. In the *Breviloquium* the extent of papal power is treated as a matter of general public interest, and on some questions Ockham seems genuinely open-minded. As its title indicates, however, the work is concerned with the '*tyrannical* government *usurped* by some who are *called* supreme pontiffs' – hardly a topic for a developing moderate. The *De Imperatorum et Pontificum Potestate*, possibly Ockham's latest work, seethes with righteous anger at the 'ecclesia Avinionica' for its unwarranted and destructive interference in imperial and Italian politics.[82] If we add that each of these works, as well as the *Octo Quaestiones*, includes direct references to the errors of John XXII, the idea that Ockham mellowed in his old age is seen to derive little support from his writings. It thus appears that we should seek to understand Ockham's turn towards institutional analysis as an outgrowth of his personal political commitments, not as a tacit repudiation of them.

To some extent, no doubt, Ockham's change of focus can be explained by his association with Ludwig of Bavaria. In the early years at Munich, Ockham wrote only about poverty and papal heresy, but at the same time he may have developed an interest in his protector's problems and the rights of the Roman Empire – an interest which then expressed itself in works written after 1337.

---

[81] Baudry, *Guillaume d'Occam*, pp. 210–12. Miethke, *Ockhams Weg*, pp. 117–21. Miethke (p. 117) calls attention to the specifically historical character of these missing treatises.

[82] *Imp. Pont. Pot.*, cc. 1, 7, 15–27; pp. 454–5, 460–1, 470–80.

However this may be, his initial, practical project would have carried him in an institutional direction even if he had been personally indifferent to the empire's problems, for that project rested on implicit general or institutional principles which, as it turned out, badly needed defending. Ockham ultimately called on every Christian individual to take action against papal heresy, yet he proceeded as if such an appeal were consistent with the acknowledged institutional principles of medieval Christian society. To be sure, he recognized that there were no regular or formal institutional safeguards available for coping with so fundamental a crisis, but he mistakenly assumed that there were underlying attitudes which could be used as a basis for mobilizing irregular or 'casual' corrective forces. Hence, if the interpretation offered here is near the truth, no new theory of secular or ecclesiastical government is propounded in I *Dialogus* because none was thought necessary. In fact, however, Ockham's flexible, cognitive approach to the problem of papal heresy challenged prevailing attitudes towards authority rather than appealing to them. The crisis of the times extended far beyond the question of John XXII's orthodoxy or the finer points of Ludwig of Bavaria's title to the empire. It involved disagreements about the basis and functions of the major institutions of Christian society. Ockham found, then, belatedly, that in order to take effective action in the present or in the future concerning particular, personal political problems it would be necessary to resolve these underlying general disagreements. For this reason, if for no other, he was forced to carry his political thought to a new level of abstraction.[83]

A sign of the need to move from the history of *gesta* to the theory of institutions is provided by the ambiguous status of each of the individuals Ockham intended to treat in III *Dialogus*. It is a striking fact that the official positions of all six were in dispute. Dissension about John and Benedict was not on the question, whether they were good or bad popes. The issue was whether they were popes at all. The dissension about Ludwig of Bavaria did not concern his justice or ability in discharging the duties of the imperial office. The question was not whether he was a *bonus imperator*, but whether he was a *verus imperator*. Again, was Michael of Cesena the legitimate minister

---

[83] Ockham did not desert the plane of particulars entirely, however, as witness the *Consultatio de Causa Matrimoniali* and *De Electione Caroli Quarti*.

general of the Franciscan order or was Guiral Ot? It needs little stretching to bring the sixth individual, Ockham himself, under the same rubric. We have seen that Ockham viewed his role in the process of correction partly as an official function, the discharge of a teacher's office. Since the verdict on his theology delivered at Avignon was relevant to his holding this 'office', we may say that Ockham's position, too, was characterized by a basic ambiguity of 'official' status. [84] In a world in which everyone's position is uncertain, including one's own, the need for an acceptable account of these positions is more than academic.

[84] In the prologue to III *Dialogus* (fol. 181r*a*), Ockham himself calls attention to the ambiguous official status of the other individuals he planned to discuss. He tells us that the third tract will be concerned with the *gesta* of John XXII, 'quem nonnulli putant propter haereticam pravitatem diu antequam de hoc mundo migraret, *omni dignitate ecclesiastica* fuisse *privatum*. Alii ipsum fuisse catholicum et *in vero papatu* finisse dies suos existimant.' The fourth tract will be about Ludwig of Bavaria, 'quem aliqui *verum imperatorem* non reputant, alii contrarium arbitrantur'. The fifth will be about Benedict XII, 'quem multi sed non omnes *tamquam summum pontificem* venerantur', the sixth about brother Michael of Cesena and the seventh about Gerald Odonis, 'quorum unum quidam alii alium *verum generalem ordinis fratrum minorum* affirmant'. The eighth tract will be about the deeds of brother William of Ockham.

Chapter 3

THEORY OF INSTITUTIONS:
SECULAR AND SPIRITUAL GOVERNMENT

Ideo negatur illa: 'Nulla communitas potest esse optime ordinata nisi uni supremo iudici sit subiecta' . . . *quia in tali communitate posset iste supremus iudex iustitiam in ruinam et etiam in perniciem totius communitatis delinquere, quod optimae ordinationi communitatis cuiuscunque repugnat.*

Hence, that [proposition] is denied: 'No community can be best ordered unless it is subject to one supreme judge . . . because in such a community that supreme judge could destroy justice by his wrongdoing and even endanger the whole community, which is repugnant to the best ordering of any community whatever.'

Octo Quaestiones III, 3; *OP* I, 104f.

Ockham's initial project of exposing and removing John XXII raised important questions in spite of itself. For although the goal was a change of persons rather than offices, this could be achieved only if offices and official responsibilities were regarded in a more flexible way than Ockham's contemporaries found tolerable. Hence, while he did not abandon his attack on the Avignonese popes, Ockham devoted more attention after 1337 to the papal office than to its occupants. Similarly, although he defended particular actions of Ludwig of Bavaria and his allies in this period, Ockham's main writings on secular politics were also pitched at a more general, institutional level. Following Ockham's own order of thought, then, we must go on to consider the basis, functions and proper relations of supreme spiritual and secular power.

The main outlines of Ockham's position are easy enough to draw. Except in a few passages, he clearly advocated a 'regular' dualism of secular and spiritual government, supplemented by a doctrine of 'casual' power in which lay and ecclesiastical authorities could in exceptional cases act outside their ordinary jurisdictions. Thus, the pope 'does not regularly have from Christ the power to dispose and order the temporal matters acknowledged to pertain to kings and other lay rulers'. '*Casualiter*', however, if there is a grave crisis in temporal affairs and no laymen can or will take action, 'the pope would by divine right have power in temporal matters to do whatever right reason dictated to him was necessary'.[1] Conversely, the pope is normally exempt from the power and jurisdiction of the supreme secular ruler, but 'by reason of a delict, not any delict at all . . . but a grave and enormous one, especially if often repeated', and assuming that the appropriate clerics are negligent or powerless, it seems reasonable to Ockham that 'judgment about the pope . . . pertains to the supreme [secular] ruler'.[2]

Ockham himself did not regard such views on papal and imperial government as revolutionary. So far as the main outlines of his position are concerned, this seems a reasonable estimate. To be sure, the idea that the emperor might judge the pope even in extraordinary circumstances was anathema to the curialists. We have seen evidence of papal attitudes in Clement VI's selection of this as the one specific error of Ludwig of Bavaria and Michael of Cesena which Ockham had to repudiate if he wished to make peace with the church.[3] Yet this idea was hardly new. Not to mention the distant historical precedents provided by emperors like Constantine, Justinian, and Otto I, we may note that so reputable a scholastic as John of Paris

[1] 'Et ita in tali casu haberet super temporalia quodammodo et secundum quid plenitudinem potestatis . . . Quae quamvis non sit plenissima potestas, est tamen grandis, singularis et quam magna. Per ipsam enim potest in casu imperia et regna transferre reges et principes et aliumque laicum quemcunque temporalibus iuribus et rebus privare, aliisque conferre. In spiritualibus etiam omnia potest in casu.' III *Dialogus* I, I, xvi, fol. 188vab.

[2] 'Ratione delicti non cuiuscunque, ne ipsius auctoritas contemptibilis videatur et ne pro parvo commisso, forsitan emendato, ab utilitate communi valeat impediri, sed gravis et enormis, praesertim saepius iterati, quod in discrimen notabile, praecipue communis boni, redundaret, expedit ut papa humano iudicio destitui valeat et deponi, maxime si appareat incorrigibilis et de ipso scandalizetur ecclesia.

Videtur autem rationabile ut huiusmodi de papa iudicium primo spectet ad aliquas certas personas de clero; quibus deficientibus, sive per malitiam sive per dampnabilem negligentiam sive per impotentiam, hoc ad supremum principantem pertineat, si fidei et Christianae religionis sincerus est et fervidus aemulator.' OQ III, 12; OP I, 121–2. If the supreme ruler is deficient, the passage continues, deposition or detention of the pope pertains to the *universalem congregationem fidelium* or to any of the faithful who may have sufficient temporal power. If temporal force is lacking, one must imitate Jeremiah and sit alone, full of bitterness.

[3] See above, p. 25.

commended certain papal depositions at the hands of the people or the emperor.[4] Philip the Fair and his henchmen were less devout but no more revolutionary when they proclaimed the king's right to summon a heretical pope before a general council.[5] As to the crucial term 'casualiter', it had a thoroughly respectable history, even by the most hierocratic standards, for it had been progressively exploited by popes since Innocent III to justify intervention in cases for which no ordinary precedent could be alleged.[6] To be sure, there was no suggestion from this quarter that laymen might have even casual power over the pope, and for many defenders of the papacy the distinction between regular and casual papal jurisdiction was a matter of practical convenience for a universal ruler who could not do everything himself, not a constitutional limitation. Nevertheless, it would be unhistorical to lay at Ockham's door the principle that some part of a duly established institutional order might need to be set aside in exceptional circumstances.[7] The most that can be said is that he took a weapon from the curialist armory to strengthen an anti-curialist position that was already within the range of orthodox opinion.

Ockham's attempt to maintain a balance of spiritual and temporal power could claim to be orthodox, then. But was it likely to prove effective? This is a more difficult and more rewarding question, and will serve as a useful guide in dealing with the complexities of Ockham's later thought. Instead of adding up affirmations and

---

[4] John of Paris, *Tractatus de Regia Potestate et Papali*, ed. F. Bleienstein, *Johannes Quidort von Paris über königliche und päpstliche Gewalt (De Regia Potestate et Papali)*, Frankfurter Studien zur Wissenschaft von der Politik (Stuttgart, 1968), c. 22, p. 196. For John's spirited opposition to a papal absolutism immune from coercive correction, see Tierney, *Foundations of the Conciliar Theory*, pp. 171–8.

[5] The king's claims follow a tradition which dates back to Frederick I's attempt to convoke councils at Pavia and Avignon to decide the disputed papal election of 1159. Wilks, *Sovereignty in the Later Middle Ages*, p. 517, n. 3, with references.

[6] See Wilks, *Sovereignty in the Later Middle Ages*, pp. 271–3, including citation of Innocent III's seminal claim (*Decretales* IV, xvii, 13) 'quod non solum in ecclesiae patrimonio, super quo plenam in temporalibus gerimus potestatem, verum etiam in aliis regionibus, *certis causis inspectis*, temporalem iurisdictionem *casualiter exercemus*'.

[7] Ockham's contention that in the most extreme crises virtually all normal institutions may need to be supplemented by *individual* action is a different matter. See above, pp. 72–3. Cf. the continuation of the passage cited in note 2 of this chapter.

rejections of tradition in his institutional writings, it will be better to ask why so clear-headed and intrepid a thinker took up dualism in a perplexed age that tended increasingly towards unitary political extremes. Immersed as he was in a thoroughly non-academic political milieu, how could he hope to gain general acceptance for a position that struck so many of his contemporaries as logically incoherent and practically futile?[8]

The turmoil of the fourteenth century has been subject to unusually disparate interpretations both from without and within. Such terms as 'disintegration', 'decay', 'waning', 'harvest', and 'forward movement' have all been applied to the period by historians, and equally divergent estimates were made at the time. To assess the true import of what was written in this period, including its political theory, would be hard enough if there were only these different answers to substantive questions to contend with, but in addition we face a wide range of attitudes towards discourse itself: credulity, anti-intellectualism, mysticism, a more or less cynical distinction between 'real' and 'verbal' power, technically brilliant developments in logic and the arts of language, and an unprecedented use of complex argumentation to engage the loyalties of an ever more literate and ever more skeptical public. Obviously, then, an attempt to indicate the major ideas and arguments in a collection of political treatises can yield only partial understanding of Ockham and his contemporaries. Nevertheless, if sustained political argument is not always a major force in human affairs, it can count for something, and even the claim that it is special pleading or 'mere' ideology needs to be supported by an understanding of the inner logic of the argumentation being attacked. In these terms, the political unrest of the early fourteenth century comes to light as a conflict between

---

[8] Ockham's hopes for a general consensus about the nature and extent of papal power are indicated in the first book of the *Breviloquium*. He argues that it is necessary for both the pope and his subjects to 'know' the *quam* and *quantam* of his office (*Brev.* I, 3–4, pp. 43–5), and presents these as subjects for expert inquiry (c. 5: 'Papa non debet moleste ferre, si periti diligentissime investigant, quam et quantam habeat potestatem'). Indeed, in a rare venture in speculative history, he suggests that God may have permitted the usurpations of recent popes so the skill of experts can bring to light hidden truths which will benefit all humanity and by which a bridle may be placed on supreme pontiffs who try to rule tyrannically (*Brev.* II, I, pp. 53–4).

two concepts of law and government.[9] Both the difficulty and the interest of Ockham's institutional thought depend on understanding it in terms of this conflict.

On one side, political power and authority were seen as coming 'from above', ultimately from God himself, but for practical purposes from God's unique representative on earth, the pope. Such later exponents of this theme as Egidius Romanus, Augustinus Triumphus, Alvarus Pelagius, and Guido Terreni built on a long tradition, in which the papal government functioned as the soul of Christian society, 'animating' by its activities the *corpus* of all believers. From this standpoint, the papacy was in essence a royal or judicial office, while papal legislative and judicial activities were the source of all other legitimate power. There was no true and legitimate jurisdiction outside the church, and no autogenous rights within it. Everything was derived from above, from the church's *caput*, the pope. As Egidius Romanus expressed it, the pope's power gave weight, measure, and number to all other authority without itself being weighed, measured, or numbered.[10] Not surprisingly, Egidius could find no adequate analogy for such power in the created order. The papal *plenitudo potestatis* could be compared only with the power of God himself. As the power (*posse*) of all agents is reserved in God, who can thus do without secondary agents whatever He can do with them, so the whole power (*totum posse*) of the church is found in the pope, who can also do without a secondary cause whatever he can do with it.[11] Concerning the need to derive all other earthly power from the pope, Egidius' successors made no substantial modifications in this position.[12] As against the 'descending' view of law and

9 On medieval descending and ascending political theories, see Ullmann, *Government and Politics in the Middle Ages, passim*, especially pp. 19–26. For the situation in the early fourteenth century, see Wilks, *Sovereignty in the Later Middle Ages*, pp. 15–63.

10 Egidius Romanus, *De Ecclesiastica Potestate*, ed. R. Scholz (Weimar, 1929), p. 206.

11 *Ibid.*, pp. 190–1, 193. I have discovered no clear reference to Egidius in Ockham's political writings. It is more than possible that he was acquainted with the *De Ecclesiastica Potestate*, perhaps through his association with Marsilius of Padua at Munich. In any case, Egidius provides an outstanding example of the political mentality to which Ockham was opposed. (For E. A. Moody's contention that Egidius was Ockham's arch-opponent in speculative matters, see above, pp. 4–5.)

12 Augustinus Triumphus and Alvarus Pelagius, the leading curialist writers at the time of John XXII, were much readier than Egidius Romanus to admit differences between the pope and God. For practical purposes, however, the dependence of

government, however, other writers held that political authority came from below. According to this second, 'ascending' or secular viewpoint, power ultimately resided in the community. The principle of legitimacy for emperors, kings, and other rulers was the derivation of their power from the people, not approval by the pope. On such a basis, the legists of Philip the Fair resisted papal interference in secular affairs and even advanced to the attack, asserting the king's rights over the *temporalia* of the clergy in his dominions. The purest exponent of the ascending theme in the later middle ages was Marsilius of Padua. Going far beyond the idea of an original derivation of power from the political *corpus* to its ruling head, Marsilius insisted that government be subject to the active will of the people at all times.[13] The Marsilian doctrine of popular sovereignty, then, was a nearly perfect antithesis to the hierocratic view of power as descending from above.

Secularists and papalists did have in common an insistence on ultimate governmental unity. 'No man can serve two masters.' 'A house divided cannot stand.' 'No community can be perfectly ordered unless it is subject to one supreme judge.' However expressed, this axiom of political monism had a compelling force. Unfortunately, it drove hierocrats and lay writers in opposite directions, leading each side to demand that the other be ordered to its own basic principle. So far as events were to be determined by the theories of these authors, there were only two alternatives. Either the papal government must succeed in dominating the emerging secularism, in which case temporal affairs would be controlled by considerations of eternal salvation, or else Marsilianism must triumph, and the church become a department of state.

Ockham's espousal of dualism in this situation requires explanation. Most sensible men must have been repelled by the extremes of

secular on papal power was as great in their theories as it had been for Egidius. Thus, for example, Alvarus Pelagius continues to insist that all jurisdiction is from the pope, who receives it immediately from God (*De Planctu Ecclesiae*, c. 18, pp. 32–3), and Alvarus applies this principle at length to the pope's relationship to the empire (c. 37, pp. 42–58).

13 For Marsilius as an exponent of the ascending theme, see Ullmann, *Government and Politics in the Middle Ages*, pp. 269–79. On the continuousness of popular control over government in Marsilian theory, see Gewirth, *Marsilius of Padua and Medieval Political Philosophy*, pp. 237–42, 244–8.

curialism and secularism and wished for a way between. But where could such a way be found? In the preceding decades, Christian Aristotelians like St Thomas, John of Paris, and Dante had made profound attempts to integrate the temporal and spiritual orders in a more or less dualistic institutional synthesis, but although these efforts have earned the admiration of centuries of scholars, their immediate impact on affairs was small, and they did not produce general agreement even in theory. Ockham could scarcely have overlooked the logical force of monism. Nor could he have hoped that the contemporary crisis would subside of itself, that a *de facto* dualism could be reestablished without basic intellectual or institutional changes. He was too directly involved in the situation for such optimism. He recognized the ambiguous official status of contemporary rulers. He saw that basic institutional questions had to be faced. Nor, finally, could he have settled into an inconclusive dualism from weakness of nerve. We have seen in the case of papal heresy how bold he could be in following his principles to their most extreme conclusions. In view of these considerations, it would be wholly inadequate to note the apparent conservatism of Ockham's major institutional conclusions and let matters rest there. To consider his position in abstraction from the basic alternatives of papalism and Marsilianism, or to explain his views by a sentiment for moderation or a vague reverence for tradition, would show a failure to appreciate either the gravity of his situation or the calibre of his mind. Ockham's dualism appears so far to be as much a problem as a solution. Until his position can be understood in terms of the specific circumstances and political debate of the time, Ockham will remain as enigmatic as ever.

The material ahead is complex. It will be well to indicate initially its main themes. One is that Ockham made a significant attempt to widen the distance between secular and spiritual government. Instead of constructing a subtle theory by which the two powers could be accommodated to one another when their concerns overlapped, Ockham sought to arrange matters so that such overlapping would seldom occur. This involved, on one hand, a thorough 'desacralization' of secular power and, on the other hand, a reduced emphasis on the juridical aspects of ecclesiastical power. This first theme is one of separatism. The other main thesis of the present

84

chapter is that Ockham substantially redefined the relation between society and government. Instead of viewing law and government as the animating force in society, the source of all order and value, Ockham regarded them as purely instrumental. The political element in human affairs becomes with him a means to the social existence of free men, but not the basis of the community or its end. Although he maintained a doctrine of original consent, however, Ockham studiously avoided other aspects of the ascending conception of political power. Hence, this second theme is not popular sovereignty. For its primary emphasis, it should be called instead an exposition of freedom. In the following pages the two themes combine with one another and with other ideas. The theme of separatism predominates in Sections 1 and 3, however, and the theme of freedom in Sections 2 and 4.

I. THE BASIS OF SECULAR POWER: REJECTION OF THE DESCENDING THESIS

'Concluons qu'Ockham entend retirer toute valeur effective à la "sacralisation" du pouvoir que la tradition ecclésiastique a imposée depuis cinq siècles.'[14] Instead of ignoring or denying this conclusion as some defenders of Ockham have attempted to do, we must try to understand it. We shall then discover that Ockham did eliminate the specifically religious basis for secular power, not only within the medieval *societas Christiana*, but in broader contexts as well. This desacralization of secular power was part of Ockham's larger effort to resolve the institutional conflicts of his age, and its ultimate motive was religious. Nevertheless, the immediate effect was a reinterpretation of certain longstanding ecclesiastical traditions, a reinterpretation which in all but the most abnormal conditions deprived them of political substance.

Laicizing secular power within the societas Christiana

Ludwig of Bavaria's contest with the Avignonese papacy set the central problems for Ockham's treatment of the basis of secular power. In the light of the papalist contention that 'imperium est a

---

papa',[15] Ludwig's failure to wait upon papal approval of his election was not merely a breach of custom, but a rebellion which robbed his administration of all claim to legitimacy. In spite of an apparent profusion of arguments scattered through many works, Ockham's answer to 'imperium a papa' can be understood as the development of only a few ideas. The significance of these ideas will be still clearer, however, if we glance first at Ockham's mature treatment of two or three less central topics.

In the *Octo Quaestiones* of 1340–1, Ockham took up the question, whether a hereditary ruler acquires any temporal power from being anointed, consecrated, and crowned by an ecclesiastic.[16] Professor Offler has shown that this and the following two *quaestiones* were framed at the prospect of Charles of Moravia's coronation as king of Bohemia,[17] not with reference to Ludwig of Bavaria. Hence, Ockham's contention here, that unction and consecration contribute a ceremonial heightening of reverence for the new ruler, but confer no temporal power,[18] cannot be interpreted as a direct assertion about papacy and empire. Nevertheless, it reveals something of Ockham's thinking about secular and spiritual power generally. The same can be said for his remarks on the coronation of a lay ruler by an ecclesiastic. Ockham concedes that such coronation can confer temporal power, but even as he makes this concession, he deprives it of all hierocratic force by the reason he gives: not nature or grace, but human decision. There is nothing in the nature of monarchy that requires endorsement from above. Monarchy does not have a 'nature' – Aristotle is astutely cited on this point – and there are presently no divinely instituted governments. Hence, although a king can receive temporal power in being crowned by an ecclesiastic or by someone else, if he does, this is purely a matter of positive, human institution.[19]

---

15 See, for example, Alvarus Pelagius, *De Planctu Ecclesiae*, c. 37, pp. 42–58.
16 *OQ* v; *OP* I, 157–68.
17 Offler, 'The origin of Ockham's *Octo Quaestiones*', pp. 329–30.
18 'Unctio vero regalis licet in Veteri Testamento fuerit ex praecepto Dei, tamen in Nova Lege est solummodo ex institutione humana ... Unctio regalis non fit frustra ... Potest enim fieri ... ut rex in maiori veneratione et reverentia habeatur.' *OQ* v, 3; *OP* I, 159.
19 *OQ* v, 6; *OP* I, 161–2. This passage is given below, p. 197. In the next question, whether a hereditary king is in some way subject to the person who crowns him, Ockham does not even pay lip-service to the idea of power descending upon the king 'from above' in the ritual of coronation.

Another clash between secular considerations and sacred rights occurs in the seventh of the *Octo Quaestiones*. The issue is, whether a king crowned by an archbishop other than one who would customarily have crowned him should thereby lose his title or power. Ockham shows some reluctance to brush aside the customary ecclesiastic's rights simply because they are irksome to those in high places, yet he contends that the ruler in question ought not to be deposed – even when he is at fault and is incorrigible – if this will bring about grave civil turmoil: 'We ought to delight more in the life of a people than in the punishment of one bad person . . . If, therefore, the scandal of deposing such a king threatens to overthrow the people . . . such severity should be abandoned.'[20] Ockham took this line in emphatic opposition to the view that ecclesiastical rights are inviolable because sacred.[21] Several of the nine arguments he offers on this point are directly relevant to the theme of laicism, hinging as they do on the clergy's obligation to keep faith with the laity and the corresponding right of the laity to resist clerical hostility.

If the churches do not give laymen what is owed them, the churches must seek in vain for their own rights to be respected by laymen. Again, laymen, especially emperors, kings, princes, and other eminent persons, who have adorned churches with honors, rights, privileges, and liberties solely from devotion, are no more subject to the churches with respect to such gifts than feudal vassals are subject to their lords . . . [But the feudal tie is mutual] . . . If the lord does not keep faith he is deprived of his dominion over the vassal, and the feudal right passes to a superior . . . Therefore, all the more can the churches justly be deprived of the honors, rights, liberties, and privileges granted to them if they are not faithful to the laymen who have granted these things. Again, faith should not be kept with a faithless enemy . . . If the churches do not keep faith with lay- men, but begin to treat them with hostility, faith should not be kept with them, and they can be deprived of those things which have been granted to them.[22]

It is unlikely that the immediate subject of these arguments was Ludwig of Bavaria. The present passage suggests, however, that Ockham would have disapproved of the papal process against

[20] *OQ* vii, 7; *OP* i, 180.
[21] 'Alia est opinio quod ius huiusmodi revocari non potest a rege, quia sacrilegus est qui revocare vult ea quae ecclesiis sunt concessa.' *OQ* vii, 4; *OP* i, 174.
[22] *OQ* vii, 4; *OP* i, 176-7.

Ludwig even if he had deemed the emperor to be in the wrong. Under positive law, the church may have rights in such matters, but it should not insist on them if this will lead to the destruction of public life. With such arguments in view, we cannot regard the laicism imputed to Ockham by scholars like Lagarde as merely a response to 'fantastic' curialist theses. The tone of these arguments is sharply out of harmony with the sacerdotalism characteristic of even moderate clerical authors in the earlier medieval period. This does not mean that Ockham's position was irreligious or, for that matter, wholly 'un-medieval'. We must not assume, however, that it was only a late and aberrant papalism that troubled him.

In spite of its apparent comprehensiveness, Ockham's opposition to papal claims over the empire can be understood in terms of a few ideas. In the first place, he sought to repulse any suggestion that the emperor was, or ever had been, a feudal vassal of the pope. Secondly, when he could not discredit papal interventions in temporal affairs as unwarranted and illegitimate, Ockham gave such actions a purely secular political interpretation, thus depriving them of hierocratic significance as surely as if they had never occurred.

Ockham's rejection of a specifically feudal conception of papal superiority over the empire was developed in answer to two particular papalist arguments, one based on the emperor Otto I's oath to John XII (as recorded in the canon law text, *Tibi domine*), and the other on a famous passage from Nicholas II. In both cases there is progressive refinement in Ockham's treatment of the problem. Thus, in such early works as the *Opus Nonaginta Dierum* and I *Dialogus*, his only real reply to the argument from *Tibi domine* is that one emperor's oath to the pope does not bind his successors.[23] By the time he wrote III *Dialogus* II, however, he had learned the

---

[23] In I *Dialogus*, Ockham has not yet found the distinction between an oath of faithful defense and an oath of homage, a distinction which does not occur in *OND*, c. 93; *OP* II, 688–9 either. He concedes that someone who freely swears an oath does render himself inferior in some respect to the person to whom he swears (I *Dialogus* 6, ix, fol. 55rb). Accordingly, besides the usual insistence that such an oath by one emperor does not bind his successor, he presents the fanciful and not repeated construction: 'ex ordinatione Romanorum a quibus imperator suam habuit iurisdictionem potuit imperator papae iurare et in hoc tenuisset papa non vicem beati Petri, ne[c] in hoc fuit vicarius Christi, sed in hoc fuisset commissarius Romanorum'. It is not to the pope as a *persona spiritualis* that the emperor swears, but to the pope as delegate of the Roman people.

distinction between an oath of homage and an oath of faithful defense. After quoting the Ottonian oath in full from *Tibi domine*, he produced two typical oaths of vassalage from Hostiensis and pointed out several differences between them.[24] He employed the same distinction in the *Octo Quaestiones*, more succinctly than in III *Dialogus*, but with a clearer statement of its general significance. Otto's oath was of the same sort that other rulers offer in their realms, he argues – they swear to defend the church faithfully, although they hold their realms from no church *in feudum*.[25]

A second major hierocratic argument for 'imperium est a papa' was based on a decretist text from Nicholas II claiming that Christ had committed to blessed Peter the laws (*iura*) of both earthly and heavenly empire.[26] As with *Tibi domine*, Ockham's successive refutations of this argument focus more and more clearly on the relationship of feudal superior and vassal. In the *Opus Nonaginta Dierum* he only points out that the passage from Nicholas must somehow be reinterpreted, since it would be absurd to attribute jurisdiction over the church triumphant to St Peter. He suggests that the heavenly and earthly empires of the text could be good and bad persons belonging to the church militant, but he does not develop this, and in particular does not attempt to specify the pope's relation to these *boni* and *mali*.[27] In III *Dialogus* II and the *Breviloquium*, not one but two absurdities are said to follow from the papalist interpretation[28] and, more important, Ockham gives some indication of the *iura terreni imperii* that are at stake. Thus, in III *Dialogus* he denies the pope *dominium* over the earthly empire, but concedes that he has 'some right' (*aliquod ius*) in it. The pope has spiritual power over the emperor and a right to bodily sustenance from the empire to which he ministers spiritually.[29] This position is further clarified in the

---

[24] III *Dialogus* II, 1, xxi.   [25] *OQ* II, 12; *OP* I, 93.

[26] 'Illam [Romanam ecclesiam] solus ipse instituit et fundavit et supra petram fidei mox nascentis erexit, qui beato Petro, aeternae vitae clavigero, terreni simul et coelestis imperii iura commisit.' *Brev.* VI, 1, p. 194 (Gratian, I, Dist. 22, c. 1; ed. Friedberg, I, col. 73).

[27] *OND*, c. 93; *OP* II, 688.

[28] The new absurdity is that '*omnia regna sunt a papa*'. III *Dialogus* II, 1, xix, pp. 239va–240ra. *Brev.* VI, 1, pp. 194–5.

[29] 'Papa habet aliquod ius in terreno imperio, quando a Christiano gubernatur. Tum quia habet potestatem spiritualem super imperatorem. Tum quia habet ius participandi carnalia ab imperio cui ministrat spiritualia.' III *Dialogus* II, 1, xix, fol. 240ra.

Breviloquium, where the absurdity of the kingdom of heaven being 'from' the pope is spelled out in explicitly feudal terms. On the papalist reading, everyone who attained the kingdom of heaven would be obliged to acknowledge *as a vassal (tamquam eius vassalus)* that it was from blessed Peter and the pope.[30] A refinement is also added to Ockham's own doctrine of papal rights in the earthly empire, for these are now said to depend on the acceptance of the catholic faith by those to whom it is preached.[31] This condition makes the empire still less 'from' the pope than before, since now even the pope's spiritually based powers are made contingent upon the emperors' voluntary conversion to Christianity.[32]

Ockham's concentration on a feudal interpretation of *imperium a papa* was a tacit disengagement from the terms of reference usual in hierocratic writings. He made no pretense of discussing the vast literature in which speculative theology and metaphysics had been used to establish the general superiority of sacerdotal to secular power on the basis of its greater age, nobility, dignity, and spirituality. This omission contributes to the impression one has of moving into a different world when reading first Augustinus Triumphus or Alvarus Pelagius[33] and then Ockham. The hierocratic writings are

30 Ockham adds acidly that if the least in the kingdom of heaven is greater than John the Baptist, then all the more is he greater than the pope, who is often the wickedest of men. *Brev.* VI, 1, pp. 194–5.

31 'Potest dici, quod Christus commisit beato Petro . . . ius et potestatem docendi et praedicandi eis [imperatoribus] catholicam fidem; *quam si reciperent,* dedit beato Petro ius et potestatem in spiritualibus super imperatorem et ius recipiendi carnalia pro sustentatione sua et executione officii sui.' *Ibid.*, p. 197. This corresponds with the qualification in III *Dialogus* (note 29 above) that the pope has a certain *ius* in the empire 'when it is governed by a Christian'.

32 The language of the *Octo Quaestiones* is still more feudal. The absurd consequence that all realms are from the pope is said to be prejudicial to all rulers who do not do formal homage to the pope for their realms, and it is denied that the pope has either heavenly or earthly empire *in feudum.* OQ II, 7; OP I, 83–4.

33 Ockham's method is to explore a few crucial propositions, in the process alleging and interpreting (sometimes originally) a great many Biblical and legal texts. The *Summa de Potestate Ecclesiastica* of Augustinus Triumphus, on the other hand, is a confidently systematic work in which nearly every aspect of ecclesiastical institutions is handled on the basis of philosophical and theological first principles. Alvarus Pelagius begins the *De Planctu Ecclesiae* with a series of claims supported by references to canon law, but he hardly hits full stride until chapter 36, in which he shows at length how the church began in Adam and thence came to be in Eve, an investigation in theological genealogy very different from anything found in Ockham.

intellectually more stimulating, and the Augustinian vision of heavenly and earthly societies to which these thinkers appealed has a depth and vividness not present in Ockham. Yet much can be said for Ockham's austerity. The progressive legalization of papal authority since Innocent III had made the connection between papal governmental practice and the ideal hierarchies of papalist theory harder and harder to discern. A direct attack on the ideals of unity and order would have been out of place, however, and Ockham was not prepared to dispute the unique authority of the papacy in purely spiritual matters. By focusing on the specifically legal relationship of vassalage, and by arguing literally and almost legalistically himself, Ockham avoided confronting the hierocrats on their speculative home ground. No doubt this was an evasion not only of abstract metaphysics but also of what many thinkers regarded as the main social issue, the need for effective, comprehensive institutional embodiment of the larger cosmic order. As a result of such evasion, however, the structure of purely spiritual authority was spared attack and the extreme position of secularists and many Spiritual Franciscans was avoided. As we shall see, Ockham's conception of papal government even in the ecclesiastical sphere differed from that of the papalists. It remains significant, however, that he was able to admit readily that hierocratic comparisons of the relationship between emperor and pope to those between son and father, student and master, lead and gold, and moon and sun did indeed have a valid application: 'not because of the empire or temporal matters, but because of spiritual matters, *in which* [the emperor] *is* subject to the pope'.[34]

---

[34] *OQ* II, 14; *OP* I, 95. There is a revealing confusion in Ockham's reply, earlier in the *Octo Quaestiones*, to arguments for papal power based on the relations of soul and body. 'Respondetur quod quantum ad multa sicut anima se habet ad corpus, sic spiritualia se habent ad corporalia sive temporalia; *sed non quantum ad omnia*, quia sicut anima est nobilior corpore, ita spiritualia sunt digniora temporalibus, et sicut anima quantum ad multa regit corpus, ita temporalia in multis sunt secundum exigentiam spiritualium disponenda, *et sicut anima rationalis non habet plenissimam potestatem super corpora, quia quamplures operationes habet corpus quae non sunt in potestate animae rationalis, ita habens potestatem in spiritualibus non habet plenissimam potestatem in temporalibus*' (*OQ* I, 14; *OP* I, 58). Ockham seems to have begun writing this passage with an inclination to reject, or at least limit, the soul–body analogy but then to have noticed that it could be applied in reverse to support his own position, since the natural independence of some physical operations from rational psychological control resembles the rightful independence of

The same policy of disengagement emerges in Ockham's treatment of the pope's supposed right to depose emperors or other secular rulers, or to transfer their dominions from one people to another. Thus, according to one view presented in the *Opus Nonaginta Dierum*, only the mildest restriction is placed on the pope's right to depose secular rulers: 'In a case of crime (*ratione criminis*) a Christian emperor is subject to the pope, and the same may be said about other rulers. In case of crime, then, the pope has jurisdiction over emperors and kings.'[35] As the experience of a century had shown, however, a *crimen* or *peccatum* of some kind could be alleged for almost any case in which the papacy desired to intervene. The secular power allowed the pope was thus 'indirect' only in name. Although Ockham insisted on the spiritual superiority of pope to emperor, he could not in the end allow this superiority to be used as a pretext for constant papal incursions into secular affairs. Hence, although he never abandoned the doctrine of casual papal power, he placed greater stress in later treatises on the principal responsibility of the laity, not only in ordinary affairs of government, but also in matters such as the correction or deposition of secular rulers.

On this basis, Ockham was able to mount a powerful two-pronged attack on the hierocratic arguments based on past papal interventions. His first and most basic contention was that such acts as the deposition of the Frankish king Childeric in the eighth century were valid only if they had been done *auctoritate populi*, not *auctoritate papali*.[36]

many temporal affairs from ecclesiastical control. If he had found this whole style of argument more congenial, he might have attempted to draw some conclusions from his own view of the 'sensitive', or sensory, soul as a single kind of entity homogeneously extended throughout the animal body, with its 'powers' (sight, hearing, etc.) depending on the part of the body in which it happened to be placed rather than on an intrinsic psychological differentiation (*Sent.* II, q. 26 E). This could be taken to suggest that the difference between a private person and an ecclesiastical or secular official was merely a matter of circumstance, and this underlying equality might in turn support some of the radical ideas surveyed in the last chapter. Such was not Ockham's manner of argument, however.

On the relation between the pope's spiritual superiority and the homage due him in political contexts, cf. Buisson, *Potestas und Caritas*, pp. 216–347.

35 *OND*, c. 93; *OP* II, 688.

36 This view is presented even in the *OND* (c. 93; *OP* II, 688), along with the *ratio criminis* argument. In explaining the papal deposition of Childeric as an action performed *auctoritate populi*, Ockham always cites the gloss to the canon law text *Alius* (Gratian, II, C. 15, q. 6, c. 3; ed. Friedberg, I, col. 756): 'Dicitur deposuisse, quia deponentibus consensit.'

Ockham oscillates between the view that Pope Zachary merely consented to Childeric's deposition as a *fait accompli* and the view that he was given power by the Franks to effect the deposition himself. This is a minor uncertainty, however, for in either case, Ockham insists, the pope did not exercise a specifically papal power. Such cases, then, establish no claims for the papacy as an institution. Instead of being accepted as vivid, immediately compelling manifestations of an eternal hierarchical order, historical incidents like this are analysed by Ockham as deeds of individual popes acting in individual circumstances. Perhaps the best expression of Ockham's mature view is found in the *Octo Quaestiones*. There the pope is said to have deposed Childeric by consenting to the act and by counseling the Franks that they should not fear to exercise 'their own power . . . against the king for the common utility of all' (*potestatem suam . . . contra regem pro communi utilitate omnium*).[37] In other words, he acted in an advisory capacity, reassuring the people concerning their own rights. But even here he did not act *as pope* in any important sense. In going to Rome for advice the Franks approached the pope, says Ockham, 'as a wise man and as having with him men wiser than they were themselves (for there was not yet a University of Paris)'. On this interpretation of the Frankish case, the pope's function could as well have been served by any person possessing the relevant legal or moral wisdom. Ockham's reference to the University of Paris, though perhaps partly ironic, brings this point out clearly. It would be understandable that laymen in primitive France – before the university was established – should have sought such wisdom at Rome, but this accident of history should not be taken as a precedent for *ex officio* action by the holy see. Accordingly, Ockham immediately refers to a more recent case (apparently the deposition of Edward II) in which men who had no doubts about their own power formally (*sententialiter*) deposed their king without having any recourse to the pope. This, indeed, would seem to be the more natural procedure, according to Ockham, because neither the institution nor the removal of kings pertains to the pope if such an action can be taken without danger by laymen and if the laymen involved are not culpably negligent.[38]

[37] *OQ* II, 9; *OP* I, 87.
[38] *OQ* II, 9; *OP* I, 87. For further references, see note 175 below. Ockham's treatment

93

The second prong to Ockham's anti-hierocratic account of historic papal interventions in secular politics was an attack on their validity. In III *Dialogus*, it is suggested that Pope Zachary may have usurped power in deposing Childeric, for the papacy has often acted 'in praeiudicium laicorum'. Whether laymen are negligent or not, it is said, the pope grants letters against them to the clergy every day.[39] The theme of usurpation recurs in the *Octo Quaestiones* in the discussion of papal proceedings against the emperors Otto IV and Frederick II,[40] and it is the major burden of the *Breviloquium*[41] and the *De Imperatorum et Pontificum Potestate*.[42]

Ockham never denied the pope's ultimate jurisdiction in secular

of the translation of the empire from the Greeks to the Germans is less detailed than his discussions of papal depositions of secular rulers, but he usually takes the same line. In the *OND*, I *Dial.*, and III *Dial.* II, he denies that the pope can make such a transfer by his own authority and suggests instead that the pope acted 'auctoritate Romanorum qui sibi potestatem huiusmodi concesserunt' (*OND*, c. 93; *OP* II, 688), or 'qui sibi ex causa rationabili potestatem huius contulerunt' (I *Dialogus* 6, ix, fol. 55rb). He did not make the transfer by any authority or power given him by Christ but by authority given him by the Romans, 'tanquam *personae* excellentiori *inter* Romanos' (or, it is suggested, the pope consented to a transfer actually made by the Romans) (III *Dialogus* II, 1, xx). A different position is favored in *OQ* II, 10, however. Instead of suggesting that the pope acted by authority properly belonging to others, a somewhat strained idea in this case, Ockham brings the notion of casual power into play. The pope cannot transfer the empire (for a secular crime) by his own authority unless the Romans or others are culpably negligent. The implication is that in case of negligence he can act by his own authority.

39 III *Dialogus* II, 1, xviii, fol. 239rab.
40 'Alii dicunt quod uterque [papa] male processit usurpando sibi potestatem quam non habuit . . . Propter quam usurpationem dicunt ordinem Christianitatis esse confusum, quia omnis ordo confunditur, si unicuique sua iurisdictio non servatur.' *OQ* II, 9; *OP* I, 88.
41 See especially *Brev.*, *Prologus*, p. 39; II, 1, pp. 53–4; and the full title of the work (above, p. 21n., p. 75).
42 See especially *Imp. Pont. Pot.*, c. 1, p. 455: 'Si reges et principes ecclesiarumque praelatos ac Christianos ceteros non lateret, quod Christianitas cunctis agitatur angustiis et pressuris ac incessanter omnibus premitur importabilibus et iniustis propter hoc, quod nonnulli Romani pontifices vel pro Romanis pontificibus se gerentes, *terminos transgredientes antiquos, ad aliena manus impias extenderunt,* et quod super omnes illos ecclesia Avinionica in Christianos nostris periculosis temporibus saevius debacchatur, puto, quod plurimi eorum eidem ecclesiae Avinionicae non faverent, sed futuris casibus affectarent prudenter occurrere et ne incepta mala praevaleant praecavere.'

affairs. In case of grave crisis, if no layman can or will take adequate action, the pope has a divine right to do whatever is necessary. In Ockham's argumentation, however, the requirement that laymen be negligent or powerless before the pope may intervene on his own initiative leads to a much more restricted doctrine of casual power than in the hierocratic version of the same idea. For with Ockham it is not merely the secular judge or ruler who must be defective if the pope is to act. There must also be a failure on the part of the local community or of those particular laymen who might be expected to act for the community. Extraordinary corrective action in secular affairs should come from the lay ruler's subjects, those below him, not from his spiritual superior, the pope. In thus construing secular politics as a properly self-corrective process, Ockham provided a natural complement to his denial that the pope stood to lay rulers in a regular relationship of feudal superior to vassal. Both in ordinary circumstances and in all but the most hopeless of extraordinary circumstances, the basis for secular power in Christian society was to be non-clerical.

'Concluons qu'Ockham entend retirer toute valeur effective à la "sacralisation" du pouvoir que la tradition ecclésiastique a imposée depuis cinq siècles.' The passages we have examined amply confirm this conclusion of Lagarde's. Within the precincts of the *societas Christiana*, Ockham denied the dependence of secular on ecclesiastical power. It must again be emphasized, however, that, 'radical' as this denial was in terms of papalist political theory, Ockham did not present it as a departure from tradition. He was indignant at the papacy's attempt to subjugate secular rulers and still more indignant at the claim that such subjection was the usual state of affairs. This is most evident in the *Octo Quaestiones*, in his response to a set of arguments from Ptolemy of Lucca's *Determinatio Compendiosa*, the gist of which was that papal claims to *plenitudo potestatis* could be proved by the acknowledgment of the superiority of priests by secular rulers throughout the course of history. Ockham's reply was a withering case-by-case rebuttal. Such emperors as Constantine, Justinian, and Charlemagne were devout towards all clerics, but they never regarded themselves as their subjects 'in imperialibus'. Ockham provides particulars in each instance. He finds it especially astonishing that Justinian should be adduced here, 'since there was never a Christian emperor who so expressly attributed to himself such great superiority, jurisdiction, and power over the affairs and persons of pope and clergy as Justinian'. With ironic charity, Ockham wonders whether those who argue for papal supremacy on this basis can actually have read Justinian's laws. His own citations are most effective in evoking the state of imperial authority prior to the growth of papal government in the West.[43]

In terms of the perennial tension between clerical and lay classes in medieval society,[44] Ockham was squarely on the side of the laity in the matter of papal overlordship of the empire and of secular jurisdictions in general. When this is said, however, we have only begun to grasp the meaning of his desacralization of the basis of secular power. To speak of 'laicism' is to suggest a contrast with one form or another of 'sacerdotalism', a contrast drawn within a specifically religious structure of ideas. Now in the special domain of Christian concepts, opposition to sacerdotalism takes on a purely negative character. It has the guise of rebellion against the high and holy. Such rebellion can perhaps be justified if the spiritual authorities are corrupt, if in fact they are not holy, as in the case of papal heresy. Yet so long as the contest for power is seen as a struggle between two classes within the church – clergy and laity – there is something ultimately futile about the 'lay' thesis. Who is to say what are the boundaries of various jurisdictions within the church, after all, if not the clergy? It is in the light of such questions that we must consider a further stage in Ockham's desacralization of the basis of secular power. Beyond offering legal and historical arguments vindicating the independence of the lay power against various excessive clerical claims, he attempted to deal with contemporary conflicts by giving secular power a basis outside the church.

Dominium extra ecclesiam – imperium tempore Christi

In his attempts to establish the independence of the empire from papal approval or control, Ockham often availed himself of Biblical texts recognizing legitimate *dominium* or jurisdiction among

---

[43] *OQ* I, 12; *OP* I, 54–6 (Constantine on pp. 53–4, Charlemagne on p. 56).
[44] This is the starting point of Lagarde's study. *La naissance*, new edition, I, *Bilan du XIIIe siècle* pp. ix–x. Cf. Boniface VIII, *Clericis laicos*.

non-believers. In the *Breviloquium* he is especially emphatic about Biblical contributions to the imperial cause, claiming that the empire's rights are *principally* to be fortified by holy writ. To presume against these rights involves not only iniquity, injustice, and error, but also heresy.[45] In the *Octo Quaestiones* he is hardly less extreme. It appears to him that contemporary emperors derive more stability and vigor from their succession to the first Roman emperors – especially those in the time of Christ and the apostles – than from succession to Charlemagne. It is more certainly known that those unbelievers were true emperors than that Charles was a true emperor, because we have greater testimony about their empire than his, since God's testimony is greater than that of men: 'testimonium Dei maius sit quam testimonium hominum'.[46] Such passages lend themselves to the view that Ockham rejected the papal–hierocratic sacralization of all power, only to prepare for a sacralization of his own: a Biblically based descending conception of authority, in which power would be derived from God, not through the pope as intermediary, but by direct positive command. It was perhaps this derivation of modern imperial authority from the divinely approved pagan emperors which led Scholz to place a theological positivism at the center of Ockham's political thought.[47] A closer examination of Ockham's use of Scripture reveals, however, a very different situation. Far from using the Biblical record as a means of divinizing or glorifying the Roman Empire, or regarding it as a direct fulfillment of divine will, Ockham employed 'God's *testimony*' to legitimate a conception of empire drastically less sacred than that held by his contemporaries.

[45] *Brev.* IV, 1, p. 141.
[46] *OQ* IV, 3; *OP* I, 129–30. Ockham made this assertion in the course of respectfully but firmly rejecting the contemporary German jurist Lupold of Bebenberg's distinction between the emperor's national and universal authority. Lupold hoped to secure the German and Italian portions of the empire against papal claims by basing title to these lands on succession to Charlemagne as king of the Romans, a position he could be said to have held prior to his coronation as emperor in St Peter's. Lupold could then allow that universal jurisdiction (succession to Charlemagne as emperor) did depend on papal approval and coronation. Ockham, on the other hand, was not only committed to a universal rather than national conception of the empire (Lagarde, *La naissance*, IV, 15), but was also oriented towards the pre-Christian empire. This needs explanation. Ockham discusses Lupold at *OQ* IV; *OP* I, 126–57, and *OQ* VIII, 3–5; *OP* I, 184–202.
[47] See above, pp. 35–7. See also Lagarde's view, p. 31 above.

In the great majority of cases, Ockham appealed to the Bible as an unimpeachable source of information rather than law. Thus, although some of the Old Testament passages cited refer to particular divine grants of temporal power to individuals *extra ecclesiam* (in the sense of *extra populum Dei*, not belonging to God's people), most merely acknowledge the legitimacy of such *dominium* without specifying its origin.[48] In the New Testament passages this is universally the case.[49] The words and deeds in the New Testament recognizing the imperial regime's legitimacy in no sense created that legitimacy for Ockham. Rather, as he interpreted the situation, Christ and His disciples were confronted by a world government which they had had no share in making and which admitted no need of their acknowledgment or blessing.[50] On these terms, however, they accepted the imperial jurisdiction, not merely *propter iram* but *propter conscientiam*. It was clear to Ockham, for example, that St Paul considered himself a Roman citizen only by the authority and privilege of the Romans. He must have held, therefore, that the Romans had a true 'conceded' power in these matters, not a merely permitted power.[51] The direction of the inference is crucial. Paul acquired his status as a citizen from the authority of the Romans. The Romans acquired no legitimacy from being endorsed by Paul. Or again, in the fairly detailed treatment of Romans 13: 1–2 in the *Breviloquium*, there is not a word as to *how* the higher powers are ordained by God. There is certainly no reference to a special divine ordination of either the personnel or the institutional structure of the Roman Empire.[52] The point is of some importance in view of the

48 *Brev.* III, 2, pp. 110–13. III *Dialogus* II, i, xxv, fol. 243v*ab*. *OQ* I, 10; *OP* I, 43–4. Ockham refers to the divine grants of power to unbelievers recorded in the Bible, not as the basis of his own position, but 'quia posset *cavillose* dici, quod tales contractus inter fideles et infideles [as are mentioned, e.g., in Genesis] non erant veri contractus' (p. 111).

49 *Brev.* III, 3, pp. 113–18. III *Dialogus* II, I, xxv, fols. 243v*b*–244r*b*. *OQ* I, 10; *OP* I, 44–5.

50 The issue concerns Christ's authority only insofar as He was a mortal man. For John XXII's claim that Christ was given universal temporal authority by God the Father from the instant of His conception, see *OND*, c. 93; *OP* II, 670–705.

51 *Brev.* III, 3, p. 117–18. According to Innocent IV, imperial authority had merely been permitted to exist *de facto* up to the time of Constantine, when its Christianization transformed it into a positively conceded power. Ockham uses this claim to state the problem of political legitimacy at *ibid.*, I, pp. 107–8. Cf. III *Dialogus* II, I, xviii, fol. 238v*b*.   52 *Brev.* III, 3, pp. 115–17.

natural desire of imperialist political writers to find as firm a divine foundation for their own claims as the theological warrants adduced by their papalist opponents. Dante, for example, had a more exalted view of the empire and was, indeed, more of a theological positivist here than Ockham. He saw Christ's birth under the empire, 'in plenitudine temporis', as a tribute to Roman civilization[53] and took as the first principle of his demonstration that the Roman people had assumed the office of empire rightfully the thesis that, 'that which God wills in human society is to be accepted as truly and wholly right'.[54] Accordingly, he then searched Roman history for signs of the divine will. Such a synthesis of humanism, theology, and speculative history has no parallel in Ockham. In legitimating the empire he made no attempt to glorify it. Or again, Ludwig of Bavaria asserted in the constitution *Licet iuris* that the imperial dignity 'proceeded from the beginning' immediately from God alone and that through the emperor and kings of the world 'God bestowed' rights on the human race.[55] Such phrases convey a much more active sense of God's involvement in imperial affairs than can be found anywhere in Ockham. To him, 'imperium est immediate a Deo' meant merely and precisely that the emperor was not regularly *subject* in temporal affairs to anyone under God.[56]

---

[53] 'A lapsu primorum parentum . . . non inveniemus, nisi sub divo Augusto Monarcha; existente Monarchia perfecta, mundum undique fuisse quietum. Et quod tunc humanum genus fuerit felix in pacis universalis tranquillitate, hoc historiographi omnes, hoc poetae illustres, hoc etiam Scriba mansuetudinis Christi testari dignatus est.' *Monarchia*, in Dante's *Opere*, ed. E. Moore and P. Toynbee, 5th ed. (Oxford, 1963), Book I, c. 16, p. 350.

[54] 'Illud quod Deus in hominum societate vult, illud pro vero atque sincero iure habendum sit.' *Ibid.*, II, 2, p. 352.

[55] Berthold, *Kaiser, Volk und Avignon*, p. 282. The Augustinian text on which this portion of *Licet iuris* was modeled (from Gratian, I, Dist. 8, c. I ed. Friedberg, I, col. 13) is cited by Professor Ullmann as a neat statement of the *descending* thesis of government and law (*Government and Politics in the Middle Ages*, p. 21). Nothing suggests more clearly a basic difference in political orientation between Ockham and his protector. While it may be correct to speak of the strong influence of Ockham's *Contra Benedictum* on Ludwig's official statements (Becker, 'Das Mandat *Fidem Catholicam*', p. 474) or of the reciprocal bearing of those statements on theses developed in Ockham's later works (*ibid.*, pp. 490–1), the distinctive ways in which Ockham understood imperial problems and policies (and tried to get others to understand them) must always be borne in mind.

[56] *Brev.* IV, 5–8, pp. 149–58. *OQ* II, 3–6; *OP* I, 74–81. In the *Breviloquium*, Ockham considers the possibility of a positive divine origin for the empire but rejects this

In sum, Ockham contended that in the authentic tradition of the church, as recorded in the Bible, non-Christians are generally recognized as persons with legitimate legal standing. There is no suggestion of a metaphysical distinction between nature and grace that can be drawn within the same person, and which could thus be used to argue that Christianity 'perfects' the jurisdiction of non-believers by subordinating it to specifically religious ends. Rather, the Bible refers to concrete individuals – some *fideles* and some *infideles* – who are not systematically distinguished *vis-à-vis* property and legal standing by their religious status. Just as papacy and empire are not feudal superior and inferior within the *societas Christiana*, so believers and non-believers are not 'ordered' as temporal superior and inferior in the Biblical record. But the basis for this equality of rights is not in most cases found in special divine collations of power upon the infidels. Ockham accepted the general equation of true and legitimate jurisdiction with jurisdiction ordained and conceded by God, but his interpretation of the Biblical sources strikingly avoids any claim that secular power is itself sacred in nature or in its particular origin.[57]

What did the empire's legitimacy consist of *in tempore Christi*? The answer is apparently that the imperial government had exclusive rights to the administration of justice, at least in cases where severe penalties were likely. Thus, when Ockham discusses Paul's advice to the Corinthians about settling disputes that might arise among them, he insists on an interpretation without prejudice to the *iura* of the (pagan) secular judges. In particular, he questions whether the early

idea for lack of a scriptural foundation (*Brev.* IV, 10, p. 162). Having established the empire's legitimacy in the time of Christ and the apostles, he expresses doubt as to how or when it began to be legitimate. Perhaps the Romans began their domination tyrannically and only later had true empire. Christ and the apostles have said nothing on this matter (*ibid.*, p. 161). There may be a trace of impatience in Ockham's continuation: 'Quod autem illi non diffinierunt, nec ego diffinire praesumo.'

57 If the medieval emperor's 'succession' to his earliest predecessors is viewed purely temporally, as the preservation of an unbroken chain of legitimacy, then Ockham's argument is certainly liable to the ridicule Lagarde (*La naissance*, IV, 261) heaps upon it: 'Comment a-t'il pu se convaincre, un instant, des droits de cet empire maintenus inviolés depuis le Christ?' If, however, the *successio* to the pagan emperors in Ockham's thought concerns his conception of what imperial jurisdiction is and how it is related to the church, rather than a historical myth about its descent from one generation to another, the subject becomes more interesting.

Christians had power to exercise the full measure of justice among themselves.[58] The other leading example of legitimacy as involving the right to dispense 'complete' justice is the situation of Christ before Pilate. Christ's acceptance of Pilate's jurisdiction over Him was consistent with His denial that He was a king in any sense that prejudiced the rulership of Caesar.[59] This did not involve approving the moral character of the Roman administration or endorsing its particular legal judgments. It simply acknowledged the imperial official's unique right to administer the severest penalties of criminal justice.

Ockham did not regard it as normal that secular government be hostile to the church, but in other respects, the *tempore Christi* situation of Christianity and the empire served him as a paradigm for the relations of temporal and spiritual power in general. To be sure, just as he did not directly attack the metaphysical foundations of papalism, so he did not always emphasize the lack of sacred foundations for the empire, but the underlying idea is often clearly visible. A wholly non-Christian conception of empire stands out, for example, in the *Breviloquium*, when Ockham defends the legitimacy of Julian the Apostate's government, pointing out that it is only *iure humano* that heretics are incapable of exercising jurisdiction. In Julian's time no such law had been made. Hence, his subjects were bound to obey him, as one having true dominion and power, except in things contrary to their faith.[60] Although Ockham did not

---

58 'In multis enim casibus, *salvo omni iure superioris*, potest iniuriam patiens atque fraudem nolle apud superiorem iudicare et contendere coram eo' (*Brev*. v, 9, p. 187). 'Sed adhuc forte quaeret aliquis, an licuit, illis, quibus scribebat apostolus, de omni negotio emergente inter ipsos facere iustitiae complementum, etiam secundum rigorem. Cui potest responderi, quod hoc non licebat eis de omni negotio, quia forte non habebant merum imperium, et per consequens non licuit eis penam mortis vel membri truncationem inferre; quibus etiam non licebat iniuriantibus irrogare penam, per quam impedirentur principibus infidelibus *servitia debita* et obedientiam exhibere, quia *non debebant eos* per talem modum *iure, quod* in delinquentibus *habebant, privare*, reddendo subditos eis ad obediendum et reddendum debita impotentes' (*ibid.*, pp. 189–90). Cf. *OND*, c. 113; *OP* ii, 797. iii *Dialogus* ii, 2, xviii, fol. 255rab. *OQ* i, 11; *OP* i, 45–9 (with sharp criticism of Innocent IV, pp. 48–9). In some of his discussions of this and related topics, Ockham applies the dictum of Ambrose, 'Christiana religio privat neminem suo iure', to the jurisdiction of pagan judges – this jurisdiction is considered to be a *ius* of the judge.
59 *OND*, c. 93; *OP* ii, 675–80. *OQ* iii, 12; *OP* i, 122. iii *Dialogus* ii, 3, xxiii, fols. 275vb–276ra.   60 *Brev*. iii, 4, p. 120.

question the laws against heretics passed after Julian's time, he believed that contemporary unbelievers were still capable of exercising legitimate jurisdiction. Thus, he argued that the papalist denial of any *dominium* outside the church was prejudicial to unbelievers and so was an occasion for their not becoming converts.[61] He even went on to extend the capacity for property and jurisdiction to unbelievers remaining in their unbelief (*infideles infidelitate manente*).[62] In the same vein are his suggestions in III *Dialogus* II that an emperor need not be a Christian (except insofar as every rational adult ought to be a Christian)[63] or that a world community comprising Christians and non-Christians in which an *imperator infidelis* presided over all mortals might be expedient in the future as it was in the past: 'Believers ought not to bear the same spiritual yoke with unbelievers; nevertheless, they can licitly bear the same temporal yoke with them, whence there are many believers in both the New and the Old Testament who bore the same temporal yoke with unbelievers and obeyed an infidel ruler. Believers can licitly have community and peaceful association (*communionem et pacificam societatem*) with unbelievers, too ... and so it could even be expedient *in casu* that one infidel emperor preside over all mortals.'[64] Such conclusions are not often stated by Ockham. They had little practical importance in the circumstances for which he wrote. He faced difficulties enough in defending the jurisdiction of a Christian emperor over Christians without emphasizing the political rights of Moslems or the unconverted Lithuanians, let alone pressing the legitimacy of a world order in which non-Christians might actually have supreme secular authority. Nevertheless, such assertions are consistent with his basic principles and have a theoretical interest far beyond their immediate significance in practice.[65]

---

[61] *Ibid.*, 5, p. 124. [62] *Ibid.*, 6, pp. 124–5.

[63] III *Dialogus* II, I, xiv, fol. 236vab.

[64] *Ibid.*, I, xi, fol. 235vb. At OQ III, 12; OP I, 123, Ockham is even ready to grant an *imperator infidelis* authority in religious disputes in so far as they endanger the common good: 'Coram autem imperatore infideli causa fidei non inquantum respiceret solummodo veritatem divinitus revelatam, sed inquantum posset tangere mores et reipublicae derogare et bono communi aut alicui personae iniuriam irrogare posset tractari.' On this point, however, see below, pp. 131–3. On the possibility of genuine moral virtue among pagans (and the inexcusability of idolatry), see I *Dialogus* 6, lxxvii, fol. 90rb–91ra.

[65] On both the rights of unbelievers and the legitimate authority of pagan emperors, Ockham was more enlightened than St Thomas. The latter, too, held that

'The faithful emperor succeeds the infidel empeior, therefore he ought to have the same rights as the infidel.'[66] Current emperors have more stability and vigor as successors to the first emperors, especially those in the time of Christ and his apostles, than as successors to Charlemagne.[67] Ockham's immediate motive in such assertions was his desire to free the empire from subservience to the Avignonese papacy. At a deeper level, however, his view of secular government in the first century provides the pattern according to which the whole dualistic structure of his political thought is built. His denial that Christ's advent transformed the basis or nature of imperial power is only the most vivid expression of a more general refusal either to accept the hierocratic conversion of secular power to direction by Christ's vicar, or to provide the present imperial government with a sacral ideology of its own. Either of these courses would have exacerbated the conflicts Ockham was concerned to allay. Considering the deep sources of those conflicts, we should perhaps not be surprised that he was driven to seek a model for his own position in a pre-medieval historical setting.

Imperium a Deo per homines?

It seems fair to sum up what we have so far observed of Ockham's theory of government as an emphatic negation of the descending thesis of law and government, the claim that all authority is derived from God himself through a specially appointed vice-gerent on earth. Ockham's contrary position can be seen in successively broader contexts: within the boundaries of Christendom, as a

---

dominium was introduced *iure humano* and that the distinction between believers and unbelievers did not in itself abolish that human right. He maintained, however, that the church, which has God's authority, can take away from unbelievers at least their *dominium* over believers, for by their infidelity unbelievers deserve to lose power over those who have become children of God: 'Potest tamen iuste per sententiam vel ordinationem Ecclesiae, auctoritatem Dei habentis, tale ius dominii vel praelationis tolli; quia infideles merito suae infidelitatis merentur potestatem amittere super fideles, qui transferuntur in filios Dei' (*Summa Theologiae*, IIa IIae, q. 10, a. 10, *resp.*). Again, St Thomas treated Julian the Apostate's *dominium* as something 'tolerated' by the church solely from lack of coercive power: 'Illo tempore Ecclesia . . . nondum habebat potestatem terrenos principes compescendi. Et ideo toleravit fideles Iuliano Apostatae obedire in his quae nondum erant contra fidem, ut maius periculum fidei vitaretur' (*ibid.*, q. 12, a. 2, *ad* 1).

[66] OQ II, 6; OP I, 80. [67] OQ IV, 3; OP I, 129.

rejection of papal demands for effective control of secular politics; in terms of the relations between Christian and non-Christian political orders, as a denial of the inherent political superiority of the former over the latter; in the setting of the pre-Constantinian era of early Christianity in the Roman Empire, as a rejection of any attempt to transform the *prima facie* condition of poverty and power-lessness of Christ and the apostles into one of even *de iure* secular political authority. We may add that Ockhamist political authority does not descend from above in the sense of belonging to those who morally deserve to have it.[68] A more thorough rejection of the descending theme as a general explanation of political authority would be hard to imagine.[69]

Should Ockham therefore be credited with an ascending conception of political legitimacy? It is clear that he regarded popular consent as the normal original basis for legitimate secular authority: in accord with natural law a people lacking a ruler can provide one for itself.[70] Pope Zachary advised the Franks that they should not fear to exercise *their* authority for the common good.[71] The question,

---

[68] The moral dimension of the problem of legitimate political authority is raised by St Augustine's assertion that all things belong to the just – 'cuncta iustorum sunt' (Epistle 93, c. 12, *Patrologia Latina*, XXXIII, col. 345). Ockham's most illuminating discussion of this proposition is in the *Breviloquium*. After pointing out that there are many 'impii' and 'iniusti' among believers, who do not lose their property on that account, he goes on to develop an 'orthodox' interpretation of Augustine's words which reduces personal justice to a purely moral consideration having no political effects on either side of the Christian–non-Christian religious boundary: 'Iure divino cuncta sint non solum fidelium in Christum credentium, sed etiam iustorum, qui iustificati sunt per gratiam gratum facientem, *non quoad dominium et proprietatem* . . . *sed quoad dignitatem possidendi, habendi et utendi*, hoc est: *soli iusti digni sunt possidere, habere et uti rebus temporalibus* . . . Quamvis infideles et univer-saliter impii indigni sint iurisdictione huiusmodi, tamen veram iurisdictionem huiusmodi possunt habere tam infideles, quam peccatores fideles' (*Brev*. III, 12, p. 133). Ockham's praise of the Romans elsewhere in the *Breviloquium*, though supported by Augustinian texts, implicitly rejects Augustine's contention that the pagan empire was based purely on lust for domination. Ockham goes so far here as to contrast the public-spirited Romans of old with the popes of his own day. It is the latter whom he accuses of *libido dominandi*. *Ibid.*, II, 19, pp. 97–8. See Lagarde, *La naissance*, IV, 212–14 for useful discussion and references.

[69] The descent of authority by direct divine mandate was a possibility Ockham explicitly recognized (see notes 48 and 56 above and note 72 below), but this could be invoked only on the basis of a particular revelation and was relevant only to cases specifically mentioned in the Biblical text.

[70] *Brev*. IV, 10, p. 161. III *Dial*. II, 3, vi, fol. 263vb.   [71] *OQ* II, 9; *OP* I, 87.

'a quo est imperium Romanum?', is to be answered, 'a Deo *per homines*', and the function of the *homines* in Ockham's interpretation of this phrase was not to obey the promptings of divine inspiration, but to act on their own initiative in setting up the imperial government, or voluntarily becoming subject to the empire once it had been established.[72] More important than these separate examples is Ockham's exposition in the *Breviloquium* of a general doctrine of the natural human powers involved in instituting legitimate governments.[73] Before the fall, according to Ockham, there was no private property or political rulership. The human race did have a *dominium* (*potestas dominandi*) over the rest of creation, but this was a natural right possessed by the human race in common. After the fall, a second power was conferred by God, a power to appropriate temporal things to determinate persons and to set up rulers. This power, too, was conferred upon the human race in common, however, not on particular persons. Accordingly, when Ockham speaks of *dominium* and *iurisdictio* as being introduced by human law,

---

[72] Ockham's clearest treatment of these matters is in the *Breviloquium*: 'Tertio potest intelligi aliqua iurisdictio vel potestas esse a solo Deo, non quando datur vel confertur, sed postquam data est, ut scilicet, quando datur ... vere detur vel conferatur etiam ab alio, quam a Deo; tamen postquam collata est, a solo Deo dependet ita, quod fungens ea ipsam a nullo alio, quam a Deo, tamquam a superiori, regulariter recognoscit' (*Brev.* IV, 5, p. 150). 'Imperium est a solo Deo tertio modo, quia, scilicet fuerit sic a Deo, quod humana ordinatio concurrebat ita, ut homines habentes potestatem conferendi alicui iurisdictionem temporalem, vere conferebant imperatori iurisdictionem, quemadmodum vere conferebant sibi et transtulerunt a se in eum potestatem condendi leges' (*ibid.*, c. 6, p. 151). 'Narrabo modos, quibus poterat fieri verum imperium, non obstante infidelitate imperantium. Quorum unus poterat esse absque omni violentia per consensum liberum et spontaneum populorum voluntarie subdentium se Romanis. A Deo enim et a natura habent omnes mortales, qui nascuntur liberi et iure humano nequaquam alteri sunt subiecti, quod sponte possunt sibi rectorem praeficere ... Et ita omnes populi poterant voluntarie subdere se Romanis et unum verum imperium constituere Romanorum; quod semel poterat fieri et successive, ita ut Romani prius reciperent verum imperium super unam regionem quam super aliam' (*ibid.*, 10, p. 161). As alternative modes of constituting *verum imperium*, Ockham considers conquest in just wars and special divine *ordinatio*, revealed in a special miracle. About this last mode he says, however, that, 'non videtur concurrisse ad constitutionem Romani imperii, quia de hoc in scripturis divinis nihil habemus' (*ibid.*, p. 162). Cf. *OQ* II, 3–6; *OP* I, 74–81.

[73] *Brev.* III, 7–11, pp. 125–32. Cf. *OND*, c. 88; *OP* II, 655–63. For more detailed expositions of Ockham's doctrine, see Boehner, 'Ockham's political ideas', pp. 454–8 (for the *Breviloquium*); and Miethke, *Ockhams Weg*, pp. 467–77 (for the *Opus Nonaginta Dierum*).

he clearly regards this *ius humanum* as the joint exercise of a common power.

In spite of this forthright doctrine, severe qualifications must be attached to the description of Ockham as the advocate of an ascending conception of law and government. We must reckon, for example, with the following passage, which he offered as one possible explanation of how the Romans came to be rulers of the world:

The Romans saw that it was necessary for the common utility of the whole world that one emperor rule over (*dominari*) all mortals. Hence, since those who opposed unity of empire were obstacles to the common good, the power of establishing the empire (*potestas ordinandi de imperio*) devolved upon the Romans and others who consented with them in this. Hence, the Romans could licitly subjugate opponents and rebels to their empire.[74]

Although this passage is by no means typical, and the view it expresses is not advanced by Ockham *in propria persona*, it cannot be entirely discounted.

A more important indication of Ockham's unwillingness to make popular consent the sole principle of political legitimacy is his repeated denial that a community may at its own discretion withdraw power from the government it has established. Once an emperor is elected he has no regular superior on earth. In this sense (though not in the sense of a special divine mandate) his power is *a solo Deo*. Hence, he cannot validly be deposed without cause or fault. This is one of the points at which Ockham's ideas were directly relevant to current political reality. The attempts of the papacy and of Baldwin of Trier to depose Ludwig of Bavaria in the years around 1345 could be made more acceptable to the imperial electors if they were persuaded that they had the power to depose the emperor and elect a successor at their own discretion.[75] The electors would naturally have been reluctant to concede that their original election of Ludwig was invalid, but no such concession was required

---

[74] III *Dialogus* II, 1, xxvii, fol. 245ra. But cf. *Brev.* IV, 10, pp. 161–2 for possible alternative origins of imperial power (see above, notes 56 and 72).

[75] On Baldwin of Trier see E. E. Stengel, 'Baldewin von Luxemburg, ein grenzdeutscher Staatsmann des 14. Jahrhunderts', in *Abhandlungen und Untersuchungen zur mittelalterlichen Geschichte* (Cologne, 1960), pp. 180–217, especially 207ff. For further references see Miethke, *Ockhams Weg*, p. 131nn.

by a theory of electoral discretion. It is likely enough that Ockham's rejection of this theory in the *Breviloquium* was directed against electoral pretensions to sovereign power.[76] Its relevance to German politics does not make this limitation of the doctrine of consent inconsistent with the basic principles of Ockham's own thought, however.[77] If we search his writings from one end to the other, we find almost nothing to suggest that the continuing participation and consent of the governed is an essential principle of political legitimacy.

Ockham's sympathetic consideration of conciliarism in I *Dialogus*[78] might seem to indicate that he regarded the express agreement of the community of believers or its representatives as an all-important factor in the life of the church – and one could go on to imagine implications for secular politics as well. In I *Dialogus*, however, Ockham was concerned with the abnormal case of a heretical pope. What he says about councils in this context has little tendency to show that representative bodies have a decisive part to play in the normal affairs of government.

Whatever might be made of I *Dialogus*, there is no doubt about Ockham's attitude towards popular government in his later works. In III *Dialogus*, he carefully investigated whether either the church or the world would be better governed by one or by many. He treated this as an issue between monarchy and aristocracy, however, and did not even consider a popular regime.[79] In discussing govern-

---

76 *Brev.* IV, 12–13, pp. 165–6. The probable date of the *Breviloquium* rules out direct reference to the machinations resulting in Charles of Moravia's election in 1346. As Scholz points out, however (*Wilhelm von Ockham*, p. 14), Ockham had the possibility of electoral challenges to the emperor's authority in mind elsewhere in the work (VI, 2, pp. 198–9), when he denied that the electors automatically have power to correct or depose the emperor. If they have this power it is only because it has been given them *auctoritate imperatoris vel populi*.

77 See especially III *Dialogus* II, I, viii, xxix and xxxi.

78 I *Dialogus* 6, xii–xiii and lxxxiv–lxxxvi. To show that laymen (and women) may interest themselves in a general council and can even convene one when necessary, Ockham makes insistent use of the medieval axiom of consent, 'quod omnes tangit, ab omnibus tractari et approbari debet' (*ibid.*, lxxxv, fols. 97rb–98rb). By 'conciliarism' is meant here only the thesis that a general council has power to inquire into the pope's orthodoxy and punish papal heresy. For Ockham's rejection of conciliar infallibility, see I *Dialogus* 5, xxv–xxviii and III *Dialogus* I, 3, v–xx.

79 The single reason given for the expediency of rule by many is that there would be fewer errors and sins 'si plures *sapientes et virtuosi* dominarentur universitati mortalium' (*ibid.*, II, I, iv, fol. 232va). Although Ockham's review in III *Dialogus* I

ment by many ruling together, he took into account arguments advanced by Aristotle in support of popular assemblies. Nevertheless, his conclusion that monarchy is preferable to aristocracy was partly based on the fact that a monarch can call on popular assemblies when he needs their counsel or favor, but need not use them otherwise, whereas a regime of many must consult all of its members, even when it is unnecessary or inexpedient to do so.[80] Thus, the function of popular assemblies in Ockham's preferred form of government is somewhat *ad hoc*. It certainly cannot be said that he was in favor of a mixed regime, let alone that he would have regarded the popular component of such a regime as the decisive one.[81]

When we add to the preceding positive points the fact that Ockham never once discussed specific means by which the will of the people should be determined in the process of establishing a government, we must conclude that his doctrine of consent was far less developed than that of some contemporaries.[82] This is a fact which needs to be explained. In particular, we must ask what protection Ockham offered against the ultimate misuse of a secular power which he had so completely deprived of a religious basis. By espousing and further developing the negative, desacralizing portion of laicism, he removed a traditional restraint on the brutality of Western

of the various species of constitution recognized by Aristotle includes democracy and 'polity' (*ibid.*, 2, viii, fol. 193vab), his discussion of constitutional change in that tract is framed entirely in terms of monarchy and aristocracy.

80 *Ibid.*, xviii, fol. 197va, disscussed further below, pp. 160–1. Also see *ibid.*, xix, fols. 197vb–198vb, quoted in part by Gewirth, *Marsilius of Padua and Medieval Political Philosophy*, p. 236n.

81 Cf. Thomas Aquinas, who held that popular choice of rulers was an important part of the best constitution: 'Dicendum quod circa bonam ordinationem principum in aliqua civitate vel gente, duo sunt attendenda. *Quorum unum est ut omnes aliquam partem habeant in principatu* . . . Talis enim est optima politia, *bene commixta ex regno* . . . *et aristocratia* . . . *et ex democratia, idest potestate populi, inquantum ex popularibus possunt eligi principes, et ad populum pertinet electio principum*' (*Summa Theologiae* ɪaɪɪae, q. 105, a. 1, *resp.*).

82 For St Thomas, see the preceding note. Although the primordial consent of the community remains an important basis for legitimacy in Ockhamist thought, it is misleading to combine Ockham with Marsilius as an exponent of popular sovereignty. So far as I have been able to determine, Ockham never construes political consent as a matter of individual agreement to the powers and laws of government, nor, in particular, do I know of any text which suggests that all have to agree upon what the dictates of right reason are. For differences between Ockham and Marsilius on this matter, see above, pp. 61–2.

European politics. He did not, however, attempt to fill the resulting moral vacuum by a full-fledged acceptance of the positive side of laicist or Aristotelian thought. He did not develop a detailed theory of popular sovereignty or republican institutions, as did Marsilius of Padua, nor did he found his conception of political institutions on a theory of the needs and fulfillments of human nature, as did St Thomas and his followers. To be sure, there was still room for a theory of casual papal intervention in secular affairs in extreme emergencies, but the reduction to merely ceremonial value of the pope's normal role in instituting lay rulers should make us skeptical about the effectiveness of casual papal action once the ruler was established. Yet Ockham was more sensitive than any of his contemporaries to the danger of concentrating all power in one place. 'In a community subject to one supreme judge, that judge could by his wrongdoing destroy justice and even endanger the whole community, which is repugnant to the best ordering of any community whatever.' In view of Ockham's sensitivity to the misuse of power, his failure to embrace a consistent ascending theory after rejecting the theocratic descending theme constitutes a major problem in the interpretation of his thought.

2. THE FUNCTIONS OF SECULAR POWER

In trying to state Ockham's view of the basis for legitimate secular power, we have reached an impasse. On one hand, he rejected the traditional idea that all political legitimacy depends on participation in divine justice mediated by the holder of the divinely created papal office. He stressed instead the strictly human origin of current distributions of property and jurisdiction. On the other hand, he was so far from espousing a theory of government based on the continuing consent of the governed, that he cannot be described as an unqualified supporter of ascending ideas of law and government.

As a way out of this impasse, it will be helpful to consider another question raised earlier: what, for Ockham, are the functions of secular political power? He himself indicates that the questions of basis and function are connected. As he puts it at the beginning of his discussion of world government, if it is inexpedient that the human race be ruled by one supreme governor in *temporalia*, then the so-called rights (*iura*) of the Roman empire would not be rights but positive wrongs (*iniuriae*).[83] In other words, claims to legitimate authority are hardly worth discussing if the power to be legitimated serves no useful function. Conversely, if we can determine the duties of secular government, this may shed light on the basis Ockham provides for political legitimacy.

Ockham's clearest discussions of the functions of secular power are found in the treatment of world government just referred to and in the third of the *Octo Quaestiones*, where he considers what is required by, inconsistent with, or compatible with, the best form of government. Other passages will be referred to for clarification of details.

In accord with the assumption that political legitimacy depends at least partly on the usefulness of the institution in question, the first thing Ockham asks about the rights of the Roman Empire is whether it pertains to the 'commodity' and 'utility' of all mankind for the world to be subject in temporal matters to one emperor or secular prince.[84] Five opinions are examined, the first of which answers the question affirmatively.[85] Although, as we shall see, Ockham did not accept so simple an answer without important qualifications, the functions he attributed to secular power are well revealed in the eleven reasons given for this opinion. In outline, the arguments run as follows. The regime of one secular prince is best because:

(1) By such a regime evildoers could be coerced more easily, beneficially, effectively, justly, and severely, and the good could live more quietly among the bad.[86]

(2) Temporal matters should be ordered by secular rulers and

---

83 'Romani iura imperii non iura, sed iniuriae et iniustitiae ac crudeles tyrannides non indigne censeri deberent, si nullatenus expediret unum imperatorem seu principem cunctas mundi provincias gubernare. Cum Romani super universum orbem sibi usurpaverunt principatum.' III *Dialogus* II, 1, i, fol. 230rb.

84 'De iuribus imperii Romani plurima quaesiturus et ante omnia, an expediat esse unum imperatorem totius orbis interrogare decrevi, aut ad totius generis humani commodum et utilitatem pertineat totum orbem terrarum in temporalibus uni imperatori seu principi saeculari subesse.' *Ibid.*

85 'Per unum principem saecularem qui non incongrue imperatoris nomine censetur, mundus quoad temporalia optime regeretur. Nec sufficienter paci et quieti totius societatis humanae potest per aliud regimen provideri.' *Ibid.*

86 'Per regimen unius principis saecularis qui super universum orbem habeat potestatem, mali facilius, salubrius efficacius, iustius ac severius coercentur, et boni quietius vivunt inter malos.' III *Dialogus* II, 1, i, fol. 230va.

laymen in the same way spiritual matters are administered by priests and ecclesiastics. But even if the whole world were converted to the faith, it would be expedient for all believers to obey one supreme pontiff in spiritual matters. Therefore, it is expedient for the whole world to be under one emperor in temporal matters.[87]

(3) Just as it is expedient for any part of the world to be subject to one secular ruler, so it is for the whole world.[88]

(4) All those who have – or can have – communication with one another in temporal matters should be subject in these matters to one supreme ruler. But all mortals can have such a relation with one another, no matter how far apart they are in space. Wherefore, all ought to have one secular ruler.[89]

(5) Discord would be more effectively abolished among mortals if all were subject to one secular ruler.[90]

(6) Disputes and litigations are more conveniently decided if the parties have a common judge or ruler.[91]

(7) If all rulers were subject to the emperor, not only inferiors but superiors, too, could be corrected for wrongdoing.[92]

(8) In order for true concord to grow and for everyone to give proper respect or affection to everyone else, there ought to be a

---

[87] 'Sicut spiritualia per sacerdotes et viros ecclesiasticos ministrantur et temporalia per principes saeculares et laicos disponuntur . . . Sed quamvis totus mundus esset ad fidem conversus universitati fidelium expediret uni summo pontifici in spiritualibus obedire . . . Igitur universo orbi expedit uni imperatori in temporalibus subesse.' *Ibid.*, fol. 230vab.

[88] 'Simile iudicium tenendum est de toto et de parte, in magnis et in parvis . . . Sed cuilibet regno partiali quod est pars mundi expedit quod uni principi saeculari sit subiectum . . . Igitur similiter . . .' *Ibid.*, fol. 230vb.

[89] 'Omnes qui communicationem in temporalibus habent ad invicem aut habere possunt, ut quilibet posset iuvare [reading *iuvare* for Trechsel's *invenire*] pariter et nocere non optime gubernantur, nisi uni summo principi quoad temporalia sint subiecti . . . Sed omnes mortales quocunque spatio terrarum distantes ad invicem possunt habere communionem . . . Quare . . . unum principem saecularem debet habere.' *Ibid.*, fols. 230vb–231ra.

[90] 'Si universitas fidelium uni principi saeculari fuerit subiecta efficacius tolletur inter mortales discordia, quam si plures fuerint principes unum superiorem non habentes.' *Ibid.*, fol. 231ra.

[91] 'Convenientius iurgia et litigia inter litigantes si unum habuerint iudicem vel dominum aut principem deciduntur quam si habuerint plures qui uni minime sint subiecti.' *Ibid.*, fol. 231rb.

[92] 'Si omnes reges fuerint imperatori subiecti, non solum inferiores, sed etiam superiores si deliquerint poterunt legitime castigari.' *Ibid.*

connection among all mortals such that each man is related to each other as his superior, his inferior, or as a common inferior to the same superior. But there will be no such connection among all mortals unless one presides over all the others.[93]

(9) The regime which God abolished because of the sins of the multitude is better than that which he introduced to punish those sins. But God ordains that many should rule over all mortals, rather than one, as punishment for men's sins.[94]

(10) If it were inexpedient that there be one emperor, this would be either because no one sufficient for the office could be found, or because of the excessive force that a single lord of all would have at his disposal, by which he could devastate his subjects at will. But neither of these is a sufficient impediment.[95]

(11) If it were not expedient that there be one emperor over the whole world, it would not be just. But if it were not just it would be wrong, and then it would be against the law (*contra ius*). It is not against the law, however, either natural law or positive law. Therefore, it is not wrong for one man to hold empire over the whole world. Hence, it is expedient.[96]

These arguments present numerous points of interest. However, it seems possible to formulate the essential features of Ockham's position in the following three theses: (1) The chief aim of secular

---

93 'Inter omnes mortales debet esse connexio ut quilibet respectu alterius sit inferior vel superior aut ambo inferiores respectu eiusdem ut inter omnes vera fiat concordia, et quilibet cuilibet reverentiam vel dilectionem impendat . . . sed talis non est inter cunctos mortales connexio, nisi unus praesideat omnibus aliis.' III *Dialogus* II, 1, i, fol. 231rb–va.

94 'Illud regimen quod Deus inter mortales propter peccatum multitudinis non permittit sed aufert, est melius illo, quod Deus propter peccata multitudinis punienda introducit. Sed quod supra universitatem mortalium non dominetur unus sed multi, ordinat Deus propter peccata mortalium punienda.' *Ibid.*, fol. 231va. The reference is to Proverbs 28: 2.

95 'Si non expedit universitatem mortalium uni imperatori subesse, aut hoc est propter insufficientiam humanam, quia nullus poterit sufficiens reperiri . . . aut propter nimiam potentiam temporalem unius domini totius, qua posset secundum libitum in subiectos debacchare. Sed insufficientia non impedit . . . Nec nimia potentia impedit . . .' III *Dialogus* II, 1, i, fol. 231va.

96 'Si non expediat universo orbi unum imperatorem praeesse, non est iustum . . . si autem non est iustum nec expediens, est iniquum . . . sed non est iniquum, quia esset contra ius . . . sed non contra ius naturale . . . Nec etiam contra ius positivum . . . Igitur non est iniquum unum super universum orbem habere imperium, quare expediens est censendum.' *Ibid.*, fol. 231vab.

government is the negative one of preventing or punishing injustice. (2) The proper beneficiaries of political thought and action are concrete individuals rather than abstract corporate wholes. There is a corporatism in Ockham, but it is one of human solidarity rather than a priority given to the social or political whole over its individually insignificant parts. (3) Since governments are to be assessed primarily for their instrumental value in promoting ends beyond themselves and not for the degree to which they themselves embody permanent metaphysical or religious values, different regimes may be expedient in different circumstances.

(1) The essentially negative function of secular government is revealed most clearly in the first of Ockham's eleven arguments: The most expedient regime is that which best controls evildoers and allows good men to live more quietly among them. All that is asked for the 'good' is that they be able to live among the 'bad' 'more quietly'. There is no thought of contributing to their good life in a positive fashion. The business of government is rather with the 'bad', who must be coerced. The New Testament passages appealed to here include a positive component for the *boni*, namely, that they should receive 'praise' or 'good' from the government,[97] but Ockham does not pick this up. Rather, after citing additional authoritative support, he adds a further negative qualification in stating the minor premise of the argument: 'By the regime of one secular ruler with power over the whole world, evildoers would be more easily, beneficially, effectively, justly, *and severely (severius)* coerced.'[98]

The fifth, sixth, and seventh arguments are also based mainly on this negative or peace-keeping function of secular government: the removal of discord is primary in the fifth, as much as is possible in the present life. The sixth goes into more detail as to the greater equity and convenience with which disputes and law-suits (to which the nature of mortals is prone) can be decided when the litigants have safe recourse to a common judge.[99] The seventh argument, again, is not concerned with achieving the coordination of great powers

---

[97] 1 Peter 2: 14 and Romans 13: 3–4. III *Dialogus* II, 1, i, fol. 230rb.
[98] *Ibid.*, fol. 230va.
[99] 'Si enim litigantes quorum unus alteri damnum vel nocumentum intulit aut ius suum pluribus regibus vel principibus superiorem non habentibus sint subiecti facilius poterit periclitari iustitia nec apparet sub quo iudice tutum sit utrique parti litigare'. *Ibid.*, fol. 231rb.

for positive ends. It is a matter, rather, of providing means by which the great powers, as well as those subject to them, can be punished if they are delinquent, for when there are many kings or rulers without a superior in different parts of the world, they can disturb the peace and the rights of lesser folk freely and with impunity (*libere et impune pacem et iura minorum perturbare valebunt*).[100]

The minimal character of secular governmental functions is still more salient in *Octo Quaestiones* III, where an emphasis on punishment as the ruler's principal task is crucial in resolving the issue of papal power. In this important discussion, which may well be regarded as the central text in Ockham's defense of dualism, the question is whether all mortals ought to have one supreme judge in both *temporalia* and *spiritualia*. In explicit contrast with the monistic answers to this question, Ockham presents the complex opinion that both pope and lay ruler may have universal coercive power, the pope in spiritual matters and another judge only in temporal matters, and that notwithstanding this, the community of mortals could still be optimally ordered (*tamen communitas mortalium hoc non obstante poterit esse optime ordinata*).[101] As he immediately points out, the proposition that no community can be best ordered unless it is subject to one supreme judge is rejected here. In place of this monistic axiom – the piece of common ground on which Marsilius of Padua and the papalists may be said to have fought all their battles – it must be established that regular exemption from the coercive jurisdiction of a supreme judge is possible in a well-ordered community so long as the person involved is subject to that jurisdiction casually, when the common good would otherwise be endangered.[102] The establishment of a thesis at once so reasonable and so potentially anarchic is no simple matter. It calls for a general examination of what is required for the best government, prelacy, leadership, or regime, what is repugnant to it, and what things should be regarded as compatible with it.[103] We find Ockham's clearest brief statement of the functions of secular government at the end of this inquiry. For it to be evident what is compatible with the best government, although not essential to it ('licet ad essentiam eius nequaquam pertineant, sed sibi adesse valeant et deesse'), it must be known before all that,

---

[100] *Ibid.*
[102] *OQ* III, 3; *OP* I, 105.
[101] *OQ* III, 3; *OP* I, 104.
[103] *OQ* III, 4–10; *OP* I, 105–15.

although many things pertain to the kind of rulership under discussion – namely, to grant and preserve everyone's rights, to enact necessary and just laws, to establish lower judges and other officials, to direct what arts ought to be practised in the community subject to it and by whom, to enjoin the acts of all the virtues, and many other things – yet it seems to be most principally instituted for this, that it may correct and punish wrongdoers (*tamen ad hoc videtur principalissime institutus ut corrigat et puniat delinquentes*). For in a community in which no one needed to be punished for a fault or a wrong act, a monitor and teacher of the good would suffice, and a ruler would be wholly superfluous, which is gathered from the holy scriptures. For law and the ruler seem to be most principally instituted for the same things. The law, however, is not instituted because of the good, but for correcting and punishing the bad, as the apostle testifies in 1 Timothy 1: [9] 'The law is not laid on the just but on the unjust and rebellious.'[104]

On the basis of this conception of the *principalissima* function of secular government, Ockham is able to establish his striking denial of the unitary thesis that no community is well governed unless it is subject to one supreme judge. For so long as the pope does not commit crimes, there is no reason to regard him as under the secular prince. The independence of spiritual authority is achieved by emphasizing the negative, peace-keeping function of temporal authority. *Per contra* this effect is achieved by ignoring other possible functions of secular government, in particular the last three items on the list: the establishment of lower judges *and other officials*, direction of the arts, and the promotion of virtue.[105] For it is these items at the ethically elevated end of politics that verge into the spiritual domain and seem to require either a subjugation of church to state or state to church. By treating these as, in effect, non-essential functions of secular rulership, matters which may be present or absent in the operations of government in various circumstances, Ockham provides a buffer zone between the necessary business of temporal

---

[104] *OQ* III, 8; *OP* I, 112–13.
[105] *OQ* III, 8; *OP* I, p. 113. Cf. the much more inspiring purposes for world monarchy envisioned by Dante, for whom the emperor was to lead men to an earthly blessedness according to philosophical teachings (*Monarchia*, III, 16, pp. 375–6) or promote the 'finis universalis civilitatis humani generis', that is, the full realization of the understanding in both speculation and practice ('actuare semper totam potentiam intellectus possibilis, per prius ad speculandum, et secundario propter hoc ad operandum per suam extensionem') (*ibid.*, I, 4, p. 343).

politics and the higher activities of Christian religious institutions.[106] This text from the *Octo Quaestiones*, to which we shall return in other connections, thus confirms the conclusion suggested by the arguments for world government in III *Dialogus*: a certain negative emphasis is an important component of Ockham's conception of the functions of secular government.

(2) In several of the arguments for world monarchy in III *Dialogus* II as well as elsewhere, Ockham shows more interest in the concrete body of individuals living under various conditions of government than in sovereignty or political unity as values in themselves. He observes, for example, that the absence of a single ruler encourages promptness and audacity in carrying on feuds and wars, and that wars among kings, princes, and counts who refuse to submit to one government tend to be more dangerous and cruel than differences among subjects of a single ruler. It is not only a matter of disorder among abstract institutions. Ockham is evidently concerned with the destructive effects of war on human beings. In time of war the evil grow insolent and the good are disturbed in many ways – *insolescunt mali et boni multipliciter turbantur.*[107] An orientation towards individual rights and wrongs rather than formal political structures is also apparent in Ockham's second and fourth arguments for world monarchy. In form, the second argument is an elegant piece of scholastic parallelism which derives the right order in *temporalia* from the right order in *spiritualia*: papal monarchy in one suggests that imperial monarchy is best in the other. In its conclusion, however, the argument is an attack on clerical immunities for secular crimes and thus challenges the traditional hierarchical ordering of society by classes: for Ockham's contention is that the whole earth should be under one secular ruler in temporal matters, not only as such matters concern laymen, but also inasmuch as they concern pope and clergy.[108] Instead of construing political problems in

---

[106] None of this implies that politics is amoral. As we have seen (pp. 98, 100–1), the early Christians were morally obliged to respect pagan judges as dispensers of justice, not because resistance would bring retribution. Similarly, the function of secular rulers in the negative arguments just examined is to punish 'the bad', or wrong-doers, and to settle disputes equitably as well as conveniently.

[107] III *Dialogus* II, 1, i, fol. 230va.

[108] 'Sed quamvis totus mundus esset ad fidem conversus universitati fidelium expediret uni summo pontifici in spiritualibus obedire non solum inquantum spiritualia concernunt clericos, sed etiam inquantum concernunt laicos.' *Ibid.*, fol. 230vb.

terms of the relations among orders in a corporate hierarchy, Ockham treats them in terms of the common needs of the entire range of individuals making up society. It is important to recognize, though, that we are not confronted here with a politics of atomic or isolated individuals. Ockham's fourth argument for world monarchy is especially helpful on this point, because of its emphasis on corporate humanity. Ockham is corporatist, however, in a pre-political way. The 'corpus' in question is a concrete body of individuals: the human community, mankind, not legally organized society.

The major premise of this fourth argument is that all who have or can have temporal activities in common with one another (*communicationem in temporalibus . . . ad invicem*) are best governed only if they are subject in these matters to one prince. Ockham gives several proofs for this premise, arguing that all who can have such *communicatio* make up or can make up one people, one fold and flock, one city, company, family, or realm. In each case there is a need for unity.[109] These proofs make the need for government depend on concrete possibilities for communication among individuals, rather than upon the aesthetic or ideal attractiveness of a well-ordered political structure. Ockham's treatment of the minor premise of this argument further strengthens the 'pre-political' character of the community he is concerned with. It is necessary to show that all mortals, by whatever portion of earth they are distant from one another, can have communion (*communionem*) with one another, so that they become – or are able to become, unless malice disjoins them – one people, one fold, one flock, one body, one city, one company, one family, one realm.[110] This is established by reference to Scripture, but not by citing Biblical endorsements of the Roman Empire or any other political unit actually embracing the world.

109 *Ibid.*, fols. 230vb–231ra. The argumentation here is unusually traditional and metaphorical in tone: for one flock there ought to be one pastor, a body or city with no head or more heads than one is 'monstruosum', and so on. Still, those who can have temporal contact with one another seem to *be* a body for Ockham with or without a head – the head does not so much make them one as secure them from becoming many.

110 *Ibid.*, fol. 231ra. The negative final clause should be noted. The primary function of government is not to promote *communicatio* directly, but to prevent disintegration of the conditions which make *communicatio* possible.

Instead, Ockham sets out, as the basis and goal of government, the ideal notions of the organic interdependence of the human race, universal brotherhood and the unity of the whole world as a kingdom of God:

Thus the Apostle in Romans 12: [5] 'we are all one body in Christ, each a member of the other', manifestly suggesting that just as all mortals, not only believers but unbelievers, ought by renouncing the devil through faith and love to adhere more firmly to Christ, so all, if they were well ordered, ought to be one body. Solomon, too, says in Proverbs 10 [actually Proverbs 18: 19], 'A brother aided by a brother is as a firm city', intimating that, just as all mortals of the world are brothers, so, unless malice impedes them, they ought to become one city. Thus the wise man says in Wisdom 6 [4–5], rebuking wicked kings, 'Power has been given you by the Lord and strength by the most high, who will ask about your works and search into your thoughts, since when you were ministers of that realm, you did not judge it rightly.' From which words it is given to be understood that, although there are many rulers established by the Lord . . . yet the whole world is one realm.[111]

In view of such arguments, it is impossible to describe Ockhamist political institutions as purely conventional constructions of permanently isolated individuals. It is precisely to avoid becoming isolated – to avoid being disjoined by malice – that mortals who are already together set up governments. Ockham had in mind corporate but non-political reference points for evaluating the benefits of various forms of government. Instead of viewing society as the source of moral personality or status, he found such values in man's situation prior to the establishment or activities of any government, yet there is no ground for attributing to him the view that pre-political man exists in a state of radical ethical separation from his fellows. On the contrary, it is because all men are brothers that they should form a city. It is because all humanity already forms one kingdom in an informal sense that the existing political situation (where there are many kings) should be transcended. The values appealed to here are social, not individualistic. Under suitable political conditions these values are likely to flourish; the possibilities of *communicatio* can be realized. Under adverse political conditions they will be menaced; in times of war the bad grow insolent and the good are disturbed.

111 *Ibid.*, fol. 231ra.

In both suitable and adverse conditions, however, the specifically political component in human affairs, the apparatus of law and government, will be distinct from and secondary in value to the larger human *corpus* which it regulates.

Perhaps the clearest expression of this idea of an autonomous communal life 'subject' to government but at the same time moved by its own impulses and possessing intrinsic value is Ockham's defense of liberty. Once again, the central text is his discussion in *Octo Quaestiones* III of what is required by, repugnant to, or compatible with, the best form of government. There we learn that the best form of government cannot be exercised exclusively over the unfree – over slaves and servants (*servi*). Indeed, Ockham reports, some find it incompatible with the purity of the best government for *any* subject to be a *servus* without his own fault, especially against his will.[112] He supports this position by three arguments which reveal both the temper of his concern for liberty and also the tension between his ideas and traditional medieval views. The first argument rests on the assumption that government over the unfree is always despotic, that is, operates principally for the good of the ruler. On this assumption, such a regime is obviously not optimal, since the best regime is instituted for the good of the subjects.[113] This is ultimately a fair enough rendering of Aristotle,[114] but it ignores the Platonic and hierocratic assimilation of political rule to the father's care for his family, with its associated concept of freedom as subordination to the good.[115] On such a view, one cannot speak of the subject as a slave or servant, or of government as despotic, and yet the idea of comprehensive direction from above plays a central and positive

[112] *OQ* III, 6; *OP* I, 111. In suggesting that it may be incompatible with the best regime that there be *any servi* under it, Ockham goes well beyond Aristotle.
[113] *OQ* III, 6; *OP* I, 111.
[114] Aristotle, *Politics*, III, 6–7, 1278*b*–1279*b*.
[115] Plato, *Republic*, I, 342a–345e; *Statesman*, 267a–d, 293b–e. For freedom in the Augustinian and Platonic traditions more generally, see R. P. McKeon, *Freedom and History* (New York, 1952), pp. 48ff. For the contrast between papalist and Marsilian conceptions of freedom, see Gewirth, *Marsilius of Padua and Medieval Political Philosophy*, pp. 221–2. Ockham differed from both Marsilius and the papalists in construing the individual's political freedom as an absence of interference *from* government, not in terms of a positive relation *to* government (as either an efficient cause in legislation or as an ordered part of the corporate whole).

part. Although Aristotle criticized this conception of political authority, he himself used it in his treatment of monarchy.[116] Here Ockham departs still further from Plato than does Aristotle.[117] He accepts the paternal model for papal government, though with important restrictions as to its consequences, but in the secular sphere this model is not even mentioned.[118]

Ockham's second argument in favor of free subjects also depends on a significant assumption, namely, that prospective rulers are not likely to be radically superior to all their subjects in virtue and wisdom – or at least not to what their subjects can become. On this assumption, it is obvious that government exercised exclusively over *servi* is against nature and unjust, for it is unjust and against nature that anyone should rule as slaves his betters in virtue and wisdom, or his equals, or even those who can reasonably be hoped to become his betters or equals in the future.[119] Ockham's assumption here is important in view of Aristotle's use of the same moral point as an argument justifying constitutional government. If the citizens are equal in virtue and wisdom, Aristotle argued, they should take turns at ruling and being ruled.[120] Ockham, as we have seen, did not favor regular changes of rulers, but he used the rough equality between

[116] Aristotle, *Politics*, I, 12, 1260b 10–18; *Nic. Ethics*, VIII, 10, 1160b 24ff. Aristotle criticizes Plato in *Politics*, I, 1, 1252a 7–18.

[117] Ockham's conception of freedom also differs from Dante's. Dante agreed that freedom involved existing for one's own sake, not for another ('illud est liberum quod suimet et non alterius gratia est', *Monarchia*, Book I, c. 12, p. 347). Since, however, he held that a man is free only when judgment moves appetite ('si . . . ab appetitu . . . iudicium moveatur, liberum esse non potest, quia non a se, sed ab alio captivum trahitur') he did not conclude that freedom was to be achieved by leaving men alone. On the contrary, he argued that the greatest freedom would exist under a world monarchy because a monarch would want all men to become good ('cum Monarcha maxime diligat homines . . . , *vult omnes homines bonos fieri*').

[118] See below, pp. 156–9. On the 'non-naturalness' of even a monarchical constitution, see above, p. 86.

[119] 'Iniustum est et contra naturam ut quis maioribus aut aequalibus et sibi similibus vel de quibus spes probabilis esse potest quod futuri sunt maiores aut aequales et sibi similes virtute et sapientia, principetur tanquam servis, ut Aristoteles . . . videtur asserere. Quod etiam Ieronymus testari videtur, cum dicit . . . "Vilissimus computandus est nisi praecellat scientia et sanctitate, qui est honore praestantior." Hinc Sapiens Ecclesiastici [32: 1] . . . rectorem et principem instituens et informans, ait: "Rectorem te posuerunt, noli extolli; esto in illis quasi unus ex ipsis."' *OQ* III, 6; *OP* I, 111.   [120] Aristotle, *Politics*, II, 2, 1261b 1–5.

ruler and subjects as a basis for arguing that monarchy should have some of the characteristics of constitutional government. It should not be permeated by a sense of the overall superiority of rulers. Ockham makes a somewhat strained use of Jerome here which provides a vivid illustration of his own convictions. Where Jerome had apparently believed that only exceptionally learned and holy men should be made rulers, Ockham alleges him to show that a ruler should not be 'honored' above his subjects unless he is also their superior in these other respects. More happily, Ockham cites Ecclesiasticus to show that the ruler should be regarded as someone placed in office by the people. He should bear himself, therefore, as if he were one of them, *quasi unus ex ipsis*. Such sentiments are in sharp contrast with the hierarchical spirit of political Augustinism.

The third argument for liberty is taken from Aristotle and is one to which Ockham attached some importance, for he also developed it elsewhere. He asserts that the quality of a form of government depends on the quality of its subjects: the better the subjects, the better the regime. Since free men are better than unfree, the 'best' regime will be over the former. Hence, it is repugnant to the best regime to be entirely over *servi*.[121] In this argument, Ockham once again differs from Plato and Augustine, for whom the best regime is that in which the best element is dominant. For this tradition, the quality of a community thus depends on the quality of its rulers. For Ockham the reverse is the case. As he puts it elsewhere, although a despotic regime is in some quantitative sense 'greater' and 'more perfect' than a royal government because in a certain way it extends to more things, yet for this very reason it is simply speaking less perfect: 'In a despotic government there is harm to many *just from this*, that the despot *can* use his subjects and their goods for his private benefit.' The contrast is not merely between governments which aim, respectively, at the ruler's good and the good of his subjects, but between regimes which are permitted even as a possibility to 'use' their subjects as *servi* and those whose subjects enjoy their natural liberty.[122]

---

[121] 'Melior est principatus qui est meliorum subiectorum, sicut melior est principatus hominum quam bestiarum. Liberi autem meliores sunt quam servi.' *OQ* III, 6; *OP* I, 112.

[122] 'Principatus despoticus est quodammodo maior, quia ad plura quodammodo se extendit, sed ex hoc ipso est imperfectior ... In principatu autem despotico est

Taken together, the pre-political corporatism noted earlier and the defense of freedom just discussed yield a remarkably balanced conception of the relation between governments and subjects. On this basis, we may begin to answer some of our questions about the secular side of Ockham's institutional dualism. It seems clear, for example, that the restraining influence traditionally exerted on secular rulers by the papacy is continued in Ockham's scheme by a self-consciously free body of subjects. There is no reason to think of these free men as selfish individualists, but their collective attitude towards those in authority would be anything but servile. For Ockham, it would be nearer the truth to say that government should be the servant of the community, rather than the reverse. To be sure, the Ockhamist community does not have a unilateral right to withdraw its obedience from one government and establish another. Even with this important qualification, however, Ockham's conception of government remains predominantly an instrumental one. The view that government exists for the sake of the governed gains considerable support from Ockham's exaltation of the governed as a community of free men.

(3) The eleven arguments for world monarchy at the beginning of III *Dialogus* II support a limited and instrumental conception of secular government. Although the community is not regularly master of its government, government is nevertheless meant to serve the interests of the community. Implicit in this notion of government as merely an effective means of promoting the public interest is the suggestion that regimes failing to achieve this goal are therefore inexpedient. The expediency of a regime will be contingent upon its performance in actual circumstances and may, accordingly, vary. In explicitly accepting this consequence of his earlier analysis, Ockham differed from most of his contemporaries, who tended to ascribe a high intrinsic value to some one permanently valid regime. For just as the papalists construed the ideal of human or Christian solidarity in terms of an organized body, so the head of this organic structure, the papal government, was viewed as having unique and unsurpassed value in itself. To be sure, in this way of thinking the

detrimentum multorum ex hoc ipso quod despotes potest uti sibi subiectis et bonis eorum ad propriam utilitatem . . . Propter quod principatus despoticus. . . esset simpliciter imperfectior principatu . . . regali.' III *Dialogus* I, 2, vi, fol. 193r*ab*. Cf. *Imp. Pont. Pot.*, c. 6, p. 462.

papacy served vital functions, and it was an instrument of God – but it was an instrument which actually embodied divine characteristics.[123] Hence, relative to the body of Christians it was by no means a merely utilitarian institution. Accordingly, in a direct comparison of the head and members of the church, Augustinus Triumphus could conclude that the papal head was of greater value than all the members combined: 'Since the good of the church does not exist except because of the good of the pope, the pope's good is greater than that of the whole church.'[124] The situation is to some extent similar at the opposite end of the political spectrum with Marsilius of Padua. Marsilius' political doctrine is like Ockham's in the moderateness of its goal, the preservation of a rather mundane state of peace. For Marsilius, however, there was a necessary and invariable connection between this goal and the means to be employed in attaining it. Popular legislative control of government was as essential in his system as monarchic control from above was in the systems of his papalist opponents.[125] Again, Dante, along with a more elevated conception of the aims of secular government than Ockham's, put forward more speculative reasons for supposing that this aim would be best achieved by monarchy. We find him commending unity on metaphysical grounds or as a way for the human race to attain a maximum assimilation to God or to the heavens.[126] Even Dante's pro-monarchical use of the principle of parsimony makes this a matter of metaphysical propriety rather than practical efficiency: superfluity is bad because it is displeasing to God and nature.[127] Ockham's position, like that of St Thomas,[128] allows for

---

[123] On the distinction between instruments which embody the characteristics of the agent employing them and those which are neutral or even capable of acting contrary to their principal agent's intentions, see Wilks, *Sovereignty in the Later Middle Ages*, pp. 493–8.

[124] Augustinus Triumphus, *Summa de Potestate Ecclesiastica*, q. 6, a. 6, *ad* 2; cited and discussed by Kantorowicz, *The King's Two Bodies*, pp. 264–5.

[125] Although the people are the only holders of ultimate constitutional power for Marsilius, he was 'quite indifferent as to the "species of temperate government" which the state may have' (Gewirth, *Marsilius of Padua and Medieval Political Philosophy*, pp. 172–3), so long as the law by which that government acted was made by the people.   [126] Dante, *Monarchia*, Book I, cc. 5, 8–9.

[127] *Ibid.*, c. 14, p. 348: 'Omne superfluum Deo et Naturae displiceat, et omne quod Deo et Naturae displicet sit malum.'

[128] *Summa Theologiae*, Ia IIae, q. 97, a. 1, *resp.*: 'Lex recte mutari potest propter mutationem conditionum hominum, quibus secundum diversas eorum conditiones

basic constitutional variation in accord with changing circumstances. Instead of unqualifiedly accepting monarchy as the best form of government, he develops the more complex thesis that 'it is expedient to vary the regimes or dominions of mortals according to the variety, quality, and necessity of the times. Sometimes it may be expedient to have one secular or ecclesiastical ruler over all mortals, sometimes many secular or ecclesiastical rulers governing together; sometimes, indeed, it may be useful for many rulers not having a superior to preside over the different parts of the world.'[129] A brief examination of Ockham's grounds for this opinion will complete our survey of the proper functions of secular government.

The first and most substantial argument for the variable expediency of different constitutions is an appeal to the common utility.[130] Ockham did not rate all governments equal. Although he lacked the absolute commitment to a single regime that animated most contemporary political thought, he held that monarchy was usually best. Yet because Ockham's preference for monarchy was based on utilitarian rather than metaphysical or aesthetic considerations, on its effectiveness in providing just and peaceful conditions for communal life and not on its inherent excellence, his later qualification of this preference is readily intelligible. Such contingencies as the corruption of rulers and the shifting willingness of the multitude

diversa expediunt. Sicut Augustinus ponit exemplum in I *De Libero Arbitrio*, quod "si populus sit bene moderatus et gravis, communisque utilitatis diligentissimus custos, recte lex fertur qua tali populo liceat creare sibi magistratus, per quos respublica administretur. Porro si paulatim idem populus depravatus habeat venale suffragium, et regimen flagitiosis sceleratisque committant; recte adimitur populo talis potestas dandi honores, et ad paucorum bonorum redit arbitrium."'

[129] III *Dialogus* II, I, v, fol. 232vb. This is evidently Ockham's own position, since the arguments for the other opinions are all answered from the viewpoint of this fifth one, whereas the reasons given for this opinion are left standing. From the student's remarks at the beginning of chapter 6, it is reasonable to say that Ockham accepts the first (monarchical) opinion, but only as understood in terms of the fifth. 'Ista [quinta] opinio cum aliis opinionibus contrariis quantum ad aliqua concordare dinoscitur a quibusdam etiam in multis discrepare videtur, *vel forte a prima secundum intellectum aliquorum in nullo discordat*, licet quantum ad verba ei obviare videatur.' *Ibid.*, vi, fol. 233ra. Cf. OQ III, II; OP I, 115–16.

[130] 'Nam sicut leges pro communi utilitate debent institui . . . sic principes rectores et domini, tam saeculares quam ecclesiastici pro communi utilitate prae ceteris sunt praeponendi, quam etiam ipsi magis quam propriam procurare tenentur. Si enim utilitate communi propriam praeposuerint non rectores seu principes vel domini, sed tanquam tyranni sunt censendi.' III *Dialogus* II, I, v, fol. 232vb.

to sustain one or another government do not alter the ideal value of a monarchic regime, but may easily spoil it as a means to the common utility. In some conditions another regime might do better.[131] This is also the rationale of Ockham's reply to the first of the eleven arguments offered earlier for monarchy alone. It is regularly and frequently true, he concedes, that the bad are more strictly coerced and the good live more quietly when one secular ruler has dominion over all, yet in special cases this fails to be so (*hoc tamen in casibus specialibus fallit*).[132] One of these cases occurs when a substantial and powerful part of the world maliciously refuses to obey a single ruler and stirs up sedition and war. If the malicious would desist from these activities given independent rulers in different regions, world monarchy would in this case be inexpedient.[133] A universal monarchy would also become undesirable if the monarch used his power tyrannically, attacking good men who loved the republic and promoting evil men who aided him in his tyranny. Ockham notes that we can read about many such tyrants in the history books.[134] His discussion suggests, then, that monarchy is best if general agreement to it can be obtained and trustworthy rulers found. This position is not anarchic or disordered, though it does take serious account of changing circumstances without attempting to fit those circumstances into a systematic metaphysical or historical pattern.

Ockham's indications of cases in which world monarchy is inexpedient are given in connection with his argument from the common utility. This first argument for the variable expediency of different regimes gains further significance from comparison with the principal arguments accompanying it. The first of these is theological, its major premise being that the best government for all mortals will be most like that by which God disposed the people of Israel. But God disposed the Israelites sometimes to be ruled by one secular ruler, sometimes by one priestly ruler, and sometimes by several independent kings.[135] Ockham has previously given specific

---

[131] 'Nonnumquam autem magna multitudo mortalium nullatenus sustineret dominium unius, sed voluntarie se subderet dominio multorum vel simul regentium vel diversarum provinciarum curam gerentium et per consequens tunc per plures melius procuraretur communis utilitas quam per unum solum.' *Ibid.*, fol. 233r*a*.
[132] III *Dialogus* II, 1, vi, fol. 233r*b*.   [133] *Ibid.*
[134] III *Dialogus* II, 1, vi, fol. 233r*b*–v*a*. Nero and Domitian are given as examples.
[135] *Ibid.*, v, fol. 233r*a*.

arguments from the Old Testament for and against specific regimes.[136] These arguments and the one just cited express, in effect, a stand-off, one with which Ockham seems content. Accepting the general conclusion that different governments are right for different times, he does not pursue the matter further from the standpoint of Biblical theology. To speak of political Ockhamism as an attempt to fulfill the positive revealed will of God can thus be seriously misleading if it is meant to imply that concrete constitutional decisions are to be made by consulting Biblical texts.

The brief third argument for the variability of expedient regimes also comes to a stand-off, this time with respect to justice; for sometimes the world has licitly and justly been subject to the regime of one ruler, occasionally to the regime of many.[137] It would be wrong to say that Ockham found considerations of justice (in the sense of legitimacy) irrelevant in determining what government is expedient in given circumstances. Nevertheless, the purely instrumental principle of promoting the common welfare is predominant. In this connection it deserves mention that, although the place of traditional feudal institutions and ideas in Ockham's thought and the influence of English constitutional experience deserve study, he never appealed to mere custom as a basis for settling fundamental political questions. Quite the contrary, his only general discussion of *consuetudo* is an enumeration of ways in which an appeal to it may be refuted. The first such way is simply by showing that the custom alleged is unreasonable.[138]

---

[136] For an argument in favor of monarchy based directly on Biblical precedent see argument (9) above, p. 112. The corresponding anti-monarchical argument is given at III *Dialogus* II, I, ii, fol. 231vb: 'illud cuius contrarium est a Deo ordinatum, non est mundo expediens . . . Sed divisio regnorum ita ut diversis regibus non habentibus superiorem subsint non est a Deo vetitum sed ordinatum, ut patet III Regum xii et xiii.'

[137] *Ibid.*, v, fol. 233ra. No details are given for the minor premise.

[138] 'Et certe multae consuetudines, quas ecclesia Avinionica pro se allegat contra imperium, duabus viis principalibus, includentibus quam plurimas, possunt faciliter reprobari et annullari, ostendendo videlicet, quod vel non sunt rationabiles, vel quod nequaquam legitime sunt praescriptae. Potest autem ostendi, quod consuetudo non est rationabilis, si esset contra ius divinum vel contra bonos mores, si est periculosa, si est scandalosa, si est praeiudicialis bono communi vel etiam alicui personae, cui non possunt licite tolli iura et libertates suae, et aliis modis. Quod etiam consuetudo nequaquam legitime sit praescripta, potest multis modis ostendi, sicut per iura canonica et civilia liquet aperte.' *Imp. Pont. Pot.*, c. 19, p. 473.

Our survey has picked out three major aspects of Ockham's view of secular government. One, which may be described as a principle of moderation, locates the chief functions of government at the lower end of the range of activities statesmen and political thinkers have traditionally attended to. The clearest expression of this principle is the thesis that secular rulers are instituted 'most principally' to correct and punish wrongdoers. A second major component of Ockham's position is his use of non-political reference points for evaluating the benefits of government activity. This principle is at work most directly in his defense of personal liberty as a value to be respected by even the best of regimes, or rather, especially by the best regime. It also underlies several of his arguments for world government, as well as the qualifications he later adds to those arguments. Finally, we have pointed to an emphasis on contingent circumstances in Ockham which distinguishes his conception of government from most contemporary views, which emphasized the intrinsic value of some one preferred constitution. For Ockham, government is to be functional in a far more circumstantial and utilitarian way than for other writers, a fact indicated by his detailed development of the thesis that the most expedient form of government varies according to the needs of the times.

What bearing does such a moderate, instrumental, and circumstantial approach to the functions of secular power have on the problems arising from Ockham's desacralization of the basis of that power? Two suggestions may be made. One is, that Ockham lacked a doctrine of continuing participation in politics because of the primarily negative functions he assigned to government. Since no conspicuous degree of moral elevation or human fulfillment is to be found in punishing criminals, Ockham's failure to encourage broad participation in political affairs is a natural enough consequence of his view of what political affairs are like. Second, we may suggest that Ockham provided against the dangers of secular tyranny by his emphasis on personal liberty and his insistence on the circumstantial value of particular regimes. A community of free men under no ideological illusions about the eternal validity of their government should be harder to reduce to slavery than other populations. Such a community might set up rulers strong enough to coerce all classes of evildoers efficaciously without undue fear of the coercion becoming universal.

With regard to the basic problem of this chapter, the nature of Ockham's institutional dualism, the principle of moderation seems most important. In stressing the least elevated functions of secular government, Ockham presents a conception of lay power which ought normally to separate it from religious affairs. To this extent, Ockham's dualism consists of a disengagement of the two powers, rather than a plan for their harmonious cooperation. Instead of adding another theory determining what should be done in situations when both secular and spiritual interests were involved, Ockham attempted to limit the occurrence of such borderline cases. This, at least, is the conclusion from our examination of the secular side. Before we go on to consider ecclesiastical government, however, it will be well to test this conclusion by asking directly whether Ockham attributed specifically religious functions to secular rulers.

Spiritual functions for secular rulers?

The surest indication that Ockham did not intend secular rulers to have regular spiritual functions is found in the independent, extensive, and divinely ordained power he constantly attributed to the office of pope.[139] In none of his many discussions of papal

---

[139] 'Christus constituit beatum Petrum caput, principem, et praelatum aliorum apostolorum et universorum fidelium, dans ei regulariter in spiritualibus quoad omnia quae propter regimen communitatis fidelium quantum ad bonos mores, et quascunque necessitates spirituales fidelium sunt de necessitate facienda, vel omittenda, omnem potestatem in hiis quae non periculose sed provide, et ad utilitatem communem committerentur uni homini, ac libertatem et iurisdictionem etiam coactivam absque omni detrimento ac dispendio notabili et enormi iurium imperialium, regum, principum et aliorum quorumque laicorum vel clericorum quae eis iure naturali gentium, aut civili ante vel post institutionem legis evangelicae competebant . . . Et hanc potestatem . . . habent nunc regulariter ex iure divino successores beati Petri, scilicet Romani pontifices' (III *Dialogus* I, I, xvii, fols. 188vb–189ra). This passage is taken as an authentic expression of Ockham's views by both Jacob and Boehner (see above, pp. 38 and 40). Any doubts which might remain on this point can be removed by reading the passage in the full context of III *Dialogus* I. This will be attempted below, pp. 149–68. For similar passages, see *An Princeps*, c. 6; *OP* I, 255. *OQ* I, 7; *OP* I, 34–5. *Brev.* II, 20, pp. 99–100 (identified as Ockham's own opinion by Scholz). *Imp. Pont. Pot.*, cc. 8–10, pp. 465–6. Also see the passage quoted in note I above. In the personally bitter *Imp. Pont. Pot.*, c. 6, p. 460, Ockham emphasized the nobility of the 'mini-

plenitudo potestatis did he agree with Marsilius of Padua in denying all coercive power to the papacy, [140] and on more than one occasion he directly asserted the pope's superiority in *spiritualia* to all Christians, including, in particular, secular rulers.[141] Hence, it is impossible to agree that the claim to independence from secular jurisdiction which Ockham makes on behalf of the papacy in the *Octo Quaestiones* is an 'étrange plaidoyer'.[142] On the contrary, Ockham's contention that the best form of government allows for some power or jurisdiction in the community to be normally independent of the supreme secular ruler[143] seems not merely consistent with his other views, but a central pillar of his position. Certainly, Ockham recognized clearly enough that this contention contradicted the unitary principle, common to papalists and extreme secularists alike, that a well-ordered community must be subject to a single supreme judge. The guiding problem of the present chapter has been to understand his reflections on government as a response to conflicting applications of this monistic thesis. In the light of our interpretation, papal independence from secular jurisdiction appears as an integral part of Ockham's whole effort, not as a vestige of tradition. In the same light, the exclusion of secular rulers from regular control of ecclesiastical affairs also appears as a natural consequence of basic Ockhamist principles. To be sure, Ockham was severe in reserving to the lay government an ultimate jurisdiction over the church's temporal goods – 'especially superabundant goods'[144] – and he had

strativus' character of the papal office: 'In quo . . . maxime assimilatur, plus quam alius principatus saecularis institutus de facto, nobilissimo modo principatus regalis, qui forsitan numquam nec a Deo nec ab hominibus fuit super homines institutus, *et in quo superat dignitate omnes alios principatus*.' For the sense in which the papacy is *a solo Deo*, see below, note 207.

140 The Marsilian view is frequently presented but never accepted. III *Dialogus* I, I, xiii and xv, fols. 187vb–188ra and 188rb–va. *Ibid.* 4, x, fol. 224rab. *OQ* I, 7; *OP* I, 34, ll. 12–22. *Brev.* II, 20, p. 99, ll. 21–6.

141 In addition to the passages cited in note 139 see *OQ* II, 14; *OP* I, 95 (cited above, p. 91). *Imp. Pont. Pot.*, c. 12, p. 468: 'Quia in omni causa necessario diffinienda per iudicem regulariter vel casualiter iure divino potest esse iudex, ideo concedendum est, quod papa sub Christo est caput et iudex summus *omnium* fidelium. Non sic imperator . . .' For the continuation of this passage, see below, note 152.

142 Lagarde, *La naissance*, v, 258. See above, p. 32.

143 *OQ* III, 9; *OP* I, 113–15.

144 He was especially trenchant on this point in the *An Princeps*, a work in which Professor Jacob has found a strongly Erastian note ('Ockham as a political

some inclination to bring the clergy under secular jurisdiction for secular crimes.[145] A fair assessment of these matters would, however, need to consider his own conception of the proper functions of ecclesiastical government.[146] Another apparent sign of Erastianism is the sympathetic discussion in III *Dialogus* of a possible imperial right to choose the pope. A careful reading of the text shows, however, that Ockham did not consider such a right an essential part of the imperial office. Although he rejected any view of the papacy as a self-perpetuating institution competent to determine its own election procedures as it pleased, Ockham located the 'natural' right to elect the pope in the people over whom he was to exercise jurisdiction, not in the emperor. Hence, although it would not have been directly contrary to Ockham's principles for a Christian emperor to choose the pope, such a right could be renounced by the emperor, or it could be placed by popular consent in some person or group other than the emperor.[147]

> thinker', p. 101). 'Praelati et clerici regi Anglorum subiecti res non possident temporales, *praesertim superabundantes*, iure divino, sed iure humano ab ipso rege manante' (*An Princeps*, c. 7; *OP* I, p. 256). Ockham first supports this position with the negative contention that God has given no special possessions to ministers of the new law, and then fills the resulting legal vacuum by appeal to the principle, 'unusquisque in traditione seu collatione sive donatione rei suae potest legem quam vult imponere, dummodo nihil imponat quod sit lege superiori prohibitum' (*ibid.*, p. 257). From this he infers that the English churches are bound to respect the reasonable conditions for use of their property laid down by kings and other lay donors 'de necessitate salutis'.
>
> [145] See the second argument for world monarchy in III *Dialogus* II, cited above, pp. 110–11, discussed pp. 116–17. Also see below, pp. 136–7, where Ockham again seems to assume that all of the severest criminal punishments should be dispensed by secular rulers, no matter who the criminals are. In the first two books of III *Dialogus* II, Ockham carefully avoids asserting imperial jurisdiction over the clergy. This was to be among the topics treated in the (presumably unfinished) third book of the tract.
>
> [146] See below, pp. 133–49.
>
> [147] Ockham's thesis in a well-known chapter on *ius naturale* in III *Dialogus* II is that the *Romani* have a 'divine' right to elect the pope, since *ius divinum* can be extended to all *ius naturale*, and *ex iure naturali* a *people* lacking a ruler have the right to choose one. III *Dialogus* II, 3, vi, fols. 263ra–264rb. The emperor's (possible) right in papal elections is based on this natural–divine right of the Roman people to choose their own spiritual leader. The emperor's possession of this right is thus contingent on its not having been conceded to someone else: 'Imperator eo ipso quod est Christianus catholicus discretus et Romanus habet ius eligendi summum pontificem, *nisi eidem iuri tacite vel expresse renuntiet vel electio summi pontificis vel potestas et ius eligendi de consensu Romanorum alicui personae vel personis determinatae vel*

It seems clear, then, that for Ockham regular control of spiritual affairs was not essential to secular power. But what of the secular ruler's 'casual' jurisdiction in such matters? Can it not be said that Ockham's wholesale appeals for action by lay rulers in the case of papal heresy inevitably pointed towards the lay state? There is no denying the risk here, though a fair estimate demands that papal heresy should also be considered a grave danger. Even in the heat of his struggle to bring down John XXII, however, Ockham was careful to place strict limits on the secular judge's right of casual intervention. Thus, there is no suggestion in I *Dialogus* that the pope may be deposed simply because he is useless or mildly harmful to the church.[148] It is papal heresy that is at issue. But here, too, Ockham exercised caution when it came to lay intervention, for he distinguished sharply between cases of explicitly condemned heresy and cases in which the pope's heresy was not 'certain', because the doctrine involved had not been previously condemned by the church. Only in cases of the first sort can laymen coerce a pope whom the clergy will not or cannot depose. When the heresy in question has not already been condemned (or the contrary catholic truth explicitly approved), the case pertains to the universal church and a general council, or the Roman pontiff. It cannot be brought before a secular court: 'talis causa nunquam deferenda est ad iudicium saeculare'.[149]

determinatis concessa extiterit ita ut Romani non habent a papa potestatem ius eligendi summum pontificem' (*ibid.*, v, fol. 262rb).

[148] If, as Tierney concludes (*Foundations of the Conciliar Theory*, p. 175), John of Paris presented papal jurisdiction as 'a mere delegation from the Church', it is easy to understand why he sometimes seems to advocate deposing a pope in less extreme circumstances than are required in Ockham's doctrine. Thus, John argues that, 'efficacior est *consensus populi* in casu tali ad deponendum eum etiam invitum, si *totaliter inutilis* videatur, et ad eligendum alium, quam e converso voluntas ad renuntiandum populo nolente' (*Tractatus de Potestate Regia et Papali*, ed. Bleienstein, c. 24, p. 201). On the normal irrevocability of grants of secular power for Ockham, see above, pp. 106–7.

[149] 'Causa haeresis sicut causa fidei duplex est, quandoque enim vocatur causa haeresis, quando quaestio agitatur de aliquo quod manifestum est esse haeresim, quia est haeresis explicite condemnata... et ideo haec causa in casu speciali potest competere laicis super papam haereticum quem clerici nolunt vel non possunt coercere. Alia est causa haeresis sive fidei, quando quaestio de aliquo efficitur, quod non est certum esse haeresim, quia non est haeresis explicite condemnata, nec eius contrarium est veritas catholica explicite approbata et *talis causa haeresis vel fidei inter causas maximas computatur, nec diffinitio seu determinatio talis causae unquam spectat ad laicos illiteratos*, sed solummodo spectat ad ecclesiam universalem et

In such a situation, if the clergy fail to provide a properly ecclesiastical judgment, the matter must simply be left unresolved.[150] Thus, even at a time when he must have been tempted to ascribe as much power as possible to any enemy of John XXII, Ockham claimed only that the Christian secular ruler was obliged to defend truths already certified as authentically Christian by non-secular processes. Ockham firmly excluded the formulation of Christian truth by lay rulers either for their own ends or for the good of the church.

Even the right to intervene in clear cases of heresy came, however, to seem too great a concession to secular power as such. Here we have one of the few points on which a significant difference can be exhibited between Ockham's earlier and later convictions. In I *Dialogus* he had contended that a Christian emperor could intervene in ecclesiastical affairs as emperor, notwithstanding that in this capacity he succeeded pagans.[151] In III *Dialogus* II and in his latest important work, the *De Imperatorum et Pontificum Potestate*, he took the opposite view, contending that the Christian emperor has a right to casual intervention in ecclesiastical affairs only because he is a Christian, not insofar as he is emperor – for as emperor he succeeds pagans.[152] The factor Ockham had minimized near the beginning of his polemical career came to seem essential. For practical purposes, the difference was slight. The measures actually open to a secular

concilium generale, vel Romanum pontificem, *et ita talis causa nunquam deferenda est ad iudicium saeculare.*' I *Dialogus* 6, c, fol. 112vb. For the important distinction between implicitly and explicitly condemned heresy, see *ibid.*, 2, xvii–xxiv.

150 'Si tamen iudicium ecclesiasticum propter infidelitatem clericorum deficeret, talis causa tunc minime est tractanda.' *Ibid.*, 6, c, fol. 112vb.

151 Since the pagan emperors were obliged, as men, not as pagans, to worship God and abandon idolatry, it also pertained to them, as emperors, not as pagans, to defend catholics. Hence it pertains to those who succeed them in the imperial office (not in their paganism) to correct papal heresy if the clergy cannot or will not do so. *Ibid.*, fol. 113ra.

152 'Ideo concedendum est, quod papa sub Christo est caput et iudex summus omnium fidelium. Non sic imperator, quia *imperator, inquantum imperator*, cum multi veri imperatores fuerint infideles, *non debet se etiam casualiter spiritualibus immiscere*, licet si est fidelis, *in quantum fidelis, de multis causis spiritualibus* in multis casibus *se intromittere teneatur*, et praecipue de fidei causa, quae ad omnes omnino pertinet Christianos.' *Imp. Pont. Pot.*, c. 12, p. 468. The same distinction between *imperator inquantum imperator* and *imperator inquantum Christianus* is applied at III *Dialogus* II, 3, iv, fol. 261vab, to the emperor's right in papal elections. As against this, however, see the passage from the *Octo Quaestiones* quoted above, note 64.

ruler in such situations would have been substantially the same, whether he acted *qua* Christian or *qua* secular ruler. Nevertheless, there is a great difference in concept. Significantly enough, Ockham's final position on this point was less favorable to secular domination of the church than the view with which he started.

Ockham's changed position did not result from a general mellowing of his attitude to papalist ideas. In the *De Imperatorum et Pontificum Potestate* it was presented side-by-side with his bitterest denunciations of the *ecclesia Avinionica*. It seems more plausible to say that this final desacralization of the imperial office (though not of its Christian occupants) expressed an acceptance of consequences towards which his principles had been leading him for some time. If this interpretation is correct, our consideration of Ockham's apparent Erastianism confirms the general interpretation of his institutional thought put forward in this chapter. The secular side of Ockham's institutional dualism has presented a more and more clearly non-sacral character at every stage of analysis.

3. THE FUNCTIONS OF ECCLESIASTICAL GOVERNMENT

We have now observed Ockham's disengagement of secular and ecclesiastical government from the secular side, discovering that his rejection of a hierocratic origin for lay authority rested on a non-sacral conception of secular governmental functions. We must now consider how this disengagement is supported by a markedly non-secular conception of the proper functions of ecclesiastical government. There are two themes here. One is the traditional plea that the government of the church should avoid entanglement in secular politics, a plea whose most prominent exponent in the medieval period was Bernard of Clairvaux. Beyond this, however, Ockham sought to diminish the legalistic quality of papal government even within its own sphere. His efforts here were based on an ideal of evangelical liberty strikingly parallel to the freedom he defended in the secular area.

'No one fighting for God entangles himself in secular business'

Although Ockham continually used the contrasting terms 'spiritual' and 'temporal', he attempted only once – in III *Dialogus* II – to determine a clear meaning for the distinction. Even here an important interpretive question remains, but the passage deserves to be cited.

There are some who say that these words, 'temporalia', 'carnalia', 'spiritualia', and so on, are used equivocally in different writings, but are restricted to one meaning when it is asked what power laymen have in *temporalia* and in *spiritualia*, so that by *temporalia* may be understood those things that pertain to human government or [the government] of the human race insofar as it is established solely in its natural condition without any divine revelation, which things would be observed by those who recognized no law beyond natural and human positive law and on whom no other law was imposed. By *spiritualia*, however, are understood those things that concern the government of believers insofar as they are instructed by divine revelation.[153]

The restriction of the spiritual to what concerns believers only, in contrast with a mankind uninstructed by revelation, is already significant. There is a problem, however. Are we to understand by *spiritualia*, things found only in divine revelation, or does the term include whatever is in principle discoverable without revelation even if it is also, in fact, found in the Bible? The latter, broader conception of the spiritual was the basis for St Thomas Aquinas' brilliant accommodation of Aristotelian naturalism in an intellectual synthesis which was comprehensive while remaining theological.[154] Ockham himself could scarcely have intended to prohibit theologians

153 'Sunt quidam dicentes quod praedicta vocabula, scilicet temporalia, carnalia, spiritualia, et cetera in diversis scripturis accipiuntur aequivoce, qui tamen cum quaeritur quam potestatem habent laici in temporalibus et in spiritualibus, ad unam significationem restringuntur, ut per temporalia intelligantur illa quae respiciunt regimen humanum, vel humani generis in solis naturalibus constituti absque omni revelatione divina quae servarent illi qui nullam legem praeter naturalem et positivam humanam susciperent et quibus nulla alia lex esset imposita. Per spiritualia autem intelliguntur illa quae conspiciunt regimen fidelium inquantum divina revelatione instruuntur.' III *Dialogus* II, 2, iv, fol. 248va.

154 That is, faith, grace, and revelation not only transcend reason for St Thomas, but also include and perfect it. *Summa Theologiae*, I, q. I, aa. I and 8; IIa IIae, q. 2, aa. 3–4.

and preachers from discussing Biblical doctrines which were also accessible to unaided human reason.[155] Nevertheless, in his political writings he tends to use the first, narrow notion wherever it is at all tenable. From being an essentially comprehensive idea, the concept of the spiritual becomes a basis for specialization.

The most direct evidence of this comes from Ockham's discussion in the *Breviloquium* of the crimes for which an emperor should be deposed. These may be either secular or ecclesiastical. A *crimen ecclesiasticum*, we are told, is one which is directly contrary to the Christian religion and is only by it regarded as a crime worthy of condemnation.[156] If the emperor deserves to be deposed for such a crime, it seems likely to Ockham that the pope should examine the case but that sentencing and the execution of punishment would pertain to the Roman senate or people.[157] In case of secular crimes, however, all aspects of the case are normally the responsibility of the people or those to whom they have given power.[158] Clearly, this treatment of ecclesiastical and secular crimes corresponds with a narrow use of the term 'spiritual'. The spiritual here is what remains after the natural or secular is taken away.

A specialized concept of the spiritual is also evident in Ockham's constant use of II Timothy 2:4 against the papalist idea of *plenitudo potestatis*. No one fighting for God should become entangled in secular business. The thesis that spiritual and temporal are 'distinct' powers and should normally be exercised by distinct persons[159]

---

[155] The fact that Ockham wrote in times of crisis must again be emphasized. His arguments for the separation of secular and spiritual government, which grew out of concern with actual conflicts of power, were not endorsements of lay–clerical antipathy or indifference.

[156] 'crimen ... ecclesiasticum, quod scilicet est directe contra religionem Christianam, et quod a sola religione Christiana crimen dampnatione dignissimum reputatur'. *Brev.* VI, 2, p. 198.   [157] *Ibid.*, p. 200.

[158] *Ibid.*, p. 198. On p. 199 Ockham seems to put off the question of whether the pope has even casual jurisdiction in cases of secular crime: 'Utrum autem *in aliquo casu* huiusmodi habeat potestatem, non est discutiendum ad praesens.'

[159] 'Nemo militans Deo implicat se negotiis saecularibus' (II Timothy 2:4) (OQ I, 4; OP I, 21). 'Triplex invenitur ratio, quare Christus ordinavit istas duas potestates supremas distinctis competere debere personis. Prima est, ne si imperator vel pontifex haberet utramque, superbiret et in infernum demergeretur ... Secunda ratio est, ut distinctae personae distinctas potestates supremas habentes ... se invicem debeant indigere. Tertia ratio, quae in scriptura sacra, sicut et allegatio praecedens fundari videtur est, ut militans Deo se saecularibus negotiis non

replaces the idea of one power comprehensively including all that pertains to the other.[160] Whereas such hierocratic authorities as Innocent IV had used the greater 'spirituality' of the new law of the gospel as a basis for claiming greater clerical control over secular affairs than under the old law, Ockham used the same commonplace to urge exactly the opposite policy.[161]

The pope, and the clergy in general, have a natural right to receive material sustenance and support for their work from those to whom they minister.[162] As a result of Ockham's restricted conception of *spiritualia*, however, the clerical right to lay support is a modest one. Partly, no doubt, because of his Franciscan background, Ockham was convinced that an uncorrupt ecclesiastical government could exercise all necessary spiritual power without great expense or significant physical force.[163] Here again, the principally punitive function of secular authority is crucial. Because of it the imperial office

implicet et ut saecularibus intentus negotiis supremam in spiritualibus non habeat potestatem' (*OQ* I, 4; *OP* I, 23). Cf. *Brev*. II, 7, pp. 65–6. III *Dialogus* I, I, ix, fols. 185vb–186ra. *Imp. Pont. Pot.*, c. I, pp. 455–6.

160 Cf. Alvarus Pelagius, *De Planctu Ecclesiae*, c. 56, p. 152: 'Institutio potestatis temporalis, materialiter, et inchoative habet esse a naturali hominum inclinatione ... Perfective autem, et formaliter habet *esse* a potestate spirituali.' Because of this, Alvarus is able to compare the two powers 'secundum *continentiam*', with the conclusion that, 'temporalis potestas ... *continetur* in potestate spirituali' (p. 153).

161 Ockham comes to grips with Innocent in the *Octo Quaestiones* (I, 2 and 10; *OP* I, 17 and 42–5). Also see *Brev*. III, I, pp. 108–9. III *Dialogus* II, I, xviii, fol. 238vb.

162 'Aliquando vocatur ius divinum; quia multa sunt consona rationi rectae acceptae ex illis, quae sunt nobis divinitus revelata, quae non sunt consona rationi pure naturali: sicut consonum est rationi rectae acceptae ex credibilibus quod Evangelium praedicantes, saltem qui non habent unde sustententur aliunde, de bonis illorum, quibus praedicant, sustententur; hoc tamen per rationem puram naturalem probari non potest: sicut per talem rationem probari sufficienter non potest quod illa, quae praedicant, sunt vera, utilia et necessaria illis, quibus praedicant.' *OND*, c. 65; *OP* II, 575. See above, pp. 89–90.

163 Although he never demanded that the clergy give up all property Ockham clearly believed that the apostles had done well without it and that it was a superfluity which should not be sought by dedicated ministers of the gospel (*OND*, c. 106; *OP* II, 776). To the argument that the apostles had compelling reason to seek property – so that they might give alms or administer things for the common good (*propter temporalia pro bono communi utiliter dispensanda*) – he replied that they were more usefully occupied with prayer and preaching: 'circa orationem et praedicationem Evangelii fuerunt utilius occupati' (*ibid.*, p. 777). For a good discussion of Ockham's treatment of ecclesiastical property in the *OND*, see Miethke, *Ockhams Weg*, pp. 458–66.

differs sharply from the papal in its need for riches and power. Without *divitiae* and *potentia*, according to Ockham, the imperial office cannot be well administered, for jurisdiction is nothing without coercion – the imperial authority especially requires it – but coercion cannot be exercised without force, which an emperor must therefore have. Force, however, is greatly strengthened by riches, since it cannot last without friends, or at least subordinates, but these are acquired with riches.[164] Ockham's use of the term 'potentia' in this argument is noteworthy, for he is ordinarily concerned with spiritual and temporal 'potestas'. In the present passage, however, temporal 'potestas' is regarded more analytically as an 'auctoritas' whose essentially coercive nature requires that it be bolstered by 'potentia', which in turn requires wealth. Ockham's position on the supposed need for a wealthy papacy is in direct contrast with this. It turns on the fact that Christians are not exempt from secular power (*potestas*) and jurisdiction. For this reason their ecclesiastical head does not regularly have power to punish secular wrongs with death or other corporal punishments. But it is principally to carry out such punishments that temporal force and riches are necessary (*propter quas taliter puniendas principaliter potentia temporalis et divitiae sunt necessariae*). The pope can regularly correct wrongdoers solely with spiritual punishment, and hence it is unnecessary that he excel in temporal force or have an abundance of riches. It is enough if Christians promptly obey him.[165] Although the theologian or social historian is free to take issue with Ockham on the true relations between spiritual *potestas* and temporal power, it would be a mistake to interpret this passage and others like it[166] as cynical attempts to weaken the church. Ockham's convictions on these matters were

---

164 '*Iurisdictio* sine coertione nulla est censenda . . . multo magis imperialis *auctoritas* absque coertione nulla est, coertio autem sine *potentia* exerceri non potest. Igitur potentia in imperatore requiritur, *potentia* autem maxime roborari videtur per divitias eo quod *potentia* absque amicis aut saltem obedientibus non videtur posse persistere, amici autem et obedientes divitiis acquiruntur.' III *Dialogus* II, 1, xvii, fol. 238*va*.

165 'Per legem Christianam et solam ordinationem Christi a *potestate* et iurisdictione saeculari Christiani minime sunt exempti . . . propter quod caput Christianorum non habet regulariter *potestatem* puniendi saeculares iniquitates poena capitis et aliis corporalibus poenis . . . et ideo non est necessarium quod *temporali potentia* [papa] praecellat vel temporalibus abundet divitiis, sed sufficit quod Christiani sibi prompte obediant.' *Ibid.*, 1, 2, xxix, fol. 204*vab*.

166 See above, note 144.

religious convictions. They provided a specifically religious basis for de-secularizing ecclesiastical government.

Does the doctrine of casual power undo all this? According to Ockham, Christ willed that supreme spiritual and lay power should regularly be separated, yet the two are not so opposed *ex natura rei* that they cannot possibly belong to the same person.[167] Ockham consistently reserved to the papacy a power of casual intervention in secular affairs.[168] Does this represent a failure to carry papal disentanglement from worldly matters to its proper conclusion? No doubt, the doctrine of casual power involves sacrificing a certain theoretical simplicity, but this may be a dangerous simplicity. In stopping short of complete 'spiritualization' of the papacy,[169] however, Ockham did not in fact significantly weaken his emphasis on the need for regular disengagement from the secular. In the first place, his doctrine does not leave decisions about secular interventions solely to the pope's discretion. The papalists themselves admitted that the pope might intervene mistakenly, even in such a way that he committed mortal sin, but they held such papal actions to be legally binding nevertheless.[170] They thus ascribed to the pope a great amount of real temporal power. For Ockham, on the other hand, papal interventions are not automatically binding. If the pope usurps the jurisdiction of a secular ruler, his acts are null, and Ockham says little to suggest that such invalid acts should be respected from a sense of propriety. Thus, for example, although he is willing to give

---

[167] 'Alia est opinio quo modo media via inter praedictas opiniones incedens . . . quod de facto potestas spiritualis et potestas suprema laicalis non cadunt simul in eundem hominem nec cadere debent . . . sed . . . quod illae duae potestates non in tantum ex natura rei distinguuntur quin formaliter simul cadere possent . . . nam omnis potestas spiritualis, quae competit fungenti potestate spirituali, aut competit sibi ratione ordinis aut ratione administrationis; sed potestas laicalis nec ordini nec administrationi repugnat.' *OQ* I, 3; *OP* I, 19–20.

[168] See the passage quoted above in note 1. Cf. *OQ* I, 7; *OP* I, 34–5. *Imp. Pont. Pot.* c. 12, p. 468; *ibid.*, c. 13, pp. 468–9 (quoted below, note 177).

[169] Ockham several times presented the Marsilian view, that the pope has no *iure divino* power except *in foro poenitentiali*, but never accepted it. See above, note 140.

[170] Alvarus Pelagius, writing in defense of the irascible John XXII, tried especially hard to show that even a pope thought to be in the wrong should be obeyed (*De Planctu Ecclesiae*, cc. 4, 7–8, 25–8, 34). The distinction between the papal office and its imperfect occupant goes back to Leo I (see above, pp. 72–3) and is expressly taken for granted in Ockham's formulation of the extreme papalist position in the *Octo Quaestiones* and *Breviloquium* (*OQ* I, 2; *OP* I, 15–16. *Brev.* II, 1, p. 54).

the papacy the benefit of the doubt regarding the legitimacy of the translation of the empire from the Greeks to the Germans, this is only because we ought to presume in favor of any judge.[171] Certainly, Ockham argued in the *De Imperatorum et Pontificum Potestate*, there are many exceptions to the canonist principle that the sentence of a pastor is to be feared whether it is just or unjust.[172] That principle is regularly true, but it fails in many cases, even when the pastor is a true pastor. It fails, for example, when the sentence in question is contrary to law or canons, contains intolerable error, is given in a case in which the subject is exempt or not a subject or is superior to the pastor, or when the subject has made a legitimate appeal, and so on.[173] Elsewhere in the same work, Ockham showed some willingness to obey even invalid papal commands from reverence or a sense of propriety if obedience was not troublesome.[174] In view of traditional images of the pope as something less than God but more than man, this limited deference in unimportant matters is almost as striking as defiance of unjust papal commands in matters of substance. A second feature of Ockham's doctrine of casual power that must be recalled here is its dependence on a thorough breakdown of secular political processes. The pope is by no means a regular appellate judge in secular affairs. He may intervene only when the lay authorities are negligent and those who should

---

171 'Pro facto papae praesumendum sit, nisi possit probari contrarium, quemadmodum pro quocunque iudice praesumendum sit, donec probatur contrarium' (*OQ* II, 10; *OP* I, 89–90).

172 'Sententia pastoris sive iusta sive iniusta timenda est' (Gratian, II, xi, 3; ed. Friedberg, I, col. 642).

173 *Imp. Pont. Pot.*, c. 14, pp. 469–70. 'Licet illa verba Gregorii sint regulariter vera, tamen secundum iura in multis casibus fallunt, etiam loquendo de sententia veri pastoris et non solum de sententia illius qui putatur esse pastor et non est. Fallunt enim, si sententia etiam veri pastoris lata est contra leges vel canones . . . Ex quo conclude, quod sententia etiam veri vicarii Christi non est timenda, si contra ius divinum vel contra ius naturale feratur . . . Fallunt etiam, quando sententia continet intollerabilem errorem . . . Adhuc fallunt, quando sententia lata est in eo casu, in quo subditus est exemptus . . . Et ita fallunt, quando fertur sententia contra quemcunque in illa causa et in illo casu, in quo non est subditus . . . Ad hoc fallunt verba praedicta Gregorii, quando sententia lata est contra subditum in causa, quantum ad quam subditus est maior pastore suo . . . Fallunt etiam, quando sententia lata est post appellationem legitime interdictam . . . Hiis modis et forte aliquibus aliis fallunt verba praedicta Gregorii, quando sententia lata est a vero pastore.' Cf. *OQ* I, 17; *OP* I, 60–6, especially 63–6. On the nullity of papal directives commanding works of supererogation, see below, pp. 145–6.

174 *Imp. Pont. Pot.*, c. 5, p. 459.

normally correct them are unwilling or unable to act.[175] This is a far cry from the developed papalist doctrine of casual power, which could be used to justify almost any papal intervention *ratione peccati*.[176] As Ockham himself was ready to admit, it may be impossible to formulate a rule stating with certainty when the pope may act and when he may not.[177] There can, however, be no uncertainty about the substantially non-interventionist character of Ockham's own views.

'The gospel's law is a law of freedom'

Beyond disengaging the ecclesiastical hierarchy from secular affairs, Ockham sought to diminish the juridical character of church government within its own sphere. The characteristic style of his argumentation tends to obscure this point. Because of the polemical need to argue in legalistic terms throughout his political works and owing also to his use of Aristotle's *Politics* in discussing church government, it is easy to suppose that Ockham regarded the church as preeminently a juristic entity, disagreeing with his papalist opponents only on the location of sovereign authority within that entity. Hence, it is not surprising to find a respected student of John Hus laying at the door of 'scholastic or nominalistic theology' the fact that Hus

---

[175] 'Illa autem sententia tenet quod, quia papa in temporalibus praeter ius exigendi necessaria nullam habet potestatem a Christo nisi salvis non solum iuribus, sed etiam libertatibus aliorum, ideo quia papa etiam illa quae necessaria sunt reipublicae in temporalibus minime potest quamdiu sunt alii qui ipsam possunt vel volunt utiliter expedire ... Unde et universaliter dicunt isti quod papa ... temporalibus quibuscunque se non debet implicare negotiis quamdiu inveniuntur laici qui ea volunt et possunt rite et legitime expedire.' *OQ* II, 2; *OP* I, 72–3. Cf. III *Dialogus* I, I, xvi, fol. 188 *vab* (quoted above, note I). *OQ* II, 9–10; *OP* I, 87–91. *OQ* VIII, 6; *OP* I, 203–8. *Brev.* VI, 2, pp. 197–201. See above, pp. 92–4.

[176] On the irrelevance of the secular ruler's sinful intentions as a basis for papal intervention, see above, note 68.

[177] 'Non liqueat, qui sint casus, in quibus licent sibi illa, quae nequaquam sibi regulariter sunt concessa. Et forte de eis non potest dari certa regula generalis, sed in eis est cum maturitate maxima procedendum iuxta discretionem et consilium sapientissimorum virorum iustitiam sincerissime, sine omni personarum acceptione zelantium, si possunt haberi, sive pauperes sint sive divites sive subiecti sive praelati. Si autem talium copia haberi non possit, supersedendum est, ne papa ex ignorantia, qua de facto saepe laborat, periculose terminos transgrediatur antiquos et sententias ferat, quae ipso iure divino sunt nullae.' *Imp. Pont. Pot.*, c. 13, pp. 468–9. Cf. III *Dialogus* I, I, xvi, fol. 188vb.

was tried by men who 'regarded the Church mainly as a legal corporation'.[178] Although recent scholarship has tended to minimize Ockham's conciliarism, the more basic assumption of legalism underlying this remark has not been seriously examined. Limitations of space prohibit a thorough investigation, but we may consider in detail one major theme, Ockham's appeal to the gospel as a law of freedom.

'Lex evangelica est lex libertatis.' This constitutes one of Ockham's chief objections to the extreme papalist conception of *plenitudo potestatis*.[179] In contrast with some of his other arguments against an unrestricted *plenitudo potestatis*, however, Ockham's appeal to evangelical liberty does not merely exclude the papacy from intruding in secular affairs. It also expresses an affirmative conception of how ecclesiastical government should operate in its own sphere. When we have stated Ockham's argument and determined what sort of freedom is involved in it, we may go on to consider these broader implications for the church. The picture to emerge will not be one of anarchy. Yet Ockham's treatment of evangelical liberty clashes sharply with the hierocratic ideal of comprehensive direction of man's spiritual life from above.

As stated in III *Dialogus* I, the essential argument is as follows:

The Christian law is by Christ's institution a law of freedom in comparison with the old law, which by comparison was a law of servitude. But if the pope had such a plenitude of power from Christ that he could do anything not contrary to divine law or the law of nature, then the Christian law would be by Christ's institution a law of unbearable servitude, of much greater servitude than the old law. Therefore, the pope

178 Matthew Spinka, *John Hus at the Council of Constance* (New York, 1965), p. 74.
179 The argument that unrestricted *plenitudo potestatis* is incompatible with the liberty of the gospel is, as far as I have been able to determine, original with Ockham. It first occurs in the *Contra Benedictum* of 1338 (Book VI, c. 4; *OP* III, 275)after several other arguments. It moves up to first place in the *An Princeps* (c. 2; *OP* I, 233–5) and III *Dialogus* I, where its exposition occupies Ockham for three substantial chapters (Book I, cc. 5–8). It retains this position in the *Octo Quaestiones* (*OQ* I, 6; *OP* I, 28–9) and *Breviloquium* (II, 3–4, pp. 56–9; and see II, 17–18, pp. 90–5). In the *Imp. Pont. Pot.* (cc. 1 and 3; pp. 456, 457–8) it comes third, behind the argument from II Timothy 2: 4 (see above, note 159) and an argument based on the ministerial character of papal government. Both the originality of this argument from gospel liberty and its importance in Ockham's writings justify paying it the closest attention.

does not have from Christ such a plenitude of power in spiritual and in temporal matters.[180]

What kind of freedom is involved here? Is it a matter of purely moral and spiritual liberation, or something more concrete? Ockham himself raises the question, as he recognizes that a papalist might find gospel freedom compatible with the most detailed regulation of human life by superior authority: for it might seem that the new law should be called a law of freedom not because it frees Christians from universal subjection to the pope, but because it frees them from servitude to sin (*non quia fiant liberi, ne sint subiecti in omnibus summo pontifici, sed quia efficiuntur liberi a servitute peccati*).[181] In other words, Christian freedom would have little to do with the individual's right to lead his life as he chose. On the down-to-earth level of daily life, Christianity would leave things substantially unchanged. Or again, perhaps Christian liberty amounts to nothing more or less than freedom from the specific provisions of the Mosaic law.[182] In this interpretation, the crucial texts would be read concretely but denied universal significance. Here, too, there would be no challenge to the ideal of obeying the pope 'in omnibus'. This was not Ockham's idea of freedom.

In order to combat the hierocratic concept of freedom as obedience, Ockham relied heavily on the circumstantial character of the scriptural texts under discussion.[183] He assumes that the burdensomeness of a state of subjection should be measured by the quantity of external regulations one is bound to obey. It also seemed clear to him that the Christian converts whose liberty the texts described would hardly have leaped for joy, as they are reported to have done, if their 'liberation' had been an exchange of one state of subjection for another equally great. With these premises, the passages at hand

---

[180] 'Lex ... Christiana ex institutione Christi est lex libertatis respectu veteris legis, quae respectu novae legis fuit lex servitutis. Sed si papa haberet a Christo talem plenitudinem potestatis, ut omnia possit quae non sunt contra legem divinam nec contra legem naturae, lex Christiana ex institutione Christi esset lex intolerabilis servitutis, et multo maioris servitutis quam fuerit lex vetus; ergo papa non habet a Christo talem plenitudinem potestatis.' III *Dialogus* I, I, v, fol. 183va.

[181] *Ibid.*, vi, fol. 184ra.

[182] 'Per eam Christiani efficiuntur liberi a servitute peccati vel legis Mosaicae.' *Ibid.*

[183] In addition to James 1: 25, the main texts cited by Ockham are Galatians 2: 3–4 and 5: 12–13, and Acts 15: 10, 19–20, and 28–34.

take on a significance at once concrete and far-reaching: however much the gospel liberated Christians from servitude to the Mosaic law in particular, it could not be called a law of freedom if it bound them to *any* external servitude as great or greater than that of the old law.[184] Or again, for Ockham the Council of Jerusalem was not primarily concerned with a metaphysical or purely spiritual transformation of the religious life, but with lifting a yoke that was 'heavy' and hard to bear. It is clear from the account in Acts, he says, that the apostles by the inspiration of the Holy Spirit declared the gentiles free from the yoke of servitude in order to comfort them, so they would not grieve and be troubled. But if these converts had been liberated from servitude to God's law and yet subjected to Peter and his successors in a greater servitude, they would deservedly have grieved and had no ground for consolation.[185] It is thus in a universal but almost tangible sense that Ockham interpreted the scriptural references to gospel liberty. We must now trace the implications of this interpretation for ecclesiastical government.[186]

Although the gospel is not itself a source of servitude for Ockham, he denied that his conception of evangelical liberty abolished all existing servitude among men or prohibited new servile relations from arising, if there was just cause for them.[187] Certainly, if we shift

184 'Si enim Christiani quacunque servitute quoad opera exteriora tanta vel maiori quanta fuit servitus veteris legis per legem evangelicam tenerentur, non posset lex evangelica magis dici lex libertatis quam lex Mosaica, quantacunque liberati essent a servitute Mosaicae legis. Qui enim liberatur ab una servitute et premitur alia aequali vel maiori, non est magis liber quam prius extiterat. Sicut qui liberatur ab uno vinculo coporali et alio aequali vel fortiori constringitur non est solutus, sed magis ligatus.' III *Dialogus* I, I, vii, fol. 184rb.
185 *Ibid.*, fol. 184vab.
186 It is because Ockham interprets evangelical liberty as precluding any servitude as great as that of the old law that he can use it in refutation of extreme papalism. If the papalist doctrine of *plenitudo potestatis* were true, all Christians would be *servi* of the pope in the strictest sense: 'Lex nova sive evangelica esset intolerabilis servitutis et maioris quam fuerit lex vetus, si papa haberet ex institutione Christi talem plenitudinem potestatis ... Si enim hoc esset, omnes Christiani essent servi, et nullus esset liberae conditionis, omnes enim essent servi summi pontificis' (III *Dialogus* I, I, v, fol. 183vb). 'Quod non omnes Christiani sint servi summi pontificis secundum strictissimam significationem huius nominis servus, quod tamen ... sequeretur si papa haberet tam in temporalibus quam in spiritualibus huiusmodi plenitudinem potestatis multis modis ostenditur' (*ibid.*, viii, fol. 185va).
187 'Lex Christiana non dicitur lex libertatis quia liberat Christianos ab omni servitute, sed quia non premit Christianos tanta servitute quanta pressi fuere

our attention from the relation of servitude to the very different one of political subjection, it becomes clear that for Ockham the *lex libertatis* was not meant to menace the jurisdiction of lawful secular governments. Ockham evidently believed, furthermore, that Christian liberty was compatible with differences in power and authority within the church itself. Indeed, as we shall see, he held that the gospel actually requires all Christians to be subject to the pope. We may note for the present his emphatic assertion that the 'sheep' in the primacy text 'Pasce meas oves' were meant to be tended 'powerfully' and 'with authority':

The word 'tending' means not only tending others by word and example and physical assistance, but also with power and authority (*potestative et cum auctoritate*), especially as the word 'tending' is used in the sacred scripture and the expositions of the holy fathers. This could be shown copiously, but it may suffice to adduce a few [Biblical texts] . . . From these words of Christ and the others which follow, it is gathered that a shepherd of Christ's faithful is likened as concerns his office to a shepherd of irrational sheep. But from his office such a shepherd has some power and authority over his lord's sheep. Therefore, the shepherd of Christ's sheep, the faithful, also has power and authority over them from his office. This is so patently and evidently found in the expositions and assertions of the holy fathers that it seems completely superfluous to prove it by them.[188]

In view of Ockham's usual willingness to overwhelm his reader with citations and arguments on doubtful points, his assertion that texts are superfluous here is the strongest possible testimony that he accepted the need for authority in the church. Marsilian assertions

Judaei, et ideo licet regibus et aliis Christianis servos habere licet per legem Christianam nullus Christianus *fiat* servus cuiuscunque. Et ad beatum Iacobum dicitur quod non intendit legem Christianam esse legem perfectae libertatis ut nullus Christianus cuicunque homini sit subiectus, Christiani enim papae sunt subiecti, et multis principibus et aliis Christianis subduntur. Sed ideo dicit eam esse legem perfectae libertatis, quia per eam religio Christiana paucis sacramentis et sacramentalibus seu cerimonialibus ex institutione divina subiicitur, et *per ipsam nullus Christianus servus cuiuscunque mortalis efficitur*, nec etiam nisi in his quae spectant ad necessitatem vel utilitatem ipsius aut reipublicae alicuius hominis subditur potestati' (*ibid.*, vii, fol. 185rb).

188 III *Dialogus* I, 4, x, fol. 224rab. Cf. *OQ* I, 7; *OP* I, 34. In III *Dialogus* I, I, again, Ockham considers the view that the pope has no coercive power *ex ordinatione Christi* (cc. 13–15), but goes on to develop his own opinion in the following two chapters.

of the *ex officio* equality of all priests are repudiated here as patently false to Christian tradition. From Ockham's acceptance of the necessity of *potestas* and *auctoritas*, however, it does not follow that he considered these factors to be the church's heart and soul, or that he regarded the church as essentially a legal corporation.

In the simplest terms, Ockham held that the exercise of power and authority in the church should be kept to a minimum. This does not mean that the pope or the church generally should be quiescent or withdrawn in relation to the faithful, but that there are limits on the right to issue binding commands. Ockham emphasizes the pope's obligation to respect the rights of others, insisting that he seek his subjects' voluntary cooperation and avoid needlessly harsh means of governing them.

The picture of apostolic government in the primitive church which Ockham presents in discussing evangelical liberty, and which he takes as the model for his own conception of papal power does contain elements of coercion. They are, however, minimal. The apostles laid down many laws (*plures canones condiderint*) and directed many things (*praeceperint multa*), but not without their subjects' knowledge and consent, except in matters of divine law and natural right or those demanded by necessity or public utility, whose direction could not be omitted without doing harm. In such matters, Ockham observes, the supreme pontiff holds similar power now.[189] Ockham relates this picture of the apostles' government to a later exposition of his own views on papal power,[190] thus providing further evidence of the centrality of the *lex libertatis* in his thought and entitling us to take seriously his more extensive development of the idea elsewhere. In the *Breviloquium*, for example, the liberty of the gospel is said to prohibit the pope from infringing the freedom granted by God and nature,[191] or from employing too onerous and heavy a mode of ordering and doing what actually pertains to the papal office.[192] These restrictions are not offered merely as counsels of perfection. The pope has no right to ignore the law of liberty under which he operates. Just as Ockham had taught that papal usurpations

---

[189] III *Dialogus* I, I, vii, fol. 184vb.
[190] '*Discipulus*: Istud . . . non potest . . . verbis brevibus explicari, ideo ipso dimisso ad praesens, quia de ipso post tractabimus . . .' *Ibid.* The promise is fulfilled at III *Dialogus* I, I, xvi–xvii, fols. 188va–189va.
[191] *Brev.* II, 17, pp. 90–3.   [192] *Ibid.*, 18, pp. 93–5

in secular affairs could licitly be resisted, so he contended that it is unnecessary to obey papal commands in spiritual matters if they are needlessly severe. Such orders are null and void by divine law itself, even though given by one who is a proper judge in other cases, since he is not a proper judge in this case, and hence in this case his sentence is null.[193] It should be noted, too, that the pope cannot plead for an excessively burdensome government on the ground that it serves the good of his subjects, in the sense of promoting their perfection. That is not enough to warrant an authoritative command. It is required, rather, that the command be a matter of 'urgens necessitas' or 'manifesta utilitas', that the things commanded be 'necessaria' or 'de necessitate salutis'. Only in such cases does the pope have power to command his subjects against their will.[194]

Ockham's liberal conception of church government was based not only on scriptural texts mentioning evangelical liberty, but also on the words and deeds of Christ. Thus, in a passage repeated almost verbatim in the *Breviloquium* and the *Octo Quaestiones*, he sharply

---

[193] *Ibid.*, p. 94. The contrast between gospel liberty and Mosaic servitude is made explicit at the end of the chapter. Cf. *Imp. Pont. Pot.*, c. 5, p. 459: 'Supererogatoria etiam excipi debent [a potestate papae] . . . et si iniunxerit, alius tunc nequaquam ei astringitur obedire, quia talia iniungere ad eius non pertinet potestatem, et ideo si contra aliquem nolentem in huiusmodi obedire faceret quemcunque processum vel faceret sententiam, huiusmodi processus et sententia, tanquam a non iudice in huiusmodi causa factus et lata, esset ipso iure nullus et nulla esset.' For other references to the nullity of unjust papal commands, see above, note 173.

[194] '*Haec est enim libertas evangelicae legis*, quod observatoribus eius sine culpae eorum extra articulum urgentis necessitatis et manifestae utilitatis, ipsis invitis, nihil praecipue grave, quod supererogationis est, vel non est de iure naturali nec de iure divino expresso, potest imponi virtute eiusdem legis' (*Brev.* II, 17, p. 91). On other occasions, too, Ockham cites works of supererogation as clear exceptions to papal *plenitudo potestatis*, though not always in connection with the *lex libertatis*; III *Dialogus* I, I, xvi, fol. 188va. *OQ* I, 7 and II, 2; *OP* I, 34 and 71. *Imp. Pont. Pot.*, c. 5, p. 459. Even a papacy which prescribed such works for the good of its subjects would fall under Ockham's strictures. On this, see especially *Brev.* II, 17, p. 91. In the *Octo Quaestiones* he is somewhat less extreme on a similar point. 'Esto quod talis plenitudo potestatis in summo pontifice non esset periculosa perfectis voluntarie obedientiae perfectissimae se subdentibus, esset tamen periculosa multis imperfectis, quibus etiam ad obedientiam perfectissimam obligari discriminosum esse videtur. Cum igitur in congregatione fidelium multi imperfecti existant, non expedit ut papa respectu omnium fidelium talem habeat plenitudinem potestatis' (*OQ* I, 8; *OP* I, 38).

contrasted Christ's giving of life with the capital punishment and other bloodshed incident to secular government – 'He raised three men from the dead but punished no one, no matter how wicked, with death or mutilation' – and explicitly applied this contrast to the present government of the church.[195] Equally non-juristic in tone is Ockham's account of Christ's refusal to judge the woman taken in adultery. Again there are parallel passages in the impersonal *Octo Quaestiones* and the unguarded *Breviloquium*. Christ suggested the limits of papal power by example, according to Ockham, when He rejected a lordly (*dominativum*) mode of ruling consisting principally of severe physical punishment, even when it was offered Him by others. In order to show perfectly that the judgment of blood was not to be exercised either by Himself as a mortal man, or by His vicar, He was unwilling either to give sentence on the woman Himself or to commit her to another for the full measure of justice, or even to say what punishment should be inflicted on this sort of woman by an appropriate judge. By this example, Peter and all his successors who wish to follow in Christ's footsteps were instructed not to exercise such judgment regularly, either personally or through another.[196] Although Ockham's immediate purpose in this passage was to demonstrate that Matthew 16: 19 ('*Whatever* you bind ... or loose ...') must be understood with exceptions, his reasoning has broader and more constructive implications. It is not a matter of condemning secular government as sinful or immoral. In the *Breviloquium*, at least, Ockham distinguishes between tyrannical and non-tyrannical secular power, but maintains that Christ forbade the apostles to exercise either the one or the other.[197] What remains, then, as a compelling model for the normal operations of papal

---

[195] *OQ* I, 4; *OP* I, 25. Cf. *Brev.* II, 19, p. 96. Christ taught by example, however, that prelates may make use of light corporal punishments.

[196] *Ibid.*, pp. 95–6. Cf. *OQ* I, 4; *OP* I, 25.

[197] 'Nec omnes principes saeculi, etiam infideles, tyrannice principati fuerunt ... Christus autem non solum principatum saeculi tyrannicum et iniustum, sed etiam legitimum atque iustum penitus refutavit' (*Brev.*, II, 19, pp. 97–8). Cf. *Imp. Pont. Pot.*, c. 7, pp. 461–2: 'Christus non omnem principatum seu praelationem interdixit apostolis, sicut aliqui male intelligentes affirmant, cum quia ipse seipsum ponat in exemplum, quia fuit verus praelatus ipsorum et super ipsos etiam inquantum homo veram habens praelationem ... Sed interdixit eis principatum dominantium ... qui ... est respectu servorum.' There can hardly be any doubt that Marsilius of Padua is included among the *male intelligentes*. See above, pp. 128–9, 144–5.

government is a mild pastoral care, a *ministerium*[198] which explicitly allows for acts of power but only when these are urgently necessary for the good of the church. This view stands in marked contrast with the traditional hierocratic contention that judicial power is the essence, and its exercise the glory, of the papal office.[199]

We shall see in the next section that an ideal of evangelical freedom for spiritual leadership is accompanied in Ockham by a somewhat dry and functional view of the formal relations between the papal government and the body of believers. In some respects, therefore, Ockham's account of ecclesiastical government will be shown to resemble his treatment of secular government. His vision of spiritual leadership as 'non-dominative' is distinctive, however, as is his interpretation of the gospel as a law of freedom. Ockham, then, in the midst of bitter and legalistic polemics, also called for an important shift of ideals. For him the image of Christ as judge and ruler is largely replaced by the image of a shepherd and liberator. To be sure, even the gospel, although it is a perfect law of liberty, is not 'perfectissima'. Such is not available in this life.[200] Even the relatively mild government proper to the church seems to have struck Ockham as a regrettable necessity. Far from reflecting the permanent

---

198 Ockham avoids the term *iurisdictio* in connection with papal power even when developing a positive interpretation of traditional primacy texts like Matthew 16: 18–19 (III *Dialogus* I, 4, xii–xx, fols. 224va–227va). On the *ministrativus* character of papal government, see especially *Imp. Pont. Pot.*, c. 6, p. 460, quoted in part above, note 139.

199 Thus, Egidius Romanus begins his *De Ecclesiastica Potestate* by establishing 'quod summus pontifex est tantae potentiae, quod est ille spiritualis homo, qui *iudicat* omnia et ipse a nemine *iudicatur*' (I, 2, pp. 6–9). The guiding idea of James of Viterbo's *De Regimine Christiano* was his comparison of the church to a kingdom, with the attribution of royal powers to its head (see especially Book II, c. 9, pp. 267–78). The jurisdictional character of the papal office is especially prominent in Augustinus Triumphus (Wilks, *Sovereignty in the Later Middle Ages, passim*). It should be noted, however, that Ockham, like Augustinus Triumphus (*ibid.*, pp. 530–7), held that the distinctively papal power of *administratio* could be held by a layman, since it was distinct from the sacerdotal power of binding and loosing which Christ conferred on all the apostles together (III *Dialogus* I, 4, xvii, fol. 226rab). For early canonist accounts of the sacramental and governmental implications of Matthew 16: 18, see Tierney, *Foundations of the Conciliar Theory*, pp. 25–36, especially pp. 33–4n.

200 'Debet dici lex perfectae libertatis . . . non tamen dicitur lex perfectissimae libertatis, in perfectione enim sunt gradus, quare non omne perfectum est perfectissimum reputandum, perfectissima autem libertas in hac vita mortali nequaquam habebitur.' III *Dialogus* I, I, vii, fol. 185rb.

metaphysical structure of reality, it stands in contrast with both the state of innocence and the state of glory. Just as there would have been no secular emperor if men had remained in a state of innocence, so in the state of glory there will be no government or prelacy, but everyone will rule himself.[201] By papalist standards, this is no doubt a strange idea of the state of glory, yet it belongs to a consistent and passionately Christian conception of ecclesiastical government. Ockham delivered no wholesale condemnations of the institutional church, nor did he set his hopes on the advent of an angel pope or a new age. His sense of the limitations of this mortal life was too strong for such enthusiasms. Within these limits, however, he fervently advocated a less juridical and more spiritual ecclesiastical government.

4. THE BASIS OF ECCLESIASTICAL GOVERNMENT

The last book of III *Dialogus* I is devoted to the question whether Christ in fact established blessed Peter as ruler and prelate over the other apostles and all believers.[202] The structure of the book leaves no doubt about Ockham's answer. Arguments against Peter's primacy are presented at the beginning,[203] but later they are all answered.[204] Careful development of the affirmative position occupies twenty-two chapters in between. For the most part, Ockham builds on the classical primacy texts, John 21: 15–17 ('Feed my sheep'), Matthew 16: 18–19 ('Thou art Peter'), and Luke 22: 32 ('I have prayed for you, Peter'), but he also appeals to the sense of

---

[201] In his discussion of secular world government, Ockham rejects the idea that 'illud regimen est magis expediens universitati mortalium in statu culpae quod magis assimilatur regimini quod fuisset si homines in statu innocentiae permansissent (quia illud quod magis assimilatur meliori est magis expediens)' (*ibid.*, II, I, ii, fols. 231vb–232ra). Instead of assimilating monarchy to an ideal state of affairs, he emphasizes the non-ideal character of any government whatever: 'propter *diversitatem* inter statum innocentiae et naturae lapsae non semper illud regimen est melius in statu naturae lapsae quod magis assimilatur illi regimini quod fuisset in statu innocentiae, sicut nec regimen illud est melius in statu naturae lapsae quod magis assimilatur regimini quod est in statu naturae gloriae, *quia tunc melius esset quod quilibet regeret seipsum et quod nullus regimen super alios seu praelationem haberet, quia regimen seu praelatio non erit in statu gloriae*' (*ibid.*, xi, fol. 235va).

[202] III *Dialogus* I, 4 is Ockham's most extensive treatment of this question. The basis of papal authority is also discussed at I *Dialogus* 5, xiv–xxi, fols. 40rb–43b.

[203] III *Dialogus* I, 4, i–ii, fols. 218va–220ra.   [204] *Ibid.*, xxv, fols. 243rb–244va.

Peter's superiority shown by Christians 'in a continuous series ...
from the time of the apostles up to our time'. 'The church's prelates
and the peoples subject to them from those times up to this have
held and believed (*tenuerunt et senserunt*) that Peter was superior to the
other apostles.'[205] The superiority of monarchy as a form of government is also adduced. Many objections are raised along the way, but
they are all met. The affirmative answer to the main question of the
book is thus left in sole possession of the field. The final chapter
builds on this basis in raising the further questions, 'whether it can
be found in any authentic source that Peter sometimes used his
power over the other apostles?'[206] This question, too, is answered
affirmatively. All of this places ecclesiastical government on an
essentially different basis from that underlying secular government.
The papal office exists *iure divino*, whereas currently existing secular
governments are of purely human institution. This contrast in the
origins of papal and imperial authority is clearly laid down in
Ockham's exposition of the ways in which power or jurisdiction may
be said to be *a solo Deo*. The power held by St Peter himself was
'from God alone' in the strongest possible sense, 'without any
human ordination, election, or assistance (*absque omni ordinatione,
electione et ministerio humano*)'. Even the power held by succeeding
popes is from God in a distinctly stronger sense than applies to
imperial power. It is God who actually confers power on each
pope – the electors act only as his ministers. In the secular case,
however, power is actually conferred by men. It is first possessed by
those who institute the ruler, and then transferred from them to
him.[207]

---

205 *Ibid.*, xxii, fol. 228ra.   206 *Ibid.*, xxvi, fol. 229vab.
207 'Aliqua enim iurisdictio est a solo Deo absque omni ordinatione, electione et
ministerio humano ... Sic ... beatus Petrus potestatem, quam habuit per illa
verba Christi *Pasce oves meas* a solo Deo recepit. Aliter potest aliqua iurisdictio vel
potestas intelligi esse a solo Deo, quia a solo Deo confertur, non tamen absque
omni ministerio creaturae vel hominis. Sic gratia in baptismo ... Sic potestas
conficiendi corpus Christi in sacerdote ... Isto modo videtur aliquibus, quod
potestas papalis est a solo Deo in omni summo pontifice post beatum Petrum;
quia licet Christus absque omni ministerio hominis beato Petro papalem contulerit
potestatem, tamen successoribus eius potestatem huiusmodi absque electione
canonica minime confert. *Electores enim summi pontificis nullam sibi tribuunt potestatem, sed Deus solus dat sibi potestatem*, non tamen, nisi illi canonice eligant personam
capacem huiusmodi potestatis.' *Brev.* IV, 5–6, pp. 149–50. Cf. *OQ* II, 3–6; *OP* I,
74–81. For the mode in which *imperium* is *a solo Deo*, see note 72 above.

In view of the clarity and emphasis of these distinctions, we cannot avoid asking how such heterogeneous bases of authority can be accepted together in a coherent scheme of political thought. The basis of papal power seems to have an absoluteness which removes it utterly from the realm of utilitarian moderation governing Ockham's treatment of secular power. In Lagarde's eyes, this problem was insoluble: 'Ockham croit que l'ordre du Christ instituant la primauté est formel, mais l'état contemporain de la chrétienté le persuade que ses effets sont provisoirement néfaste. Et il essaie de trouver une impossible issue à cette impasse.'[208] In different terms, Ockham's problem was to preserve the balanced dualism required both by his own principles and by the crisis of his age when one element in the balance could plausibly claim an infinite weight because of its unique, divine origin. Unless a way of handling this difficulty could be found, his 'dejuridization' of papal governmental functions would amount to little more than an expression of pious sentiment.

The solution to this problem is found in the three earlier books of III *Dialogus* I, where Ockham laid a subtle groundwork for his later exposition of the Petrine commission. These books exhibit important structural analogies between secular and spiritual government. When the original warrant for papal primacy is interpreted in terms of these analogies, the gulf between absolute theological positivism and utilitarian human action is considerably diminished. Ockham's conception of the basis of papal power had both conservative and revolutionary aspects. It can be adequately understood only if we resist the temptation to build our interpretation on a few selected passages. To trace the argument of an entire tract of III *Dialogus* is a difficult process, but it is the only way to form a fair estimate of Ockham's position.

Ockham begins by examining five opinions concerning papal *plenitudo potestatis*, ranging from the extreme hierocratic view that the pope can do anything not expressly contrary to divine or natural

---

[208] *La naissance*, V, 126. The problem was in a way more severe for Ockham than for John of Paris. As Tierney notes (*Foundations of the Conciliar Theory*, p. 175), John believed that *papatus*, the papal office, was *a solo Deo*, but that since its being held by any particular person was due to human cooperation, so it could be taken away by human action (*Tractatus de Potestate Regia et Papali*, ed. Bleienstein, c. 25, p. 202). For Ockham the inherence of papal power in individual popes would seem to be more exclusively due to divine action.

law, to the Marsilian view that he has no coercive power at all. Ockham's criticism of the despotic implications he saw in extreme papalism is important,[209] for it limits what can rightly be deduced from his later treatment of the classical primacy texts. The situation at the end of this first book is, however, somewhat undecided. Extreme papalism has been rejected, and an alternative to Marsilianism has been presented in the mediating opinion expounded in general terms at the end of the book.[210] Yet no defense of this unquestionably Ockhamist position has been offered. This is the work of Book 2.

The second book of III *Dialogus* I commences an 'exquisite' discussion of the mediating opinion on *plenitudo potestatis* previously stated, beginning with its first particular, that Christ did in fact make blessed Peter 'head, ruler, and prelate of the other apostles and of all believers'.[211] This is, of course, an exact statement of the thesis defended two books later. We must pay the utmost attention, therefore, to Ockham's way of conveying a fuller understanding (*intelligentiam pleniorem*) of this *prima particula*, for it could scarcely be clearer that he intended his later treatment of the Petrine commission to be taken in terms of this book. Here is the foundation on which he built his own positive interpretation of 'Pasce oves meas', 'Tu es Petrus', and the other traditional arguments for papal primacy.

The principal question of III *Dialogus* I, 2 is whether it is expedient for the whole community of believers to be subject to one head, prince and faithful prelate under Christ.[212] Even a cursory examination of this book shows it to be a distinctly political treatment of ecclesiastical government, almost fully comparable in structure to the treatment of world secular government in Book I of the following tract. To be sure, as we have already seen, Ockham thought of the two governments as normally being concerned with entirely different matters. In a formal or structural sense, however, Ockham's

---

209 III *Dialogus* I, I, v–viii, fols. 183rb–185vb.

210 *Ibid.*, xvi–xvii, fols. 188va–189va.

211 III *Dialogus* I, 2, i, fol. 189vb. See note 139 above for the rest of the opinion of which this is the first point.

212 'Ad cuius [an Christus constituerit beatum Petrum caput principem et praelatum . . .] intelligentiam pleniorem ante omnia conferendo scrutemur, an expediat toti communitati fidelium uni capiti principi et praelato fideli sub Christo subiici et subesse.' *Ibid.*, fol. 189vb.

approach to government is similar in both areas. III *Dialogus* I, 2 resembles III *Dialogus* II, I with respect to the problems raised, the principles used in resolving those problems, and the solutions reached.

(1) The chief question in each book concerns the expediency of a certain form of government in relation to the needs of a given community, in one instance the community of believers, in the other, all mankind.[213] This question of expediency for the community is explicitly connected with the question of legitimacy or governmental right in the secular case, for Ockham contended that the rights of the empire would become injuries, injustices, and cruel tyrannies if world monarchy were wholly inexpedient.[214] The connection is not so straightforward in the ecclesiastical case; Ockham nowhere asserts that the legitimacy of papal monarchy would be destroyed if it were inexpedient for the *congregatio fidelium* to be under one head. Nevertheless, since the question of expediency is raised to provide a fuller understanding of the original basis of papal government, the logic of the discussion obliges us to complete the parallel. Ockham proposes to mark off the topic of expediency as distinct from legitimacy but closely related to it. He means to discuss the Petrine commission in the light of an independent examination of various possible regimes with a view to their usefulness to the communities subject to them.

A further similarity between the problems raised in Ockham's treatments of ecclesiastical and secular government concerns constitutional change. By any standard, the most radical portion of the tract on church government is the series of chapters on this topic. 'Is it expedient for the community of believers that they have power to change an aristocratic government into a regime similar to royal government and conversely, so that they would have power to establish one supreme pontiff who would be over all the others, and also power to establish or elect several supreme pontiffs with equal power . . . so that it would be possible to change one government into another indifferently (as might seem expedient)?'[215] When we recall Ockham's emphasis on the variability of expedient secular regimes,[216]

213 III *Dialogus* II, 1, i, fol. 230rb. See above, pp. 109–10.
214 *Ibid.*, fol. 230rb.
215 III *Dialogus* I, 2, xx, fol. 198vb. This question is the subject of cc. 20–8.
216 See above, pp. 122–6.

his discussion of constitutional change in the church appears all the more striking, especially when put in terms of action by the community (of believers, in this case) as shall seem expedient. Ockham himself immediately brings out the 'political' character of the problem by framing it in comparison with constitutional changes made by the ancients. Is it expedient, he asks, for the *communitas fidelium* to be able to change regimes 'in the way in which the gentiles reasonably changed aristocratic into royal government, and conversely (*ad modum quo gentes principatum aristocraticum rationabiliter transmutarent in regalem et econverso*)?'[217]

When he comes to arguments in favor of one regime or another for the church, Ockham again shows a strong tendency to analogize ecclesiastical and secular governmental problems. Thus, the last two of the ten arguments he gives in favor of one head for the whole congregation of believers explicitly link the considerations relevant to constitutional questions in the two areas. It is expedient for the community of believers to be governed in things pertaining to the Christian religion by that regime which is most like the best secular polity ('quod politia optima saeculari maxime assimilatur'). A kingdom is the best among all polities, so it is expedient for the whole multitude of believers to have one ruler above all.[218] Ockham's enumeration of types of government in the course of this argument leads logically to a detailed examination of certain parts of Aristotle's *Politics* a few chapters later, a revealing analysis to which we shall soon give attention. The final argument for ecclesiastical monarchy also has a strong logical connection with other political discussions. No less unity is required at the head of the community of believers, the master asserts, than in the whole body of mortals. Since it is expedient for the latter that one man rule over all, it is also expedient for the former. The student is quick to see the large field of relevant considerations opened up by this *ratio*. On the basis of this reasoning, he gathers, it should be easy to gauge what can be alleged for both sides on the present issue from what will be said about secular world monarchy in the next tract, 'for all those things or many of them can be applied to this matter'.[219]

(2) Following the leads Ockham himself has given, let us turn

---

[217] III *Dialogus* I, 2, xx, fol. 198vb.   [218] *Ibid.*, i, fol. 190vb.
[219] *Ibid.*, ii, fols. 190vb–191ra.

now from problems to the principles appealed to in their solution, the specific considerations about the nature and aims of government which determine the best choice of regime. The student's sweeping statement that many or all of the arguments concerning secular monarchy can be applied in the assessment of monarchy as a form of ecclesiastical government may seem surprising, for according to Ockham, as we have seen, the central concerns of secular and ecclesiastical government are quite different. Notwithstanding this important difference in sphere of action, certain tasks of ecclesiastical government resemble the moderate or negative tasks of secular government. The student's assertion of an analogy between the two is especially easy to understand in connection with these functions. Thus, the arguments for ecclesiastical monarchy include the following, which anticipate both in tone and substance the secular political reasoning of III *Dialogus* II.

[4] It is expedient for a community that cannot best be ruled by a multitude of judges who can disagree among themselves concerning cases and other business, and whose quarrels can even be dangerous to the whole community, that it be under one supreme leader and head, who can indicate to all the truth of judgment.[220]
[6] It is expedient for those who are under different judges capable of erring about important matters to have one head, to whom these important matters may be referred and by whom they may be justly and properly judged.[221]
[7] It is not expedient for the community of believers that many among them, and especially those having power over others, should be able to do wrong insolently and without any fear of correction and temporal punishment . . . wherefore, since the prelates of the faithful are prone to evil, just as others are . . . it is expedient that some faithful prelate have power in such matters over the others.[222]

The basis for each of these arguments is an appeal to specific functions government must serve, not any intrinsic metaphysical excellence possessed by unity as against plurality. In all three arguments, furthermore, the functions appealed to are negative rather than constructive ones: the resolution of judicial conflict, the correction of judicial error, and restraint of the excesses of those in high places.

A somewhat negative conception of governmental functions

[220] *Ibid.*, i, fol. 190ra.   [221] *Ibid.*, fol. 190rb.   [222] *Ibid.*, fol. 190vab.

becomes apparent even in the most metaphysical reason Ockham presents for ecclesiastical monarchy. This is the argument that the church as one body must have one head, for it would be imperfect with none and monstrous with more than one. In the hands of a hierocratic writer, such a line of thought would end by ascribing extensive positive powers to the pope as principal and noblest member of the ecclesiastical organism. Ockham's very different attitude becomes evident in his reply to the objection that Christ alone should be head, with no single head under him. To be sure, Ockham says, Christ is indeed head of the church, but it is necessary that there be another head to bear its care under Christ, for there ought to be a vicarious leader physically present to the church, who may rule it visibly, and to whom believers, when necessary, can have physical access for various necessities. Christ, however, does not rule the church in this way. Except in special cases (*in casu*) he rules only invisibly.[223] The inference seems to be that, if it were not for various 'necessities' which may 'need' to go before a visible head, Christ's invisible headship would be sufficient. The visible 'principal member' of the church thus seems restricted to primarily utilitarian functions by Ockham even in the context of the traditionally broad and speculative organic analogy.

As has been noted already, Ockham's initial arguments for and against ecclesiastical monarchy led him to a detailed exposition of parts of Aristotle's *Politics*. Space does not permit an adequate discussion of these chapters. We can only note the major points that emerge and briefly indicate their bearing on Ockham's political treatment of ecclesiastical government.

Ockham's main aim in the exposition of Aristotle is to distinguish and evaluate various types of '*politia*' such as monarchy and aristocracy. He begins, however, with an account of two pre-political 'communities', the household and, much more briefly treated, the village.[224] Although his analysis of the human relationships making up a household yields politically important principles, one of its chief effects is to emphasize differences between the lesser communities and such greater communities as the *civitas*, *regnum*, or *ducatus*.

---

223 'Ecclesiae esse debet vicarius rector . . . ad quem fideles (cum necesse fuerit) pro variis necessitatibus corporaliter possint accedere.' *Ibid.*, fol. 189vb.
224 III *Dialogus* I, 2, iii–iv, fols. 191vb–192va.

The similarity of royal power to the father's power in the family is close enough to support a later commendation of monarchy because it is more assimilated to a 'natural' regime and government,[225] but analogies between household and political community are as a rule ignored by Ockham, and his discussion of ecclesiastical government rarely points to paternalism.

Ockham recognized that for Aristotle the ideal regime was a monarchy unlimited by purely positive human law or custom, a regime in which the king ruled for the common good of all but according to his own will, limited only by the laws of nature.[226] Superficially, this appears to support a rather extreme form of ecclesiastical monarchy. In fact, however, Ockham sets up two important obstacles to the deduction of hierocratic conclusions from Aristotle's *Politics*. In the first place, the proviso that the ruler govern 'propter commune bonum omnium' distinguishes Aristotelian ideal monarchy from extreme papalism in its very concept. Aristotle's ruler can indeed be said to have a *plenitudo potestatis*, but only with respect to what concerns the common good, not private good ('respectu eorum quae bonum commune respiciunt, non privatum').[227] It is not monarchy but the despotic rule of master over slave which corresponds with Ockham's usual formulation of papalism.[228] The despot, assuming that his power is legitimate, may use his *servi*, not only for the common good, but also for his own good (*bonum proprium*) so long as he attempts nothing against divine or natural law.[229] By contrast, the ruler in Aristotle's best form of monarchy cannot use his subjects and their goods as it pleases him for his own advantage. They are not slaves but enjoy their natural liberty, and it pertains to liberty that no one should be able to use free men for his own ends ('ad naturalem libertatem spectat, ut nullus possit uti liberis propter utilitatem utentis').[230] Like the pope of hierocratic theory, then, a pure monarch would be restricted only by natural and divine right, not by human law or

---

[225] *Ibid.*, ix, fols. 193vb–194va.   [226] *Ibid.*, vi, fols. 192vb–193ra.
[227] *Ibid.*, fol. 193ra.
[228] For the rule of master over slave, see III *Dialogus* I, 2, iii, fol. 192rab. On Ockham's principles, such domination is not always unjust but is 'repugnant' to the best form of government (see above, p. 121). For Ockham's contention that extreme papalism makes all Christians slaves 'in the strict sense', see above, note 186.
[229] *Ibid.*, vi, fol. 193ra.   [230] *Ibid.*

custom. He would be regularly above the law. In contrast, however, with the hierocratic pope generally depicted, and opposed, by Ockham, Aristotle's ruler would have such power only in matters concerning the common good. The difference is between a despotic and a truly royal *plenitudo potestatis*. By thus using his exposition of the most powerful (*potissimus*) mode of Aristotelian monarchy as an occasion for contrasting liberty and servitude, Ockham sharply distinguished Aristotelianism from papalism at what may be called the ideal level of political theory. As it happens, however, pure monarchy was not the Aristotelian regime that Ockham considered most relevant to the circumstances of his own day. Hence, in a second, practical respect his monarchist analysis of the *Politics* also leads away from papalism, not towards it.

Other forms of monarchy differ from Aristotle's ideal form either in their intention or in their power (*quantum ad potestatem*). To the extent that a regime is established for the special benefit of the ruler and not wholly for the common good, it deviates from the ideal in the direction of tyranny or despotism.[231] Ockham nowhere suggests that this sort of departure should be instituted in either ecclesiastical or secular affairs. There is, however, another property which differentiates certain monarchical regimes from the strongest or ideal form, the amount of power possessed by the ruler. The monarch may be formally bound to observe specific human laws and customs. Such a royal government is called legal (*secundum legem*), for although one man rules he does not do so according to his own will but is limited by certain humanly introduced laws and customs which he is formally obligated to observe. The more such laws and customs the ruler is bound to observe, the more his regime recedes from the first form of royal government.[232] Assuming, then, that a despotic *plenitudo potestatis* is to be rejected, which form of genuine monarchy is preferable, one in which the ruler pursues the common good

---

[231] III *Dialogus* I, 2, vi, fol. 193rb.

[232] 'Principatus autem unius interdum deficit a saepe dicto principatu regali quantum ad potestatem, quia scilicet non habet illam plenitudinem potestatis quam habet principatus regalis praefatus. Et talis principatus regalis dicitur secundum legem, quia licet unus principetur, non tamen principatur secundum voluntatem, sed quibusdam legibus et consuetudinibus humanitus introductis astringitur, quas tenetur servare et ipsas se servaturum iurare vel promittere obligatur, et quanto-plures tales leges et consuetudines servare tenetur, tantomagis recedit a memorato principatu regali.' *Ibid.*

limited only by divine and natural right, or one in which he is further limited by human law and custom? More important still for our purposes, what reasons can be given to support one or the other regime?

Ockham's response to these questions is clear. It immediately follows the passage just cited. 'The more such laws and customs the ruler is bound to observe, the more his regime recedes from the royal government mentioned before, and hence in these days perhaps there is not such a government – namely, the first form of royalty – in the whole earth.'[233] At first glance, the assertion that no contemporary government enjoys a regular *plenitudo potestatis* seems merely descriptive, an observation, of dubious accuracy in the case of papal government, that existing regimes are in fact all formally bound by positive law and custom. It soon becomes clear, however, that the irrelevance of ideal monarchy to actual conditions has philosophical as well as historical grounds. Following Aristotle once more, Ockham contends that no man deserves to be given such full power unless he is outstandingly eminent (*superexcellat*) in wisdom, virtue, and all good qualities of both body and soul, even including external goods such as friends and riches. Otherwise, it must be feared that he will turn to tyranny.[234] Such cautionary remarks might well dissuade men from reducing historic limitations on governmental power, or even persuade them that formal limitations should be imposed where they do not already exist. At the very least, Ockham's arguments suggest the need for a certain shrewdness in suiting political institutions to the moral and other traits of the persons available to operate them. Such considerations are decidedly foreign to the climate of hierocratic thought. On both the ideal and practical levels of political theory, therefore, Ockham's astute analysis of the varieties of monarchy provides important groundwork for his distinctive treatment of the papal office.

After expounding the Aristotelian species of *politia* Ockham turned to the personal qualifications necessary in a monarch. The main issue is, whether a prospective monarch must excel everyone else in virtue and wisdom. Just as Ockham's discussion of various possible monarchical constitutions avoids endorsing a supra-legal form of royal power that could safely be put in operation only with

[233] *Ibid.*   [234] *Ibid.*

ideal individuals as rulers, so his treatment of the personal qualifications for rulership implicitly assumes a constitution that can tolerate imperfect officials. He proposes, in essence, that if an exceptionally wise and virtuous man is available when a ruler of the church is to be elected, then he certainly ought to be chosen. If, however, no such individual can be found, it is better that some ordinarily good man be elected than that the church be without a head.[235] Ockham's approach to the problem of personal qualifications for the papacy thus slips quietly between two temptations. On the one hand, there was the temptation to suppose that only a charismatic individual, an 'angel pope', could alleviate the church's perils. Ockham avoided this by not insisting on a 'super-excellent' man for the office. On the other hand, by his balanced, matter-of-fact discussion of the problem, he also avoided mystically exalting the papal office so far above its merely human occupants that their character and policies could become matters of no consequence.

Ockham concluded his general comparison of different types of government by commending monarchy over aristocracy on grounds of efficiency. 'I want you to say for what utility . . . it is more expedient for the community of believers to be ruled by one than by many', the student asks.[236] The master's reply is more than generous. There are many utilities, he says, and proceeds to enumerate no fewer than five. There is easier access to one ruler than to many, because many could not always be in the same place. One ruler can ordinarily give judgment, do justice, and avoid dangers more easily than many when the need occurs, for with many rulers it is necessary for each to wait on the others even when matters must be dealt with quickly and delay would be dangerous. A third utility is that one man can be corrected more easily than many if he should

---

235 III *Dialogus* I, 2, xv, fol. 195va. Ideal ethical considerations are overridden here by considerations of public utility: 'In distribuendo autem honores et dignitates quandoque solum attenditur meritum et dignitas illorum quibus debent distribui, quia tunc iniustum est ut aequalibus inaequalis honor seu dignitas tribuatur . . . Quandoque autem non solum attenditur meritum et dignitas honorandorum, sed etiam attenditur utilitas publica quae melius procuratur principaliter per unum quam per plures, et tunc quia maior respectus habendus est ad bonum commune quam ad meritum et dignitatem honorandorum, iustum est ut aequalibus et similibus secundum virtutem non aequalis honor et virtus tribuatur' (*ibid.*, fol. 196ra). Cf. *OQ* III, 6; *OP* I, 111; discussed above, p. 120.

236 III *Dialogus* I, 2, xviii, fol. 197rb–va.

go astray, because a regime of many rulers would have more defenders than one. No large community can be ruled well without many counselors, but it is better if one rules the others and can arrange the time and place of council and other details (for example, who is to be admitted or excluded) than if many ruled, one of whom could not easily exclude another from council and from other affairs even if he were plotting evil to the republic. Finally, one man can deal with (*expedire*) more affairs in more ways and with less labor than many, because all sorts of impediments can arise to prevent many men from deciding such affairs together.[237] Always bearing in mind the mildness to be practiced in ecclesiastical government, we cannot fail to be struck by this emphasis on sheer efficiency. John XXII's streamlining of papal government evidently did not offend Ockham in itself.

Some of the utilities of monarchy are explained further in the next chapter, which is devoted to answering arguments in favor of the rule of many. Efficiency is again the keynote. Thus, to the Aristotelian argument that the judgment of the multitude is superior to the judgment of one man, Ockham replies that one *optimus* or *bonus* can call upon all or some of the many when it is expedient.[238] Similarly, although many eyes and ears perceive more and better than the two eyes and ears of one man, this does not count heavily against one-man rule, for one good and wise man ruling the faithful could use the organs of many when it was expedient and his own organs alone when *that* was expedient. Such arguments are an appropriate end to a strikingly functional defense of monarchy as normally the most expedient of ecclesiastical regimes.[239]

(3) Having noted the similarity of problems and examined the similarity of principles appealed to in Ockham's ecclesiastical and secular political theory, we can better understand his conclusions.

---

[237] *Ibid.*, fol. 197va.
[238] In the regime of many, on the other hand, 'necesse esset saepe omnes convenire pro negotiis, quae possent expediri per paucos.' III *Dialogus* I, 2, xix, fol. 197vb.
[239] *Ibid.*, fols. 197vb–198ra. The anti-Marsilian character of Ockham's position is especially clear on fol. 198rb–va, where the impervertibility of the people's will, a fundamental principle in Marsilius' defense of popular sovereignty (Gewirth, *Marsilius of Padua and Medieval Political Philosophy*, pp. 58–9, 185, 204, 209, 211) is rejected. Ockham concedes that the multitude is less liable to total corruption than one man, but the will of one man is less pervertible 'secundum partem'. It is necessary, however, that a ruler be less pervertible even in this partial sense.

Although Ockham's analysis fitted some aspects of current papal practice, considerations such as ready accessibility and efficiency in doing justice are scarcely mentioned in hierocratic defenses of papal monarchy,[240] while the third *utilitas* on Ockham's list, the relative ease of correcting one man 'si exorbitaverit', would have been unthinkable in a work of Egidius Romanus or Augustinus Triumphus. For them, the natural context in which to discuss the papal office was not political, but metaphysical. At least in normal circumstances, Ockham agreed with such writers that papal monarchy was the only proper ecclesiastical government. However, the premises that he provided for this apparently conservative conclusion affected the meaning of the conclusion in important ways in both normal and abnormal circumstances.

As concerns normal conditions, we must recall that the whole treatment of ecclesiastical government in terms of expediency was intended to provide fuller understanding of the first particular of Ockham's conception of papal *plenitudo potestatis*. This was the assertion that Christ had in fact made the apostle Peter head, prince, and prelate of the other apostles and of all believers. When we come to Ockham's treatment of the Petrine commission in Book 4, then, we can only interpret it in terms of the argumentation of Book 2. This means that for Ockham, clearly, Christ's act in instituting a monarchical form of government for His church is to be understood in terms of the considerations so carefully examined earlier with the aid of Aristotle's *Politics*. Seen in this light, the Petrine commission is by no means opposed to the dictates of political reason. Quite the contrary, the papal primacy receives extensive support from this analysis. On Ockham's interpretation, Christ's act was not an arbitrary fiat, but an intelligible way of providing for the needs of His church. It is thus a mistake to construe Ockham's treatment of the classical primacy texts in Book 4 as the reluctant acceptance of a divine command contrary to reason.

240 Thus, for example, James of Viterbo concluded his metaphysically subtle treatment of the unity of the church and the Petrine basis of this unity (*De Regimine Christiano*, Book I, c. 3, pp. 106–21) by remarking almost casually that from this and similar 'conditions' it follows that the church is peaceful (*pacifica*), 'nam unitas causa est pacis' (p. 120). Why? Not from utilitarian causes, but because 'pax effectus amoris [est], cuius est unire'. See *ibid.*, Book II, c. 5, pp. 205 and 211 for further metaphysical arguments for 'unum primum et summum' in the church.

Ockham gave an affirmative sense to these texts, not from a commitment to theological positivism, but in light of the most advanced rational theories of government available to him. Although, however, the papal primacy gains support from Ockham's earlier, political analysis, it takes on a significance very different from that accorded it by hierocratic writers. By substituting rational, utilitarian considerations for the cosmic and theological analogies of the papalists, Ockham effectively decreased the specifically religious meaning of the institutions of church government. It is not necessarily a matter of reducing the pope's power, but of changing its character. Ockham saw the pope as chief pastor, and, when necessary, judge, but not as the *fons et origo* of all that is Christian. In normal circumstances, then, Ockham's position on ecclesiastical government would be conservative in the sense of endorsing an undivided papal primacy *ordinatione Christi*. His way of understanding this primacy was, however, significantly more down-to-earth than that of his papalist opponents.[241] The pope receives his power immediately from God and not from his subjects – in this he differs from present-day secular rulers – but in spite of this the pope and his subjects are in important respects on the same level.

In abnormal conditions, Ockham's rational, utilitarian approach to ecclesiastical institutions could be used to justify temporary but radical change. For he answered the question posed in III *Dialogus* I, 2, xx by asserting that it *is* expedient for the community of believers to be able to change the church's form of government, and he was ready to specify some circumstances in which this should be done.[242] Here is where a disparity seems to arise between Ockham's use of divine–positive and human–utilitarian bases of authority. The crucial issue is stated in the first argument against the possibility of ecclesiastical constitutional change: the disciple is not above the master, nor the servant above his lord, but all Christians are disciples and servants of Christ, who has ordained and willed that there should be one

---

[241] 'Les thèses d'Ockham sur le magistère doctrinal de l'Église et de la papauté ... sont révolutionnaires, moins par leurs conclusions les plus directes ... que par le raisonnement qui les fonde.' Lagarde, *La naissance*, v, 128. Ockham's conception of the papal office was also more down-to-earth than that of many earlier Franciscans, including Peter Olivi. On the attitudes of Bonaventure and Olivi towards the papacy, see Tierney, *Origins of Papal Infallibility*, pp. 82–130.

[242] III *Dialogus* I, 2, xxviii, fol. 204ra–va.

highest pontiff and head of all Christians, which He in fact showed when He ordained blessed Peter alone as highest priest.[243] If there is no conflict between rational expediency and Christ's positive ordinance in normal circumstances, such a conflict would surely seem to occur in the abnormal case where expediency might dictate change and Christ's will forbid it.

It is important to see that Ockham's treatment of this issue is integral with his defense of papal monarchy as normally the best church government. If the papacy's normal superiority is understood in terms of its benefits to the community of believers, then an appeal to necessity or utility as a warrant for dispensing with that government in abnormal circumstances is no departure from principle.[244] Indeed, Ockham takes as a general rule for interpreting Christ's precepts that exceptions in cases of urgent necessity or evident utility are *always* to be understood (if the exceptional action is consistent with natural law) unless explicitly disallowed by Christ himself:

Notwithstanding that all Christians are Christ's disciples and servants and are not above Him, yet from necessity or utility they can act against His order – that is, against the surface meaning of His words and deeds, though not against His intention – because He himself meant that urgent necessity and evident utility be excepted when He ordered or did anything whose contrary is not against natural law and did not explain that necessity and utility ought not to be considered.[245]

There is no thought of questioning Christ's divine right to issue absolute, exceptionless commands. Very shortly after the passage just cited, Ockham discusses in another connection God's command to Abraham to sacrifice his innocent son. It does not matter that this action would have been contrary to natural law if it had not been

---

243 *Ibid.*, xxi, fol. 200r*a*.
244 For the appeal to necessity and utility, see *ibid.*, xx, fols. 199r*b*–200r*a*; xxviii, fol. 204r*a*–v*a*.
245 'Et non obstante, quod omnes Christiani sint discipuli et servi Christi, et non sint supra ipsum, tamen ex necessitate vel utilitate possunt aliquid contra ordinationem eius. Hoc est contra verba et facta eius secundum quod prima facie sonare videntur. Non tamen contra intentionem quia ipse vult quod in verbis eius urgens necessitas et evidens utilitas sint exceptae ubi aliquid ordinat vel facit cuius contrarium legi naturali minime adversatur, et ipse non explicat quod necessitas et utilitas nullatenus recipi deberent.' *Ibid.*, xxii, fol. 200v*a*, deleting Trechsel's parentheses around 'quia ipse . . . vel facit', following Ms. Paris Mazarine 3522 (478), fol. 218r.

divinely commanded. The fact that it was unambiguously ordered by God made it obligatory.[246] But is the Petrine commission to be understood on this model, as a trial of heroic faith? Ockham himself did not raise the question. Instead, he pointed out that there are other dominical precepts more absolute in expression than the passages containing the Petrine commission, to which everyone would allow special exceptions.[247] All the more, then, is it licit to make exception in cases of manifest necessity or evident utility to Christ's order concerning the monarchic government of the church.[248] Again, the crucial point is that Ockham appealed to the same basic principle both in interpreting Christ's order for normal circumstances and in arguing for a departure from it in times of crisis: 'Concerning Christ's order establishing one supreme pontiff, that should be observed which is best for the church (*quod magis prodest ecclesiae*), for whose utility he ordered that one supreme pontiff should be established (*pro cuius utilitate ordinavit unum summum pontificem constituendum*).' But this implies, according to Ockham, that many pontiffs should be set up to rule the church aristocratically when it is expedient for the church that there be many.[249] Thus, Ockham's rational justification of ecclesiastical monarchy was integral with his calm consideration of constitutional revolution in the government of the church. In neither case can his position be fairly described as an arbitrary positivism.[250]

---

[246] 'Alium intellectum non potuit elicere ex verbis praecepti nisi quem primo sonabant. Et ita erant expressa omni ambiguitate carentia quod non erat ibi locus interpretationi, nec aliquem alium intellectum potuit elicere. Ex quibus verbis Dei nec etiam per rationem potuit alium elicere intellectum, cum non ignoraverit Deum esse dominum vitae et mortis ... Si [praecepta] enim sint simpliciter praecepta iuris naturalis, nullus casus excipi debet, propter quamcunque necessitatem vel utilitatem, nisi Deus specialiter aliquem exciperet, quemadmodum non obstante praecepto iuris meri naturalis de nullo innocente scienter interficiendo Deus praecipiendo Abrahae ut immolaret fillium suum specialem exceptionem fecit. Si autem sint praecepta mere positiva casus necessitatis et utilitatis, ita debet excipi ... nisi ex scripturis specialiter colligi possit, quod in aliquo tali praecepto non est excipiendus casus necessitatis et utilitatis'. *Ibid.*, xxiv, fols. 201v*b*–202r*a*.

[247] For the need to interpret the Matthean 'quodcunque' with exceptions even in normal circumstances, see *Brev.* II, 14–19, pp. 81–98, and *OQ* I, 7–9; *OP* I, 33–41.

[248] Exceptions are allowed to Christ's precepts concerning patience, taking oaths, and the non-possession of gold and silver. III *Dialogus* I, 2, xxii, fols. 200v*b*–201r*a*.

[249] *Ibid.*, fol. 200v*b*.

[250] The intelligibility of the Petrine commission bears on Ockham's discussion of the 'power' of interpreting it, for if the relevant texts were utterly mysterious, they

Besides inquiring into the theoretical coherence of Ockham's views, the historian must also ask how radical they were in their practical implications. Did Ockham seriously expect a change from a 'royal' ecclesiastical government to an 'aristocratic' one? Did he himself wish for such a change? Or were the revolutionary final chapters of III *Dialogus* I, 2 written more in hope of reforming papal government than of overthrowing it?

Ockham's discussion of conversion to an aristocratic ecclesiastical regime was so detailed on some points[251] that we can hardly doubt he regarded such change as a possibility deserving serious practical consideration. Given his conviction that John XXII and his successors were manifest heretics, the first case Ockham suggests in which it would be licit for Christians to set up many non-apostolic primates is especially significant: if pope and cardinals became heretics and the Romans favored them or were unwilling to elect a catholic supreme pontiff, it would then be licit for whatever and however many provinces and regions as might agree in the matter to elect a primate for themselves to preside over their spiritual causes. In this way, if some provinces agreed on one such primate and others on others, it would come about that Christians would be ruled by many primates without a superior (none of them an *apostolicus*, however)

could not be interpreted without a new special revelation. As it is, however, there are many experts who understand the Biblical passages bearing on papal government and are thus in a position to interpret them to other Christians, for such interpretation is only the expression of a true understanding of God's commands. 'Multi autem periti sciunt verum intellectum praeceptorum Dei et Christi. Et ideo praecepta illa possunt interpretari illis qui nesciunt, quia huiusmodi interpretatio non est nisi expositio vel declaratio, seu manifestatio veri intellectus praeceptorum Dei. Et ita Christiani habent potestatem interdum interpretandi praeceptum divinum, quando scilicet sciunt verum intellectum illius. Si autem nesciretur verus intellectus alicuius praecepti Dei, quia nesciretur intentio Dei in praecipiendo, nec per rationem nec per scripturas alias sed solummodo per revelationem Dei possit sciri, sicut secundum quosdam verus intellectus litteralis multarum prophetiarum, quae ponuntur in libro Apoc. et aliis scripturis propheticis, non potest sciri nisi per revelationem novam, tunc interpretatio talis praecepti expectanda est a solo Deo. Sed intellectus praeceptorum sive ordinationum Dei de patientia conservanda, iuramento non praestando, de non portando sacculo sive pera, et de summo pontifice constituendo et multorum aliorum et scitur a pluribus Christianis et sciri potest per rationem et scripturas.' III *Dialogus* I, 2, xxiv, fol. 201va.

251 In this connection, his defense of the thesis that 'absque unitate summi pontificis potest unitas ecclesiae [Trechsel: summi pontificis] perdurare' is of interest. *Ibid.*, xxv, pp. 202ra–203ra.

until such time as the whole body of believers could be otherwise provided for.[252] In view of these plain and apposite words, we can hardly say that Ockham's discussion of radical change in ecclesiastical institutions was idle speculation.

On the other hand, there is good reason to deny that he wished for a permanent abolition of the papal office – nor is this denial a matter of imputing a vague traditionalism to him. There is no speculative philosophy of history in Ockham, and particularly no vision of the coming church as one in which a unified government is unnecessary. There should be 'perfect' liberty in the church, but a liberty which is *perfectissima* is not a genuine option in the conditions of this life. Hence, the reasons Ockham gave for indefinitely suspending papal government had nothing to do with a progressive view of human nature or the spiritual development of the church. On the contrary, the election of a pope should be deferred, not because papal government is unnecessary, but for just the opposite reason, because it is impossible, either due to the absence of a suitable candidate or because no candidate would be generally accepted by the multitude of Christians. In other words, although the existence of government for the church is made necessary by man's fallen condition, the absence of papal government would not be due to an improvement of the human condition but, more nearly, to a further deterioration. Under the circumstances, Ockham's rationally grounded attachment to monarchy would combine with his affirmative interpretation of the Biblical primacy texts to suggest that suspension of the papal regime could by rights be only temporary. It must be stressed again that this is a matter of principle, not sentiment.

In conclusion, then, the supposed incoherence between theological positivism at the basis of papal government and utilitarian rationalism underlying secular government in Ockham's thought is more apparent than real. Since the *congregatio fidelium* does not depend on government for its corporate being, any more than does mankind

252 'Liceret quibuscunque et quotcunque provinciis et regionibus (quae hoc concorditer vellent) sibi unum primatem eligere qui in causis spiritualibus omnibus aliis praesidere et ideo si aliquae provinciae concordarent in unum et aliae in alium possent plures tales primates non habentes superiorem quorum nullus esset apostolicus praeesse Christianis quouscunque de alio provideretur universitati fidelium.' *Ibid.*, xxviii, fol. 204rb.

in general, grave failure of government does not signal the end of the world but the need for action. There should be greater reluctance to set aside a divinely established government than one of purely human institution, but the fact that both can be understood as normally expedient means to the welfare (spiritual and temporal, respectively) of their subjects implies that either can be temporarily modified in abnormal circumstances – in circumstances, that is, when the 'best' form of government is ineffective or positively harmful. In both areas, Ockham contended, it must be possible for a community to take constructive action when its government is inadequate. Unless the Petrine commission is interpreted as comparable to God's paradoxical command that Abraham sacrifice his innocent son, it cannot be used as an excuse to ignore intolerable evils in the church which are due to its own government. On the other hand, a reasonable regard for the spiritual welfare of the *congregatio fidelium* will always lead towards a normalization of church government in accordance with the abiding *prima particula* in this matter, Christ's injunction to Peter and to him alone, 'Pasce oves meas.' Just as everyone zealous for the common good should work to bring the whole world under one monarch in secular affairs,[253] so, it would seem, every zealous Christian should work to bring about the government of the whole church by an uncorrupt and generally acceptable successor of St Peter.

INSTITUTIONAL CONCLUSIONS

Ockham's attempt to disengage secular and ecclesiastical government instead of ordering them in a complex institutional synthesis took account of the conflicting political monisms of his day without being dominated by them. To be sure, he did not accept the Marsilian bifurcation of temporal and spiritual power into totally separate spheres of 'this-worldly' and 'other-worldly' effects. Accordingly, he could offer no guarantee that the directives of the two governments would never collide, and no simple rule of procedure for cases in which such collisions took place. Ockham conceived of

---

253 'Non est verus zelator boni communis, qui non desiderat et non laborat, quantum sibi licet pro gradu suo, ut totus mundus uni monarchae sit subiectus.' *Brev.* IV, 13, p. 166.

secular and spiritual affairs as sufficiently distinct, however, so that conflicts between them should be rare, especially since, on his view, neither government could justify intervening in the other's area by any pretense to universal regular jurisdiction.

A second factor marking off Ockham's position from other systems of medieval political thought was its emphasis on personal freedom. Ockham did not attempt to set up formal procedures whereby the members of a community might appraise the performance of their rulers and take action if it was defective. The right to change an inadequate government is inherent in the community on Ockhamist theory, however, and Ockham's emphasis on individual liberty of action must be viewed as in part a way of making this informal communal right effective in practice. When, for example, he defended monarchy on the ground that bad monarchs are easier to depose than bad factions, he obviously assumed that government would not have a monopoly of power. In place of the schemes of supra-personal 'powers', 'offices', or 'orders' characteristic of so much earlier thought, he assumed a world in which individuals had sufficient scope to find out what their rights were and to take action if those rights were violated. Hence, his essentially traditional view of the level at which secular government was to operate led him neither to quietism nor to an acceptance of ecclesiastical control over secular institutions. He could insist that the minimal goals of secular government should in fact be attained, but assign the main burden for seeing that this was done, not to the lay ruler's spiritual superiors, but to the body of his free subjects.

Ockham considered the lack of effective imperial jurisdiction in secular affairs to be a major problem of his age. On grounds of efficiency in maintaining justice in the present, not from reverence for the past, he contended that the peace and quiet of mankind could not be sufficiently provided for unless the whole world was subject to one lay ruler. Although this contention has been disparaged as unrealistic, it can as well be said that the subsequent history of the West has been 'unrealistic' in that it has confirmed the wisdom of Ockham's thesis. But even as he emphasized the need for institutions that could effectively achieve the minimal goals for which governments are instituted, Ockham implicitly displaced legal and political relationships from the center of human life. Given the more elevated conception of the political community held by Christian Aristotelians like Thomas Aquinas, John of Paris, or Dante, it is natural to regard active participation in that community as an important fulfillment of human potentialities. For Ockham, on the other hand, politics was not intrinsically attractive. Free men should know their rights and duties under law, and they have an informal responsibility to take remedial action in times of crisis, but here their participation in formal political processes is likely to end. In the religious sphere, similarly, Ockham's conception of evangelical liberty lessened in importance the juridical bond of superior and inferior between the pope and his subjects. In neither domain did Ockham indulge in an easy polarization of freedom and authority as respectively good and evil, but he deliberately substituted the value of freedom for the value of comprehensive direction 'from above' even in spiritual matters. In the area of secular politics, the relation of ruler and subject was to be even less charged with ethical significance, since rulers are not presumed to be radically different from their subjects in virtue, and since the good people in a community should depend upon their government for nothing more inspiring than peace and quiet. Ockham at no point recommended atomic individualism – on the contrary, he had a strong sense of human solidarity. Time and again, however, he refused to tie basic secular or religious values to the acceptance of one or another governmental institution.

If the positive ethical content of juridical relations is diminished when Ockham's views of secular and ecclesiastical government are considered separately, it is lessened still further by the impossibility of combining these two perspectives in a single vision of higher and lower grades of authority. As Ockham willingly conceded, it is contradictory to hold that one man can be both superior and inferior to another at the same time and in the same respect. There is no logical difficulty, however, in the first individual's being superior to the second in one respect (*in spiritualibus*, for example) but not superior in another respect (*in temporalibus*), or superior at one time (*regulariter*) but inferior at another (*casualiter*). The separatist or non-interventionist form in which Ockham developed these distinctions was well suited to the practical problems of his day. In its long-term effect, however, acceptance of Ockham's dualism between spiritual and temporal power would surely tend to dilute the inner human significance of relations of rank. If a man needed always to ask in what respect or for what purposes he was inferior to another, his inferiority could hardly pertain to his essence as a human being.

What, then, can be said of the coherence of Ockham's institutional dualism? In an important sense, Ockham did not wish the major governmental institutions of Christendom to be coherent with one another, for he was sensitive to the dangers of excessive concentrations of power and did not believe that any government, even one divinely instituted, was immune from these dangers. If coherence means an ultimately unitary system of government, Ockham's position was not coherent. But it is at least debatable whether coherence in this sense is a virtue.

In other senses, coherence, along with justice, is a prime desideratum in politics. Men want institutions which, taken together, will foster peace and concord. We might speak, then, of the coherence of mankind as a chief goal of politics, and ask that a political thinker provide a coherent scheme for attaining it, that is, ideas which are theoretically consistent and likely to be effective in practice. Was Ockham's dualism coherent in this sense? In theory, perhaps so. In point of historical fact, certainly not. When he put forth a desacralized view of secular political institutions, Ockham was, in Bochner's words, 'a brilliant man whose political views were in advance of his time'.[254] Indeed, the need for demythologizing secular politics without sinking into brutality or an amoral skepticism is as urgent now as in Ockham's day. On the ecclesiastical side, Ockham was sorely mistaken if he counted on gaining general acceptance for an essentially pastoral conception of the papal office. He was even more mistaken if he expected that the religious unity of the medieval church would in fact be preserved through an extended period in which large bodies of Christians set aside papal government. But with after-the-fact observations like these we go beyond the bounds of fair appraisal. It is easy enough to blame the disengagement of secular and ecclesiastical government and an emphasis on personal freedom for much in the modern world that clashes with medieval values. Certainly the application of such principles risks consequences

---

[254] Boehner, *The Tractatus de Successivis*, p. 15.

which Ockham himself would not have welcomed. We must ask, however, whether a consistent son of St Francis would not have thought the risk worth taking. Christ and the apostles had brought salvation to the world without assuming the rights of secular rulers or exercising despotic rule over their own followers. Where could one find better models of spiritual power?

Chapter 4

POLITICS AND PHILOSOPHY: NATURAL RIGHT AND THE ETHICAL BASIS FOR OCKHAM'S POLITICAL IDEAS

Hoc est elicere conformiter rationi rectae, velle dictatum a ratione recta propter hoc, quod est dictatum . . . ad hoc quod velim virtuose illud dictatum a ratione recta oportet necessario quod velim rectam rationem per eundem actum.

To elicit an act conformably to right reason consists of willing what right reason dictates because right reason dictates it . . . In order for me to will virtuously what right reason dictates, it is strictly necessary for me to will right reason [itself] in the same act.

Sent. III, 12, DDD

Ockham's philosophical and theological writings are difficult to interpret; they contain little that is directly concerned with politics, and Ockham himself seldom referred to them in the polemical writings central to the present study. For these reasons, and fortified by the example of such scholars as Boehner, Jacob, and Bayley, we have attempted in the preceding chapters to understand Ockham's political thought in its own terms, with little reference to his predominantly earlier work in other fields. This course has led to a surprisingly clear view of the territory so far explored. That we have been proceeding in a reasonable direction is also attested by the moderate, somewhat anti-metaphysical character of Ockham's chief constitutional doctrines. Yet, if it would be an 'adventure' or a 'construction of the writer', as Boehner has it, to develop Ockham's political ideas from his 'so-called metaphysics', it does not follow that there is no significant connection between the academic and political phases of his thought. Whether or not Ockham himself called attention to the fact, his nominalism and his political thought might still be 'rigorously parallel', as Lagarde has contended. Even though Ockham avoided a Platonic or Augustinian deduction of political power from a comprehensive speculative vision of the cosmos, he still said and did many things in his career as a political writer that call for philosophical or theological explanation. To the extent that our analysis in the last two chapters has brought into sharper focus the most distinctive aspects of Ockham's political ideas – what most needs fundamental clarification or justification – it should help in the attempt to understand his thought as a whole and certainly should not be taken as a rejection of that project.

The essential philosophical problem is to assess the turbulent mixture of objectivity and individualism in the political works. Ockham, as we have seen, was prepared to stand alone against the world, advocating a revolutionary change in ecclesiastical government. At the same time he claimed the permanent values of justice and moderation for his own. He composed an extended defense of papal as well as imperial monarchy, but demanded as much freedom as possible for the subjects of monarchy. His insistence on presenting 'what the learned think' about important practical issues and his minute dissection of arguments for all positions fit well with his earlier mode of life at Oxford, but these techniques of the academic establishment are used to attack traditional views about traditional governmental institutions. There is much in Ockham's speculative writings to illuminate such contrasts. While a detailed treatment of the relevant passages would be highly desirable, the material is sufficiently extensive and intricate to rule out adequate discussion in the space available. Hence, in order to avoid cryptic abstractions or misleading slogans, it will be well to select a more limited subject for analysis. An appropriate theme is provided by Ockham's conception of natural right, which, when properly understood, sheds light on his political thought and at the same time poses significant questions about his earlier work in moral philosophy. In pursuing this theme we shall largely ignore such important matters as Ockham's treatment of universals, his logic and epistemology in general, and his extensive discussion of ethical and psychological questions, but it may be better to look closely at part of the elephant than to grope blindly over his every aspect.[1]

There is no doubt that Ockham had a conception of natural right,

[1] A wider-ranging yet detailed and sound treatment of relevant speculative passages is provided by Miethke, *Ockhams Weg*, 137–347.

and a distinctive one. In the last book of the *Dialogus*, he defends the right of the Roman people to elect the pope[2] by proposing a three-fold division of *ius naturale* which the student has never heard before and accordingly asks about at some length.[3] No less a person than Cardinal d'Ailly later found this new way of distinguishing natural right 'tremendous' (*valde bonam*).[4] Nevertheless, a sympathetic interpreter of Ockham's novel division has concluded that it is of only limited significance in his work.[5] The major interpretations of Ockham's political thought reviewed earlier suggest even less hopeful conclusions. For example, Lagarde's view of Ockham as a voluntarist has little place for the rationality of the natural law tradition, while the theological positivism central to Scholz's interpretation seems to rule out a genuinely 'natural' natural right. Scholz's study also raises another question. How can the essentially objective, external orientation of natural law be reconciled with Ockham's emphasis on individual intention as the sole criterion of moral worth? If external behavior has no intrinsic value, what can be the moral significance of laws bearing on it?

Space does not permit a full discussion of even the issues most relevant to the topic of natural law. We can give no direct attention, for example, to the much discussed question of the contingency of natural law on God's will. It has been argued that Ockham made *ius naturale* a wholly arbitrary divine fiat.[6] The God of nominalism does not impress all scholars as equally irrational in His relation to natural law,[7] but the question remains an interesting one for philosophical theology. As the course of the present chapter will make clear, however, the issue of God's willfulness in relation to natural law is of only marginal bearing on Ockhamist political thought, since Ockham's appeals to *ius naturale* in his political writings are based on its

---

[2] For the polemical context, see above, pp. 130–1, n. 147.

[3] III *Dialogus* II, 3, vi, fol. 263rab.

[4] 'Sextum capitulum ostendit quod extendendo ius divinum ad omne ius naturale Romani ex iure divino habent ius eligendi summum pontificem et ibi novam distinctionem de iure naturali valde bonam.' D'Ailly's abbreviation of the *Dialogus*, Paris, Bibliothèque Nationale, Ms. Lat. 14579, fol. 101r.

[5] W. Kölmel, 'Das Naturrecht bei Wilhelm Ockham', *FzS*, xxxv (1953), 39–85; p. 56.

[6] F. Oakley, 'Medieval theories of natural law: William of Ockham and the significance of the voluntarist tradition', *Natural Law Forum*, vi (1961), 65–83.

[7] For a less threatening view see Oberman, *The Harvest of Medieval Theology*, pp. 90–119.

rationality (in explicit contrast with positive law). Hence, the possibility that natural law is itself positive at some^higher level is not of direct concern to us.[8] A topic more germane to the political interests of this study is Ockham's treatment of *ius naturale* in the *Opus Nonaginta Dierum*. From the standpoint of political theory, the most important single issue between Ockham and John XXII concerned the logical and moral possibility of a mode of using material things which involved no (positive) legal *iura* and yet was not *iniustus*. The relevance of natural law to this issue is clear when we consider that Ockham attempted to construe the *licentia utendi* granted to the Franciscans with regard to food, clothing, and so on, not as conferring a *ius*, but as removing an impediment to exercise of the common *natural* right to use such things. Evidently, then, if there were no natural rights, Ockham's case would be seriously damaged. Only lack of space can excuse the omission of a detailed treatment of this matter.[9]

Some insight into the philosophical basis of Ockham's political ideas may be gained, however, from pursuing the following questions: (1) Are there significant reflections of Ockham's new division of *ius naturale* in III *Dialogus* elsewhere in his political works? Can he fairly be described as a constructive natural law thinker? (2) Is the idea of an objectively valid natural right consistent with the account of morality and virtuous action developed in Ockham's academic works? In other words, assuming that Ockham did make significant use of natural law in his political writings, was this only a tactical device, basically at odds with his individualistic or voluntarist ethics, or were there essential elements in his early ethical thought which demanded an appeal to objective, rational norms in politics?

[8] For Ockham's significant distinction between natural and positive parts of *ius divinum*, see above, p. 136, n. 162.

[9] A good account is given by Miethke (*Ockhams Weg*, pp. 458–502). Also see above, pp. 10–12 and 15–16. The central passages in the *OND* are cc. 2, 61–2, 65, and 87–92; *OP* I, 299–313; *OP* II, 558–70, 573–80, 653–70.

OCKHAM'S DIVISION OF 'IUS NATURALE' AND ITS PLACE IN HIS POLITICAL THOUGHT

The master begins by distinguishing three kinds (*modi*) of natural right.

In one way that is called natural right which conforms with a natural reason which in no case fails... In another sense, natural right is what should be observed by those who use only natural equity, without any human custom or constitution... In a third way, that is called natural right which is gathered by evident reason from the law of nations or some human deed, unless the contrary is established by consent of those concerned. This last can be called suppositional natural right (*ius naturale ex suppositione*).[10]

About the first of these three modes little need be said. There is no reason to think that Ockham regarded even 'unfailing' natural reason as setting limits on *God's* right to command any action whatsoever.[11] Ockham's brief account of first-mode *ius naturale* shows, however, that aside from express divine commands to the contrary, he regarded certain norms – two of the ten commandments are offered as examples[12] – as absolutely valid: 'naturale est immutabile primo modo et invariabile ac indispensabile'.[13] Ockham's constant reference to *ius naturale* as setting limits to papal power[14] can most readily be understood in terms of the unchangeable, 'indispensable' norms of the first mode. Although his use of higher law in restraining papal action broke with the hierocratic tendency to regard the pope as a uniquely competent interpreter of higher law, Ockham himself did not make anything of this difference. He assumed, on the whole correctly, that his opponents did not wish to

---

[10] 'Uno enim modo dicitur ius naturale illud quod est conforme rationi naturali, quae in nullo casu fallit ... Aliter ius naturale est, quod servandum est ab illis qui sola aequitate naturali absque omni consuetudine vel constitutione humana utuntur ... Tertio modo dicitur ius naturale illud, quod ex iure gentium vel aliquo facto humano evidenti ratione colligitur, nisi de consensu illorum quorum interest, statuatur contrarium, quod potest vocari ius naturale ex suppositione.' III *Dialogus* II, 3, vi, fol. 263rab.

[11] *Ibid.*, I, 3, xxiv, fol. 202ra (in connection with God's command to Abraham to sacrifice Isaac), quoted above, p. 165n. Ockham's reference to God as the *dominus* of life and death is no departure from tradition. Cf. Thomas Aquinas, *Summa Theologiae*, Ia IIae, q. 94, a. 5, *ad* 2.

[12] 'Non mechaberis, non mentieris.' III *Dialogus* II, 3, vi, fol. 263ra.

[13] *Ibid.*, fol. 263rab.   [14] See above, chapter I, p. 21.

Politics and philosophy

place the pope *above* natural and divine law.[15] The vital issue for Ockham and for almost all of his contemporaries, Marsilius being the great exception, was not whether there are unalterable norms accessible to natural reason. The question was whether the pope's power was limited *only* by such norms.[16] Accordingly, the first member of Ockham's division of *ius naturale* is more significant as an acknowledgment of common ground with the previous tradition than as an original contribution. The other modes of *ius naturale* are of more interest, both in themselves and in their special bearing on Ockham's political thought.

The second kind of natural right consists of that which should be observed by men living on the basis of natural equity, without any human custom or constitution. In contrast with the immutable norms of the first mode, second-mode natural rights, such as community of possessions and universal freedom, can licitly be modified by positive law. This kind of right is natural, according to our texts and manuscripts,[17] because it is against the original condition of human nature ('quod ideo est naturale, quia est contra statum naturae institutae') and because it would not need to be observed if everyone lived according to natural reason or divine law.[18]

---

[15] On the relations between law and judgment in the medieval tradition and in Marsilius, see Gewirth, *Marsilius of Padua and Medieval Political Philosophy*, pp. 170ff. For Marsilius' drastic reinterpretation of natural law as a species of human positive law, see *ibid.*, pp. 147–52.

[16] Ockham's formulation of the problem of papal *plenitudo potestatis* (p. 21 above) is quite close to Augustinus Triumphus' articulation of the issue, though their solutions were opposed: 'Illa, quae papa praecepit vel clauduntur sub iure naturali, vel sub iure positivo. Si clauduntur sub iure divino, non est obediendum papae, si mandaret aliquid contra illa . . . Si autem clauduntur sub iure naturali, et papa mandaret aliquid contra illa fieri . . . similiter in talibus sibi obediendum non est. Sed si illa, quae praecepit, clauduntur sub iure positivo, cum omne ius positivum ab ipso dependeat . . . in talibus si aliquid mandat contra ipsa, vel aliter interpretaretur, quam scripta sint, sibi obediendum est' (*Summa de Ecclesiastica Potestate*, q. 22, a. 1, *resp.*). For other references to the limitation of papal plenitude of power by divine and natural law, see Gewirth, *Marsilius of Padua and Medieval Political Philosophy*, p. 170, n. 25, and Tierney, *Foundations of the Conciliar Theory*, pp. 88–90.

[17] I have consulted the following mss.: Ms. 517, Bibliothèque de l'Arsenal, Paris; Ms. 3522 (478), Bibliothèque Mazarine, Paris; Mss. Lat. 14619 and Lat. 15881, Bibliothèque Nationale, Paris; Mss. Lat. 4098 and 4115, Biblioteca Vaticana, Rome.

[18] 'Aliter ius naturale est, quod servandum est ab illis qui sola aequitate naturali absque omni consuetudine vel constitutione humana utuntur, quod ideo est naturale, quia est contra statum naturae institutae, et si omnes homines viverent

178

Calling a law natural *because* it is contrary to nature and would be unnecessary if everyone followed nature is odd, to say the least. It is tempting to emend the text to give the opposite sense: if everyone followed natural reason after the fall of man, we *would* observe norms which were *not* contrary to our original condition.[19] With less alteration of the text, however, we may take Ockham to mean that the second mode is natural because it operates by natural equity alone and without positive law, *although* (referring 'ideo' to the preceding clause and reading 'quamvis sit' for 'quia est') it is against the original state of nature and would be unnecessary if everyone lived rationally, that is, if we were not liable to moral defects consequent upon the fall.[20]

Thus, when Ockham asserts later that all things are common by second-mode natural right because all were common in the original state of nature and would remain so if everyone lived according to reason after the fall, he can be read as saying that fallen man has a choice, in principle at least, between continuing to live without property or setting up economic institutions defined by positive law.[21] If men decided to do without property, however, they would need to observe principles of equity which took account of the needs and shortcomings of their fallen state. In fact, of course, all men do not live according to reason after the fall (even by a reason tempered with equity), and so, *propter iniquitatem*, private property is introduced. However we interpret or rewrite the initial definition, Ockham's account of second-mode *ius naturale* defines a framework of norms sufficient for a community of reasonable men. The life of such men would be 'natural' at least in the sense that it was not governed by formal institutions or arbitrary custom. Quoting

secundum rationem naturalem aut legem divinam non esset faciendum nec servandum.' III *Dialogus* II, 3, vi, fol. 263ra.

[19] This emendation is incorporated by F. Oakley in his translation of the text in R. Lerner and M. Mahdi (eds.), *Medieval Political Philosophy: a Sourcebook* (New York, 1963), p. 500.

[20] The emendation suggested here would bring the text more into line with the interpretation of R. McKeon, 'The development of the concept of property in political philosophy: a study of the background of the constitution', *Ethics*, XLVIII (1938), 297–366; 333–4: 'This is natural law in the sense of those equitable readjustments made necessary by consideration of human needs and weaknesses, but unaffected by particular conventions.'

[21] III *Dialogus* II, 3, vi, fol. 263ra.

Isidore of Seville again, Ockham cites universal freedom and community of possession as examples of second-mode *ius naturale*.[22] The ideal aspect of this state of nature is yet more prominent, however, in a later remark. The right to repel violence with force would not exist among those who lived according to reason and natural equity, the master asserts, 'because among them ... [no one] would use force against another'.[23] The 'natural' (pre-political) condition of man is presented as a potentially desirable one. The view that property and government were introduced *propter iniquitatem* has as its converse the notion that natural equity alone would suffice to regulate human affairs if men, with all their limitations, lived as reasonably as they could.

Although Ockham's two examples of second-mode *ius naturale –* *communis omnium possessio* and *omnium una libertas –* are both taken from the Isidorian text at the beginning of the *Decretum*,[24] we should not overlook the peculiar importance of these values in Ockham's own political career. In his first polemic he defended a life without property, and elsewhere he placed unusual emphasis on personal liberty in both ecclesiastical and secular political contexts.[25] In view of Ockham's sustained commitment to such values, it is worth asking what practical political relevance he attributed to the second mode of *ius naturale*. As it happens, this issue, though not essential to the polemical task at hand, is briefly raised in the text which we have been discussing. To begin with, second-mode natural right is distinguished from the first mode on the ground that it can licitly be contravened.[26] Does it not follow then, that the supposed natural rights of freedom and common property are mere verbiage? Possibly with this thought in mind, the student objects to calling such rights natural, since, according to Isidore, natural right is universal, 'commune omnium nationum'.[27] The master's reply is in line with the critical rationalism which we have observed in Ockham's treatment of government. The second mode of *ius naturale is* common to all nations, he says, in the sense that all nations are bound to it unless

---

22 'Isto modo loquitur Isidorus ... cum dicit, quod secundum ius naturale est communis omnium possessio et omnium una libertas.' *Ibid.*, fol. 263ra.
23 *Ibid.*, fol. 263rb. 24 Gratian, I, di. I, c. 7; ed. Friedberg, I, col. 2.
25 See above, pp. 9–16, 119–22 and 140–9.
26 'Non est immutabile; immo bene licet contrarium statuere ut iuri fiat contrarium.' III *Dialogus* II, 3, vi, fol. 263rb. 27 *Ibid.*, fol. 263rb–va.

the contrary is ordained for some reasonable cause.[28] In other words, although norms of this type are not 'immutabile ... invariabile ac indispensabile', as are the absolute norms of the first mode, neither are they 'mere' ideals, to be set aside by popular agreement or the arbitrary stipulation of those in power. If that were so, the student's objection would be justified. In fact, however, substantial justification is required for departing from this kind of *ius naturale*, and failing such justification, all societies are obliged to observe it.

This answer is briefly given, but it sheds light on an important aspect of Ockham's political thought. Ockham believed that there was reasonable cause for establishing systems of property and even, on occasion, for imposing the yoke of servitude on men who are by nature free. Nevertheless, his defense of Franciscan poverty and emphasis on personal liberty cannot be viewed simply as expressions of pious sentiment or subjective, personal aspiration. In the former case, to be sure, the ideal natural 'right' to be poor was defended only for a select minority, not used as the basis for a new social order. In the case of freedom, too, Ockham was far from insisting upon the universal implementation of the natural ideal. In both cases, however, he claimed a more than hortatory force for his position. The Franciscans must be allowed to be poor.[29] The subjects of government in a good society must be free. The papal government must regularly respect the individual Christian's gospel liberty. Ockham's attitude on all these important matters is well conveyed by the assertion that all communities are genuinely bound by an ideal natural

---

[28] 'Sic est commune omnium nationum quod omnes nationes nisi ex causa rationabili ordinetur contrarium tenentur ad ipsum' (*ibid.*, fol. 263va). 'Habetur nisi contrarium aliquo iure humano *ex causa rationabili* constituatur' (*ibid.*, fol. 263vab). It is clear from Ockham's discussion of the same canonist text in the *OND* (c. 65; *OP* II, 577–8) that even reasonably made property divisions do not completely abolish the underlying natural community of ownership: 'Non tamen istud ius naturale potest totaliter evacuari, quia nunquam sic possunt temporalia appropriari, quin tempore necessitatis debeant esse communia ... Et ideo tempore necessitatis extremae potest quilibet iure poli uti qualibet re temporali, sine qua vitam suam conservare non posset.' St Thomas, too, held that it is licit to use someone else's property in case of extreme need (*Summa Theologiae*, IIa IIae, q. 66, a. 7), but he did not base this conclusion on Isidore's text, which he treated briefly and without positive emphasis elsewhere (*ibid.*, Ia IIae, q. 94, a. 5, *ad* 3).

[29] In their life of poverty the friars had returned to the condition of Adam and Eve so far as property was concerned. See above, p. 176, and *OND*, cc. 14 and 25–8; *OP* II, 430–40 and 482–94.

law unless there is reasonable cause to the contrary. Hence, although there is no direct reference to second-mode *ius naturale* elsewhere in Ockham's writings, his remarks on this class of norms in III *Dialogus* give systematic expression to a major theme in his thought, the commitment to essentially non-political values as an effective standard for human relations.

The third mode of natural right, *ius naturale ex suppositione*, may be said to begin where the second mode ends, for the same examples which show what would be missing from human affairs in a pre-political state illustrate the suppositions on which this type of natural norm is based. Suppositional natural right is that which may be deduced by evident reason from the law of nations or from some human deed, unless the contrary is established by the agreement of those concerned. Suppose for example, that goods and money have been assigned to (*appropriatae*) different parties by the *ius gentium* or some human law, then it is gathered by evident reason that deposits and loans ought to be given back. Or again, suppose that someone violently injures another – a supposition which is not based on *ius naturale* but is against it – then evident reason shows that such violence may licitly be repelled by force.[30] The people's right to choose the pope, the polemical occasion for the whole discussion, provides a further example of *ius naturale* in its third sense. It is 'ex iure naturali tertio modo dicto' that the Roman people have the right to choose the pope, for this situation falls under the principle that any people lacking a ruler (this is the supposition) has a natural right to choose one.[31]

Suppositional natural right is 'gathered by evident reason'. In this respect it is on a footing with the absolute natural right of the first mode, which 'conforms to natural reason which in no case fails'. As Ockham's examples show, however, acts dictated by suppositional natural right are distinguished by being rational responses to non-rational and contingent circumstances. Thus, unprovoked violence is flatly contrary to reason. Such violence is,

---

[30] III *Dialogus* II, 3, vi, fol. 263rb.
[31] 'Supposito enim, quod aliquibus sit aliquis praelatus vel princeps vel rector praeficiendus evidenti ratione colligitur, quod si per illum vel per illos cuius vel quorum interest non [aliter?] ordinetur illi quibus est praeficiendus habent ius eligendi et praeficiendi eum [for *eis*], unde nullus dari debet ipsis invitis.' *Ibid.*, fol. 263vb.

however, a 'supposition' for the natural right to repel violence with force. Or again, although there are rational principles relevant to the choice of a ruler or the distribution of property there is also, according to Ockham, an arbitrary element in such actions: rulers must be *chosen*,[32] it is 'de *consensu* hominum' that goods are appropriated.[33] Finally, some third-mode natural obligations come into play only when acts have been performed (e.g., lending money) that flow from the private choice of the individuals concerned. Hence, although the element of rational deduction gives third-mode norms universality in the sense of objective validity, they do not have the universality of application of absolute norms or the universal ideal relevance of the second mode. Where special justification is required for departing from the second type of natural right (nothing would justify deviations from the first type), special circumstances are required for the third kind to become applicable. The third type of *ius naturale* is 'common to all nations', then, but it is common to all only conditionally.[34]

The third mode of natural law bears on two important features of Ockham's political thought, his readiness to grant that exceptional circumstances require special action and his insistence that such actions be rational rather than arbitrary or authoritarian. Since most of the conclusions reached earlier in this study can be cited in connection with one or another of these points, it would be a long and perhaps unnecessary task to indicate all the places at which Ockham's polemic corresponds with his doctrine of suppositional natural right. On the other hand, it would be difficult to determine exactly when Ockham began to regard his approach to the problems

---

[32] 'Quia non est iustum naturale ut magis isti principentur quam illi, necesse est quod per iustum positivum determinetur quod isti principentur, vel simpliciter secundum totam vitam suam vel ad tempus. Et sicut non obstante quod non sit iustum naturale ut iste principetur secundum totam vitam suam sibi similibus et aequalibus, qualiter intelligit Aristoteles, tamen ex causa fieri potest iustum positivum, quod Aristoteles negare non intendit . . . Quare possibile est quod *aliquem* debere principari sibi similibus sit iustum naturale, et tamen non est iustum naturale *istum* debere principari sibi similibus, et sic de singulis.' III *Dialogus* I, 2, xvii, fol. 196vb. The appeal to formal logic in this passage and in the sequel is rare.

[33] 'Omnia sunt communia antequam de *consensu hominum* appropriarentur.' *Ibid.* II, 3, vi, fol. 263va. See above, pp. 105–6.

[34] 'Ius vero naturale tertio modo dictum est commune omnium nationum ex suppositione si scilicet omnes nationes statuerunt vel fecerunt illud quo ius illo modo dictum evidenti ratione colligitur.' *Ibid.*, fol. 263va.

of his time as the application of a new and distinct mode of *ius naturale*.[35] Since he did not give a systematic exposition of this concept in III *Dialogus*, it is also a delicate matter to work from the formulation there to particular passages in other works. The examples offered in III *Dialogus* give some indications of a systematic structure, however, and when these indications are followed out, it becomes evident that the third branch of Ockham's division is *par excellence* the normative basis for each crucial stage in the development of legitimate government. First, the need for government rests, according to Ockham, on the supposition that human nature is prone to evil due to the fall. The precept to establish rulers, the initial norm for practical politics, is thus *iure naturali ex suppositione*. Given that rulers are to be instituted, a further stage of supposition, it is naturally right that they should be chosen by the agreement of those concerned. Finally, 'supposing' that a positive legal and political order has been duly established, then respect for that order is not merely a requirement enforced by the order itself but an obligation of natural law. Ockham himself did not arrange his examples in this sequence or otherwise systematically articulate his conception of suppositional natural right. Hence, we can hardly be confident that he would accept the notion of three and only three essential 'stages' of political development in accord with suppositional natural right. Furthermore, problems arise to which this outline gives no solution, for example, the problem of determining what is to be done when men contravene one or another principle of natural right. Yet, just as the general theme of rational response to non-rational contingencies is found throughout Ockham's political writings, so the subordinate ideas of our subdivision also recur: the idea that political institutions are made necessary by defects in human nature, that consent is the natural basis of legitimacy, and that duly established institutions merit conscientious respect and are not legally subordinate to extrapolitical powers. It seems clear, therefore, that the third mode of *ius naturale*, like the first two, is coherent with the balance of Ockham's political thought.

[35] A clear distinction between absolute and conditional natural right is drawn at III *Dialogus* II, 1, x, fol. 235ra and is later applied to the *ius gentium* (*Ibid.*, xi, fol. 235vab) For a possible source of Ockham's doctrine, see Thomas Aquinas, *Summa Theologiae*, Ia IIae, q. 94, a. 4, *resp.*

Considering all three senses of *ius naturale*, the absolute, the ideal, and the suppositional, we may fairly assert that Ockham's position on the abstract, philosophical topic of natural law has important connections with his approach to practical politics. He always proceeded as if the rights and liberties of rulers and subjects or the comparative usefulness and justice of various constitutions were objective matters that could be correctly determined by expert analysis, although he rejected positive law and custom as ultimate normative principles. It is in just such a situation that we might expect to find reliance on natural law. In Ockham's case, the application of natural norms was not a process of mechanical deduction from comprehensive principles. Hence, he spent little effort in articulating a complete system of such norms. His attachment to natural law was not, however, as casual as this lack of explicit system implies. We have seen that the scheme of *ius naturale* so tersely offered in III *Dialogus* II corresponds with the most distinctive recurrent features of his large polemical output. The tension between an acceptance of certain values as absolute, devotion to a lofty human ideal, and sensitivity to the needs of particular circumstances accounts for much that is complex and obscure in Ockham, but also for much that is permanently valid in his thought. Whether this use of natural law was consistent with the principles of his own earlier moral philosophy remains to be investigated in the following sections.

MORAL VIRTUE: INDIVIDUALISM

Ockham's extensive discussions of ethical and psychological questions deserve detailed study.[36] It will be prudent here, however, as

[36] Among the central texts for Ockham's ethics are *Sent.* I, di. I; III, qq. 11-15; IV, 14 and *dubitationes additae* 3-6. *Quodlibeta Septem* I, 20; II, 16; III, 13-14; IV, 6. Although he found no valid reason to question their authenticity, Boehner adduced convincing manuscript evidence against regarding *Sent.* III, qq. 12-15 and the *dubitationes additae* as parts of Ockham's commentary on the *Sentences* (*Quodlibeta Septem* IV, 6, which is almost identical with *Sent.* III, 12, is also missing from the oldest manuscripts of the *Quodlibeta*). These questions 'seem to be the nucleus of another work by Ockham, which probably could be called *Quaestiones Disputatae Ockham*' (P. Boehner, 'The *notitia intuitiva* of non-existents according to William Ockham with a critical study of the text of Ockham's *Reportatio* and a revised edition of *Reportatio* II, Qq. 14-15', *Traditio*, I (1943), 223-75; reprinted in Boehner, *Collected Articles on Ockham*, pp. 268-300; pp. 296-8). Ockham's

in the last section, to discuss only a few especially pertinent points, merely sketching the surrounding context.

Perhaps the best known thesis in Ockhamist ethics is that only acts of will are intrinsically virtuous or vicious: 'nullus actus alius ab actu voluntatis est intrinsece virtuosus vel vitiosus'.[37] On one side, this thesis is to be understood as denying that overt behavior has its own proper moral goodness or badness. The moral value of *actus exteriores* depends entirely on the intentions with which such acts are performed. Thus, the act of walking to church will be morally good if done for the honor of God, but not if it is done out of vainglory. Or again, in the hypothetical case of a man who throws himself over a cliff but repents of his suicidal intention in mid-fall, the first part of his descent is morally vicious, the second part not. Ockham's thesis involves a further contrast, however, besides the one already drawn between 'outer' and 'inner'. For the inner side of human action is itself complex, involving not only choices and habits of the will but also cognitive factors, especially acts of understanding. Ockham found it conceivable that God could have created a world in which acts of understanding were intrinsically virtuous or vicious rather than acts of will, but did not believe He had done so.[38] A man deserves praise or blame for volitions rather than acts of understanding. Cognitive acts are purely 'natural'; they are not in

ethical writings deserve further study. The accounts of A. Garvens ('Die Grundlagen der Ethik Wilhelms von Ockham', *FzS*, XXI (1934), 243–73, 360–408) and L. Vereecke ('L'obligation morale selon Guillaume d'Ockham', *La vie spirituelle*, *Supplément*, No. 45 (2e trimestre 1958), 123–43) exaggerate Ockham's formalism. A more balanced presentation is given by Miethke (*Ockhams Weg*, pp. 300–35). In a detailed recent study of 'William of Ockham on right reason', *Speculum* XLVIII (1973), 13–36, David W. Clark has arrived at conclusions substantially agreeing with those reached in the following pages.

37 *Sent.* III, 12, G.
38 And yet, even though God *could* 'accept' acts of understanding as He now accepts acts of will, the 'intrinsic' goodness thus accorded them would in that case be due to an extrinsic cause. Only an act of will can be intrinsically good from its own nature: 'Tale [formaliter et intrinsece bonum] nihil potest esse *ex natura sua* nisi solus actus voluntatis, licet aliquis [alius?] actus posset dici intrinsece bonus et virtuosus ex causa extrinseca acceptante, quomodo Deus solum acceptat actum voluntatis, quia si acceptaret actum intellectus sicut voluntatis, tunc ita posset actus intellectus dici bonus intrinsece sicut voluntatis.' *Quodlibeta Septem* IV, 6 (argument against the second Scotist reply to the first objection raised after the main discussion). The version here is somewhat clearer than the parallel text at *Sent.* III, 12, XX.

our power to perform or not to perform and hence are not intrinsically meritorious or culpable. Taking both contrasts into account, we may say that Ockham's ethical voluntarism consisted of a double emphasis on the will as the exclusive locus of moral evaluation, first in comparison with external behavior, but also in comparison with the intellect. It is this distinctive position which must be related to the objective natural-law orientation surveyed in the last section. Before proceeding to this problem, however, we may note certain broader connections between Ockham's voluntarism and his political thought.

The emphasis on the individual's inner states in Ockham's academic ethical writings supports the concept of legitimate correction he developed in his campaign against papal heresy. As we have seen,[39] Ockham contended that an erring Christian needed to have his error clearly explained to him before he was obliged to recant. In the circumstances, this was a radical claim. It played a vital conceptual role in Ockham's attempt to turn the tables on those in power. This position on legitimate correction was, however, thoroughly consistent with Ockham's earlier attempts to show that the quality of an individual's intention is ultimately the sole determinant of the moral worth of his actions. The individual who alters his religious professions to please his superiors and not from respect for the truth would be comparable, for Ockham, to the man who goes to church *propter vanam gloriam* rather than *propter Deum*. Although his behavior might be objectively correct – the superior may be orthodox, just as going to church is a proper thing to do – the ill-intentioned act is not even morally good, let alone obligatory.

Another point at which Ockham's ethical voluntarism provides support for his political thought is in his attitude towards experts,[40] which depends in turn on the importance he attached in certain circumstances to individual character. While Ockham stressed the need for expert knowledge in political affairs, he never proposed a constitution in which experts were given political authority. This was partly because he had a bitter appreciation of the extent to which questionable volitional factors rather than purely rational considerations determine who is actually given the position of expert

[39] See above, pp. 53–7.
[40] See above, pp. 59–67, 81 n , and 140, n. 177.

in any society.[41] Beyond this, however, was his recognition that even those who deserve to be regarded as experts because of their intellectual qualifications may be useless or positively harmful in practical matters because of moral defects. Ockham's treatment of understanding and will is relevant here, particularly his thesis that the will has power (although not, as we shall see, the moral right) to reject any course of action dictated by the understanding, no matter how objectively reasonable it may be.[42] To put the matter in slightly different terms, Ockham's celebrated fallibilism was based less on skepticism about the understanding than on sober caution about the human will. An expert may be relied upon to know the truth, but there is no guarantee that he will act upon it.[43] This does not mean, however, that we have no grounds for trusting anyone. On the contrary, for all of its emphasis on spontaneity, Ockham's ethical theory provides a quite definite basis for forming expectations as to how men will act in important situations. Ockham argued at length that at certain levels all the moral virtues are 'connected'[44] and that habits generated by our actions are themselves causative of further similar acts.[45] That is, a man who has one virtue (in addition to prudence) will have some inclination to perform acts appropriate

---

[41] See above, pp. 60–1.
[42] 'Quantumcunque ratio dictet aliquid, potest ... voluntas hoc velle vel nolle' (*Quodlibeta Septem* I, 16). This proposition, which he held to be certain from experience, was Ockham's basis for asserting the freedom of the will. For the thesis that prudence (= *recta ratio agibilium*) can be present without moral virtue, see *Sent.* III, 12, OO–TT. Cf. Ockham's intricate discussions of the will's contingency and freedom in the enjoyment of its ultimate end in *Sent.* I, di. 1, q. 6 (*Opera Theologica*, ed. Gál and Brown, I, 486–507), *Sent.* IV, 14, and *dubitatione additae* 3–4. The spontaneity of voluntary activity in Ockham's thought appears even more impressive when contrasted with his thoroughgoing (more than Aristotelian) determinism with respect to nature. On this see F. Corvino, 'Il significato del termine *natura* nelle opere filosofiche di Occam' in *La filosofia della natura nel medioevo: atti del III congresso internazionale di filosofia medioevale, Passo della Mendola (Trento)*, 1964 (Milan, 1966), pp. 605–15.
[43] Ockham's attitudes on these matters were shaped in part by personal experience: 'Puto enim in istis quattuor annis ultimis [1329–33] plura de moribus nunc viventium evertisse, quam si cum eis extra istam brigam xl annis conversationem continuam habuissem' (*Epistola ad Fratres Minores*; *OP* III, 16–17).
[44] *Sent.* III, 12, U–BB. On this matter Ockham took issue with St Thomas, who had argued (*Summa Theologiae*, Ia IIae, q. 65, a. 1, *ad* 1) that virtues such as magnificence and magnanimity, which pertain only to special states of life, are not linked with virtues bearing on the general condition of man.
[45] *Sent.* III, 4, F; cf. *ibid.*, 12, B, J, and O.

to any of the others when circumstances require it.[46] This has some tendency to support the idea that in an emergency any good person may rightly be called on to act in public affairs. Similarly, Ockham's acceptance of the causality of virtuous habits helps explain the emphasis he placed on *bona fama* as a basis for deciding who ought to be believed in cases of conflicting testimony on such matters as papal heresy. A man's institutional status, the office he holds, may be a less reliable guide to his credibility than his reputation as an individual.[47] This would make sense if the reputation were founded on his actually having performed virtuous actions.

Perhaps the most important political implications of Ockham's voluntarism are found in his attitudes towards government. His limited conception of governmental functions is a natural consequence of the view that virtue and vice are centered in an inner region that the external coercion of secular power does not touch. Ockham's opposition to the notion of comprehensive papal regulation of behavior and his attempt to build a more pastoral conception of the papal office point in the same direction. Secular government must control behavior which seriously disturbs public order, but the development of higher moral and spiritual values in a community lies in the choices made by individuals, not in a pattern of correct behavior enforced from above. Accordingly, Ockham's emphasis on personal liberty and his insistence that free men are better than unfree should not be understood in purely negative terms or attributed solely to his reading of Aristotle's *Politics*. In terms of his own philosophy, the demand for freedom of action was an intensely moral demand, such freedom being in his view a necessary precondition for significant human existence.[48]

MORAL VIRTUE: RATIONALITY

Ockham was a voluntarist in believing that only acts of will could have intrinsic moral value. Was he also a voluntarist in the more extreme sense of exalting volition as opposed to rationality? Did he

[46] *Sent.* III, 12, U.
[47] See above, pp. 70–1. Ockham's views on the virtue ordinarily required in an office-holder were, however, moderate. See above, pp.120–1, 159–60.
[48] Cf. St Augustine's argument that since man cannot act rightly unless he wills to do so, it was good that God gave him freedom of choice (*De Libero Arbitrio*, II, I, v).

hold that things are good only because they are desired, that the virtuousness of an act is purely personal, independent of whether the act is directed towards some objectively valuable end? Was his criticism of traditional social structures a 'willful' revolt against reason in public affairs? It is hardly a sufficient response to these questions to point out that Ockham himself often claimed to seek 'rational' solutions to public problems and avoided extreme positions. Granting that the moderate or constitutionalist aspects of his political thought are more prominent than has often been recognized, and even granting his sincerity in appealing to natural law, one may still doubt that these traits were consequences of his earlier ethical discussions. A thoroughly subjective moral philosophy, an ethics of personal authenticity, is, after all, logically compatible with 'rational' as well as 'irrational' outward behavior. The point is, that such a moral philosophy makes the choice between reason and unreason itself a matter of personal impulse. At the deepest level, then, nominalism might have an anarchic influence even if the chief nominalist was by preference a practical conservative. If a significant connection is to be asserted between Ockham's ethics and the rationality of his politics, it must be shown that the former not only permits but requires rationality in public action. This can, however, be shown. For, first, in his academic writings as well as in later appeals to natural law, Ockham clearly accepted the concept of 'objective' value common to the scholastic tradition. Second, he thoroughly integrated the principle of ethical objectivity – or rationality – with the voluntarism surveyed in the last section. Both points deserve emphasis.

Just as Ockham accepted the basic validity of the scholastic tradition of natural law, so, in his most important discussion of moral and theological virtue, he also accepted without question the idea that some actions are generally good and others bad. Giving alms, for example, is *ex genere* a good act, while stealing and wanting to commit fornication are bad. The types of action men have to choose among (including inner acts of will as well as external behavior) are not in themselves of equal value. It is not as if the moral agent with a good will were at liberty to attach this will to any course of action whatever and could thus, by a kind of volitional magic, change a bad or indifferent act into a good one. On the contrary, setting aside the special good or bad circumstances surrounding a particular choice, Ockham claimed that there are certain actions 'about which the philosophers and saints say that from their very description they are involved in malice'.[49] This is only one of several passages in which Ockham accepted without a trace of skepticism the traditional scholastic view of the objectivity of values.[50]

By itself this acceptance goes some way to allay suspicion about the character of Ockham's position, but doubt may remain. The political writer who now and then appeals to natural law may not be a natural-law thinker. The ethicist who now and then pays allegiance to the objectivity of values may not be a thorough objectivist. The question is how well his objectivity or rationality is integrated with other relevant principles. As we have seen, Ockham considered and rejected the notion that the understanding is the locus of intrinsic moral value. This suggests that the relation between will and reason (given that reason exists) is a contingent one, that it will be purely accidental if the morally virtuous good will happens to be conjoined with a right reason directing it to objectively good outer acts. If this connection were indeed purely accidental, then public anarchy would be a natural consequence, since there would be no common basis on which even good men could live in concord. In this situation, uncritical submission to ecclesiastical officials, blind reliance on custom, a positivist public reason, or some other non-rational agency would be needed to provide effective law.

Although there is not the slightest indication that Ockham had political considerations in mind when he lectured on the *Sentences*,

[49] 'Aliquis actus est bonus ex genere vel malus... Exemplum... quantum ad actum bonum ex genere... dare elemosinam... Exemplum quantum ad actum malum ut furtum facere velle fornicari absolute sine aliqua circumstantia bona vel mala de quibus dicunt philosophi et sancti quod statim nominata convoluta sunt cum malitia.' *Sent.* III, 12, N.

[50] Ockham sharply distinguished between the good as *honestum* or *delectabile*, and the good as *volitum*, and also between things which are *realiter* and *apparenter* good or evil (depending on the rightness of the judgment of the intellect) (*Sent.* III, 13, S). At *Quodlibeta Septem* II, 14, he defended the possibility of a demonstrative science of morals, 'deducens conclusiones syllogistice ex principiis per se notis vel per experientiam scitis', in explicit contrast with 'moralis scientia positiva, cuiusmodi est scientia iuristarum'. Cf. *OND*, c. 65, *OP* II, 574–5. I *Dialogus* I, vii–x (see above, p. 67, n. 59).

that work contains passages highly relevant to these questions. As if wishing to restrain his hearers from the irrational voluntarism he himself was to be so often charged with, he argues with considerable persistence that rationality – *recta ratio* – is an integral requirement of genuine virtue, not a contingent addition from outside. The decisive passage concerns the question, whether *recta ratio* is included in the 'object' of a virtuous act.[51] In other words, if we assume that a virtuous act is one produced by a good will, the question is: in such an act must the agent intentionally aim at doing what is most rational, or is its rationality an incidental feature of his act, something with which the agent is not directly concerned? The thrust of Ockham's complex repsonse is that his own previously established principles entail the closest possible bond between goodness of will and rationality in the object of will. He rejects other arguments and proposes instead that 'a better and stronger argument to prove [that] right reason or prudence [is] an object of the virtuous act' is to show that the denial of this thesis contradicts important conclusions established earlier in his own analysis. For unless right reason is included in the object of the virtuous act, then no act would be necessarily and intrinsically virtuous but only contingently so. Furthermore, a non-virtuous act would become virtuous by the addition of something merely natural and not in our power. But the opposite of these consequences has been proved earlier.[52]

The essential function of *recta ratio* in the production of virtuous acts appears with special clarity in Ockham's discussion of the first 'inconvenient' consequence just mentioned. No act of will lacking right reason for an object can be intrinsically virtuous, he argues, because it cannot satisfy the general principle that a virtuous act must be elicited 'conformably' to right reason, for an act of will directed towards any object other than right reason itself can be elicited without the mediation of right reason as well as with it; hence, no such act can be intrinsically virtuous.[53] Ockham evidently

---

[51] *Sent.* III, 12, CCC–FFF.
[52] Similarly, a non-meritorious act would become meritorious by the addition of something natural and not in our power. *Sent.* III, 12, DDD.
[53] 'Quemcunque actum respectu quorumcunque obiectorum exceptaa ratione rect in ratione obiecti potest voluntas elicere mediante recta ratione potest elicere sine ea . . . quaero si illa volitio sit virtuosa intrinsece vel non. Non potest dici quod sic, quia non elicitur conformiter rationi rectae.' *Sent.* III, 12, EEE.

has in mind here the will which produces actions materially conforming to rational principles without itself paying attention to those principles or being determined by them. One thinks here of the church-goer who simply wills to go to church, not out of vainglory perhaps, but not from the love of God or regard for right reason, either. Although his outer act might conform to right reason, the volition behind it does not, and hence his act cannot be intrinsically virtuous. As Ockham himself puts it, it does not suffice for virtue if the objects actually willed are those that right reason *would* dictate. Such an 'aptitudinal' conformity is lacking in its own terms, since right reason would dictate that the agent perform a certain action *because* it is dictated by right reason. From this it follows that an actual exercise of *recta ratio* is required in every virtuous action. Even this statement of the matter, however, is not sufficiently stringent to mark the strength of Ockham's commitment to rationality, for the mere presence of right reason does not guarantee that the action is done because of, or for the sake of, right reason. It is necessary that the act have *recta ratio* itself for an object.[54] To continue our example, if a man goes to church when he ought to, knowing the right reason for this act and actually having it in mind as he goes, he may yet fail of virtue unless to some extent the very object of his act – what he wills to do – consists of going-to-church-because-it-is-rational-to-do-so. As Ockham explains in a slightly earlier passage, 'to act conformably to right reason consists of willing what right reason dictates because right reason so dictates. It is impossible, however, that someone will one thing because of another unless he wills that other, because if he does not will it or wills it not to be, then he wills the first thing more for its own sake than because of the other. Therefore, in order to will virtuously what right reason dictates, it is strictly necessary that I will right reason [itself] by the same act and not by another.'[55] It is ironic, to say the least, that a thinker who

---

[54] 'Pono quod *coexistat* actus prudentiae. Et quaero tunc utrum ille actus volendi coexistente actu prudentiae sit virtu[osu]s vel non. Si non patet discurrendo per singulas causas huius, quia nulla esset causa huius nisi quia illa volitio non habet rectam rationem *pro obiecto*, quia per hypothesim nullum aliud obiectum requisitum deficit et ratio recta *coexistit*, et omnia talia.' If it is said that the bare presence of prudence makes the act virtuous, the argument goes back to the preceding stage: an otherwise non-virtuous act would become virtuous by the addition of something merely natural. *Ibid.*   [55] *Sent.* III, 12, DDD.

---

insisted so vehemently on the moral necessity of 'willing' rationality should be stigmatized as a skeptic and the apostle of arbitrary, unrestrained will.

Instead of ascribing to Ockham a simple dualism between 'inner' and 'outer', in which moral evaluations based on personal integrity or purity of intention have no reliable connection with the rational assessment of overt behavior, it is more correct to say that the good will at the heart of Ockham's conception of morality is itself oriented outward. As Ockham states matters, a will like ours, which of itself can act well or badly, stands in need of a rule or reason beside itself ('alia a se') to direct its actions.[56] Accordingly, we may speak of commitment to rationality as an essential component of moral virtue for Ockham. 'For this, that a right act be elicited by the will, it is *necessarily* required that there be some right reason in the understanding.'[57] Accordingly, *recta ratio* is involved in each of the five grades of moral virtue distinguished in Ockham's massive question on the connection of the virtues.[58] Rationality carries the

---

[56] 'Illa voluntas quae potest quantum est de se bene agere et male, quia de se non est recta necessario ad hoc quod recte agat indiget aliqua regula dirigente alia a se.' The point is made clear by contrast with the divine will, which does not stand in need of external direction because it is itself the first directive rule and cannot act badly: 'Voluntas divina non indiget aliquo dirigente, quia illa est prima regula directiva et non potest male agere, sed voluntas nostra est huiusmodi, quia potest recte et non recte agere, igitur indiget aliqua ratione dirigente.' *Sent.* III, 13, B.

[57] 'Ad hoc quod actus rectus primo eliciatur a voluntate necessario requiritur *aliqua recta ratio* in intellectu.' *Ibid.*

[58] *Sent.* III, 12, substantially identical with *Quodlibeta Septem* IV, 6. 'Primus gradus est quando aliquis vult facere opera iusta *conformiter rationi rectae dictanti* talia opera esse facienda . . . et voluntas elicit actum volendi talia opera conformiter *iuxta dictamen intellectus. Secundus gradus* est quando voluntas vult facere opera iusta *secundum rectum dictamen praedictum et* propter [read: praeter] hoc *cum intentione nullo modo dimittendi talia pro quocunque quod est contra rectam rationem* et non pro morte *si recta ratio dictaret* tale opus non esse dimittendum pro morte . . . *Tertius gradus* est quando aliquis vult tale opus facere *secundum rectam rationem* praedictam . . . et propter [read: praeter] hoc *vult tale opus* secundum circumstantias praedictas *facere praecise et semel, quia est sic dictatum a recta ratione. Quartus gradus* est quando vult illud facere secundum omnes conditiones et circumstantias praedictas et praeter hoc propter amorem Dei praecise, *puta quia sic dictatum est ab intellectu* quod talia opera sunt facienda propter amorem Dei praecise, et ita universaliter est perfecta et vera virtus moralis de qua sancti loquuntur' (*Sent.* III, 12, K). The fifth grade, heroic virtue, presupposes the previous conditions except for the end in view, when the act 'indifferenter potest fieri propter Deum tanquam propter

194

outward orientation proper to human will still further, for *recta ratio* is concerned not only with self-evident principles of conduct and their general, logical consequences, but also with particular circumstances. As Ockham makes clear in discussing the problems of misinformed conscience, ignorance does not always excuse a man from moral blame. It does so only if due care has been taken in investigating the circumstances of action. The good will is one which undertakes appropriate investigation, seeking to discover those things which it ought to know.[59] Such a process necessarily involves it in the outer world of times, places, and other particulars.[60] In an important sense, then, the *recta ratio* of Ockham's academic ethics provides a philosophical basis for that concern with contingent circumstances which we have already noted as a distinguishing trait of his political thought. More generally, what might be called the rationalism of Ockham's voluntarism – the requirement of some exercise of *recta ratio* for any good act and the demand that due care be taken to find the 'right' right reason – strongly supports the use of natural law examined in the first part of this chapter.[61] While he was acutely sensitive to the possibility of misapplying expert ethical and political knowledge, it seems never to have occurred to Ockham that a virtuous man might wish to act in defiance of such knowledge. Acknowledgment of non-conventional norms for human conduct is essential to Ockham's 'good will', and it follows that a good person will do his best to deal with practical issues in an objective and reasonable way. Sustained analysis may be required, however, to determine what is reasonable in a particular situation, and this

finem, vel propter honestatem, vel pacem, vel aliquid tale ... et praeter hoc elicit tale opus facere actum imperativo formaliter ... quod ... excedit communem statum hominum' (*Quodlibeta Septem* IV, 6).

59 Ockham's resolution of the question, whether a virtuous act of will is compatible with intellectual error concerning the object of the act, turns on a distinction between the agent whose ignorance is culpable ('puta quia fuit negligens ad investigandum id quod tenetur scire'), and the agent who has made an investigation 'per omnem viam possibilem', but is deceived by something hidden, which it was not in his power to know. *Sent.* III, 13, J–K.

60 The frequent references in I *Dialogus* to what various persons are obliged to know (*tenetur scire*) must be understood in terms of this distinction between culpable and blameless error. While he did not, of course, assert that everyone was bound to know that the pope was a heretic (if this was the case), Ockham did insist that every Christian was in some circumstances obliged to give ear to those offering to prove such a charge. See above, p. 69n.   61 Above, pp. 177–85.

necessary analysis may be beyond the ordinary man's powers. Consequently, when a variety of both natural and positive norms are involved and the facts of the case are complicated as well, a man of good will may need expert advice of various kinds. From the moral side this cooperation of virtue with expertise is no accident.

Ockham rejected Neoplatonism in both speculative and practical matters. Accordingly, one should not expect him to propound a scheme of law, government, and society deduced by metaphysical analogy from a comprehensive vision of the universe. Furthermore, the character of Ockham's writings was determined to an unusual extent by circumstances not in his power to control, most notably by the state of the church and of European politics, but also by his virtually unavoidable temperamental reactions to personal theological censure and to papal attacks on common Franciscan beliefs and values, and by his association with Ludwig of Bavaria. As we have seen in the present chapter, however, the striking individualism of Ockham's political works and their equally striking objectivity both indicate a continuing attachment to his earlier philosophical positions. We have examined only a small portion of his academic thought and even in connection with the few topics considered have had to pass over many problems. Our investigation has shown, however, that Ockham's references to an objective natural law, his insistence that the rights and wrongs of political questions could be impartially known, and his opposition to purely authoritarian acts of power were not solely matters of circumstance or temperament. These central features of his political thought are proper consequences of a moral philosophy based on the principle that right reason should be followed, not only in some cases as it suits private interests or the individual's impulses, but always and for its own sake.

Chapter 5

POLITICS AND THEOLOGY: SECULAR
POLITICS AND CHRISTIAN VIRTUE

*Nullus . . . principatus regalis est a natura, quamvis principatus regᵭlis assimiletur
in multis principatui naturali: sed omnis principatus regalis est ex institutione
positiva, divina et humana. De divina patet in libro Regum in quo habemus
quod Deus per Samuelem instituit principatum regalem pandendo quod deberet
esse ius regis qui instituendus erat . . . [P]rincipatus regalis humanitus institutus,
cuiusmodi est omnis principatus qui etiam in praesentia habetur, pendeat et
procedat ex ordinatione humana quae ex causa rationabili variari potest.*

No . . . royal government exists by nature, although royal government is in
many ways like a natural government: but every royal government is based
on positive institution, divine and human. About the divine it is clear in the
book of Kings, in which we read that God instituted a royal government
through Samuel by showing what ought to be the law of the king who
was to be instituted . . . Humanly instituted royal government, of which
sort is every government which still exists at present, depends and
proceeds from human ordination, which from reasonable cause can be
varied.

OQ v, 6; *OP* I, 161–2

*Aliquis . . . vult . . . propter amorem Dei praecise . . . quia sic dictatum est ab
intellectu . . . ita . . . est perfecta et vera virtus moralis de qua sancti loquuntur.*

Someone . . . wills . . . precisely from the love of God . . . because the
understanding so dictates . . . Such is the complete and true moral virtue
of which the saints speak.

Sent. III, 12, K

Scholars have often approached Ockham's politics by way of his
theology, beginning their studies with surveys of his distinctive
views on the status of theology as a science, or divine omnipotence,
or the distinction between God's absolute and ordained power
(*potentia absoluta* and *potentia ordinata*). Yet Ockham himself con-
spicuously failed to claim formal theological support for his political

ideas. He made constant use of Biblical and patristic texts in the political writings, but he used these authorities largely to attest the legitimacy of an empire which itself had no religious orientation,[1] and even for this purpose he made little appeal to academic or systematic theology of any kind, let alone to a specifically Ockhamist theology. To be sure, certain negative traits of his theology are reflected in his political thought. For example, the absence of Neoplatonism in Ockham's theology helps explain his unwillingness to emphasize the intrinsic religious significance of the papal office at a time when its individual occupants seemed to him manifestly dangerous to the Christian community.[2] Again, the lack of a speculative theology of history in Ockham's academic writings helps explain his readiness to deal with political problems as they arose, in terms of their effects on the individuals concerned, not in terms of general ideas about the rise and fall of empires or the earthly destiny of the human race.[3] On the positive side, however, there is little to be said. In his political writings, Ockham placed no special emphasis on God's omnipotence[4] and strenuously denied omnipotence to anyone else, including the heads of church and empire. The important theological distinction between God's *potentia absoluta* and His *potentia ordinata* is scarcely mentioned by Ockham after the *Opus*

[1] See above, pp. 96–103 and 125–6.
[2] It should be remembered here that Ockham did not directly attack the philosophical underpinnings of extreme papalism (see above, pp. 90–1). It can hardly be said, therefore, that his opposition to realism on the question of universals drove him to a rejection of 'realist' institutions of government simply because of their theoretical foundations. It was the performance of the papacy, not its metaphysical basis, that drove him to a life of opposition.
[3] For the historical dimension of Dante's imperialism, see above, p. 99. On the opposed views of history underlying the conflict between the papacy and the Franciscan Spirituals, see E. Benz, *Ecclesia Spiritualis: Kirchenidee und Geschichtstheologie der franziskanischen Reformation*, 2nd ed. (Stuttgart, 1964), especially pp. 418ff. Ockham heartily desired reforms of the papal church, but he did not tie the ideal of reform to a prophetic attitude towards history. In reporting that 'some estimate' that Olivi's doctrines contain nothing heretical, but 'multa . . . falsa et fantastica', especially when he predicts the future, Ockham may well have been stating his own opinion (1 *Dialogus* 2, xxiii, fol. 13vb. See above, p. 13).
[4] In the *Breviloquium* (III, 6, p. 124), Ockham remarks that without God's mercy unbelievers would instantly descend to the pains of hell, but even here God's generosity is emphasized more than his power. For an account of the God of nominalism as less arbitrary and threatening than is often claimed, see Oberman, *The Harvest of Medieval Theology*, esp. pp. 30–56, 90–119.

Nonaginta Dierum.[5] In the case of Christ's commission of the church
to Peter, Ockham rationalized the divine will rather than absolutizing
it.[6] Similarly, his most novel contribution to the theory of natural
right was the recognition of non-absolute ideal and suppositional
norms, both evident to reason.[7] As to the scientific status of theology,
the political works make no appeal to a distinctively Ockhamist
theological epistemology.[8] If Ockham can be said to have criticized
the papal *magisterium*, it is not because he advocated skepticism about
matters of faith or, on the other hand, because of faith in the infallibility of theologians, but because he was convinced that John XXII
and his successors were heretics.[9] As other scholars have made
clear, however, papal heresy was considered a genuine possibility by
most canonists and theologians when Ockham wrote, and the
suspicion that John XXII had realized this possibility was hardly
restricted to nominalists. Again, therefore, a formal link between
theology and polemic is hard to find.

Superficially, then, the present study is finished. Our initial doubts
about the existence of a distinctly 'political' component in Ockham's
thought have been resolved in earlier chapters, and although future
research may reveal interesting connections between Ockham's
earlier and later thought, it seems clear that a straightforward
deduction of one from the other is not to be expected. It would be
wholly unsatisfactory to leave matters at this, however. For we
cannot help seeking an explanation for the *absence* of a deductive
link between theology and political thought. Is Ockham's

[5] Ockham accused John XXII of denying the distinction between God's *potentia
absoluta* and *potentia ordinata* (*OND*, c. 95; *OP* II, 719), but not in a political context.
To my knowledge, Ockham's single use of the term 'potentia absoluta' in connection with *papal* power was in his first formulation of the thesis of extreme papalism,
in the *Contra Benedictum* (Book VI, c. 2; *OP* III, 273). The *absoluta–ordinata* distinction does not correspond at all well with Ockham's distinction between regular and
casual power. To name but one important difference, Ockham denied that it was
within the pope's own discretion whether to use his casual power (see above, pp.
138–40).   [6] See above, pp. 162–5.   [7] See above, pp. 178–84.
[8] Ockham's objective view of theological truth and his conception of the universal
church as *regula fidei* are among the most important topics left to one side in the
present study. The most important texts are I *Dialogus* 2, fols. 5vb–17vb; *ibid.*, 6,
lvii–lxv, fols. 76va–81va. III *Dialogus* I, 3, fols. 205rb–218va. *Contra Ioannem*, cc. 14–15;
OP III, 62–74. *Contra Benedictum*, Book IV, c. 10; *OP* III, 260–1. Also see van
Leeuwen, 'L'Église, règle de foi', pp. 249–88; Oberman, *The Harvest of Medieval
Theology*, pp. 361–422; Miethke, *Ockhams Weg*, 245–99.
[9] See above, pp. 9–12.

desacralized politics in effect a rejection of the Christian view of man or of the medieval religious world-view? Is it a sign of the decay of faith? Or to state the problem from another angle, if Ockhamist theology indeed has no consequences for human communal life, this would seem to be a serious defect on the religious side. A closer look at government and society from a theological perspective is clearly necessary in even the most narrowly political study of Ockham.

From the standpoint of Ockhamist theology, the non-theological character of government is a contingent matter of fact, not a necessity. It depends on God's ordering of the world – or rather, on God's present abstention from ordering the political world – and this could be different. God could govern secular affairs by supernaturally revealed positive precepts, nor did Ockham regard this as merely an abstract possibility; such special divine interventions in political matters are reported in the Old Testament.[10] However, in the present state of the world, so far as the organization of property and government is concerned, mankind is left to its own reasonable devices. Every presently existing government depends and proceeds from human ordination.[11] Ockham even went so far as to define temporal affairs as 'those things pertaining to the government ... of the human race insofar as it is established solely in its natural condition without any divine revelation'. '*Spiritualia*', on the other hand, 'pertain to the government of believers insofar as they are instructed by divine revelation'.[12]

These definitions suggest an almost suspiciously simple and yet remarkably accurate way of determining the relationship between politics and theology. We need only ask: what theological truth can be discovered by men *in solis naturalibus constituti* without divine revelation? For if secular government is to be dealt with on the basis of unaided human reason, formal politics will have a significant religious basis only so far as unaided reason can reach substantive theological conclusions.[13] As is well known, however, the scope of

---

[10] See above, p. 98, n. 48. [11] See above, pp. 104–6, 197.

[12] III *Dialogus* II, 2, iv, fol. 248va. See above, pp. 134–5.

[13] In this case at least, Grabmann's thesis that the positions on papal and lay power in temporal affairs held by medieval writers parallel the writers' views on the relations between faith and reason seems correct ('Studien über den Einfluß der aristotelischen Philosophie auf die mittelalterlichen Theorien über das Verhältnis von Kirche und Staat', *Sitzungsberichte der bayrischen Akademie der Wissenschaften, Philosophisch-Historische Abteilung*, 1934, II). For criticism of other appli-

Ockhamist natural theology is extremely limited. According to Ockham, only probable arguments, not demonstrations, can be given for God's existence, and natural reason yields few indisputable results in its attempt to determine His nature or character. It would seem that without revelation the most defensible religious position would at best be one of hopeful agnosticism.[14] Hence, although Ockham himself never pointed out this connection between his definition of *temporalia* and the limited scope he attributed to natural theology, it seems proper to conclude that a temporal order based on an Ockhamist unassisted human reason can have no essential dependence on religion.[15] When the absence of specific political content in the Christian revelation, as Ockham interpreted it, is added to the limitations of natural theology, the inevitable conclusion is that politics must do without theological foundations. It has no such foundation either without revelation (due to the limitations of reason) or with it (due to the silence of revelation). This is not to deny that Ockham might eventually have turned his attention to political ideas if he had been left undisturbed at Oxford, or that it

cations of Grabmann's thesis, see A. Gewirth, 'Philosophy and political thought in the fourteenth century', in F. L. Utley (ed.), *The Forward Movement of the Fourteenth Century* (Columbus, Ohio, 1961), pp. 125–64.

14 *Sent.* I, di. 2, qq. 9–11; di. 3, qq. 1–4. *Quodlibeta Septem* I, 1 (discussed and in part edited by P. Boehner in 'Zu Ockhams Beweis der Existenz Gottes', *FzS*, xxxii (1950), 50–69; reprinted in Boehner, *Collected Articles*, pp. 399–420); II, 1–3; III, 1, 3; IV, 2; VII, 17–24. Ockham held that the usual philosophical argument for a first efficient cause was sound ('sufficiens', a strong endorsement), though 'more evident' if directed to proving a first conserving cause rather than a first producer. He held, however, that it was difficult to prove that there is only one such first being. *Sent.* I, di. 2, q. 10, ed. Gál and Brown, II, 354–7; cf. *Quodlibeta Septem*, I, 1. On this last point see M. Tweedale, 'Scotus and Ockham on the infinity of the most eminent being', *FcS*, xxiii (1963), 257–67. On the overall significance (or insignificance) of such philosophical results for theology, see above, chapter 1 notes 5 and 19 and also W. Creery's 1968 Yale philosophy thesis, 'The Status of Theistic Propositions in William of Ockham: a Study in the Logic of Theism'.

15 This conclusion applies at least as strongly to paganism as to Christianity. 'Secundum ista [definitions of *temporalia* and *spiritualia*] imperatores et alii infideles de multis intromiserunt se de regendo sibi subiectos quae ad temporalia vel spiritualia minime pertinebant. *Magister*: Hoc conceditur, omnia enim quae spectabant ad culturam et falsorum deorum iniquitatem, nec inter temporalia nec spiritualia sunt numeranda, sed superstitiosa sunt censenda.' III *Dialogus* II, 2, iv, fol. 248va. Cf. the interesting earlier discussion (I *Dialogus* 6, lxxvii, fols. 90vb–91ra) of the inexcusability of idolatry in pagan times given the fact that many philosophers had taught in the schools that there was no divinity in idols and that no divine honor should be shown them.

might be possible to make significant general observations *about* secular affairs from the perspective of nominalist theology. Furthermore, since the Bible itself strongly endorses the principles of natural equity in general, there is no difficulty in providing Biblical corroboration for the normative foundations of a purely rational political theory.[16] The God of Ockhamist theology is by no means a hidden God in the sense that He provides no approval or encouragement of man's own best efforts in the world. There is little reason to suppose, however, that an academic treatment of politics by Ockham would have been marked by theological positivism.

In the last analysis, the non-theological character of Ockham's secular political theory depends on the non-political character he attributed to the New Testament.[17] Building especially on the Franciscan tradition, he constructed a picture of Christ and the apostles as living independently of the secular legal and economic order, while this order in turn operated independently of them. From a hierocratic standpoint, this interpretation of the Bible is, of course, highly questionable.[18] Without presuming to endorse one or another point of view of so complex a matter, we should note that Christianity's negligible impact on political institutions is balanced in Ockham's thought by its comprehensive effect on individuals. The fact that Ockham claimed to find models for a non-political mode of life in Christ and the apostles and in St Francis should alert us to the importance of this way of life for him, and yet it is often overlooked. His overall position cannot be considered skeptical or rationalistic simply because he did not provide a religious basis for political authority. On the contrary, the theme of separatism in his institutional thought expressed not only indignation at papal interference in the normal process of secular affairs, but also a desire to free ecclesiastical leaders for full-time attention to spiritual matters. Like the apostles, they would be 'more usefully occupied' with prayer and preaching than with administering secular business.

[16] For the extension of *ius divinum* in this way to cover *omne ius naturale*, see III *Dialogus* II, 3, vi, especially fol. 263vb.   [17] See above, pp. 98, 146–8.
[18] For the Michaelists' total disagreement with John XXII on the temporal kingship of Christ, see *OND*, c. 93; *OP* II, 670–705. Ockham's literalism is relevant here. See *Brev.* V, 3, pp. 171–3 for his strictures on mystical interpretations of the Bible and *OQ* I, 2, 10, and 12; *OP* I, 16–18, 41–5, and 49–52 for the clash between figurative and literal exegesis in connection with *plenitudo potestatis*.

These spiritual functions could be highly significant, even though (indeed, especially because) exercised with a minimum of coercion. The preceding considerations suggest that the problematic relationship between theology and politics in Ockham should be approached from a new angle. Instead of trying to ground secular law and government in religion, it would be better to examine the religious grounding of the Ockhamist individual. Ockham's theology of the individual is a complex and much disputed subject.[19] To focus on a single passage will hardly do it justice, yet even this may serve to indicate the transforming personal effect Ockham contended Christianity should have and the continuity of this effect with his political ideas.

In the course of an extensive treatise on the moral and theological virtues and their connections with one another, with prudence (*recta ratio*), and with the powers of the sensitive soul, Ockham distinguished five grades of moral excellence. The ethical effect of moving to Christian faith from the agnosticism of natural reason is shown by the contrasts he draws between the fourth grade of virtue and those before it. The fourth grade is found when a person satisfies all the conditions and circumstances of the preceding grades and beyond this wills to act from love of God, his understanding dictating that he act as he does for this very reason, from love of God. Such, Ockham tells us, 'is the complete and true moral virtue of which the saints speak'.[20] The previous grade of virtue in Ockham's analysis consists, as we have seen, of action in accordance with *recta ratio* performed *because* of its rationality.[21] With the addition of the Christian idea of God, then, a new orientation and a radically new motive are added to morality (Ockham is explicit in arguing that moral, not theological, virtue is at issue): the love of God above all else and for His own sake.[22] From the standpoint of unassisted natural reason, the very existence of God is doubtful. Hence, respect for *recta ratio* at the third grade of virtue must

---

[19] Paul Vignaux, *Justification et prédestination au XIVe siècle: Duns Scot, Pierre d'Auriole, Guillaume d'Occam, Grégoire de Rimini*. Bibliothèque de l'École des Hautes Études, XLVIII (Paris, 1934); Leff, *Bradwardine and the Pelagians*, pp. 188–210; Oberman, *The Harvest of Medieval Theology*, pp. 120–248.

[20] *Sent.* III, 12, K.   [21] P. 194 above.

[22] On doing all that is in one to love God for God's sake, see Oberman, *The Harvest of Medieval Theology*, pp. 47ff., 131–60.

presumably be impersonal. There would be no moral vacuum, since self-evident ethical principles could still be apprehended and acted upon, but the basis and ultimate worth of human existence would be unknown. On the next level of ethical activity, God becomes the center of every obligation. This does not mean that everything the Christian does has a specifically religious content or object. It is rather a question of motive. Love of God for His own sake becomes the moving cause of every good act. In going beyond all lower grades of virtue, however, the fourth grade does not sweep them away in a flood of unreflective religious devotion. The characteristic ethical values of these grades are preserved. This is clear from the beginning: perfect virtue presupposes that a person wills to act according to 'omnes conditiones et circumstantias praedictas', that is, according to the conditions of the previous three grades of virtue.[23] Hence, the acceptance of the love of God as the supreme principle of morality does not abolish obligations recognized by natural reason. The dynamic spring for fulfilling those obligations is transformed, but Ockham's doctrine implies that Christians should be more rather than less prompt in applying the principles of *recta ratio* in the circumstances in which they find themselves, for they have a powerful additional stimulus to rational action beyond any impulse of reason itself. Ockham's account of Christian virtue is thus subtly balanced. On one hand, it continues his refusal to grant intrinsic moral worth to overt behavior, for by itself the love of God is an inward principle, an act or disposition of the will. On the other hand, this higher moral condition also preserves the outward orientation of the Ockhamist good will described in the last chapter. These two aspects of 'complete and true moral virtue' have distinct implications for secular life.

Ockham's emphasis on the inner relation to God provides at least indirect support for an exaltation of the free, individual 'subject'. So long as an individual does all that is in him to love God above all else and does his duty from love of God, his acts will be intrinsically valuable, whether they are externally magnificent or humble.[24] To

---

[23] The basic incompatibility of the theological virtues (faith, hope, and charity) with moral vice is also relevant here. *Sent.* III, 12, HH–KK.

[24] Indeed, Ockham believed that, other things being equal, a life of poverty undertaken *propter amorem Dei* was *better than* a life of magnificence. For Ockham's defense of Franciscan poverty as a 'status' of perfection, see *OND*, c. 76; *OP* II, 606–19.

be sure, the free Christian will show reasonable respect for his ecclesiastical and secular superiors, but his personal worth will not depend on them. Rather, the value of their government will depend on him.[25] Although Ockham never directly attacked the hierarchical order of medieval society, the effect of his doctrine is certainly to diminish the human significance of rank and privilege. It would be easy to exaggerate here what is only the development of a common Christian theme, but Ockham's habitual lack of reverence for pomp and force in the absence of integrity seems especially well rooted in just this type of moral theology.

For all of its concentration on inner processes of intention and justification, Ockham's moral theology provides the individual with no warrant for avoiding social responsibility in favor of absorption in his own psychological states or exclusive concern with his relation to God. According to Ockham, Christian virtue must meet all the conditions of the lower grades of moral virtue, but these include respect for *recta ratio* for its own sake. Hence, the specifically Christian ethical motive unquestionably directs us into the context of rationality and natural law studied in the preceding chapter. Concern with the needs and rights of others, appreciation of objectively valid social ideals, and acknowledgment of responsibility for taking action to remedy intolerable political evils are all natural consequences of a religious ethic tied as closely to rationality as Ockham's was. In neither philosophy nor theology did his ideas menace human solidarity or *communicatio*. The net effect of Ockham's ideas was, however, to diminish the normal importance of legal, economic, and political forces, to treat these varieties of power merely as background conditions for the exercise of the moral and intellectual powers of free individuals. Christian and natural human communal life, the life of society as opposed to government, should thus be a result of relatively undirected, perhaps unpredictable, voluntary individual action. As we have frequently noted, Ockham was no anarchist. Indeed, his respect for the rights of lay rulers over their subjects and his refusal to give regular power to the people seem archaic in a thinker so daring in some of his other conclusions. No doubt, Ockham was skeptical about the incorruptibility of the multitude,

---

[25] The best government is not that which has the most power, but that which is exercised over the best subjects. See pp. 121–2 above.

but a more important factor in his preference for monarchy was the desire for an efficient government that would allow men to occupy themselves with better things than politics – with important, or at least harmless, academic pursuits, with love of neighbor (especially in a life of Franciscan poverty), and finally with God.[26]

[26] Like many another Franciscan, Ockham was fascinated by the natural world and human experience. Before he was summoned to Avignon, he had made plans to comment on Aristotle's *Metaphysics*, *De Anima*, and perhaps the *Nicomachean Ethics*. He also planned to continue his work in natural science by preparing *Summulae* in physics, astronomy, and biology (including a work on plants). Baudry, *Guillaume d'Occam*, pp. 47–8, 53. Nevertheless, Ockham argued at some length that everything else can be used, but only God should be enjoyed. *Sent.* I, di. I, q. I.

CONCLUSION: OCKHAM AS A
CONSTRUCTIVE POLITICAL THINKER

Cum igitur constet, quod papa, cui dixit Christus in beato Petro: Pasce oves
meas, *de fidelibus sollicitam curam gerere teneatur* . . . *relinquitur, quod
principatus papalis institutus est propter utilitatem subiectorum et non propter
utilitatem propriam vel honorem, et per consequens non dominativus, sed
ministrativus est digne vocandus.*

Since, therefore, it is clear that the pope, to whom Christ said [in the
person of] blessed Peter, 'Feed my sheep', is bound to take sollicitous
care of believers . . . it follows that papal government was instituted for the
utility of its subjects and not for its own utility or honor, and consequently it deserves to be called not dominative but ministrative.

De Imperatorum et Pontificum Potestate, c. 6, p. 460

Ockham's political thought must be assessed as a response to the
potentialities and ideological chaos of the world in which it was
produced. The problems of Ockham's age are vividly suggested by
Pierre de Flotte's taunt at Boniface VIII, which from one standpoint
or another could have been applied to every person or institution
discussed in this study: 'Your power is verbal, but ours is real.'[1]
From a curialist point of view, de Flotte had reversed the true
situation. Supreme spiritual power, far from being merely verbal,
was more real than that of any secular government, while a ruler who
lost the papacy's favor deserved to lose even such subordinate temporal power as he had. From this viewpoint, Ludwig of Bavaria,
whose election had never been approved by the pope, was juristically
speaking a wholly unreal emperor. Even with papal approval,
however, the empire's universal power was questionable in practice.
It was defended by poets and in the verbal constructions of publicists

---

[1] As reported, among others, in Thomas Walsingham, *Historia Anglicana*, ed.
H. M. Tiley (in Rolls Series, London, 1863), at p. 85. See *Acta inter Bonifacium VIII,
Benedictum XI, Clementem V et Philippum Pulchrum regem Christianum* (Troyes,
1614), fol. 1640v.

like Ockham, who are often compared unfavorably with the more realistic lawyers of the French monarchy such as Pierre de Flotte. If the empire ought reasonably to have been an effective source of peace and order for the new secular energies of Western Europe, it was in fact often quite weak and especially subject to disturbance from the supposedly merely verbal power of the popes. The reality or unreality of papal power was, however, the most difficult issue of all. Comparisons between the genuine spirituality of earlier popes and the material involvement or merely verbal sanctity of contemporary papal government were common and made the prophetic distinction drawn by Spiritual Franciscans between a true church of the Spirit and the carnal institutional church all the more disturbing. Ockham rejected this distinction in general but was convinced of the complete inauthenticity of papal power in the particular cases of John XXII and his successors. In pertinaciously denying the real poverty of Christ and the apostles these men had, Ockham believed, cut themselves off from the church and could thus have no authority in it. Apart from this issue, the papacy's power to use its spiritual authority to direct the temporal life of Christian society was the central topic in tract after tract throughout the first half of the fourteenth century. The status of this enormous political literature was also uncertain, however, for although contemporary authors could draw on a host of well developed academic disciplines (theology, philosophy, logic, the various branches of law), their opponents could always accuse them of distorting objective principles and producing mere verbiage to serve underlying practical interests. Beyond this there was a pervasive problem of doctrinal authority: who, if anyone, had the power to determine finally that a teaching was acceptable or to condemn it as false or harmful? One or another of these uncertainties touched nearly everyone in the period, and Ockham was personally involved in them all. Some of his theological doctrines had almost been condemned at Avignon, he defended what John XXII had denounced as merely simulated Christian poverty, he was an imperial publicist, and his philosophy has been criticized for turning the real universal essences on which medieval thought was based into mere matters of language.

In a situation so perplexing there is an obvious temptation to dismiss some factors entirely or, on the other hand, become so rapt in analysing complexities that one never takes a position. Ockham, whatever else may be said of him, attempted to deal effectively with the whole range of problems confronting him. Recognizing this is the first step towards an adequate assessment of his work. The many-sidedness of Ockham's thought largely accounts for the variety of scholarly interpretations surveyed at the beginning of this study. A brief reconsideration of these interpretations will thus provide a useful basis for further discussion.

LAICIST, THEOLOGICAL AND CONSTITUTIONALIST INTERPRETATIONS RECONSIDERED

The description of Ockham as a rebel and anarchist is not only comprehensible but in essential respects accurate when applied at the level of personal, practical response to the severe problem of papal heresy. For this extraordinary case, which he thought had actually arisen, Ockham worked out a detailed theory of resistance to government which avoided placing absolute trust in any office or institutional procedure. He called for action from all Christians, whatever their rank or status. The dogmatic position Ockham defended against the papacy was a moderate one, and the general concept of papal heresy was not unorthodox. The anarchistic features of 1 *Dialogus* are due largely to Ockham's approach in practical terms to an issue which previous thinkers had left in the comparatively tranquil realm of theory. Since by definition the problem defied normal solutions, especially considering Ockham's conservative refusal to grant infallibility to a general council or the college of cardinals, his radicalism cannot by itself be regarded as an attempt to subvert an ordered Christian society. Nevertheless, his political writings are not merely suggestions for reforms to be carried out with the cooperation of established ecclesiastical authorities. They are attempts at revolution.

From a concern with Ockham's radical activities against John XXII and later popes one may easily fail to appreciate several important features of his institutional thought. For example, a more or less conscious tendency to exalt lay government at the expense of ecclesiastical institutions has been attributed to him. However, we have discovered that Ockham's assertions of independence for secular

government went hand-in-hand with a severely limited conception
of the lay ruler's rights and functions. Rather than giving secular
government an exalted status comparable to that accorded the papacy
by hierocratic writers, Ockham stressed both the human origin and
the morally moderate ends of even 'supreme' lay power. Thus, his
references to the Roman empire at the time of Christ were not
intended to demonstrate either a divine origin or a religious mission
for the empire. Although Christ and the apostles were morally
obliged to respect the jurisdiction of the imperial magistrate, whose
legitimacy did not depend on their acknowledgment, the gospel
was also independent of official secular support for its own effectiveness. Exclusive emphasis on Ockham's bitter polemics against
individual popes may also cause one to undervalue his arguments in
favor of papal government as an institution. Ockham's view of the
papacy was strikingly different from that of the hierocrats, and he was
ready to consider the expediency of temporary constitutional change
in the church, but he was genuinely committed to papal monarchy as
normally the supreme ecclesiastical office.

Ockham's struggles with the problems of his time rested ultimately on a Franciscan reading of the New Testament. To view him as a
theologian, not a political thinker, thus corresponds with his deepest
motives and with the somewhat fortuitous character of his involvement in politics. As 'one alone', fighting for Christian truth against
corruption in the center of the church, Ockham thought of himself
on the model of Athanasius and other earlier champions of orthodoxy.[2] Indisputably, his defense of Ludwig of Bavaria's empire was
stimulated by a desire to reform the church, in both the immediate
sense of expelling false popes and the broader sense of promoting an
institutional setting in which ecclesiastics could minister to the
faithful without secular distractions. One must even insist that for
Ockham the best hope of improving secular as well as religious life
lay in the increase of Christian virtue. Yet none of this implies that
distinctly theological ideas must be invoked to define secular
institutions or resolve specific secular issues. An ultimately religious
view of Ockham's motives is correct, but an exclusively religious
view of his writings fails to notice how little logical dependence there
is between his political thought and purely theological premises. If

---

[2] *Imp. Pont. Pot.*, c. 1, p. 454.

we are careful to distinguish, as Ockham did, between the philosophical and strictly theological components of his speculative thought, the position becomes still clearer. We can recognize that he appealed to the Bible in his political writings primarily to demand respect for institutions which in themselves lacked any positive 'order' to the will of God. Far from subjecting secular political processes to constant criticism in the light of revelation, he defined secular politics in a way which excluded revelation as an essential principle, and even in his discussions of ecclesiastical government made significant use of purely rational considerations. Ockham's political thought is consistent with his theology, for he believed there were compelling theological reasons for *not* deducing politics from theology, first and foremost the apolitical examples of Christian perfection provided by Christ, the apostles, and St Francis. This perfect way of life was not a withdrawal from the human community but a means of attracting as many individuals as possible to the love of God, and since Ockham held that Christian love of God led to the active pursuit of socially beneficial virtues such as courage, justice, and personal moderation, the separation of political theory and theology in his thought should be regarded positively from both a secular and a religious viewpoint. Yet there certainly is a separation. Ockham's characteristic grounds for political analysis and criticism are found in natural law and philosophical conceptions of rationality rather than in either natural or positive theology.

Constitutionalist interpreters of Ockham's thought have tended to underrate the importance of his revolutionary agitation against John XXII and later popes. Proponents of this view have, however, elucidated another important side of his overall position, a devotion to limited jurisdictions. On this point, the present study has yielded ample confirmation of earlier research. Ockham's dislike of arbitrary power, his care in limiting the functions of both ecclesiastical and secular government to matters affecting the good of the community, and his recognition of consent as normally the ultimate principle of political legitimacy all support the same general interpretation. On many such matters, furthermore, Ockham regarded himself as defending the ancient constitution of the church against modern despotism. Yet it would be wrong to take constitutionalism as the ultimate rational basis of his political theory, for this would overlook the purely contingent value he ascribed to even the best formal political arrangements. His unwillingness to propose a unitary scheme of secular and ecclesiastical government is but one important sign of Ockham's caution about institutions, even legally limited ones. Other indications are his view that the most expedient form of government may vary from time to time, his willingness to consider basic constitutional change, his refusal to endow secular government with a morally elevated mission, his disinterest in popular participation in government, and his recommendation of monarchy on grounds of efficiency rather than inherent justice. Most important of all, Ockham's use of natural law and Aristotelian political theory provided him with a rational standpoint from which all positive law and government whatever could be assessed. From this standpoint, even constitutional regimes might in some circumstances be found inadequate and 'unconstitutional' measures justified. In sum, Ockham's ideological commitment to constitutionalism, although strong, was not absolute.

Each of the interpretations we have considered casts light on one aspect of Ockham's thought but at the expense of obscuring others. As a result, even the aspect most clearly illuminated in a given view is placed in somewhat questionable perspective. Thus, for example, Ockham's personal activism presents one appearance when seen as the central element in his work but quite another when viewed in conjunction with his sober, almost tedious institutional analysis. Or again, his dedication to a seemingly artificial ideal of Christian perfection makes one impression when we think of him as 'really' an academic philosopher or theologian but quite another when we consider his capacity for dealing with practical political matters. Conversely, our view of Ockham's political involvements is affected when we see that he regarded the renunciation of positive political rights as essential to the best way of life. But the very process of seeking a truer perspective by recognizing Ockham's complexity raises a further question: how do the various aspects of his thought fit together? The more we see of him, the more difficult it is to be content with any single term such as 'traditional', 'modern', 'radical', or 'conservative' as an overall description. Yet, although his work often shows signs of strain, it does not give the impression of either confusion or a vague sympathy with each idea and interest that came to his attention. The present study suggests, rather, that Ockham considered traditional religious and governmental principles to be so gravely menaced in his time that basic analysis and reconstruction were required to restore their effectiveness. Both his treatment of secular and ecclesiastical institutions and his underlying individualism can be understood in such terms. As a preliminary to discussing these topics, we shall first consider Ockham's attitudes towards law, a field in which his combination of traditional commitments and willingness to consider innovation is particularly evident.

LAW

The first major Western theologian to oppose the papacy for more than a short time and on a variety of grounds, Ockham was a criminal in the eyes of the law throughout the period of his political writings, a state of affairs he could never ignore. From the very beginning, however, Michael of Cesena and his followers claimed that the law was on their side and conducted their case against John XXII in legal terms. Thus, for example, they contended that John's deposition of Michael as Franciscan minister general was invalid not merely because John was in truth a heretic but also because Michael had entered a technically valid appeal against John's doctrinal pronouncements before the pope deposed him. This very marked inclination to use legal arguments in defending opposition to commonly accepted legal authority is continued throughout all of Ockham's political works. He used canon, civil, and feudal legal sources even to deal with situations in which, as he saw it, there was a virtually complete breakdown of legitimate institutional authority, as well as, more naturally, to support the rights of Ludwig of Bavaria and the Roman empire. Detailed study of this aspect of his work would be highly rewarding. In the present study three basic Ockhamist attitudes towards law have appeared.

First, there is an impulse towards withdrawal. As a Franciscan, Ockham believed that the highest religious ideal included renouncing all one's legal rights. In similar though less extreme fashion, he proposed that the gospel be interpreted as a law of liberty, which meant that the positive legal apparatus sanctioned by the gospel, papal government, should be as mild and undomineering as possible.

In the secular sphere, although there could be no lessening of the qualitative harshness of law when it had to be exercised, quantitative limits could be set on the law's essential scope. Ockham did not on principle exclude ethically positive programs from the range of permissible governmental activities, but he contended that the primary function of law and government was to curb evil. Hence, a good man, even if he was not a Franciscan, would normally stay clear of the law. 'Law is made for the unjust, not the just.' In a sense, then, Ockham proposed withdrawal from law as a universal ideal.

This withdrawal was not, however, a matter of rejection. On the contrary, respect for law was also an integral part of Ockham's position. This no doubt accounts for much of his persistent effort to justify himself in legal terms. It also distinguishes his attitude towards law from the more purely democratic positions of Marsilius of Padua and later thinkers. For Ockham, it is natural that a judge or ruler be chosen by the community, but he is not chosen to execute the popular will. The function of legal institutions is to dispense justice in accordance with rational, objective principles. So long as the judge or ruler fulfills this function he is responsible solely to his legal superiors, if any, or to God. Although the relevant concept of justice was a natural rather than a revealed one, Ockham's attitude of respect for the administration of justice claimed strong religious support from his reading of the New Testament. Christ and the apostles were models not only of withdrawal from litigiousness but also of moral respect for existing law, even when it was administered by morally defective individuals. Following these examples, the church should normally respect the jurisdictions of contemporary secular rulers. Respect for law should also operate at the top of a political system. Thus, 'supreme' lay and spiritual rulers are obliged to acknowledge the rights and liberties of others, both officials and private persons. Finally, respect for the technical aspects of law operated in Ockham's own method of argument. If he often interpreted legal texts in a novel fashion, this was not part of a sweeping reconstruction, much less rejection, of jurisprudence. Clearly, he regarded the law as a legitimate discipline with its own language and procedures, a discipline with which anyone involved in public affairs had to come to terms.

Respect for law was a dominant theme in medieval political

thought of all persuasions. The ideal of withdrawal from law was in some ways new but in more fortunate circumstances need not have disturbed the order so highly valued by earlier thinkers. As we have seen, however, Ockham found the chief upholders of order in medieval society, papacy and empire, to be in profoundly unsatisfactory condition. He was thus led to radical action and significant new developments in political theory. In legal terms, this meant that the attitude of respect for law – at least positive, institutional law – had to be qualified. If only because there was so much conflict among legal authorities, a critical or innovative attitude had to be taken towards the law itself. It is possible to distinguish three levels of legal criticism in Ockham, which for convenience may be described as technical, constitutional, and social or philosophical. On the technical level, Ockham argued that the papacy of his time was an illegal government, because its authority presupposed the orthodoxy of men who had repudiated a catholic doctrine already incorporated in canon law and accepted throughout the church and also because it acted in unnecessary and flagrant disregard of the legal rights of the supreme secular ruler. At a constitutional level, he objected to the whole spirit of curialism and extreme secularism, because the comprehensiveness and at least implicit totalitarianism of these monistic political theories seemed to menace ordinary processes of law by making everything depend on the unrestrained will of a single individual or group. Most basically, Ockham's natural-law orientation and his functional view of government led him to appraise existing legal institutions in terms of their benefit to society, the *congregatio fidelium* or the *communitas mortalium*. This is to say that the final test of law was not law itself or even the general idea of legally defined due process but observable usefulness to the community. Hence, although both papal and imperial power involved regular respect for the rights and liberties of others, Ockham held that such respect ought not to be absolute. For the preservation or clear benefit of the whole community the rights and liberties of individuals and subordinate officials could licitly be overridden by government. Similarly, the powers of government itself could be curtailed, transferred, or otherwise changed if the common good required it. A political system which made provision for orderly internal change (and could thus be responsive to the legitimate needs of the times) would have much to commend it from Ockham's standpoint, and he certainly did not believe that revolutions were historically inevitable. Neither, however, did he believe that law and government inevitably improve of their own accord. Action from outside a political system may occasionally be required, and judgment of political institutions on the basis of non-institutional principles is always relevant. The problem in understanding Ockham's own treatment of papacy and empire is to see how he applied such principles, how he thought that respect for the essential functions of traditional institutions was not only compatible with, but actually required, fundamental criticism of ideas and practices currently associated with them.

INSTITUTIONS

Considered in its practical aspects and in isolation from the rest of his thought, Ockham's view of the papacy as an institution seems irreproachable by any but the most ardently curialist standards. The pope's power is 'not *plenissima* but grand, singular, and very great', divinely conferred, and of unique dignity. In denying that papal approval was necessary at the foundation of secular government, Ockham was no more radical than St Thomas, who had just been canonized by John XXII, and like St Thomas he defended the pope's emergency power to act in secular affairs. In cases of extreme political injustice, where properly secular remedies were insufficient, the pope need not stand idly by. In such cases he was implicitly empowered by Christ to 'transfer empires and kingdoms and deprive kings, princes, and any other layman whatever of his temporal rights and possessions and confer them on others', in short, to do 'whatever right reason dictates is necessary'.[3] Ockham by no means subordinated the papacy (in contrast to individual heretical or scandalously criminal popes) to any other authority, secular or ecclesiastical. Indeed, as concerns the secular ruler's power, his thought developed in the other direction, from an initial acceptance of the emperor's right to act 'as emperor' in a clear case of papal heresy to denial of that right.[4] Within the ecclesiastical order, he gave careful consideration to the expedient of a general council

[3] III *Dialogus* I, I, xvi, fol. 188vab, quoted above, p. 79.
[4] See above, pp. 132–3.

216

as a way of dealing with papal heresy but denied that anyone, including a general council, had jurisdiction over an orthodox and non-criminous pope. He also acknowledged the pope's power, in exceptional cases, to override lesser ecclesiastical jurisdictions: 'in spiritual matters, too, *in casu*, he can do everything'.[5] With a different personal history, a writer holding such views would surely be regarded as a friend, or at least a constructive critic, of papal power. If Benedict XII could have given clear approval to earlier papal endorsements of Franciscan poverty such as *Exiit qui seminat* or if Ockham had been able to find an acceptable interpretation of John XXII's pronouncements on the subject, he would probably have had the strongest inducements to make peace with the institutional church. In that case, assuming that he would not simply have returned to teaching and research in more academic subjects, he could have developed most of his political ideas with little fear of censure and a far more amiable effect on his subsequent reputation.

Accommodation on the poverty question was impossible, however, and Ockham worked out his ideas as the defender of an embattled secular ruler and the open enemy of three successive popes. One consequence of this situation was that he emphasized the powers he denied the papacy as much as those he conceded to it. In contrast with earlier writers like St Bernard, St Thomas, and to a lesser extent Dante and John of Paris, Ockham treated the secular political consequences of hierocratic theory as heretical, not merely imprudent or philosophically unnecessary, and he repeatedly asserted the right to resist improper papal actions where others had tended to emphasize the admirableness of a world in which the correct relations between secular and spiritual power were willingly maintained on all sides. The main features of Ockham's theory of secular government, its ethical moderateness and non-sacral basis, also correspond with the needs of this new situation. So long as secular and religious authorities are in practical accord with one another, it is natural to emphasize areas of shared concern even while conceding autonomous standing to each. When such practical accord breaks down, however, it becomes reasonable to look for an institutional theory which minimizes overlapping concerns instead of stressing them. The idea that secular power exists primarily to control wrongdoing was a

---

[5] III *Dialogus* I, I, xvi, fol. 188v*b*.

traditional one available for Ockham's use, but he sought a still more thorough disengagement of secular from ecclesiastical government than was warranted by this idea alone. Guided by the particular issues at stake between Ludwig of Bavaria and the papacy, he contended that not merely the functions but also the basis of legitimate secular power was non-religious. He thus arrived at a coherent view of secular politics as an independent and yet limited sphere. Ockham's ideas on this matter had a basis in the past, and he was evidently concerned to find broadly acceptable solutions to current problems, yet he took positions which were far from conventional. The desacralization of secular power which he proposed shattered the traditional ideological orientation of the secular towards higher, spiritual ends. It is not that Ockham *re*oriented secular affairs towards other spiritual aims competing with Christian values or towards some other channel of Christian endorsement competing with the traditional process of papal approbation. Rather, he '*un*-oriented' them, limiting them to matters without particular religious significance and suggesting that the pursuit of higher ends should depend on chiefly voluntary activity within the community rather than on a program enforced by secular leaders.

Ockham's separation of secular and spiritual governments was intended to benefit the properly spiritual life of the church as well as to free lay rulers from ecclesiastical interference. To be sure, his concept of a limited papal *plenitudo potestatis*, the result of a sustained attempt to determine constitutional limits to papal sovereignty, seemed a contradiction in terms from the hierocratic standpoint. Yet it did allow the pope far more power than any other ecclesiastic and subjected all Christians without exception to him in spiritual matters. Beyond this, Ockham made positive contributions towards strengthening the papacy on both a realistic and an ideal level. First, he presented, as a basis for interpreting Biblical texts establishing papal primacy, an impressive set of utilitarian or functional arguments in favor of ecclesiastical monarchy. To appreciate the constructive character of these arguments at the time Ockham wrote, we need only recall the increasing religious opposition to the institutional church which manifested itself in Spiritual Franciscan and other extreme movements. This opposition, bolstered by apocalyptic visions and welcomed by extreme secularists like

Marsilius of Padua as evidence that the church needed no governmental power independent of the state, waxed strongest at just the time when developments in administrative techniques and the general economic and social advance of the previous century had brought both greater needs and greater opportunities for sound ecclesiastical government than ever before. In this situation, Ockham's careful analysis of the usefulness of a spiritual monarchy, while it differed deliberately from the speculative expositions of hierocratic writers, was a highly relevant contribution to papal, if not papalist, theory. His discussion of the personal qualifications required for the papal office was similarly moderate. He accepted and developed the view that a heretical pope was automatically deposed and insisted that it must be possible to take action against a pontiff guilty of other serious crimes. Further, he argued that if an outstandingly virtuous man were available when papal elections were being held, he should definitely be chosen. However, failing such a candidate or given the election of someone good but not outstanding, Ockham held that the needs of the church dictated respect for the authority of lesser men. He thus took a position between radical critics of the institutional church, who insisted that ecclesiastical officials had to have personal qualities of moral excellence, charisma, and holiness in order to be legitimate holders of their offices, and conservative curialists, who for practical purposes insisted that the pope could do no wrong, that preservation of respect for the office compensated for almost any evil that could be perpetrated by its individual occupants. Ockham opposed this hierocratic indifference to the character and policies of particular popes, but he was not driven to the opposite extreme.

Ockham also contributed to papal theory on a less mundane level by emphasizing the positive values of a primarily pastoral rather than juristic view of papal government. A papacy extricated from secular affairs could devote itself to properly spiritual matters. This would involve a substantial loss of direct or indirect coercive power, but, far from being a misfortune, such a development would actually manifest the unique dignity which papal government was originally intended to have as a Christian institution. Ockham's appeal to the gospel as a law of liberty was his most significant argument against curialist views of *plenitudo potestatis*. At the same time, it provided a striking positive argument in favor of his own idea of papal power.

Conclusions

For Ockham, the papal government instituted by Christ was 'most dignified' and 'closest to the best form of royal government', precisely because its subjects were free men.[6] This conception of the dignity of papal government was very different from that found in hierocratic thought. In particular, Ockham's idea of freedom places a much greater value on individual autonomy than was usual in the medieval period. His conception of individual life must thus be examined in some detail before it will be possible to judge how faithful he was to traditional values. We may note now, however, that Ockham's opposition to curialism in his own time does not demonstrate hostility to the papal primacy which hierocratic ideas had previously supported. The very success of these ideas in earlier centuries had helped to produce conditions in which their further effectiveness was highly problematic on behalf of the papacy itself. In helping to integrate, nurture, and elevate Christian society, medieval papalism had helped to create a broadly diffused human self-confidence and self-consciousness which naturally resisted further institutional tutelage. At the same time, in working out its own implications papalism had tended towards more and more rigorously legal applications of ideas whose original appeal was less juristic than religious. The result of these developments was potentially catastrophic: a papacy insisting on its secular omnipotence collided with a laity able to criticize it even on moral and religious grounds. In terms of capacity for dealing with such a crisis, the late medieval popes can be said to have become prisoners of their own ideology. If the papacy was to regain moral authority and be as effective as possible in the spiritual government of all Christians, less emphasis on this ideology was needed, not more. In this respect, then, notwithstanding his unrelenting opposition to three popes, Ockham's pastoral conception of the papal office was in its time a constructive contribution to strong papal government, as the hierocratic ideal of juristic primacy had been in earlier periods. Ockham's curialist opponents were much closer to the past verbally, legally, and in their doctrinal presuppositions, yet from the standpoint of spiritual effectiveness it is possible that Ockham 'really' served the medieval tradition better than they, even on the issue of papal government.

6 *Imp. Pont. Pot.*, cc. 6–7, pp. 460–2; see above, pp. 121, 207.

INDIVIDUALS

Ockham sought to reduce collisions between the major institutions of his time by narrowing the essential functions of secular government on the one hand and emphasizing the specifically spiritual character of ecclesiastical government on the other. In theory at least, this also liberated much of human life from immediate institutional control of any kind. Such a result was no accident. Whether in appealing to gospel liberty or to Aristotle's unfavorable assessment of despotism, Ockham accorded great value to personal freedom. This was not merely an inner freedom to be found in subordination to higher principles and authorities but the power of individuals – free subjects,[7] who existed for themselves and not for the sake of their rulers – to be masters of their own actions, to enjoy the rights and liberties conceded to all mortals by God and nature. In this respect, Ockham's political works, especially when read in conjunction with his earlier ethical writings, are an important contribution to Western thought about human rights and the dignity of individuals. By the same token, however, although his moderate doctrine of secular government and his emphasis on inner psychological processes have clear affinities with the ideas of Augustine, Ockham's work signals the end of political Augustinism[8] and the hierocratically inspired descending thesis of government with its resulting program of moulding society from above. Does this mean a rejection, in effect if not in so many words, of classical and medieval ideals of communal wholeness, unity, and order? In Ockham's thought these ideals no longer function as principles justifying a unitary political system, but we should not conclude too hastily that they have no effective status in a world of individuals.

It seems obvious that the quality of life in any community depends

[7] Ockham speaks always of subjects rather than citizens, perhaps because he did not wish to disguise the relationship of superior and inferior obtaining between those who have power and those who do not. The idea of citizenship also loses some of its relevance in his thought because of his comparatively negative and instrumental view of government. The full-fledged member of an Aristotelian *polis* is naturally called a citizen because he achieves so much of his own fulfillment in and through the community he participates in organizing.

[8] On political Augustinism and the problem of its relation to Augustine's own thought, see H.-X. Arquillière, *L'augustinisme politique*, 2nd ed. (Paris, 1955).

on how the individuals composing the community treat one another. As far as our understanding of Ockham is concerned, this elementary insight is obscured by the readiness to speak of him as exalting 'the' individual, as if nominalism presupposed solipsism or endorsed egoism. The whole movement of Ockham's speculative philosophy was in the opposite direction: instead of the one 'Man' of Platonism, whose many particular exemplifications sometimes seemed unimportant, he insisted that there were many men. Ockham's political thought, too, is concerned with many men (and women),[9] a fact which is of the greatest significance for assessing its general moral character.

Ockham believed that the natural condition of mankind, in which the earth belonged to the human race in common and all men were free, was relevant to practical politics even after the introduction of formal human law. Such common natural rights were not to be brushed aside by positive law. They could indeed be legitimately curtailed, but only when there was good reason for curtailing them, and in some cases they could be reasserted even in the face of normally justified legal restrictions. Thus, for example, every individual has a natural right to the necessities of life which justifies using the property of another in case of extreme need even without the other's consent. There seems little ground, then, for associating Ockham's individualism with the more ferocious aspects of individualism in the eighteenth and nineteenth centuries. More generally, it is important to recognize that in Ockham's theory of natural law and his ethic of rationality the rights and liberties of other individuals are as important as one's own. While he criticized a purely institutional corporatism, Ockham assumed a corporatism of human solidarity. In this view, a person's obligations to the community, construed now as the collection of his neighbors, that is, everyone, are objective and in some cases may be substantial. Ockham had little interest in giving every individual a share of formal political power, but this was partly because he saw that human rights are morally prior to, and always remain somewhat independent of, any distribution of goods and power actually sanctioned by positive law. Individuals need not have political power to have rights, and conversely, the possession of

---

[9] For Ockham's unusual suggestion that women, too, should be represented at a general council, see 1 *Dialogus* 6, lxxxv, fol. 98r*b*.

formal political power may not guarantee them the exercise of their rights. It does not seem excessively charitable to suggest that Ockham's view of government as existing for the good of individuals – the whole community of individuals – supports as high a level of social concern as theories which magnify institutions themselves as the objects of ultimate loyalty.

If thinking of many individuals rather than 'the' individual allows us to see a solid basis for social responsibility in Ockham's ideas, the same change of focus also clarifies his distinction between the 'good' and the 'bad', whose interests and behavior he held to be fundamental for secular politics. Both are individuals. This is to say that men need protection, not from an evil world, society, or government in the abstract, but from other men, or in some cases themselves. The primary function of rulers is to provide such protection, and in discharging this task they deserve respect and cooperation. In normal conditions, the evildoers which the laws are meant to control would be criminals in the ordinary sense of the term. Rulers are also individuals, however, and are capable of misusing their power to serve their own ends. Ockham was unusually clear-headed in recognizing evildoing as a possibility for anyone, no matter what his social or political status, and he considered the problem of correcting evil in high places as important as that of suppressing purely private crime. His psychology of good and evil human behavior is another topic meriting investigation in its own right, especially in connection with the theological problem of justification, the conditions for an individual's 'acceptance' by God. It is significant that, while Ockham's Augustinian emphasis on the punitive function of the state is traditionally associated with a rather sombre view of fallen human nature, the heresy most often suspected in his own theology is Augustine's *bête noire*, Pelagianism. Ockham seems to have had a high estimate of human capabilities but without any easy faith in the automatic realization of these capabilities.

The incompatibility often thought to exist between Ockham's individualism and earlier medieval corporatist ideas has always been felt most acutely in the spiritual domain. For traditional ideas of the church as an organic body and revelation as a single universal truth Ockham is held to have substituted isolation between persons and subjectivity concerning doctrine. In this study we have found much that counts against such interpretations. Certainly, Ockham saw his own ecclesiological and dogmatic positions, not those of his opponents, as the ancient and universally accepted teaching of the church. Even on the matter of individual defense of orthodoxy against the whole world he found impressive historical precedent. Ockham's solidarity with tradition must, however, be understood in its own terms. For some, the historic tradition of the church seems to be the unfolding of ideas, an inspired process independent of those who hold them. For others, it is a history of institutions and institutional leaders. For Ockham, however, church history was the history of the *congregatio fidelium*, Christ's flock, in all too many respects comparable to irrational sheep in continuing need of shepherds with a certain amount of coercive power, but also endowed with an invincible capacity to maintain the faith and with individualized responsibilities and rights to understand it. There is, then, a certain ambiguity in Ockham's relation to corporate ecclesiastical tradition. He believed that he was at one with the historic *ecclesia universalis* but thought of this church as a community of individuals.

A new emphasis on individuals is also evident in his defense of Franciscan poverty. As we have seen, Ockham's personal requirements for ecclesiastical officials were not overwhelmingly stringent. An individual pope or bishop who lived by the Franciscan rule would no doubt have struck Ockham as a better Christian than one who did not, other things being equal,[10] but it could not be argued on Ockhamist grounds that his personally embracing poverty would add an iota to the jurisdictional superiority, perfection, or authority of an ecclesiastic's office. Christian poverty as Ockham defended it was thus not a menace to the institutional church. Yet in proposing that the fullest and most complete form of Christian life involved renunciation of economic and legal power, the Franciscan ideal did suggest especially clearly that freedom and fulfillment come through a personal way of life and not through the possession of official status in any institution. Ockham's defense of Franciscan poverty is thus the leading example of an important general tendency in his thought. While he insisted on the legitimacy of 'political' or

---

10 The Franciscans conceded that charity was the essential principle of Christian perfection and did not claim that observing the Franciscan rule guaranteed its possession. On the Franciscan way of life as a *status perfectionis* see *OND*, c. 76; *OP* II, 605–23.

governmental structures in both church and secular world, he argued for the ethical primacy of individuals who were not normally involved in such structures. For Ockham, as we have seen, the greatest contributions of Christianity to politics came through its non-political character. Religion should strengthen justice in the human community, not by formal direction of secular affairs, but by creating or reinforcing individual commitment to the natural moral virtues. It gives 'unoriented' politics direction by pointing towards a community substantially without politics. Similarly, as a commanding model of Christian perfection, the Franciscan ideal had much to contribute to the life of the church, but its essential function depended on its being in important respects non-institutional. It was a model for individuals.

Considering Ockham's attitudes towards law, his treatment of empire and papacy, and his individualism together, we may fairly describe his work as an attempt to strengthen institutions while undercutting the spirit of institutionalism. With significant respect for the texture of law on the one hand and a sometimes caustic critique of institutional self-importance on the other, Ockham's writings are an extraordinarily disciplined attempt to give effective meaning to the ideal of a human community which can use institutions without destroying them, be ruled by them without worshipping them, and live its own life in peace and freedom. In attempting to shift the center of gravity in human affairs from institutional structures to the broader context of a community of free individuals, Ockham both appealed to traditionally acknowledged principles and gave them new expression. His conception of the place which awareness of such principles ought to have in practical affairs is the final topic to which we must give attention.

KNOWLEDGE AND POLITICAL POWER

The non-metaphysical character of Ockham's political thought has been emphasized often enough in this study to require only a brief reminder here. Ockham was without a grand scheme of history, mistrusted allegorical interpretations of Scripture, and showed little fondness for the biological, psychological, astronomical, and other analogies in terms of which his papalist opponents developed their theories of government and society. If speculation is taken to be the search for a comprehensive vision of reality as a basis for all dealings with particulars, then Ockham's political thought is non-speculative. There is a narrower sense of speculation, however, which must also be taken into account. Speculative knowledge, according to Ockham, is concerned with things not in our power, whereas practical knowledge is concerned with things in our power.[11] According to this distinction, political knowledge is practical rather than speculative, for it is concerned with directing human action. It may nevertheless rest on principles which are objective and non-arbitrary. Ockham, as much as any of his contemporaries, sought to ground political action in such principles. In contrast with later attempts to base politics entirely on human agreement or treat the human spirit as fulfilling only its own inner impulses, Ockham resolutely pressed the claims of abstract reason and God, principles 'not in our power'. Thus, his rebellion against the popes at Avignon rested, at least in intention, on Christian truths beyond the power of any man or institution to abolish or modify. Again, his refutation of papalism as a political ideology and his reformulation of imperialism were based on natural law and Aristotelian political rationalism. The ideas of consent and free action were highly significant for Ockham, but he did not use them in the modern liberal manner, so well anticipated by Marsilius, as the sufficient warrant for political and even moral legitimacy. Finally, Ockham's doctrine of casual power, under which subjects might in some cases act against their rulers, or secular and religious authorities intervene in one another's affairs, depended upon the possibility of judging correctly when such exceptional cases were at hand.

Since Ockham agreed with the basic medieval assumption that action should be guided by an awareness of objective principles, one wonders how important his rejection of speculative metaphysics was, or need have been, in practice. The answer to this question lies partly in the fact that hierocratic thinkers tended to treat as part of the unchanging and unchangeable nature of things institutions to which Ockham gave a contingent, functional status. The difference is not absolute, since Ockham regarded the historical standing of the Roman empire and, far more important, Christ's commission of the

[11] *Sent.*, prologue, q. 11; ed. Gál and Brown, p. 315. Cf. q. 10, pp. 287–8.

church to St Peter as 'givens' which called for enduring respect. Nevertheless, he insisted that both papacy and empire could be understood and, if necessary, modified in the light of principles beyond themselves. From this standpoint, the inability of curialist theorists to deal effectively with the possibility of papal corruption or take adequate account of current secular realities seemed intolerable. Indeed, to Ockham the view finally adopted by one of these thinkers, Guido Terreni, must have seemed a rejection of the whole idea of grounding practice in objective knowledge. Guido found the idea of serious papal error so unassimilable that he concluded God would simply not allow the pope to fall into heresy.[12] From Ockham's standpoint, this was a juristic solution to an essentially theological problem, for, if Guido was right, one need only ascertain that an individual had been canonically elected pope to be sure that his official pronouncements were orthodox. For Ockham, on the contrary, no institutional procedure could guarantee this happy result. Judgments of orthodoxy needed a cognitive foundation rather than a legal one.

There is another side to Ockham's difference with tradition on the relation between knowledge and action. It concerns the importance of understanding being possessed by subjects as well as rulers. Ockham held that human and Christian freedom consisted of self-direction rather than unreflective participation in a broader social whole. If this is the case, it becomes essential that free individuals understand for themselves the legal, moral, and religious truths on which they ought to act. Among other things, the subject of any government ought to know in a relatively precise way the character and extent of his rulers' legitimate power over him, and the individual believer is entitled to an understanding of the Christian faith. Because the knowledge required for human life should be shared by all, it follows that those who possess such knowledge must explain it to others, not merely provide authoritative pronouncements. At the same time, because Ockham thought there was a science of morals and objective knowledge of at least some of God's intentions as revealed in Scripture, the man who has knowledge and can explain it, whether he be a prelate or an academic expert, is compelled to bring

[12] On Guido Terreni see Tierney, *Origins of Papal Infallibility*, pp. 238–69, especially pp. 245–51.

8-2

this knowledge to bear for the attainment of good ends. He cannot be the morally neutral servant of institutions which themselves determine the ends of action in arbitrary ways. Ockham was led to these conclusions partly by his own speculative principles but most immediately by the necessity he felt for dealing with the problem of papal heresy. Accordingly, his clearest account of the relations between knowledge and power is given in I *Dialogus*, a work which has impressed many readers as an attack on the foundations of medieval Christian society. It may be well to consider, however, that Ockham's defense of autonomy and self-consciousness, in spite of its modernity and potentially disruptive quality, was a genuine development of classical and medieval principles. In happier circumstances, this development might have been compatible with other traditions in practice as well as in theory.

OCKHAM AS A CONSTRUCTIVE POLITICAL THINKER

The preceding review suggests that Ockham's approach to politics was in more than one sense constructive. The basic principles on which he worked were positive rather than skeptical. They were either principles already professed by his society or, as in the case of Aristotle's analysis of royal and tyrannical government, morally positive philosophical ideas. His sharpest personal attacks were delivered on behalf of Christian orthodoxy, and his demand for institutional justice was also an attack on what he perceived as disturbances of the traditional order. Far from being a political skeptic, Ockham was so insistent on handling practical problems in a principled way and so critical of arbitrary, merely authoritarian, exercises of power that the reader may be inclined to criticize him for intolerance. He was outraged at what he took to be the irrationality of the world around him, especially of the Avignonese papacy, but rejected the cynical view that truth, justice, and sincere piety must generally be sacrificed to obtain spiritual and temporal tranquillity. Ockham demanded tranquillity and virtue as well. In this he was perhaps narrow, visionary, or naive but certainly not a skeptic.

Ockham's political work was not merely an emphatic assertion of principle, however. It was constructive in the further sense of being an attempt to promote stable and effective institutional structures. To be sure, the whole point of institutions in Ockham's view was to provide for the exercise of legitimate individual rights and freedoms, but, as we have seen, he not only denied in the abstract that life without government was possible in this world but discussed the problems of government in detail and with attention to traditional legal sources and techniques. The much debated question of his influence in the conciliar era should be approached with this aspect of his work in mind. Almost in the nature of the case, the educated and influential men who were able to put his ideas into practice in the fourteenth and fifteenth centuries were respectable ecclesiastics who would have viewed his personal history with grave misgivings. Yet precisely because of his conviction that John XXII was an obdurate heretic, Ockham became one of the few men of his time with a clear respect for orthodoxy and institutional stability who had thought through the problems posed by institutional breakdown, a combination of particular relevance in the period of the great schism. If the conciliar resolution of that crisis is seen as a constructive response by Christians of the time acting, in Ockham's terms, as 'friends' rather than officials in a non-papal ecclesiastical constitution, the relevance of his thought becomes even greater.

Finally, Ockham's work was constructive rather than merely receptive. It was a deliberate attempt to produce something new – new leadership in the church, a newly effective and newly understood central secular power, and a general conception of spiritual government in keeping with Biblical foundations and contemporary experience. In contending that papal government was properly a 'dignified' rulership over free subjects, he employed a concept of freedom different from traditional theological ideas. Besides finding support in the New Testament, however, Ockham's view of freedom as individual self-direction corresponded with current philosophical developments and with new possibilities for autonomous life actually present on the European scene. Here, as elsewhere in his political thought, Ockham's most novel ideas were a response to both the problems of the world in which he lived and its potentialities. His work was the response of a man whose commitment to traditional principles facilitated rather than hindering an awareness of existing realities.

Conclusions

None of Ockham's political writings is a harmonious *summa* in which all points of view are given thorough attention, all objections raised, and all questions answered. It is remarkable, however, if we consider the trying circumstances in which he worked, his bitter personal animosities, and his obvious temperamental preference for precise and non-conciliatory theses in academic subjects, how wide a range of ideas and attitudes he did bring together. In fashioning his own position he used elements from Augustinian and Franciscan theology, Aristotelian political science, scholastic natural law, canon, civil, and feudal law, contemporary logic and empiricism, and a strong, if inexact, sense of wholesome ecclesiastical life in earlier times. The most formidably technical of the great scholastics, he also became an *homme engagé*. As an imperial pamphleteer he elaborated a conception of world government in advance of modern as well as medieval practice. He was the sworn enemy of three popes and rejected medieval papalism as an ideology, but insisted upon the primacy and unique dignity of papal government. In defending what he took to be the traditional jurisdictional boundaries between papacy and empire, he analysed the whole apparatus of law and government as primarily an instrument for fostering non-juristic modes of communal life. While he was both an advocate and a defiant example of personal autonomy, he argued persistently and acutely for rationality in morals as well as in logic and science. He was as emphatic as Marsilius of Padua about treating secular politics in purely secular terms but found God's will the supreme ethical rule for this world as well as the next. In bringing together such contrasting ideas and attitudes he achieved on a grand scale one of his aims in the mature and complex *Octo Quaestiones*. He had written in such a way, he said, that, 'having understood what can be alleged for both sides, a sincere lover of the truth of pure reason may have occasion for discriminating the true from the false'.[13] Merely in compelling thought about fundamental political issues, Ockham's work is of real power. Beyond this, however, it presents constructive solutions to the most perplexing problems of late medieval society. Above all, Ockham achieved an extraordinarily reasonable view

---

[13] Ockham assumed the person of a 'reciter' in the *Octo Quaestiones*, 'ut pro utraque parte allegationibus intellectis veritatis sincerus amator purae rationis verum a falso occasionem habeat discernendi'. *OQ, Prologus*; *OP* I, 13.

of the legal and political domain in which so many of these perplexities arose, while maintaining a firm commitment to moral and spiritual values well beyond politics.

There is more to be said on every subject discussed in this study. In attempting to determine Ockham's political principles, we have had to treat cursorily many significant features of his own work and have been able to make only scattered comparisons with other writers. Even on this limited basis, however, it can be urged that a substantially new perception of Ockham's political thought is in order. When read carefully from its own point of view, his work seems much more defensible as authentic religious protest, much more coherent theoretically, and much more adequate to the short- and long-term demands of politics than it is typically presented as being. It is the work of a brave as well as a disturbed man, a devoted Christian, and a political thinker of major rank. Students of late medieval history need not regard Ockham as an unfortunate and enigmatic obstacle. In a time of vitality as well as disillusionment, he offers a remarkable and still instructive example of intelligent movement forward.

BIBLIOGRAPHY

I. ORIGINAL SOURCES

(a) *Manuscripts*

Michael of Cesena. *Appellatio contra Bullam 'Quia vir reprobus'* (Munich, 1330). Ms. Lat. 5154, Bibliothèque Nationale, Paris.

Pierre d'Ailly. Abbreviation of Ockham's *Dialogus*. Ms. Lat. 14579, Bibliothèque Nationale, Paris.

William of Ockham. *Dialogus*.

Ms. S. Crucis, Plut. xxxvi, dext. cod. 11, Biblioteca Laurenziana, Florence (I *Dialogus*).

Ms. 517, Bibliothèque de l'Arsenal, Paris (III *Dialogus*).

Ms. 3522 (478), Bibliothèque Mazarine, Paris (III *Dialogus*).

Ms. Lat 3657, Bibliothèque Nationale, Paris (I and III *Dialogus*).

Ms. Lat. 14313, Bibliothèque Nationale, Paris (I *Dialogus*).

Ms. Lat. 14619, Bibliothèque Nationale, Paris (III *Dialogus*).

Ms. Lat. 15881, Bibliothèque Nationale, Paris (I and III *Dialogus*).

Ms. Lat. 4096, Biblioteca Vaticana, Rome (I *Dialogus*).

Ms. Lat. 4098, Biblioteca Vaticana, Rome (I and III *Dialogus*).

Ms. Lat. 4115, Biblioteca Vaticana, Rome (III *Dialogus*).

Ms. Regin. Lat. 370, Biblioteca Vaticana, Rome (I *Dialogus*).

Expositio in Libros Physicorum. Ms. 293, Merton College, Oxford.

Quaestiones in Libros Physicorum. Ms. Lat. 17841, Bibliothèque Nationale, Paris.

(b) *Printed editions of Ockham's works*

For manuscripts and other editions of Ockham's works, see Baudry, *Guillaume d'Occam*, pp. 273–94.

Allegationes de Potestate Imperiali (attributed to Ockham with others). Ed. Scholz, *Streitschriften*, II, 417–31.

Allegationes Religiosorum Virorum (by Ockham and other Michaelist friars). BF, V, 388–96. Baluze–Mansi, *Miscellanea*, III, 315–23.

An Princeps pro suo Succursu, scilicet Guerrae, Possit Recipere Bona Ecclesiarum, etiam Invito Papa. Ed. H. S. Offler and R. S. Snape, *OP* I, 223–71.

232

Bibliography

Breviloquium de Principatu Tyrannico super Divina et Humana, Specialiter autem super Imperium et Subiectos Imperio, a quibusdam Vocatis Summis Pontificibus Usurpato. Ed. R. Scholz, *Wilhelm von Ockham als politischer Denker und sein Breviloquium de principatu tyrannico* (Leipzig, 1944; reprinted Stuttgart, 1952). Also ed. L. Baudry (Paris, 1937).

Compendium Errorum Papae Ioannis XXII. Ed. J. Trechsel, *Guillelmus de Occam, O.F.M., Opera Plurima*, II (Lyon, 1495; reprinted London, 1962). Also ed. Goldast, *Monarchia*, II, 957–76.

Consultatio de Causa Matrimoniali. Ed. H. S. Offler, *OP* I, 273–86.

Contra Benedictum. Ed. H. S. Offler, *OP* III, 157–322.

Contra Ioannem. Ed. H. S. Offler, *OP* III, 19–156.

I–III *Dialogus.* Ed. J. Trechsel, *Guillelmus de Occam, O.F.M., Opera Plurima*, I (Lyon, 1494; reprinted London, 1962). Also ed. Goldast, *Monarchia*, II, 394–957. Continuation ed. Scholz, *Streitschriften*, II, 392–5. Portions ed. and trans. F. Oakley in R. Lerner and M. Mahdi (eds.), *Medieval Political Philosophy: a Sourcebook* (New York, 1963), pp. 492–506.

De Dogmatibus Ioannis XXII Papae (printed as II *Dialogus*). Ed. J. Trechsel, *Guillelmus de Occam, O.F.M., Opera Plurima*, I (Lyon, 1494, reprinted London, 1962). Also ed. Goldast, *Monarchia*, II, 740–70.

De Electione Caroli Quarti (dubious). Found only in Conrad of Megenberg's *Tractatus contra Wilhelmum Occam*. Ed. Scholz, *Streitschriften*, II, 346–63.

Elementarium Logicae. Ed. E. M. Buytaert, *FcS*, XXV (1965), 170–276; XXVI (1966), 66–173.

Epistola ad Fratres Minores in Capitulo apud Assisium Congregatos. Ed. H. S. Offler, *OP* III, 1–17. Also ed. L. Baudry, *Revue d'histoire franciscaine*, III (1926), 201–15. Also ed. C. K. Brampton (Oxford, 1929).

Expositio Aurea et Admodum Utilis super Artem Veterem (Bologna, 1496, reprinted Ridgewood, N. J., 1965). Portions ed. E. A. Moody, *Expositionis in Libros Artis Logicae Prooemium et Expositio in Librum Porphyrii De Praedicabilibus* (St Bonaventure, N.Y., 1965). Chapter 1 of the section, *Expositio super Primum Librum Perihermenias*, ed. P. Boehner, *Traditio*, IV (1946), 320–35.

De Imperatorum et Pontificum Potestate. Ed. Scholz, *Streitschriften*, II, 453–80. Also ed. C. K. Brampton (Oxford, 1927). Continuation ed. W. Mulder, *AFH*, XVI (1923), 469–92; XVII (1924), 72–97.

Octo Quaestiones de Potestate Papae. Ed. J. G. Sikes, *OP* I, 1–221.

Opus Nonaginta Dierum. Chapters 1–6 ed. R. F. Bennett and J. G. Sikes, *OP* I, 289–374. Chapters 7–124 ed. R. F. Bennett and H. S. Offler, *OP* II, 375–858.

Bibliography

Quaestiones in Libros Physicorum. Extracts ed. F. Corvino, *Rivista critica di storia della filosofia*, X (1955), 265-88 ('Sette questioni inedite di Occam sul concetto'); XI (1956), 41-67 and XII (1957), 42-63 ('Questioni inedite di Occam sul tempo'); XIII (1958), 191-208 ('Questioni inedite di Occam sul continuo').

Quodlibeta Septem (Strasbourg, 1491; reprinted Louvain, 1962).

Quoniam scriptura testante divina (brief defense of Ludwig of Bavaria against John XXII, attributed to Ockham with other Michaelist friars). Ed. W. Preger, 'Beiträge und Erörterungen zur Geschichte des Deutschen Reichs in den Jahren 1330-1334', *Abhandlungen der historischen Classe der königlich bayerischen Akademie der Wissenschaften*, XV.2 (1880), 76-82.

De Sacramento Altaris. Ed. T. B. Birch (Burlington, Iowa, 1930).

Scriptum in Quattuor Libros Sententiarum. Ed. J. Trechsel, *Guillelmus de Occam, O.F.M., Opera Plurima*, III-IV (Lyon, 1495; reprinted London, 1962). Prologue and Distinctions 1-3 of Book 1 ed. G. Gál and S. Brown, *Guillelmi de Ockham Opera Philosophica et Theologica, Opera Theologica*, I-II (St Bonaventure, N.Y., 1967-70).

Summa Logicae, Pars Prima, Pars Secunda et Tertiae Prima. Ed. P. Boehner (St Bonaventure, N.Y., 1957-62).

Summulae in Libros Physicorum. Ed. B. Theulo, *Philosophia Naturalis Guilielmi Occham* (Rome, 1637; reprinted London, 1963).

Tractatus Logicae Minor. Ed. E. M. Buytaert, *FcS*, XXIV (1964), 55-100.

Tractatus de Praedestinatione et de Praescientia Dei et de Futuris Contingentibus. Ed. P. Boehner (St Bonaventure, N.Y., 1945). Trans. M. M. Adams and N. Kretzmann, *William Ockham: Predestination, God's Foreknowledge, and Future Contingents* (New York, 1969).

Tractatus de Successivis (attributed to Ockham). Ed. P. Boehner (St Bonaventure, N.Y., 1944).

(c) Other original sources

Alexander of St Elpidius. *Tractatus de Ecclesiastica Potestate*. Ed. J. T. Rocaberti, *Bibliotheca Maxima Pontificia* (Rome, 1698-9), II.

Almain, Jacques. *Expositio de Suprema Potestate Ecclesiastica et Laica, circa Quaestionum Decisiones Magistri Guillermi de Ockham super Potestate Summi Pontificis*. Ed. Goldast, *Monarchia*, I, 588-647.

Alvarus Pelagius. *Collirium adversus Hereses Novas*. Ed. Scholz, *Streitschriften*, II, 491-514.

De Planctu Ecclesiae. Ed. J. T. Rocaberti, *Bibliotheca Maxima Pontificia* (Rome, 1698-9), III, 23-264.

Bibliography

Amoros, L. 'Series condempnationum et processuum contra doctrinam et sequaces Petri Johannis Olivi.' *AFH*, XXIV (1931), 495–512.

Andre Ricci. *Tractatus contra Fraticellos*. Ed. L. Oliger, *AFH*, III (1910), 267–78.

Andreas of Perusio. *Contra Edictum Bavari*. Ed. Scholz, *Streitschriften*, II, 64–75.

Angelo Clareno, 'Angelus Clarenus ad Alvarum Pelagium *Apologia pro Vita sua*.' Ed. V. Doucet, *AFH*, XXXIX (1946), 63–200.

'Anonymi Spiritualis responsio *Beatus Vir* contra *Abbreviaturam Communitatis*.' Ed. A. Heysse, *AFH*, XLII (1950), 213–35.

Augustinus Triumphus. *Summa de Ecclesiastica Potestate* (Rome, 1479, 1584).

Tractatus Brevis de Duplici Potestate Prelatorum et Laicorum. Ed. R. Scholz, *Die Publizistik zur Zeit Philipps des Schönen und Bonifaz VIII* (Stuttgart, 1903), pp. 486–501.

Tractatus contra Articulos Inventos ad Diffamandum Sanctissimum Patrem Dominum Bonifacium Papam. Ed. H. Finke, *Aus den Tagen Bonifaz VIII*. Vorreformationsgeschichtliche Forschungen, II (Münster, 1902).

Bernard of Clairvaux. *De Consideratione ad Eugenium Papam*. Ed. J. Leclercq and H. Rochais, *S. Bernardi Opera*, III (Rome, 1963, 381–493.

Bernardus Parmensis. *Glossa Ordinaria ad Decretales* (Paris, 1519).

Bonagratia of Bergamo. *Appellatio contra Bullam Ad conditorem canonum*. *BF*, V, 237–46. Baluze–Mansi, *Miscellanea*, III, 213–21.

Clypeus. Ed. A. Mercati, *AFH*, XX (1927), 260–304.

Consilium Bonagratiae de Iuramento Ludowico Bavaro non Obediendi. Ed. J. F. Böhmer, *Fontes Rerum Germanicarum*, IV (Stuttgart, 1868).

Tractatus de Paupertate Christi et Apostolorum. Ed. L. Oliger, *AFH*, XXII (1929), 323–35, 486–511.

Bonagratia of Bergamo and Raymond of Fronsiaco. *Contra Responsiones ad Quatuor Supradicta Quaesita*. Ed. F. Ehrle, *Archiv für Litteratur und Kirchengeschichte des Mittelalters*, III (1887), 141–60.

Bonaventure. *Apologia Pauperum*. Ed. PP. Collegii a S. Bonaventura, *Doctoris Seraphici S. Bonaventurae Opera Omnia*, VIII (Quaracchi, 1898), 233–330.

Conrad of Megenberg. *Planctus Ecclesiae in Germaniam*. Ed. Scholz, *Streitschriften*, II, 188–248.

Tractatus contra Wilhelmum Occam. Ed. Scholz, *Streitschriften*, II, 346–91.

De Translatione Romani Imperii. Ed. Scholz, *Streitschriften*, II, 249–345.

Corpus Iuris Canonici. Ed. A. Friedberg (2 vols., Leipzig, 1879–81).

Dante Alighieri. *Monarchia*. Ed. E. Moore and P. Toynbee, *Le Opere di Dante Alighieri*, 5th ed. (Oxford, 1963).

Douie, D. L. 'Three treatises on evangelical poverty by Richard Conyngton, Fr. Walter Chatton and an anonymous . . .' *AFH*, xxiv (1931), 341–69; xxv (1932), 36–58, 210–40.

Durand of St Pourçain. *De Iurisdictione Ecclesiastica*. Ed. J. Barbier (Paris, 1506), fols. 1–8.

De Origine et Usu Iurisdictionum. *Maxima Bibliotheca Veterum Patrum* (Lyon, 1677), xxvi, 127–35.

Egidius Romanus. *De Ecclesiastica Potestate*. Ed. R. Scholz (Weimar, 1929).

Egidius Spiritalis de Perusio. *Libellus contra Infideles et Inobedientes et Rebelles*. Ed. Scholz, *Streitschriften*, ii, 105–29.

Engelbert of Admont. *De Ortu, Progressu et Fine Regnorum, et Praecipue Regni seu Imperii Romani*. Ed. Goldast, *Politica Imperialia* (Frankfurt, 1614), pp. 754–73.

Francis of Mayron. 'L'œuvre politique de François de Mayronnes', ed. P. de Lapparent. *Archives d'histoire doctrinale et littéraire du moyen âge*, xv–xvii (1940–2), 55–116 (*Quaestio de Subiectione*, pp. 75–92; *Tractatus de Principatu Temporali*, pp. 55–74; *Tractatus de Principatu Regni Siciliae*, pp. 93–116).

Francis Petrarch. *Epistolae de Iuribus Imperii Romani*. Ed. Goldast, *Monarchia*, ii, 1345–1465.

Guido Terreni. *Quaestio de Magisterio Infallibilis Romani Pontificis*. Ed. B. F. M. Xiberta, *Opuscula et Textus*, ii (Münster, 1926).

Henry of Cremona. *Non ponant laici*. Ed. R. Scholz, *Die Publizistik zur Zeit Philipps des Schönen und Bonifaz VIII* (Stuttgart, 1903), pp. 471–84.

De Potestate Papae. Ed. R. Scholz, *Die Publizistik zur Zeit Philipps des Schönen und Bonifaz VIII* (Stuttgart, 1903), pp. 459–71.

Hermann von Schilditz. *Contra Hereticos Negantes Immunitatem et Iurisdictionem Sancte Ecclesie*. Ed. Scholz, *Streitschriften*, ii, 130–53.

Hervaeus Natalis. *De Iurisdictione*. Ed. L. Hödl (Munich, 1959).

De Paupertate Christi et Apostolorum. Ed. J. G. Sikes, *Archives d'histoire doctrinale et littéraire du moyen âge*, xii–xiii (1937–8), 209–97.

De Potestate Papae. Ed. J. Barbier (Paris, 1506), fols. 139–73.

Heysse, A. 'Duo documenta de polemica inter Gerardum Odonem et Michaelem de Cesena.' *AFH*, ix (1916), 134–83.

Hostiensis. *Lectura in Quinque Decretalium Libros* (Venice, 1581).

Hugues de Digne. *De Finibus Paupertatis*. Ed. C. Florovsky, *AFH*, v (1912), 277–90.

James of Viterbo. *De Regimine Christiano*. Ed. H.-X. Arquillière, *Le plus ancien traité de l'église: Jacques de Viterbe, De Regimine Christiano* (*1301–2*) (Paris, 1926).

Bibliography

Joannes Teutonicus. *Glossa Ordinaria* to the *Decretum*. *Decretum divi Gratiani* ...*una cum variis scribentium Glossis* (Lyon, 1560).

John XXII. Constitutions and letters concerning the Franciscan order. *BF*, V–VI.

John Andreae. *Glossa Ordinaria ad Clementinas* (Venice, 1567). *Glossa Ordinaria ad Librum Sextum* (Venice, 1567).

John Branchazolus. *De Principio et Origine et Potentia Imperatoris*. Ed. E. E. Stengel, *Nova Alamanniae*, I (Berlin, 1921), 44–52.

John of Calvaruso. *Quaestio an Romanus Pontifex Potuerit Treugam Indicere Principi Romanorum*. Ed. I. Schwalm, *Monumenta Germaniae Historica, Leges*, IV; *Constitutiones*, IV.2 (Hanover, 1909–11), 1308–17.

John of Paris. *De Potestate Regia et Papali*. Ed. F. Bleienstein, *Johannes Quidort von Paris über königliche und päpstliche Gewalt (De Regia Potestate et Papali)*, Frankfurter Studien zur Wissenschaft von der Politik (Stuttgart, 1968).

Lambertus Guerrici de Hoyo. *Liber de Commendatione Johannis XXII*. Ed. Scholz, *Streitschriften*, II, 154–68.

Landulfus Colonna. *De Pontificali Officio*. Ed. Scholz, *Streitschriften*, II, 530–9.

De Statu et Mutatione Romani Imperii. Ed. Goldast, *Monarchia*, II, 88–95.

Libellus ad Defensionem Fidei Catholicae. Ed. Scholz, *Streitschriften*, II, 552–62.

Ludwig IV of Bavaria. *Briefe Ludwigs des Bayern*. Ed. J. F. Böhmer, *Fontes Rerum Germanicarum*, I (Stuttgart, 1843).

Constitutions *Fidem catholicam* and *Licet iuris*. Ed. O. Berthold, *Kaiser, Volk und Avignon* (Berlin, 1960).

Lupold of Bebenberg. *De Iure Regni et Imperii Romani*. Ed. S. Schardius, *De Iurisdictione, Auctoritate et Praeeminentia Imperali ac Potestate Ecclesiastica* (Basle, 1566), pp. 328–409.

De Zelo Catholicae Fidei Veterum Principum Germanorum. Ed. S. Schardius, *De Iurisdictione, Auctoritate et Praeeminentia Imperiali ac Potestate Ecclesiastica* (Basle, 1566), pp. 410–65.

Marsilius of Padua. *Defensor Minor*. Ed. C. K. Brampton (Birmingham, 1922).

Defensor Pacis. Ed. C. W. Previté-Orton (Cambridge, 1928). Ed. and trans. A. Gewirth, *Marsilius of Padua: The Defender of Peace*, II: *The Defensor Pacis* (New York, 1956).

De Iurisdictione Imperatoris in Causis Matrimonialibus. Ed. Goldast, *Monarchia*, II, 1386–91.

De Translatione Imperii. Ed. Goldast, *Monarchia*, II, 147–53.

Michael of Cesena. *Appellatio Avenionensis*. Extracts, *BF*, V, 341–3. Baluze–Mansi, *Miscellanea*, III, 238–40.

Bibliography

Appellatio contra Bullam Quia vir reprobus (Munich, 1330). Extracts, *BF*, v, 426–7; K. Müller, 'Einige Aktenstücke und Schriften zur Geschichte der Streitigkeiten unter den Minoriten in der ersten Hälfte des 14. Jahrhunderts', *Zeitschrift für Kirchengeschichte*, VI (1884), 83–7; E. E. Stengel, *Nova Alamanniae*, I (Berlin, 1921), 121–7.

Appellatio in Forma Maiori (Pisa, 1328). Baluze–Mansi, *Miscellanea*, III, 246–303. Extracts, *BF*, v, 408–10.

Appellatio in Forma Minori (Pisa, 1328). *BF*, v, 410–25. Baluze–Mansi, *Miscellanea*, III, 303–10.

Epistola ad Fratres Minores: Iuris divini (Pisa, 1328). *BF*, v, 347–8. Baluze–Mansi, *Miscellanea*, III, 244–6.

Epistola ad Fratres Minores Parisiis in Capitulum Convocatos. Baluze–Mansi, *Miscellanea*, III, 314.

Epistola ad Papam Ioannem XXII (1322). Ed. K. Müller, 'Einige Aktenstücke und Schriften zur Geschichte der Streitigkeiten unter den Minoriten in der ersten Hälfte des 14. Jahrhunderts.' *Zeitschrift für Kirchengeschichte*, VI (1884), 63–112; 106–8.

Litterae Deprecatoriae (Munich, 1331). Ed. Goldast, *Monarchia*, II, 1344–61.

Litterae Excusatoriae (Munich, 1331). *BF*, v, 497–500. Goldast, *Monarchia*, II, 1236–1338.

Litterae ad Omnes Fratres Ordinis Minorum (Munich, 1331). *BF*, v, 427–38. Baluze–Mansi, *Miscellanea*, III, 356–8. Goldast, *Monarchia*, III, 1338–44.

Protestation of 23 August, 1338. Ed. A. Carlini, *Fra Michelino e la sua eresia* (Bologna, 1912), 289–308.

See also Heysse, A.

Opicinus de Canistris. *De Praeeminentia Spiritualis Imperii*. Ed. Scholz, *Streitschriften*, II, 89–104.

Ot, Guiral. *See* Heysse, A.

Peter Bertrandus. *De Iurisdictione Ecclesiastica et Politica*. Ed. Goldast, *Monarchia*, II, 1361–83.

Peter de Lutra. *Tractatus contra Michaelem de Cesena et Socios eius*. Ed. Scholz, *Streitschriften*, II, 29–42.

Peter Olivi. *Postilla in Apocalypsim*. Ed. W. Lewis, University of Tübingen thesis, 1972.

Quaestio de Infallibilitate Romani Pontificis. Ed. M. Maccarrone, 'Una questione inedita dell'Olivi sull'infallibilità del papa.' *Rivista di storia della chiesa in Italia*, III (1949), 309–43.

De Renuntiatione Papae. Ed. L. Oliger, *AFH*, XI (1918), 340–66.

See also Amoros, L.

Bibliography

Peter de la Palu. *De Causa Immediata Ecclesiasticae Potestatis*. Ed. J. Barbier (Paris, 1506), fols. 24–80.

Ptolemy of Lucca. Completion of Thomas Aquinas' *De Regimine Principum*. Ed. R. M. Spiazzi, *Divi Thomae Aquinatis Opuscula Philosophica* (Turin, 1954), pp. 280–358.

Determinatio Compendiosa de Iurisdictione Imperii. Ed. M. Krammer, *Fontes Iuris Germanici Antiqui*, I (Hanover, 1909), 1–65.

De Origine ac Translatione et Statu Romani Imperii. Ed. M. Krammer, *Fontes Iuris Germanici Antiqui*, I (Hanover, 1909), 66–75.

Remigio de Girolami. *Tractatus de Bono Communi*. Extracts ed. R. Egenter, *Scholastik*, IX (1934), 79–92.

Richard Connington. *Tractatus de Paupertate Fratrum Minorum*. Ed. A. Heysse, *AFH*, XXIII (1930), 70–105, 340–60.
See also Douie, D. L., 'Three treatises . . .'

Richard Fitzralph. *De Pauperie Salvatoris*. Books 1–4 ed. R. Poole, *Wyclif's Latin Works*, VIII: *De Dominio Divino* (London, 1890), pp. 257–476.

Somnium Viridarii de Iurisdictione Regia et Sacerdotali. Ed. Goldast, *Monarchia*, I, 58–229.

Thomas Aquinas. *Contra Impugnantes Dei Cultum et Religionem*. Ed. R. Spiazzi, *S. Thomae Aquinatis Opuscula Theologica*, II (Turin, 1954), 1–110.

In Libros Politicorum Aristotelis Expositio (to 1280 a 6; completed by Peter of Auvergne). Ed. R. Spiazzi (Turin, 1951).

De Regimine Principum. Ed. R. M. Spiazzi, *Divi Thomae Aquinatis Opuscula Philosophica* (Turin, 1954), pp. 253–80. Trans. G. Phelan, revised I. Eschmann, *On Kingship to the King of Cyprus* (Toronto, 1949).

Summa Theologiae. Ed. Commissio Piana (5 vols., Ottawa, 1953).

Tractatus contra Ioannem XXII et Benedictum XII (1338). Ed. J. F. Böhmer, *Fontes Rerum Germanicarum*, IV (Stuttgart, 1868), pp. 598–605.

Traktat gegen Benedikt XII. Scholz, *Streitschriften*, II, 552–62.

Ubertino di Casale. *Arbor Vitae Crucifixae Jesu* (Venice, 1485; reprinted with introduction and bibliography by C. Davis, Turin, 1961).

Responsio ad eadem Quatuor Quaesita. Ed. L. Oliger, *AFH*, IX (1916), 27–41.

Super Tribus Sceleribus. Ed. A. Heysse, *AFH*, X (1917), 123–74.

Walter Chatton. See Douie, D. L., 'Three treatises . . .'

Zenzellinus de Cassanis, *Glossa Ordinaria* to the *Extravagantes* of John XXII. *Extravagantes . . . cum apparatu Zenzelini de Cassanhis* (Paris, 1513).

II. SECONDARY SOURCES

Abbagnano, N. *Guglielmo di Ockham* (Lanciano, 1931).

Adams, M. M. 'Intuitive cognition, certainty, and skepticism in William of Ockham.' *Traditio*, XXVI (1970), 389–98.

Adams, M. M. and Kretzmann, N. *William Ockham: Predestination, God's Foreknowledge, and Future Contingents* (New York, 1969).

Amman, E. and Vignaux, P. 'Occam'. *Dictionnaire de théologie catholique*, XI (Paris, 1931), cols. 864–904.

Baethgen, F. *Der Engelpapst: Ideen und Erscheinung* (Leipzig, 1943).

Balthazar, K. *Geschichte des Armutsstreites im Franziskanerorden bis zum Konzil von Vienne*. Vorreformationsgeschichtliche Forschungen, VI (Münster, 1911).

Baluze, S. *Miscellanea, novo ordine digesta et . . . aucta opere ac studio J. D. Mansi*, III (Lucca, 1764).

Barbaglio, G. *Fede acquisita e fede infusa secondo Duns Scoto, Occam e Biel* (Brescia, 1968).

Baron, H. 'Franciscan poverty and civic wealth as factors in the rise of humanistic thought.' *Speculum*, XIII (1938), 1–37.

Barth, T. 'Zur neuesten Ockhamliteratur', *FzS*, XXXII (1950), 164–83.
'Wilhelm Ockham und die Philosophie der Ordnungen'. *Philosophisches Jahrbuch*, LX (1950), 323–34.
'Nuove interpretazioni della filosofia di Occam.' *Studi Francescani*, LII (1955), 187–204.

Battaglia, F. *Marsilio da Padova e la filosofia politica del medio evo* (Florence, 1928).

Baudry, L. 'Fragments inconnus de Guillaume d'Occam.' *Académie des Inscriptions et Belles Lettres*, III (1927), 46–54.
'Les rapports de G. d'Ockham et de Walter Burleigh.' *Archives d'histoire doctrinale et littéraire du moyen âge*, IX (1934), 155–73.
'Le philosophe et le politique dans Guillaume d'Ockham.' *Archives d'histoire doctrinale et littéraire du moyen âge*, XII (1939), 209–30.
'À propos de G. d'Occam et de Wiclef.' *Archives d'histoire doctrinale et littéraire du moyen âge*, XII (1939), 231–51.
Guillaume d'Occam: sa vie, ses œuvres, ses idées sociales et politiques (Paris, 1949).
'Guillaume d'Occam: critique des preuves scotistes sur l'unicité de Dieu.' *Archives d'histoire doctrinale et littéraire du moyen âge*, XXVIII (1953), 99–112.
Lexique philosophique de Guillaume d'Occam (Paris, 1958).
'Les rapports de la raison et de la foi selon Guillaume d'Occam.'

Bibliography

Archives d'histoire doctrinale et littéraire du moyen âge, XXXIX (1962), 33–92.

'L'Ordre franciscaine au temps de Guillaume d'Occam.' *Mediaeval Studies*, XXVII (1965), 184–211.

Bayley, C. C. 'Pivotal concepts in the political philosophy of William of Ockham.' *Journal of the History of Ideas*, X (1949), 199–218.

Becker, H.-J. 'Das Mandat *Fidem catholicam* Ludwigs des Bayern von 1338.' *DA*, XXVI (1970), 454–512.

Belmond, S. 'Deux penseurs franciscains: Pierre Jean Olieu et Guillaume Occam.' *Études franciscaines*, XXXV (1923), 188–97.

Benz, E. *Ecclesia Spiritualis: Kirchenidee und Geschichtstheologie der franziskanischen Reformation.* 2nd ed. (Stuttgart, 1964).

Bergmann, G. 'Some remarks on the ontology of Ockham.' *Philosophical Review*, LXIII (1954), 560–71.

Berthold, O. *Kaiser, Volk und Avignon* (Berlin, 1960).

Bettoni, E. 'Guglielmo Occam appartiene alla scuola Francescana?' *Studi francescani*, LII (1955), 169–86.

Betts, R. 'The great debate about universals in the universities of the fourteenth century.' H. Seaton-Watson (ed.), *Prague Essays* (Oxford, 1948), 69–80.

Bibliographia Franciscana (Rome, 1938–).

Birch, T. 'The theory of continuity of William of Ockham.' *Philosophy of Science*, III (1936), 494–505.

Bock, F. 'Die Prokuratorien Kaiser Ludwigs IV. an den Papst Benedict XII.' *Quellen und Forschungen aus italienischen Archiven und Bibliotheken*, XXV (1933), 251–91.

'Die Appellationsschriften König Ludwigs IV. in den Jahren 1323–24.' *DA*, IV (1940–1), 179–205.

Boehner, P. 'The spirit of Franciscan philosophy.' *FcS*, II (1942), 217–37.

'The *notitia intuitiva* of non-existents according to William Ockham with a critical study of the text of Ockham's *Reportatio* and a revised edition of *Reportatio* II, Qq. 14–15.' *Traditio*, I (1943), 223–75. Boehner's essay reprinted in Boehner, *Collected Articles*, pp. 268–300.

'Ockham's political ideas.' *Review of Politics*, V (1943), 462–87. Reprinted in Boehner, *Collected Articles*, pp. 442–68.

'*In propria causa*: a reply to Professor Pegis "Concerning William of Ockham".' *FcS*, IV (1945), 37–54. Reprinted in Boehner, *Collected Articles*, pp. 300–18.

'Ockham's theory of signification.' *FcS*, VI (1946), 143–70. Reprinted in Boehner, *Collected Articles*, pp. 201–31.

'Ockham's theory of supposition and the notion of truth.' *FcS*, VI (1946), 261–92. Reprinted in Boehner, *Collected Articles*, pp. 232–67.

'The realistic conceptualism of William Ockham.' *Traditio*, IV (1946), 307–35. Reprinted in Boehner, *Collected Articles*, pp. 156–73.

'Scotus' teachings according to Ockham; I: On the univocity of being; II: On the *natura communis*.' *FcS*, VI (1946), 100–7, 362–75.

'The metaphysics of William Ockham.' *The Review of Metaphysics*, I (1947–8), 59–86. Reprinted in Boehner, *Collected Articles*, pp. 373–99.

'The critical value of quotations of Scotus' works found in Ockham's writings,' *FcS*, VIII (1948), 192–201. Reprinted in Boehner, *Collected Articles*, pp. 127–36.

'A recent presentation of Ockham's philosophy.' *FcS*, IX (1949), 443–56. Reprinted in Boehner, *Collected Articles*, pp. 137–55.

'Zu Ockhams Beweis der Existenz Gottes.' *FzS*, XXXII (1950), 50–69. Reprinted in Boehner, *Collected Articles*, pp. 399–420.

Collected Articles on Ockham. Ed. E. M. Buytaert (St Bonaventure, N.Y., 1958).

Boh, I. 'An examination of Ockham's aretetic logic.' *Archiv für Geschichte der Philosophie*, XLV (1963), 259–68.

Bonke, E. 'Doctrina nominalistica de fundamento ordinis moralis apud Guilelmum de Ockham et Gabrielem Biel.' *Collectanea Franciscana*, XIV (1944), 57–83.

Bornhak, O. *Staatskirchliche Anschauungen und Handlungen am Hofe Kaiser Ludwigs des Bayern* (Weimar, 1933).

Bosl, K. 'Der geistige Widerstand am Hofe Ludwigs des Bayern gegen die Kurie.' *Die Welt zur Zeit des Konstanzer Konzils* (Stuttgart, 1965), pp. 99–118.

Brampton, C. K. 'Ockham and his alleged authorship of the tract *Quia saepe iuris*.' *AFH*, LIII (1960), 30–8.

'Traditions relating to the death of William of Ockham.' *AFH*, LIII (1960), 442–9.

'Ockham, Bonagratia and the Emperor Lewis IV.' *Medium Aevum*, XXXI (1962), 81–7.

'The probable date of Ockham's *Lectura Sententiarum*.' *AFH*, LV (1962), 367–74.

'The probable order of Ockham's non-polemical works.' *Traditio*, XIX (1963), 469–83.

'Scotus, Ockham and the theory of intuitive cognition.' *Antonianum*, XL (1965), 449–66.

'Personalities in the process against Ockham at Avignon, 1324–1326.' *FcS*, XXV (1966), 4–25.

Bibliography

'The probable date of Ockham's noviciate.' *FzS*, LII (1969), 78–85.

Buescher, G. N. *The Eucharistic Teaching of William of Ockham* (St Bonaventure, N.Y., 1950).

Buisson, L. *Potestas und Caritas: die päpstliche Gewalt im Spätmittelalter.* Forschungen zur kirchlichen Rechtsgeschichte und zum Kirchenrecht, II (Cologne, 1958).

Burr, D. 'Ockham, Scotus and the censure at Avignon.' *Church History*, XXXVII (1968), 144–59.

Carlini, A. *Fra Michelino e la sua eresia* (Bologna, 1912).

Carré, E. *Realists and Nominalists* (Oxford, 1946).

Chambers, C. J. 'William Ockham, theologian: convicted for lack of evidence.' *Journal of the History of Philosophy*, VII (1969), 381–9.

Chauchat, P. *Cardinal Bertrand de Turre Ord. Min.: his Participation in the Theoretical Controversy concerning the Poverty of Christ and the Apostles under Pope John XXII* (Rome, 1930).

Clark, David W. 'William of Ockham on Right Reason.' *Speculum* XLVIII (1973), 13–36.

Congar, Y. M.-J. 'Incidence ecclésiologique d'un thème de dévotion mariale.' *Mélanges des sciences religieuses*, VII (1950), 277–92.

'Aspects ecclésiologiques de la querelle entre mendiants et séculiers dans la seconde moitié du XIIIe siècle et le début du XIVe.' *Archives d'histoire doctrinale et littéraire du moyen âge*, XXVIII (1962), 35–151.

Corsano, A. 'Giovanni Pico e il nominalismo occamistico.' *L'opera e il pensiero di Giovanni Pico della Mirandola nella storia dell'Umanesimo* (Convegno Internazionale, Mirandola, 1963), II, 54–42.

Corvino, F. 'Le *Quaestiones in Libros Physicorum* nella formazione del pensiero di Guglielmo d'Occam.' *Rivista critica di storia della filosofia*, XII (1957), 385–411.

'Il significato del termine *natura* nelle opere filosofiche di Occam.' *La filosofia della natura nel medioevo: atti del terzo congresso internazionale di filosofia medioevale, Passo della Mendola (Trento), 1964* (Milan, 1966), pp. 605–15.

Courtenay, W. J. 'Nominalism and late medieval religion.' C. Trinkaus and H. A. Oberman, eds., *The Pursuit of Holiness in the Late Middle Ages and the Renaissance* (Leyden, 1974) pp. 26–59..

'Nominalism and late medieval thought: a bibliographical essay.' *Theological Studies*, XXXIII (1972), 716–34.

Creery, W. E. T. 'The status of theistic propositions in William of Ockham: a study in the logic of theism.' Yale University Ph.D. thesis, 1968.

Bibliography

Day, S. *Intuitive Cognition: a Key to the Significance of the Later Scholastics* (St Bonaventure, N.Y., 1947).

Dettloff, W. *Die Entwicklung der Akzeptations- und Verdienstlehre von Duns Scotus bis Luther: mit besonderer Berücksichtigung der Franziskanertheologen.* Beiträge zur Geschichte der Philosophie und Theologie des Mittelalters, XL.2 (Münster, 1963).

Duncan, David, *Ockham's Razor* (London, 1958).

Ehrle, F. 'Petrus Johannes Olivi, sein Leben und seine Schriften.' *Archiv für Litteratur und Kirchengeschichte des Mittelalters,* III (1887), 409–552.

Der Sentenzkommentar Peters von Candia, des Pisaner Papstes Alexanders V. FzS, Beiheft IX (Münster, 1925).

'Die Spiritualen, ihr Verhältniss zum Franciscanerorden und zu den Fraticellen.' *Archiv für Litteratur und Kirchengeschichte des Mittelalters,* III (1887), 553–623.

Federhofer, F. *Die Erkenntnislehre des Wilhelm von Ockham: Insbesondere seine Lehre vom intuitiven und abstrakten Wissen* (Munich, 1923).

'Ein Beitrag zur Bibliographie und Biographie des Wilhelm von Ockham.' *Philosophisches Jahrbuch,* XXXVIII (1925), 26–48.

'Die Philosophie des Wilhelm von Ockham im Rahmen seiner Zeit.' *FzS,* XII (1925), 273–96.

'Die Psychologie und die psychologischen Grundlagen der Erkenntnislehre des Wilhelm von Ockham.' *Philosophisches Jahrbuch,* XXXIX (1926), 263–87.

Frotscher, G. *Die Anschauungen von Papst Johann XXII. (1316–34) über Kirche und Staat* (Jena, 1933).

Fuchs, O. *The Psychology of Habit according to William of Ockham* (St Bonaventure, N.Y., 1952).

de Gandillac, M. 'Ockham et la *via moderna.*' A. Forest, F. van Steenberghen, and M. de Gandillac, *Le mouvement doctrinale du IXe au XIVe siècle.* A. Fliche, V. Martin, and E. Jarry (eds.), *Histoire de l'église,* XIII (Paris, 1951), 417–73.

Garvens, A. 'Die Grundlagen der Ethik Wilhelms von Ockham.' *FzS,* XXI (1934), 243–73, 360–408.

Gewirth, A. *Marsilius of Padua: the Defender of Peace;* I: *Marsilius of Padua and Medieval Political Philosophy* (New York, 1951); II: *see under* Marsilius of Padua, *Defensor Pacis.*

'Philosophy and political thought in the fourteenth century.' F. L. Utley (ed.), *The Forward Movement of the Fourteenth Century* (Columbus, Ohio, 1961), pp. 125–64.

'Political justice.' R. B. Brandt (ed.), *Social Justice* (Englewood Cliffs, N.J., 1962), pp. 119–69.

Bibliography

Ghisalberti, A. 'Bibliografia su Guglielmo di Occam dal 1950 al 1968.' *Rivista di filosofia neo-scolastica*, LXI (1969), 273–84, 545–71.

Guglielmo di Ockam (Milan, 1972).

Gilson, E. 'La philosophie franciscaine.' *Saint François d'Assise: son œuvre, son influence* (Paris, 1927), pp. 148–75.

The Unity of Philosophical Experience (New York, 1937).

Gilson, E. and Boehner, P. *Die Geschichte der christlichen Philosophie von ihren Anfängen bis Nikolaus von Cues* (Paderborn, 1937).

Goldast, M. *Monarchia Sancti Romani Imperii* (3 vols., Hanover, 1611; Frankfurt, 1614, 1613; reprinted Graz, 1960).

Goodman, Nelson. *Fact, Fiction, and Forecast*. 2nd ed. (New York, 1965).

Grabmann, M. 'Das *Defensorium Ecclesiae* des Magisters Adam, eine Streitschrift gegen Marsilius von Padua und Wilhelm von Ockham.' L. Santifaller (ed.), *Festschrift Albert Brackmann* (Weimar, 1931), pp. 569–81.

'Studien über den Einfluß der aristotelischen Philosophie auf die mittelalterlichen Theorien über das Verhältnis von Kirche und Staat.' *Sitzungsberichte der bayrischen Akademie der Wissenschaften, Philosophisch-Historische Abteilung* (1934), II.

'Die mittelalterliche Kommentare zur Politik des Aristoteles.' *Sitzungsberichte der bayrischen Akademie der Wissenschaften, Philosophisch-Historische Abteilung* (1941), II.10.

Graf, T. *De Subjecto Psychico Gratiae et Virtutum Secundum Doctrinam Scholasticorum usque ad Medium Saeculum XIV*, I: *De Subjecto Virtutum Cardinalium*. Studia Anselmiana, II, III–IV (2 vols., Rome, 1934).

Grignaschi, M. 'La limitazione dei poteri del principans in Guglielmo d'Ockham e Marsilio da Padova. Comitato internazionale di scienze storiche.' *Atti del 10 Congresso internazionale, Rome 1955* (Rome, 1957), pp. 35–51.

Grundmann, H. *Bibliographie zur Ketzergeschichte* (Rome, 1967).

Guelluy, R. *Philosophie et théologie chez Guillaume d'Ockham* (Louvain, 1947).

Hägglund, B. 'Luther et l'occamisme.' *Positions luthériennes*, III (1955), 213–23.

Theologie und Philosophie bei Luther und in der ockhamistischen Tradition: Luthers Stellung zur Theorie von der doppelten Wahrheit (Lund, 1955).

Hamman, A. *La doctrine de l'église et de l'état chez Occam: étude sur le 'Breviloquium'* (Paris, 1942).

'La doctrine de l'église et de l'état d'après le *Breviloquium* d'Occam.' *FzS*, XXXII (1950), 135–41.

'S. Augustin dans le *Breviloquium de principatu tyrannico* d'Occam.' *Augustinus Magister*, II (1954), 1019–27.

Hay, D. *Europe in the Fourteenth and Fifteenth Centuries* (London, 1966).

Henry, D. 'Ockham and the formal distinction.' *FcS*, XXV (1965), 285–92.

Heynck, V. *Ockham-Literatur 1919–1949*. *FzS*, XXXII (1950), 164–83.

'Die unpolemischen Schriften Ockhams: Abfassungszeit, Echtheit, handschriftliche Bezeugung und Ausgaben nach Ph. Boehner, O.F.M.' *FzS*, XXXII (1950), 156–63.

Hochstetter, E. *Studien zur Metaphysik und Erkenntnislehre Wilhelms von Ockham* (Berlin, 1927).

'Nominalismus?' *FcS*, IX (1949), 370–403.

'*Viator mundi*: einige Bemerkungen zur Situation des Menschen bei Wilhelm von Ockham.' *FzS*, XXXII (1950), 1–20.

Hofer, J. 'Biographische Studien über Wilhelm von Ockham, O.F.M.' *AFH*, VI (1913), 209–33, 439–65, 654–65.

'Die Geschichte des Armutsstreites in der Chronik des Johannes von Winterthur.' *Zeitschrift für Schweizerische Kirchengeschichte*, XXI (1927), 241–63.

Hoffmann, F. *Die Schriften des Oxforder Kanzlers Johannes Lutterell*. Texte zur Theologie des vierzehnten Jahrhunderts (Leipzig, 1959).

Hofmann, F. *Der Anteil der Minoriten am Kampf Ludwigs des Bayern gegen Johann XXII. unter besonderer Berücksichtigung des Wilhelms von Ockham* (Münster, 1959).

Höhn, R. 'Wilhelm Ockham in München.' *FzS*, XXXII (1950), 142–55.

Jacob, E. F. *Essays in the Conciliar Epoch*. Rev. ed. (Notre Dame, Indiana, 1963).

Jeiler, I. Armut. 'Wetzer and Welte' *Kirchenlexikon*. 2nd ed., I (Freiburg im Breisgau, 1882), cols. 1393–1401.

Jung, N. *Un franciscain théologien du pouvoir pontifical au XIVe siècle: Alvaro Pelayo, évêque et pénitencier de Jean XXII* (Paris, 1931).

Junghans, H. *Ockham im Lichte der neueren Forschung*. Arbeiten zur Geschichte und Theologie des Luthertums, XXI (Berlin, 1968).

Kantorowicz, E. H. *The King's Two Bodies: a Study in Medieval Political Theology* (Princeton, 1957).

Käppeli, T. *Le procès de Thomas Walleys, O.P.* (Rome, 1936).

Keating, C. J. *The Effects of Original Sin in the Scholastic Tradition from St Thomas Aquinas to William Ockham* (Washington, 1959).

King, H. 'From St Thomas, Ockham and the intelligible species to Thomism, Hume and the sensible species.' *Dominican Studies*, II (1949), 93–103.

Bibliography

Klocker, H. 'Ockham and the cognoscibility of God.' *The Modern Schoolman*, XXXV (1958), 77–90.

'Ockham and efficient causality.' *The Thomist*, XXIII (1960), 106–23.

'Ockham and finality.' *The Modern Schoolman*, XLIII (1965–6), 233–47.

Knysh, Y. D. 'Political authority as property and trusteeship in the works of William of Ockham.' University of London Ph.D. thesis, 1968.

Koch, J. 'Philosophische und theologische Irrtumslisten von 1270–1329: ein Beitrag zur Entwicklung der theologischen Zensuren.' *Mélanges Mandonnet*, II (Rome, 1930), 305–29.

'Der Prozeß gegen die Postille Olivis zur Apokalypse.' *Recherches de théologie ancienne et médiévale*, V (1933), 302–15.

'Neue Aktenstücke zu dem gegen Wilhelm Ockham in Avignon geführten Prozeß.' *Recherches de théologie ancienne et médiévale*, VII (1935), 353–80; VIII (1936), 79–93, 168–97.

Köhler, H. *Der Kirchenbegriff bei Wilhelm von Occam* (Leipzig, 1937).

Kölmel, W. 'Die Freiheit des Menschen bei Wilhelm Ockham.' *Festschrift des Lessing-Gymnasiums* (Mannheim, 1952).

'Das Naturrecht bei Wilhelm Ockham.' *FzS*, XXXV (1953), 39–85.

'Von Ockham zu Gabriel Biel: zur Naturrechtslehre des 14. und 15. Jahrhunderts.' *FzS*, XXXVII (1955), 218–59.

Wilhelm Ockham und seine kirchenpolitischen Schriften (Essen, 1962).

'*Paupertas* und *potestas*: Kirche und Welt in der Sicht des Alvarus Pelagius.' *FzS*, XLVI (1964), 57–101.

'Wilhelm Ockham: der Mensch zwischen Ordnung und Freiheit.' *Beiträge zum Berufsbewußtsein des Mittelalterlichen Menschen. Miscellanea Medievalia*, III (Berlin, 1964), 204–24.

Regimen Christianum: Weg und Ergebnisse des Gewaltenverhältnisses und des Gewaltenverständnisses (8.–14. Jahrhundert) (Berlin, 1970).

de Lagarde, G. *Recherches sur l'esprit politique de la Réforme* (Paris, 1926).

La naissance de l'esprit laïque au déclin du moyen-âge. 1st ed.: I: *Bilan du XIIIème siècle* (Paris, 1934); II: *Marsile de Padoue ou le premier théoricien de l'état laïque* (Paris, 1934); III: *Secteur social de la scolastique* (Paris, 1942); IV: *Ockham et son temps* (Paris, 1942); V: *Ockham: bases de départ* (Paris, 1946); VI: *Ockham: la morale et le droit* (Paris, 1946). New ed.; I: *Bilan du XIIIème siècle* (Paris, 1956); II: *Secteur social de la scolastique* (Paris, 1958); III: *Le Defensor Pacis* (Paris, 1970); IV: *Guillaume d'Ockham: défense de l'empire* (Paris, 1962); V: *Guillaume d'Ockham: critique des structures ecclésiales* (Paris, 1963).

'L'idée de représentation dans les œuvres de Guillaume d'Ockham.' *Bulletin of the International Committee of Historical Sciences*, IX (1937), 425–51.

Bibliography

'Un exemple de logique ockhamiste.' *Revue de moyen âge latin*, I (1945), 237–58.

'Ockham et le concile général.' *Album Helen Maud Cam* (Louvain, 1960), pp. 83–94.

'La philosophie de l'autorité impériale au milieu du XIVe siècle.' *Lumière et vie*, IX (1960), 41–59.

'Marsile de Padoue et Guillaume d'Ockham.' *Études d'histoire du droit canonique dédiées à Gabriel Le Bras*, I (Paris, 1965), 593–605.

Lambert, M. D. 'The Franciscan crisis under John XXII.' *FcS*, XXXII (1972), 123–43.

Leclerc, J. 'Note sur les théories politiques d'Alvaro Pelayo: à propos d'une thèse récente.' *Recherches de science religieuse*, XXI (1931), 582–9.

Leff, G. *Bradwardine and the Pelagians* (Cambridge, 1957).

Gregory of Rimini (Manchester, 1961).

Richard Fitzralph, Commentator on the Sentences: a study in Theological Orthodoxy (Manchester, 1963).

Heresy in the Later Middle Ages (2 vols., Manchester, 1967).

'The apostolic ideal in later medieval ecclesiology.' *Journal of Theological Studies, New Series*, XVIII (1967), 58–82.

Paris and Oxford Universities in the Thirteenth and Fourteenth Centuries: an Institutional and Intellectual History (New York, 1968).

'Knowledge and its relation to the status of theology according to Ockham.' *Journal of Ecclesiastical History*, XX (1969), 7–17.

Lewis, E. *Medieval Political Ideas* (2 vols., New York, 1954).

Lieberich, H. 'Kaiser Ludwig der Baier als Gesetzgeber.' *Zeitschrift der Savigny-Stiftung für Rechtsgeschichte*, LXXXIX; *Germanistische Abteilung*, LXXVI (1959), 173–245.

Little, A. G. *The Grey Friars in Oxford* (Oxford, 1892).

Studies in English Franciscan History (Manchester, 1917).

'The Franciscan school at Oxford in the thirteenth century.' *AFH*, XIX (1926), 803–74.

Franciscan Papers, Lists and Documents (Manchester, 1943).

Longpré, E. 'Duns Scot, le nominalisme et la réforme.' *La philosophie du bienheureux Duns Scot* (Paris, 1924), 161–74.

Lottin, O. *Le droit naturel chez St Thomas d'Aquin et ses prédécesseurs*. 2nd ed. (Bruges, 1931).

Maier, A. *An der Grenze von Scholastik und Naturwissenschaft: Studien zur Naturphilosophie des 14. Jahrhunderts* (Essen, 1943).

Die Vorläufer Galileis im 14. Jahrhundert: Studien zur Naturphilosophie der Spätscholastik (Rome, 1949).

Bibliography

Ausgehendes Mittelalter: Gesammelte Aufsätze zur Geitesgeschichte des 14. Jahrhunderts (2 vols., Rome, 1964–7).

'Zwei unbekannte Streitschriften gegen Johann XXII. aus dem Kreis der Münchener Minoriten.' *Archivum Historiae Pontificiae*, v (1967), 41–78.

Marcouri, A. *Anteil der Minoriten am Kampfe zwischen König Ludwig IV. von Baiern und Papst Johann XXII.* (Emmerich, 1874).

Martin, G. *Wilhelm Ockham: Untersuchungen zur Ontologie der Ordnungen* (Berlin, 1949).

'Ist Ockhams Relationstheorie Nominalismus?' *FzS*, xxxii (1950), 31–49.

Martin, V. 'Les idées répandues par Marsile de Padoue et Occam touchant la constitution de l'église.' *Revue des sciences religieuses*, xvii (1937), 261–89.

Matthews, G. 'Ockham's supposition theory and modern logic.' *Philosophical Review*, lxxiii (1964), 91–9.

Maurer, A. 'Ockham's conception of the unity of science.' *Mediaeval Studies*, xx (1958), 98–112.

Mazzantini, C. *Il cosiddetto volontarismo dei filosofi scolastici francescani da Alessandro di Hales a Guglielmo di Ockham* (Turin, 1960).

McIlwain, C. H. *The Growth of Political Thought in the West* (New York, 1932).

McKeon, R. P. 'The development of the concept of property in political philosophy: a study of the background of the constitution.' *Ethics*, xlviii (1938), 297–366.

Freedom and History (New York, 1952).

McNamara, J. F. 'Responses to Ockhamist theology in the poetry of the Pearl-poet, Langland, and Chaucer.' Louisiana State University Ph.D. thesis, 1968.

Menges, M. *The Concept of Univocity regarding the Predication of God and Creature according to William of Ockham* (St Bonaventure, N.Y., 1952).

Michalski, K. 'Les courants philosophiques à Oxford et à Paris pendant le XIVe siècle.' *Bulletin de l'Académie polonaise des sciences et des lettres, classe d'histoire et de philosophie* (1920), pp. 59–88.

'Les courants critiques et sceptiques dans la philosophie du XIVe siècle.' *Bulletin de l'Académie polonaise des sciences et des lettres, classe d'histoire et de philosophie* (1925), pp. 192–242.

'Le criticisme et le scepticisme dans la philosophie du XIVe siècle.' *Bulletin de l'Académie polonaise des sciences et des lettres, classe d'histoire et de philosophie* (1925), pp. 41–122.

La philosophie au XIVe siècle. Reprint of the preceding three studies.

Bibliography

Ed. K. Flasch, *Opuscula Philosophica, Abhandlungen zur Philosophie und ihrer Geschichte* (Frankfurt, 1969).

Le problème de la volonté à Oxford et à Paris au XIVe siècle (Lemberg, 1937).

Miethke, J. 'Zu Wilhelm Ockhams Tod.' *AFH*, LXI (1968), 79–98.

Ockhams Weg zur Sozialphilosophie (Berlin, 1969).

Moody, E. A. *The Logic of William of Ockham* (London, 1935).

'Ockham, Buridan and Nicholas of Autrecourt.' *FcS*, VII (1947), 113–46.

'Ockham and Aegidius of Rome.' *FcS*, IX (1949), 414–42.

'Empiricism and metaphysics in medieval philosophy.' *Philosophical Review*, LXVII (1958), 145–63.

Moorman, J. *A History of the Franciscan Order from its Origins to the Year 1517* (Oxford, 1968).

Morrall, J. B. 'Some notes on a recent interpretation of William of Ockham's political philosophy.' *FcS*, IX (1949), 335–69.

'Ockham and ecclesiology.' J. A. Watt, J. B. Morrall, and F. X. Martin (eds.), *Medieval Studies Presented to Aubrey Gwynn, S.J.* (Dublin, 1963), pp. 481–91.

Moser, S. *Grundbegriffe der Naturphilosophie bei Wilhelm von Ockham: Kritischer Vergleich der Summulae in libros Physicorum mit der Philosophie des Aristoteles*. Philosophie und Grenzwissenschaften, IV.2–3 (Innsbruck, 1932).

Müller, C. *Der Kampf Ludwig des Baiern mit der römischen Curie* (2 vols., Tübingen, 1879–80).

Oakley, F. 'Medieval theories of natural law: William of Ockham and the significance of the voluntarist tradition.' *Natural Law Forum*, VI (1961), 65–83.

Oberman, H. A. 'Some notes on the theology of nominalism with attention to its relation to the Renaissance.' *Harvard Theological Review*, LIII (1960), 47–76.

The Harvest of Medieval Theology: Gabriel Biel and Late Medieval Nominalism (Cambridge, Mass., 1963).

'From Ockham to Luther: recent studies.' *Concilium*, English ed., VII.2 (1966), 63–8.

Offler, H. S. 'England and Germany on the eve of the Hundred Years War.' *The English Historical Review*, LIV (1939), 608–31.

'Über die Prokuratorien Ludwigs des Bayern für die römische Kurie.' *DA*, VIII (1950), 461–87.

'Meinungsverschiedenheiten am Hofe Ludwigs des Bayern im Herbst 1331.' *DA*, XI (1954–5), 191–206.

Bibliography

'A political *collatio* of Pope Clement VI, O.S.B.' *Revue Bénédictine*, LXV (1955), 126–44.

'Empire and papacy: the last struggle.' *Transactions of the Royal Historical Society, Series* v, 6 (1956), 21–47.

'Aspects of government in the late medieval empire.' J. Hale, J. Highfield, and B. Smalley (eds.), *Europe in the Late Middle Ages* (London, 1965), pp. 217–47.

'The origin of Ockham's *Octo Quaestiones.*' *The English Historical Review*, LXXXII (1967), 323–32.

O'Hara, G. 'Ockham's razor today.' *Philosophical Studies*, XII (1963), 125–39.

Oliger, L. 'Spirituels.' *Dictionnaire de théologie catholique*, XIV.2 (Paris, 1941), cols. 2522–49.

Ozment, S. 'Mysticism, nominalism, and dissent.' C. Trinkaus and H. A. Oberman (eds.), *The Pursuit of Holiness in the Late Middle Ages and the Renaissance* (Leyden, 1974).

Paqué, R. *Das pariser Nominalistenstatut (1340)* (Berlin, 1970).

Pegis, A. C. 'Concerning William of Ockham.' *Traditio*, II (1944), 465–80.

'Some recent interpretations of Ockham.' *Speculum*, XXIII (1948), 452–63.

Pelster, F. 'Die indirekte Gewalt der Kirche über den Staat nach Ockham und Petrus de Palude: eine Übersicht.' *Scholastik*, XXVIII (1953), 78–82.

Pelzer, A. 'Les 51 articles de Guillaume Occam censurés en Avignon en 1326.' *Revue d'histoire ecclésiastique*, XVIII (1922), 240–70.

Pernoud, M. 'Tradition and innovation in Ockham's theory of divine omnipotence: a study of possibility and singularity.' St. Louis University Ph.D. thesis, 1969.

Pesh, O. M. 'Freiheitsbegriff und Freiheitslehre bei Thomas von Aquin und Luther.' *Catholica*, XVII (1963), 197–244.

Pfeiffer, G. 'Um die Lösung Ludwigs des Bayern aus dem Kirchenbann.' *Zeitschrift für Bayerische Kirchengeschichte*, XXXII (1963), 11–30.

Pikman, E. M. *The Sequence of Belief: a Consideration of Religious Thought from Homer to Ockham* (New York, 1962).

Pleuger, G. *Die Staatslehre Wilhelms von Ockham* (Cologne, 1966).

Preger, W. 'Die kirchenpolitische Kampf unter Ludwig dem Baier und sein Einfluss auf die öffentliche Meinung in Deutschland.' *Abhandlungen der historischen Klasse der königlich bayerischen Akademie der Wissenschaften*, XIV.1 (1879), 1–70.

'Beiträge und Erörterungen zur Geschichte des Deutschen Reichs in den Jahren 1330–1334.' *Abhandlungen der historischen Klasse der königlich bayerischen Akademie der Wissenschaften*, xv.2 (1880), 1–82.

'Über die Anfänge des kirchenpolitischen Kampfes unter Ludwig dem Baier.' *Abhandlungen der historischen Klasse der königlich bayerischen Akademie der Wissenschaften*, xvi.2 (1883), 113–284.

'Die Politik des Papstes Johann XXII. in Bezug auf Italien und Deutschland.' *Abhandlungen der historischen Klasse der königlich bayerischen Akademie der Wissenschaften*, xvii.3 (1886), 499–593.

Price, Robert. 'William of Ockham and *suppositio personalis*.' *FcS*, xxx (1970), 131–40.

Rábade, R. S. *Guillermo de Ockham y la filosofía del siglo XIV* (Madrid, 1966).

Reeves, M. *The Influence of Prophecy in the Later Middle Ages: a Study in Joachism* (Oxford, 1969).

Reilly, J. P., Jr. 'Ockham Bibliography: 1950–1967.' *FcS*, xxviii (1968), 197–214.

Richards, R. C. 'Ockham and skepticism.' *New Scholasticism*, xlii (1968), 345–63.

Riezler, S. *Die literarischen Widersacher der Päpste zur Zeit Ludwigs des Bayers* (Leipzig, 1874).

Ritter, G. *Studien zur Spätscholastik*; i: *Marsilius von Inghen und die ockhamistische Schule in Deutschland* (Heidelberg, 1921); ii: *Via Antiqua und Via Moderna auf den deutschen Universitäten des XV. Jahrhunderts* (Heidelberg, 1922).

Santonastaso, G. 'Occam e la *plenitudo potestatis*.' *Rassegna di scienze filosofiche*, x (1957), 213–71.

Schlageter, J. 'Glaube und Kirche nach Wilhelm von Ockham: eine fundamentaltheologische Analyse seiner kirchenpolitischen Schriften.' University of Munich dissertation, 1969.

Schmidt, M. 'Kirche und Staat bei Wilhelm von Ockham.' *Theologische Zeitschrift*, vii (1951), 265–84.

Schmitt, C. *Un pape réformateur et un défenseur de l'unité de l'église: Benoît XII et l'Ordre des Frères Mineurs* (Quaracchi, 1959).

Scholz, R. *Unbekannte kirchenpolitische Streitschriften aus der Zeit Ludwigs des Bayern (1327–1354)* (2 vols., Rome, 1911–14).

Wilhelm von Ockham als politischer Denker und sein Breviloquium de Principatu Tyrannico (Leipzig, 1944; reprinted Stuttgart, 1952).

Schultes, R. *Fides implicita: Geschichte der Lehre von der fides implicita und explicita in der katholischen Theologie, i: Von Hugo von St Viktor bis zum Konzil von Trient* (Regensburg, 1920).

Schwöbel, H. O. *Der diplomatische Kampf zwischen Ludwig des Bayern und*

Bibliography

der römischen Kurie im Rahmen des kanonischen Absolutionsprozesses (Weimar, 1968).

Scott, T. K. 'Ockham on evidence, necessity and intuition.' *Journal of the History of Philosophy*, VII (1969).

'Nicholas of Autrecourt, Buridan and Ockhamism.' *Journal of the History of Philosophy*, IX (1971), 15–41.

Seeberg, R. 'Ockham.' *Realenzyklopädie für protestantische Theologie und Kirche*. 3rd ed., XIV (Leipzig, 1904), 260–80.

de Sessevalle, A. *Histoire générale de l'ordre de Saint François, première partie: le moyen âge (1209–1517)*, I (Paris, 1935), 571–9.

Shapiro, H. *Motion, Time and Place according to William Ockham* (St Bonaventure, N.Y., 1957).

Sharp, D. E. *Franciscan Philosophy at Oxford in the Thirteenth Century*. 2nd ed. (New York, 1964).

Sheperd, M. 'William of Occam and the higher law.' *American Political Science Review*, XXVI (1932), 1005–23; XXVII (1933), 24–38.

Sikes, J. G. 'A possible Marsilian source in Ockham.' *The English Historical Review*, LI (1936), 496–504.

Smalley, B. 'Moralists and philosophers in the thirteenth and fourteenth centuries.' P. Wilpert (ed.), *Die Metaphysik im Mittelalter*. Vorträge des 2. Internazionale Kongresses für mittelalterliche Philosophie, Köln 1961 (Berlin, 1963).

Stadter, E. 'Die spiritualistische Geschichtstheologie als Voraussetzung für das Verständnis von *fides* und *auctoritas* bei Petrus Johannis Olivi.' *FzS*, XLVIII (1966), 243–53.

Stratenwerth, G. *Die Naturrechtslehre des Johannes Duns Scotus* (Göttingen, 1950).

Suk, O. 'The connection of virtues according to Ockham.' *FcS*, X (1950), 9–32, 91–113.

Tabacco, G. *Pluralità di papi ed unità di chiesa nel pensiero di Guglielmo di Occam* (Turin, 1949).

Tarello, G. 'Profili giuridici della questione della povertà nel Francescanesimo prima di Occam.' *Scritti in memoria di A. Falchi. Annali della Facoltà di Giurisprudenza dell'Università di Genova*, III (1964), 338–48.

Teetaert, A. 'Ot, Guiral.' *Dictionnaire de théologie catholique*, XI (Paris, 1931), cols. 1658–63.

Thaddeus a New Durham. *The Doctrine of the Franciscan Spirituals* (Rome, 1963).

Thompson, K. J. 'A comparison of the consultations of Marsilius of Padua and William of Ockham relating to the Tyrolese marriage of 1341–1342.' *AFH*, LXIII (1970), 3–43.

Bibliography

Tierney, B. 'Ockham, the conciliar theory and the canonists.' *Journal of the History of Ideas*, XV (1954), 40–70; reprinted with an introduction by H. A. Oberman, Facet Books, Historical Series, XIX (Medieval) (Philadelphia, 1971).

Foundations of the Conciliar Theory (Cambridge, 1955, repr. 1969).

'Grosseteste and the theory of papal sovereignty.' *Journal of Ecclesiastical History*, VI (1955), 1–17.

'Pope and council: some new decretist texts.' *Mediaeval Studies*, XIX (1957), 197–218.

'The continuity of papal political theory in the thirteenth century: some methodological considerations.' *Mediaeval Studies*, XXVII (1965), 227–45.

Origins of Papal Infallibility, 1150–1350 (Leiden, 1972).

Torello-Barenys, R. 'El Ockhamismo y la decadencia scolástica en el siglo XIV.' *Pensamiento*, IX (1953), 199–228; XI (1955), 171–88, 259–83.

Trachtenberg, O. 'William of Ockham and the prehistory of English materialism.' *Philosophy and Phenomenological Research*, VI (1945), 212–24.

Trapp, D. 'Augustinian theology of the fourteenth century.' *Augustiniana*, VI (1956), 146–274.

Turnbull, R. G. 'Ockham's nominalistic logic: some twentieth century reflections.' *The New Scholasticism*, XXXVI (1962), 313–29.

Tweedale, M. 'Scotus and Ockham on the infinity of the most eminent being.' *FcS*, XXIII (1963), 257–67.

Ullmann, W. *Principles of Government and Politics in the Middle Ages.* 2nd ed. (London, 1966).

The Individual and Society in the Middle Ages (Baltimore, 1967).

The Growth of Papal Government in the Middle Ages. 4th ed. (London, 1970).

The Origins of the Great Schism (London, 1948, new ed. 1972).

Van Leeuwen, A. 'L'église, règle de foi, dans les écrits de Guillaume d'Occam.' *Ephemerides Theologicae Lovanienses*, XI (1934), 249–88.

Van den Wyngaert, A. 'Bonagratia de Bergame.' *Dictionnaire d'histoire et de géographie ecclésiastiques*, IX (Paris, 1937), cols. 720–2.

Vasoli, C. 'Polemiche occamiste.' *Rinascimento*, III (1952), 119–41.

Guglielmo d'Occam (Florence, 1953).

'Il pensiero politico di Guglielmo d'Occam.' *Rivista critica di storia della filosofia*, IX (1954), 232–53.

Vereecke, L. 'L'obligation morale selon Guillaume d'Ockham.' *La vie spirituelle, Supplément No.* 45 (2e trimestre, 1958), 123–43.

Bibliography

'Individu et communauté selon Guillaume d'Ockham.' *Studia Moralia*, III (1965), 150–77.

Vignaux, P. 'Nominalisme (du XIVe siècle).' *Dictionnaire de théologie catholique*, XI (Paris, 1931), cols. 733–84.

Justification et prédestination au XIVe siècle: Duns Scot, Pierre d'Auriole, Guillaume d'Ockham, Grégoire de Rimini. Bibliothèque de l'École des Hautes Études, XLVIII (Paris, 1934).

Nominalisme au XIVe siècle (Montreal, 1948).

'Sur Luther et Ockham.' *FzS*, XXXII (1950), 21–30.

Villey, M. 'La genèse du droit subjectif chez Guillaume d'Occam.' *Archives de philosophie du droit*, IX (1964), 97–127.

Vorster, H. *Das Freiheitsverständnis bei Thomas von Aquin und Martin Luther.* Kirche und Konfession, VIII (Göttingen, 1965).

Weakland, J. E. 'Administrative and fiscal centralization under Pope John XXII, 1316–1334.' *Catholic Historical Review*, LIV (1968), 39–54, 285–310.

Webering, D. *Theory of Demonstration according to William of Ockham* (St Bonaventure, N.Y., 1953).

Weinberg, J. *Nicholas of Autrecourt: a Study in Fourteenth Century Thought* (Princeton, 1940).

Weisheipl, J. A. 'Ockham and some Mertonians.' *Mediaeval Studies*, XXX (1968), 163–213.

Wilks, M. J. *The Problem of Sovereignty in the Later Middle Ages* (Cambridge, 1964).

Willemsen, C. A. *Kardinal Napoleon Orsini* (Berlin, 1927).

Zuidema, S. U. *De philosophie van Occam in zijn commentaar op de Sententiën* (2 vols., Hilversum, 1936).

INDEX OF PASSAGES IN OCKHAM
QUOTED, DISCUSSED, OR CITED

Index

Index

INDEX OF NAMES

Index

Index

SUBJECT INDEX

authority: of the master in Ockham's *Dialogus*, 17–18n., 63n., 66; maintained by Ockham as a principle, according to Lagarde, but ruined in substance by an anarchic activism, 30; and understanding in correction of doctrinal error, 48–64n.; of papal office, impediment to dealing with papal heresy, 51–2, obviously acknowledged by the church fathers, 144–5; of doctors in expounding scripture greater than that of pontiffs when the doctors use greater reason, 55; may be resisted as arbitrary even when orthodox, 58

community: of early Christians set up its own economic and legal institutions, 15; relation to government redefined in Ockham, 84–5, 122; needs of basic, in assessing forms of government, 116–19, 153; lesser communities of family and household, 156–7
conciliarism: of limited significance in Ockham, 19, 30, 107; Ockham's possible influence on, 41, 229; *see also* general council
conscience: should be followed by a pope even when all the learned doctors at a general council disagree with him, 64–5
consent: appealed to by Ockham, according to Lagarde, only to support the established order, 31; the normal original basis for legitimate secular power in Ockham, 104–6; but not regularly revocable once government has been established, 106–7; medieval

axiom of (*quod omnes tangit*) used by Ockham in discussing general councils, 107n.; means of expressing not specified by Ockham, 108; apostles governed with whenever possible, 145
constitutional variation or change, considered and, in some cases, allowed by Ockham in both secular and ecclesiastical contexts, 122–6, 153–4, 163–8
constitutionalism, in interpretation of Ockham's political thought, presented, 37–43, reconsidered, 211–12; not a solution to the crisis of papal heresy as seen by Ockham, 19, 73; in Ockham's discussion of monarchy, 158–9
correction of doctrinal error: concept of transformed by Ockham, 53–9; legitimate only when an *errans* is clearly shown that his error is contrary to catholic truth, 53–4; when legitimate obliges the *errans* to give up his error, 57; legitimate, according to the Michaelists, in their writings against John XXII, 57–8; unnecessary with regard to truths received from God or certain, 65n.–66n.; Ockham's concept of consistent with his moral philosophy, 187
custom: appeal to can be refuted in many ways, 126; formally limits ruler's power in existing monarchies, 158–9

doctor(s): not obliged to give up erroneous opinions at a pontiff's correction unless the error is shown them, 55; of outstanding knowledge and laudable life distinguished from those who

264

Index

doctor (*cont.*)
merely hold the rank or bear the name of doctor, 60–1; should be principal warriors against papal heresy, 66; sin more gravely than kings and princes in not attacking papal heresy if they can safely do so, 69n.–70n.; Ockham's function and status as, 65–7, 77

empire (Roman): last struggle with papacy, Ockham's role in, 1, 22–4, 29, 33–4, 36, 38, 41, 75, 99, 106–7; his treatment of papal claims to authority over, 21–2, 85–6, 88–96; systematic treatment of in III *Dialogus* II, 24–5; legitimacy of in the time of Christ and the apostles, 96–101; could licitly be ruled again, as in the past, by a non-Christian, 101–2; authority of requires riches and force, because of its chiefly coercive functions, 136–7
expediency *see* functions
experts: must assess legitimacy of doctrinal correction, 60; role of in Ockham and Marsilius, 60–3; Ockham's attitude towards related to his moral philosophy, 187–8; *see also* doctors

freedom: a major theme in Ockham's political thought, 85, 169, 221; of subjects, necessary for the best form of government, 119–21, obstacle to tyranny, 127–8, 169, source of the unique dignity of papal government, 220; as personal liberty in Ockham contrasted with other ideas of freedom, 119n., 120n., 142–3; of gospel, appealed to by Ockham as objection to extreme papalism and basis for his own conception of ecclesiastical government, 141–9, 219–20, compatible with servitude but not a source of it, 143, prohibits pope from infringing the freedom granted by God and nature, 145; implies that no one should be able to use free men for his own ends, 157; and natural law, 178, 180–2; of expression, 71; of the will, 188

functions: of secular power, 109–33; of ecclesiastical government, 133–49; and legitimacy of government interrelated, 109–10, 152–3; consequences of Ockham's emphasis on, 122–6, 160–5

general council: fallible, according to Ockham, 48, 107n.; and the universal church (or the Roman pontiff) to consider questions of faith not yet explicitly determined, 131–2n.; difficulty of convening during the great schism, 52n.; *see also* conciliarism

heresy: Ockham's teachings examined for at Avignon, 7–9; (presumed) of John XXII as starting point of Ockham's political works, 12, 42–3, 47, 199; pertinacity essential to, 49–50; cases in which secular rulers may give judgment concerning, 102n., 131–3; papal, as problem discussed in theory before Ockham, 51–2, the central problem of I *Dialogus*, 16–20, thought to deprive a person of ecclesiastical authority *ipso facto*, 17n., 51–2, 68, Ockham's radical practical approach to, 47, 68–9, 74, general political significance of Ockham's treatment of, 71–3

impersonality of some of Ockham's political writings: a problem, 17–18; explanation suggested for, 65–7; ways of dealing with, 18, 38n.
individuals: obliged to resist papal heresy when they can do so effectively, even if lacking official power, 69, 72–3; should not despair of victory, one alone should hope for it, 47; (free or unfree) quality of determines value of the government ruling them, 121, 220; social implications of Christianity's effects upon, 203–6; Ockham's individualism, and his moral philosophy, 174, 185–9, and corporatism, 116–19, 221–5
inquisitors: their attitudes on the rights of error compared with Ockham's,

Index

Index

papacy (*cont.*)
149–51; its origin to be understood in relation to its usefulness, 152–3; its institution by Christ rational, not an arbitrary fiat, 162; Ockham's functional account of, 152–61; consequences of Ockham's functionalism, in ordinary circumstances, 163, as regards constitutional change, 163–8; need not have an abundance of force or riches, since it can regularly use only spiritual punishments, 137–8; clearly regarded by the church fathers as having power and authority, 144; intended by Christ to be ministrative, not dominative, 147–8, 207; Ockham's conception of summarized, 216–20; *see also* heresy, papal

personal: and institutional aspects of Ockham's political thought merit distinct consideration, 27–8, 33–4, 43–4; responsibility felt by Ockham for defending Christian truth as he saw it, 12, 64–5; rather than official character of papal interventions in secular affairs as seen by Ockham, 93; qualifications for rulers, Ockham's views moderate and constructive, 159–60, 219; liberty, *see* freedom

pertinacity: essential to personal heresy, 49–51; inner and outer, 50n., 51n.; proved if an *errans* does not revoke his error after being legitimately corrected for it, 53; found in different modes in individuals holding or not holding power or authority, 63n.–64n.

philosophy and political thought in Ockham: the relationship a problem, 31–3, 173–4; some aspects of the relationship examined, 174–96; *see also* nominalism; speculative thought

plenitudo potestatis: papal, in Egidius Romanus, 82, Ockham's formulation of the papalist idea of, 20–1, papalist idea of incompatible with Christian freedom, according to Ockham, 141, 143n., limited by natural law, 177–8; of an Aristotelian ideal monarch, 157–8

potentia absoluta–potentia ordinata (of God), fundamental distinction of nominalist theology, seldom found in Ockham's political thought, 198–9

poverty, of Christ and the apostles: pattern of perfection for St Francis, 9, 204n., 224n., subject of controversy within the Franciscan order, 9–10, treated by John XXII, 10–12, without positive formal political implications in Ockham's discussions of it, 14–16, and *ius naturale*, 15, 176, 180–2, indirect social implications of, 202–6; more credence should be given to a rich and powerful pope's adversaries than to the adversaries of paupers, 71n.

power: pervasive uncertainty in Ockham's time concerning its real or verbal character, 207–8; governmental, its basis, 82–3 (medieval descending and ascending conceptions), 103–4 (Ockham's rejection of the descending thesis), 108–9 (his far from complete acceptance of the ascending thesis), its functions, often moderate or negative, 113–16, 136–7, 155–6, 189; papal, 'from God alone' (in stronger sense than imperial power), 150, extends over all believers (in contrast with the emperor, the pope is supreme head and judge of all believers), 129n., 132n., 'powerful' character of papal functions clearly recognized by the fathers, 144–5, unnecessary that the pope (in contrast with the imperial authority) have great force or wealth, 136–8; and knowledge, 14n., 53, 56, 61–3, 225–8; to interpret divine commands, 165n.–166n.; of Ockham's political thought, 230; *see also* regular and casual power

property: basis, 39, 105–6, 178–9; considered by Ockham superfluous for dedicated ministers of the gospel, 136n.; even legitimate property divisions temporarily abrogated in case of extreme need, 181n.

reason: as essential to moral virtue, 3, 173, 191–4; and ecclesiastical govern-

reason (*cont.*)
ment (rationalism of Ockham's discussion), 162–8; in politics, supported, by natural law, 183–5, by moral virtue, 194–6, by biblical endorsement of natural law, 202, by the effects of Christianity on individual morality, 204–6; and theology (the limits of natural reason in theological matters correspond with the non-sacral character of secular politics in Ockham), 200–2

regular and casual power, 76, 78–80; and natural law, 183–4; casual power of pope, more restricted in Ockham than for hierocratic thinkers, 92–5, 139–41, and its use not left to the pope's discretion, 138–9

riches: required for imperial power but not for papal, 136–8; of church (superabundant goods) within jurisdiction of lay government, 129

secular rulers: often discussed in I *Dialogus* but no systematic account of their offices given there, 19n.; as favorers or attackers of papal heresy, 69, 69n.–70n., 73; their jurisdiction in ecclesiastical matters, precedents and views before Ockham, 25, 79–80, 95–6; Ockham's view of their jurisdiction, over ecclesiastical property, 87, 129, over secular crimes of the clergy, 129–30, over the pope, 129 (pope regularly exempt from secular jurisdiction), 130 (a Christian emperor may, but need not, have power to elect the pope), over cases of heresy, 102n., 131–3; *see also* empire; spiritual and temporal

soul and body, analogy of: in hierocratic thought, 82, in Ockham, 91n.–92n.

speculative thought, Ockham's: variously interpreted, in itself, 1n.–2n., and in its relation to his political thought, 3, 28, 37–42, 44–6, 173–4, 197–9; Ockham's tacit disengagement from speculative theology and meta-

physics as basis for politics, 90–1, 196–8; speculation and action in Ockham and the tradition, 225–8

spiritual and temporal: scholarly differences as to whether Ockham arrived at the distinction, 31–2, 39; his formulation of the distinction, 134–5, corresponds with the relationship between theology and politics in his thought, 200–2; preservation of the distinction in practice a major aim of his institutional writings, 84, 90–2, 115–16, 128–9, 133–6, 168–71, 217–18

Spiritual Franciscans, 12–14, 91

status: and responsibility for resisting papal heresy, 48, 68–9; of doctors, defined by Ockham in terms of knowledge and morals rather than institutional standing, 60–1, and pontiffs compared in Ockham's interpretation of Gratian, 60; of individuals Ockham intended to discuss in III *Dialogus*, ambiguous, 76–7; of perfection (the life of poverty), 204n., 224n.; *see also* office

theology: natural, its limitations relevant to the relations of religion and politics, 200–1; positive, regarded by Scholz and Lagarde as major basis for Ockham's political thought, 31, 34–7, and legitimacy of Roman empire, 96–9, and institution of papal government, 162, 165, presence or absence in politics contingent on God's ordering of the world, 200, and particularly on the non-political character of the New Testament, 202–3, the interpretation of Ockham as a theological positivist reconsidered, 210–11; and heresy, definition of pertains principally to theologians rather than canonists, 67n., theologians sin mortally if they fail to oppose a pope whom they know to be a heretic, 69

tyranny: papal, Ockham's concern with, 75, 94 (usurpation), 158–9; secular, basis for constitutional change, 125

Index

understanding: should be possessed by those under authority as well as by those exercising it, 81n., 227–8; and authority, in the format of Ockham's works, 17n.–18n., 66–7, 230, in correction of doctrinal error, 48–63, 67n. (understanding more important than memory in determining what is heretical or orthodox); *see also* reason; virtue

unity: of all government both spiritual and temporal, common axiom of secularists and papalists, 83, rejected by Ockham as dangerous to the community, 78, 109, 129 (*see also* spiritual and temporal); of spiritual and temporal government each in its own area, *see* monarchy (regarded by Ockham as regularly the best form of government); as a metaphysical ideal, not directly attacked by Ockham, 90–1; of mankind, basis and goal in Ockham's discussion of world temporal monarchy, 117–19; of the church, can survive without unity of supreme pontiff, 166n.; (coherence) of Ockhams' institutional dualism, 171–2; (bringing together) of contrasting ideas and attitudes in Ockham's work, 230

virtue: and will, 3, 45, 185–9; and reason, 3, 45, 189–96; and heresy, 45n., 50n.; in rulers and subjects, 120–1, 159–60; as love of God above all things because the understanding so dictates, 197, 203–6 (including indirect political implications of this idea of perfect virtue)

women, not to be excluded from a general council, 222n.

269